# The Extraordinary Hidden Power of Emotional Intelligence

# The Extraordinary Hidden Power of Emotional Intelligence

Marien-Edgard Ngbali BEMI

Published by MarBe, 2025.

THE EXTRAORDINARY HIDDEN POWER OF EMOTIONAL INTELLIGENCE

**First edition. August 1, 2025.**



ISBN: 979-8231853731

Written by Marien-Edgard Ngbali BEMI.

## Also by Marien-Edgard Ngbali BEMI

Échos de l'Est de la République Démocratique du Congo : Poèmes d'une Terre en Guerre Perpétuelle.
Ecos do Leste da República Democrática do Congo: Poemas de uma Terra de Guerra Perpétua.
Echi dall'est della Repubblica Democratica del Congo: poesie da una terra di guerra perpetua.
Demokratik Kongo Cumhuriyeti'nin Doğusundan Yankılar: Sürekli Savaş Ülkesinden Şiirler.
Jesus-Christ, the Refugee!
Jésus-Christ, le réfugié!
Gesù-Cristo, il rifugiato!
¡Jesucristo, el Refugiado!
Jesus Cristo, o Refugiado!
İsa-Mesih, Mülteci!
Jesus-Christus, der Flüchtling!
The Genocide in the Democratic Republic of the Congo: Unveiling the Forgotten Tragedy.
Le génocide en République démocratique du Congo : Révéler la tragédie oubliée.
Il genocidio nella Repubblica Democratica del Congo: Svelare la tragedia dimenticata.
El genocidio en la República Democrática del Congo: Desvelando la tragedia olvidada.
O Genocídio na República Democrática do Congo: Desvendar a tragédia esquecida.

Der Völkermord in der Demokratischen Republik Kongo: Die vergessene Tragödie ans Licht bringen.

The Palestinian genocide: a scandal and a disgrace for our civilised world!

Le génocide palestinien : un scandale et une honte pour notre monde civilisé !

Echoes from the East of the Democratic Republic of Congo: Poems from a Land of Perpetual War.

Ecos del Este de la República Democrática del Congo: Poemas de una tierra en guerra perpetua.

El genocidio palestino: ¡Un escándalo y una vergüenza para nuestro mundo civilizado!

The Extraordinary Hidden Power of Indifference: Harnessing Detachment to Find Calm and Clarity.

Gaza, le nouvel Auschwitz : Comment l'histoire se répète dans l'indifférence internationale !

The Extraordinary Hidden Power of Emotional Intelligence

# Table of Contents

# Dedication

To every soul who has ever been told to hide their feelings,

To every heart that has broken and mended itself again,

To every leader who chooses compassion over control,

To every seeker who believes there is strength in vulnerability,

And to those who dare to live, love, and lead with courage, grace, and authenticity—

**This book is for you.**

May you continue to honour the extraordinary hidden power within you,

And may your light, born of wisdom and kindness,

Illumine the world in ways seen and unseen.

**With deepest respect and heartfelt hope,**

**Marien**

# Epigraphs

"*Anyone can become angry—that is easy.*

*But to be angry with the right person, to the right degree, at the right time, for the right purpose, and in the right way—that is not easy.*"

— Aristotle

"*Between stimulus and response, there is a space.*
*In that space is our power to choose our response.*
*In our response lies our growth and our freedom.*"
— Viktor E. Frankl

"*Compassion and tolerance are not a sign of weakness, but a sign of strength.*"

— Dalai Lama

"*Leadership is not about being in charge.*
*It is about taking care of those in your charge.*"
— Simon Sinek

"*Emotional intelligence is not about controlling feelings.*

*It is about learning to listen to them—and then choosing love over fear, wisdom over impulse, connection over isolation.*"

— Marien-Edgard Ngbali Bemi

# Acknowledgments

Writing a book is never a solitary journey, even when the words themselves are crafted in solitude.

Behind every page, behind every thought refined into language, there are countless silent companions—those who inspire, challenge, support, and believe.

This book would not exist without them.

First, I extend my deepest gratitude to the pioneers and scholars of emotional intelligence—**Daniel Goleman, Brené Brown, Susan David, Marshall Rosenberg, and so many others**—whose ground-breaking work illuminated paths I had not yet imagined.

To my mentors, colleagues, and friends: **thank you for your encouragement, wisdom, and belief** in the importance of emotional intelligence in a world often too hurried to feel.

Your conversations, your examples, and even your critiques became stepping stones toward clarity and conviction.

To my family:

**Thank you for teaching me, every day, the profound lessons of patience, empathy, resilience, and unconditional love.**

You have been my first and most enduring teachers in emotional intelligence.

Your presence in my life is a blessing beyond words.

To the readers:

**Thank you for choosing this journey—for believing in the quiet, transformative power of emotional growth.**

Thank you for your openness to explore yourself more deeply, to connect more authentically, and to lead with more heart.

This book was written for you, and it finds its meaning through your living it.

To those facing challenges, loss, or change:

May you find strength within your emotions and rise renewed.

Your courage is a silent revolution.

And finally, to the future:

May emotional intelligence become not just a skill we seek but **a spirit we embody**—guiding our communities, organisations, families, and souls into a world where compassion, awareness, and resilience are the foundation of all we create.

This is just the beginning.

**With gratitude, heart, and hope.**

# Introduction

Picture this: two equally brilliant minds stand at the precipice of opportunity. Both possess razor-sharp intellects, flawless academic credentials, and seemingly identical potential. Yet one will soar to extraordinary heights while the other remains perpetually grounded, forever wondering what invisible force separates triumph from mediocrity. The answer lies not in the corridors of traditional intelligence, but in a realm far more nuanced, profound, and transformative—a dimension where hearts speak louder than minds, where understanding transcends mere knowing.

Welcome to the extraordinary world of Emotional Intelligence.

In our hyperconnected, algorithm-driven epoch, where artificial intelligence threatens to eclipse human cognitive capabilities and data dictates destiny, a paradoxical truth emerges with startling clarity. The very qualities that make us most human—our capacity to feel deeply, to understand the unspoken language of emotion, to navigate the intricate web of interpersonal dynamics—have become our greatest competitive advantage (Goleman, 2020). This isn't merely poetic idealism; it's empirical reality backed by decades of rigorous scientific inquiry.

**Emotional Intelligence** or **Emotional Quotient (EQ)** —that elusive, often misunderstood constellation of abilities—represents perhaps the most significant psychological discovery of the modern era. Yet despite its profound implications, EQ remains shrouded in misconception, relegated to the periphery of educational curricula, and dismissed by those who mistake emotional sophistication for weakness (Bar-On, 2006). How tragically ironic that our most powerful tool for success remains our best-kept secret.

The genesis of this revolutionary concept traces back further than most realise. While Daniel Goleman's seminal 1995 work catapulted emotional intelligence into mainstream consciousness, the intellectual foundations were laid decades earlier (Goleman, 1995). Peter Salovey and John Mayer first coined the term in 1990, building upon Howard Gardner's ground-breaking theory of multiple intelligences (Salovey & Mayer, 1990; Gardner, 1983). But perhaps most prescient were Thorndike's 1920 conceptualisation of "social intelligence"—a visionary glimpse into what would eventually revolutionise our understanding of human potential (Thorndike, 1920).

What emerges from this rich intellectual tapestry is a startling revelation: emotional intelligence isn't simply another psychological construct. It's the master key that unlocks human excellence across every conceivable domain. Research conducted across diverse populations, cultures, and contexts consistently demonstrates that EQ predicts success more accurately than IQ, personality traits, or even past performance (Bradberry & Greaves, 2009). Fortune 500 CEOs? Their emotional intelligence quotient averages significantly higher than their purely intellectual counterparts (Cherniss, 2010). Elite athletes who transcend physical limitations? They possess extraordinary emotional self-regulation capabilities (Jones, 2003). Teachers who inspire generations of students? Their empathetic understanding creates transformational learning environments (Jennings & Greenberg, 2009).

But here's where the story becomes truly extraordinary: unlike the fixed nature of traditional intelligence, emotional intelligence represents pure potential energy waiting to be unleashed. Your IQ may be relatively static, determined largely by genetic lottery and early developmental experiences. Your EQ? That's an entirely different narrative—one where you hold the pen, where conscious effort yields measurable results, where deliberate practice transforms limitation into liberation (Cherniss, 2000).

This book—*The Extraordinary Hidden Power of Emotional Intelligence*—isn't merely another addition to the self-help pantheon.

It's a rebellion against the tyranny of purely analytical thinking. A manifesto for those who refuse to accept that success requires sacrificing humanity. An expedition into the deepest recesses of human potential, where emotion and intellect dance in perfect harmony.

Consider the magnitude of what we're discussing. Emotional intelligence encompasses five interconnected domains that collectively determine how we experience life itself: self-awareness—the cornerstone of authentic existence; self-regulation—the bridge between impulse and wisdom; motivation—the internal fire that sustains purpose; empathy—the sacred ability to truly see another soul; and social skills—the artistry of human connection (Goleman, 1998). These aren't abstract concepts floating in academic ether. They're the fundamental building blocks of everything that matters.

The neuroscientific revolution has unveiled the intricate biological mechanisms underlying emotional intelligence, revealing how our brains can literally rewire themselves through conscious emotional development (Davidson & Lutz, 2008). The prefrontal cortex—our executive command centre—doesn't simply govern rational thought; it orchestrates the delicate interplay between emotion and cognition that defines optimal human functioning (LeDoux, 2015). Meanwhile, the anterior cingulate cortex serves as an emotional thermostat, regulating our internal climate with exquisite precision (Bush, Luu & Posner, 2000).

Yet neuroscience tells only part of this remarkable story. The real magic happens in lived experience—in boardrooms where emotionally intelligent leaders inspire rather than intimidate, in classrooms where teachers create psychological safety that accelerates learning, in relationships where authentic connection transcends superficial interaction (Boyatzis, 2018). These aren't feel-good anecdotes; they're documented phenomena with measurable outcomes and transformational consequences.

The urgency of developing emotional intelligence has never been greater. We inhabit an era of unprecedented complexity, where traditional problem-solving approaches prove inadequate for navigating ambiguous, rapidly evolving challenges (Senge, 2006). Climate change, social inequality, technological disruption, political polarisation—these defining issues of our time demand leaders who can think beyond conventional paradigms, who can build bridges across seemingly insurmountable divides, who can inspire collective action toward shared aspirations (Brown, 2018).

Moreover, the digital revolution—while offering unprecedented connectivity—has created an empathy deficit of staggering proportions. Social media platforms designed to bring us together have instead fostered isolation, comparison, and superficial engagement (Turkle, 2017). Young people report higher levels of anxiety and depression than any previous generation, paradoxically feeling more alone despite being more "connected" than ever before (Twenge, 2017). In this context, emotional intelligence isn't merely advantageous—it's essential for psychological survival and social cohesion.

The journey you're about to embark upon will challenge fundamental assumptions about success, fulfilment, and human potential. You'll discover that emotional intelligence isn't about becoming more emotional—quite the opposite. It's about developing sophisticated emotional awareness that enables more strategic, intentional, and effective responses to life's inevitable challenges (Mayer & Salovey, 1997). You'll learn that vulnerability isn't weakness but rather the birthplace of innovation, creativity, and authentic leadership (Brown, 2012).

This transformation won't happen overnight. Rewiring decades of emotional patterns requires patience, persistence, and profound self-compassion. But here's what research unequivocally demonstrates: individuals who commit to developing their emotional intelligence experience improvements in virtually every area of life—enhanced relationships, increased professional success, better physical health, greater life satisfaction, and deeper sense of purpose (Petrides, 2009).

Throughout these pages, you'll encounter cutting-edge research, real-world case studies, practical exercises, and transformational frameworks designed to accelerate your emotional development. But more importantly, you'll discover something extraordinary: the person you're capable of becoming when you fully embrace your emotional potential.

The hidden power already exists within you, waiting to be acknowledged, cultivated, and unleashed. Your journey of emotional mastery begins now.

---

**References:**

Bar-On, R. (2006). The Bar-On model of emotional-social intelligence (ESI). *Psicothema*, 18, 13-25.

Boyatzis, R. (2018). *The heart of leadership: How to inspire, encourage, and motivate people to follow you.* Harvard Business Review Press.

Bradberry, T., & Greaves, J. (2009). *Emotional intelligence 2.0.* TalentSmart.

Brown, B. (2012). *Daring greatly: How the courage to be vulnerable transforms the way we live, love, parent, and lead.* Gotham Books.

Brown, B. (2018). *Dare to lead: Brave work, tough conversations, whole hearts.* Random House.

Bush, G., Luu, P., & Posner, M. I. (2000). Cognitive and emotional influences in anterior cingulate cortex. *Trends in Cognitive Sciences*, 4(6), 215-222.

Cherniss, C. (2000). Emotional intelligence: What it is and why it matters. Paper presented at the Annual Meeting of the Society for Industrial and Organizational Psychology, New Orleans, LA.

Cherniss, C. (2010). *Emotional intelligence: New insights and further clarifications*. Industrial and Organizational Psychology, 3(2), 183-191.

Davidson, R. J., & Lutz, A. (2008). Buddha's brain: Neuroplasticity and meditation. *IEEE Signal Processing Magazine*, 25(6), 176-188.

Gardner, H. (1983). *Frames of mind: The theory of multiple intelligences*. Basic Books.

Goleman, D. (1995). *Emotional intelligence: Why it matters more than IQ*. Bantam Books.

Goleman, D. (1998). *Working with emotional intelligence*. Bantam Books.

Goleman, D. (2020). *Emotional intelligence: 25th anniversary edition*. Bantam Books.

Jennings, P. A., & Greenberg, M. T. (2009). The prosocial classroom: Teacher social and emotional competence in relation to student and classroom outcomes. *Review of Educational Research*, 79(1), 491-525.

Jones, G. (2003). What is this thing called mental toughness? An investigation of elite sport performers. *Journal of Applied Sport Psychology*, 14(3), 205-218.

LeDoux, J. (2015). *The emotional brain: The mysterious underpinnings of emotional life*. Simon & Schuster.

Mayer, J. D., & Salovey, P. (1997). What is emotional intelligence? In P. Salovey & D. Sluyter (Eds.), *Emotional development and emotional intelligence: Educational implications* (pp. 3-31). Basic Books.

Petrides, K. V. (2009). Psychometric properties of the trait emotional intelligence questionnaire (TEIQue). In C. Stough, D. H.

Saklofske, & J. D. Parker (Eds.), *Assessing emotional intelligence* (pp. 85-101). Springer.

Salovey, P., & Mayer, J. D. (1990). Emotional intelligence. *Imagination, Cognition and Personality*, 9(3), 185-211.

Senge, P. M. (2006). *The fifth discipline: The art and practice of the learning organization*. Doubleday.

Thorndike, E. L. (1920). Intelligence and its uses. *Harper's Magazine*, 140, 227-235.

Turkle, S. (2017). *Alone together: Why we expect more from technology and less from each other*. Basic Books.

Twenge, J. M. (2017). *iGen: Why today's super-connected kids are growing up less rebellious, more tolerant, less happy—and completely unprepared for adulthood*. Atria Books.

# Chapter 1: Understanding Emotional Intelligence: Beyond IQ and Talent

## The Great Deception of Cognitive Supremacy

Imagine, if you will, a world where brilliance is measured solely by the cold precision of mathematical equations, where genius is confined to the sterile laboratories of pure logic, where human worth is distilled into a single, unforgiving number: The Intelligence Quotient. For over a century, this has been our reality—a civilisation obsessed with cognitive horsepower while remaining tragically blind to the engine that truly drives human excellence.

We've worshipped at the altar of IQ with religious fervour. Stanford-Binet scores became sacred texts. SAT results determined destinies. Academic achievements carved social hierarchies deeper than ancient caste systems (Sternberg, 2003). Yet beneath this gleaming facade of intellectual supremacy lurked a profound paradox that would ultimately shatter our most cherished assumptions about human potential.

Consider Albert Einstein—undoubtedly one of history's most celebrated intellects. While his revolutionary theories transformed our understanding of the universe, Einstein himself recognised something that his contemporaries missed entirely: "A person who is religiously enlightened appears to me to be one who has, to the best of his ability, liberated himself from the fetters of his selfish desires and is preoccupied with thoughts, feelings, and aspirations to which he clings because of their super personal value" (Einstein, 1954). Here was a man whose genius transcended mere cognitive ability, encompassing emotional wisdom, social consciousness, and profound empathy for the human condition.

The traditional paradigm began crumbling when researchers started examining why some individuals with extraordinary IQs lived lives of quiet desperation while others with average cognitive abilities soared to unprecedented heights of success and fulfilment. The answer, when it finally emerged, would revolutionise psychology forever: intelligence, as we had understood it, represented merely one instrument in the vast orchestra of human capability.

## The Emergence of a Revolutionary Paradigm

The seeds of this transformation were planted in 1990 when two visionary psychologists, Peter Salovey and John Mayer, dared to challenge conventional wisdom with a radical proposition. They suggested that traditional intelligence tests captured only a fraction of human intellectual potential—specifically, the ability to perceive, use, understand, and manage emotions constituted a distinct form of intelligence worthy of scientific investigation (Salovey & Mayer, 1990).

Their ground-breaking research revealed something extraordinary: individuals who could navigate the complex landscape of human emotion with sophistication and skill consistently outperformed their cognitively superior counterparts in virtually every meaningful domain of life. But it would take another revolutionary thinker to translate these findings into a language the world could understand.

Enter Daniel Goleman—journalist, psychologist, and prophet of emotional wisdom. His seminal 1995 work, "Emotional Intelligence: Why It Can Matter More Than IQ," didn't merely introduce a concept; it ignited a global awakening (Goleman, 1995). Suddenly, corporate boardrooms buzzed with discussions about EQ. Educational systems began questioning their narrow focus on academic achievement. Parents wondered whether their children's emotional development deserved equal attention to their intellectual growth.

The implications were staggering and immediate. Research conducted across diverse populations revealed that emotional intelligence predicted professional success more accurately than IQ, personality traits, or even past performance (Bradberry & Greaves, 2009). Harvard Business School studies demonstrated that executives with high emotional intelligence generated significantly better financial results than their cognitively gifted but emotionally limited counterparts (Boyatzis, 1982). Medical schools discovered that physicians with superior emotional skills had lower malpractice rates and higher patient satisfaction scores (Levinson et al., 1997).

But perhaps most remarkably, longitudinal studies following individuals over decades revealed that emotional intelligence wasn't merely correlated with success—it was the primary driver of life satisfaction, relationship quality, physical health, and psychological well-being (Bar-On, 2006).

## Deconstructing the Architecture of Emotional Excellence

What exactly constitutes this mysterious force that wields such profound influence over human destiny? Emotional intelligence, in its most precise definition, represents the sophisticated ability to recognise, understand, process, and strategically use emotional information to guide thinking, behaviour, and interpersonal interactions (Mayer & Salovey, 1997).

This seemingly simple description conceals extraordinary complexity. Unlike the relatively static nature of cognitive intelligence—largely determined by genetic factors and early developmental experiences—emotional intelligence operates as a dynamic, expandable capacity that can be cultivated throughout one's lifetime (Cherniss, 2000). It encompasses multiple interconnected competencies that function synergistically to create what we might call "emotional mastery."

Goleman's influential framework identifies five core components that together constitute emotional intelligence:

**Self-Awareness:** The foundational cornerstone of emotional intelligence, representing the ability to recognise one's emotions as they occur, understand their origins and implications, and comprehend how they influence thoughts, behaviours, and interactions with others (Goleman, 1998). This isn't merely intellectual understanding but visceral, real-time emotional recognition that enables conscious choice rather than unconscious reaction.

**Self-Regulation:** The sophisticated capacity to manage, redirect, and channel emotions productively rather than being overwhelmed or controlled by them (Gross, 2015). This component involves emotional flexibility, impulse control, stress management, and the ability to maintain composure and clarity even in challenging circumstances.

**Motivation:** An intrinsic drive toward achievement that transcends external rewards, characterised by resilience in the face of setbacks, commitment to long-term goals, and a passion for continuous improvement and growth (Deci & Ryan, 2000). This isn't simple ambition but a deeper orientation toward meaning and purpose.

**Empathy:** The remarkable ability to perceive, understand, and respond appropriately to others' emotional states, needs, and perspectives (Davis, 1983). This encompasses cognitive empathy (understanding others' thoughts), affective empathy (feeling others' emotions), and compassionate empathy (being moved to help).

**Social Skills:** The artful application of emotional intelligence in interpersonal contexts, including communication, influence, conflict resolution, leadership, and relationship building (Riggio & Reichard, 2008). These skills enable individuals to navigate complex social dynamics and inspire others toward shared objectives.

Each component represents a distinct yet interconnected facet of emotional intelligence, and mastery requires development across all five domains simultaneously.

## The Profound Limitations of Cognitive Tunnel Vision

Why has our collective obsession with traditional intelligence proven so inadequate for predicting human flourishing? The answer lies in understanding what IQ actually measures—and, more importantly, what it doesn't.

Traditional intelligence tests assess specific cognitive functions: logical reasoning, mathematical computation, linguistic processing, spatial visualisation, and pattern recognition (Sternberg, 2003). These abilities are undeniably valuable and correlate with certain types of academic and professional success. However, they represent only a narrow slice of the cognitive capabilities required for effective living.

Consider these sobering realities that emerge from decades of research:

IQ predicts only about 10-25% of career success, leaving the vast majority of achievement factors unexplained (Hunter & Schmidt, 1996). The correlation between IQ and job performance decreases significantly as career complexity increases, particularly in leadership roles where emotional and social skills become paramount (Sternberg, 2003).

Academically gifted individuals frequently struggle with practical problem-solving, interpersonal relationships, and stress management—skills essential for life satisfaction and effectiveness

(Sternberg, 1985). The phenomenon of "brilliant but ineffective" leaders populates corporate landscapes worldwide, individuals whose intellectual capabilities couldn't compensate for emotional deficiencies.

Moreover, traditional intelligence tests were designed during an era when work was primarily individual, routine, and hierarchical. Today's interconnected, rapidly changing, collaborative work environments demand entirely different skill sets—precisely those encompassed by emotional intelligence (Goleman, 2013).

## The Neuroscientific Revolution: Emotion and Cognition United

Modern neuroscience has revolutionised our understanding of how emotions and cognition interact within the brain, revealing that the traditional separation between "thinking" and "feeling" represents a fundamental misunderstanding of human neural architecture (LeDoux, 2015).

The limbic system—our emotional centre—doesn't merely influence cognitive processing; it's intimately integrated with the prefrontal cortex, our executive command centre (Davidson, 2004). This integration means that optimal decision-making requires both emotional and cognitive input. When we attempt to think purely "rationally" by suppressing emotional information, we actually impair our judgment rather than improving it (Damasio, 1994).

Antonio Damasio's ground-breaking research with patients who had suffered damage to brain regions connecting emotion and cognition revealed a startling truth: individuals who retained their intellectual abilities but lost emotional processing capacity made consistently poor decisions in their personal and professional lives (Damasio, 1994). They could analyse options logically but couldn't evaluate which choices would lead to positive outcomes because they lacked emotional wisdom to guide their reasoning.

Furthermore, neuroplasticity research demonstrates that emotional intelligence skills literally reshape brain structure through practice (Davidson & Lutz, 2008). Mindfulness meditation, empathy training, and emotional regulation exercises create measurable changes in neural pathways, increasing gray matter density in regions associated with emotional processing and decreasing activity in stress-response systems (Goyal et al., 2014).

## The Hidden Costs of Emotional Ignorance

The consequences of neglecting emotional intelligence extend far beyond individual limitation—they represent a societal crisis of staggering proportions. When we examine the challenges plaguing modern civilisation, emotional intelligence deficits emerge as underlying contributing factors across virtually every domain.

**Workplace Dysfunction:** Studies reveal that 75% of careers are derailed due to emotional incompetence rather than technical inadequacy (Centre for Creative Leadership, 2004). Toxic leadership, team conflicts, communication breakdowns, and organisational dysfunction typically stem from emotional intelligence deficiencies among key personnel.

**Educational Crisis:** Despite decades of educational reform focused on academic achievement, student anxiety, depression, and behavioural problems continue escalating (Twenge, 2017). Schools that implement social-emotional learning programmes demonstrate improved academic performance, reduced disciplinary issues, and enhanced student well-being (Durlak et al., 2011).

**Relationship Deterioration:** Divorce rates, social isolation, and interpersonal violence reflect widespread emotional illiteracy. Research consistently shows that couples' emotional intelligence predicts relationship satisfaction and longevity more accurately than compatibility, shared interests, or even communication frequency (Gottman, 1999).

**Mental Health Epidemic:** Rising rates of anxiety, depression, addiction, and suicide correlate strongly with emotional intelligence deficits (Petrides, 2009). Individuals who can recognise, understand, and manage their emotions demonstrate significantly greater psychological resilience and life satisfaction.

**Leadership Failures:** Political, corporate, and institutional leadership crises often trace back to emotional intelligence deficiencies—leaders who lack empathy, self-awareness, or emotional regulation create cultures of dysfunction that ripple throughout entire organisations and societies (George, 2000).

## The Transformation Imperative: Why Now?

We stand at a unique historical inflection point where emotional intelligence has transitioned from "nice-to-have" to "essential-for-survival." Multiple converging forces make emotional intelligence development not merely advantageous but absolutely critical:

**Technological Disruption:** As artificial intelligence assumes responsibility for routine cognitive tasks, uniquely human capabilities—creativity, empathy, complex social interaction, ethical reasoning—become increasingly valuable (Frey & Osborne, 2017). Jobs requiring high emotional intelligence are among the least susceptible to automation.

**Global Interconnectedness:** Our hyperconnected world demands sophisticated cross-cultural communication, collaborative problem-solving, and the ability to build trust and rapport across diverse populations (Livermore, 2015). These skills are fundamentally emotional intelligence competencies.

**Complexity and Ambiguity:** Modern challenges—climate change, social inequality, technological ethics—require leaders who can navigate uncertainty, build consensus among stakeholders with conflicting interests, and inspire collective action toward long-term objectives (Heifetz, 1994).

**Information Overload:** In an era of information abundance, the ability to process emotional data, maintain focus, and make values-based decisions becomes increasingly crucial for effective functioning (Goleman, 2013).

**Social Fragmentation:** Rising political polarisation, social isolation, and tribal thinking create an urgent need for individuals who can bridge differences, build empathy across divides, and foster community cohesion (Putnam, 2000).

## Dispelling the Mythology of Emotional Intelligence

Despite growing awareness, numerous misconceptions about emotional intelligence persist, creating barriers to its development and application:

**Myth: Emotional Intelligence Means Being "Soft" or "Nice"** Reality: High EQ individuals are often more direct, honest, and willing to engage in difficult conversations than their emotionally less skilled counterparts. They simply do so with greater sensitivity to impact and more sophisticated social awareness (Goleman, 1998).

**Myth: Emotions Should Be Controlled or Suppressed** Reality: Emotional intelligence involves experiencing emotions fully while choosing how to respond. Suppression typically backfires, creating greater emotional reactivity and reduced well-being (Gross, 2015).

**Myth: Some People Are Just "Naturally" Emotionally Intelligent** Reality: While individuals may have different starting points, emotional intelligence represents a set of learnable skills that can be developed through conscious effort and practice at any age (Cherniss, 2000).

**Myth: Emotional Intelligence Is Just Common-Sense** Reality: EQ involves sophisticated cognitive processes, nuanced social perception, and complex behavioural skills that require deliberate development and practice (Mayer, 2004).

**Myth: High IQ Automatically Includes Emotional Intelligence** Reality: Cognitive intelligence and emotional intelligence are largely independent. Many highly intelligent individuals struggle with emotional awareness and social skills (Mayer & Salovey, 1997).

## The Promise of Emotional Mastery

As we stand on the threshold of exploring emotional intelligence in greater depth, it's crucial to understand what awaits those who commit to this transformational journey. The research is unequivocal: individuals who develop high emotional intelligence experience profound improvements across virtually every dimension of human experience.

**Professional Excellence:** High-EQ individuals earn higher salaries, receive more promotions, demonstrate superior leadership effectiveness, and experience greater career satisfaction (Bradberry & Greaves, 2009).

**Relationship Fulfilment:** Emotional intelligence predicts relationship satisfaction, marital stability, parenting effectiveness, and social network quality (Gottman, 1999).

**Physical Health:** Studies reveal that emotional intelligence correlates with better immune function, lower cardiovascular disease risk, reduced inflammation, and increased longevity (Kubzansky & Kawachi, 2000).

**Mental Well-being:** High EQ individuals report lower anxiety and depression, greater life satisfaction, enhanced resilience, and more effective stress management (Bar-On, 2006).

**Creative Expression:** Emotional intelligence facilitates artistic creativity, innovative thinking, and the ability to inspire others through authentic expression (Mayer, 2004).

Most remarkably, these benefits compound over time. As emotional intelligence develops, it creates positive feedback loops that accelerate further growth and success.

## The Journey Ahead

The path to emotional mastery isn't always comfortable. It requires confronting uncomfortable truths about ourselves, examining long-held patterns, and developing new ways of perceiving and responding to the world. Yet the alternative—remaining trapped in cycles of emotional reactivity, superficial relationships, and unfulfilled potential—represents a far greater hardship.

In the chapters that follow, we'll explore each component of emotional intelligence in detail, examine the neuroscience underlying these capabilities, and provide practical strategies for development. You'll discover that emotional intelligence isn't merely another self-improvement concept but a fundamental shift in how you experience and interact with reality itself.

The extraordinary hidden power of emotional intelligence awaits your discovery. The only question is whether you're ready to claim it.

---

**References:**

Bar-On, R. (2006). The Bar-On model of emotional-social intelligence (ESI). *Psicothema*, 18, 13-25.

Boyatzis, R. E. (1982). *The competent manager: A model for effective performance*. John Wiley & Sons.

Bradberry, T., & Greaves, J. (2009). *Emotional intelligence 2.0.* TalentSmart.

Center for Creative Leadership. (2004). *Why executives derail: Perspectives across time and cultures.* Center for Creative Leadership Press.

Cherniss, C. (2000). Emotional intelligence: What it is and why it matters. Paper presented at the Annual Meeting of the Society for Industrial and Organizational Psychology, New Orleans, LA.

Damasio, A. (1994). *Descartes' error: Emotion, reason, and the human brain.* Putnam.

Davidson, R. J. (2004). Well-being and affective style: Neural substrates and biobehavioural correlates. *Philosophical Transactions of the Royal Society*, 359(1449), 1395-1411.

Davidson, R. J., & Lutz, A. (2008). Buddha's brain: Neuroplasticity and meditation. *IEEE Signal Processing Magazine*, 25(6), 176-188.

Davis, M. H. (1983). Measuring individual differences in empathy: Evidence for a multidimensional approach. *Journal of Personality and Social Psychology*, 44(1), 113-126.

Deci, E. L., & Ryan, R. M. (2000). The "what" and "why" of goal pursuits: Human needs and the self-determination of behaviour. *Psychological Inquiry*, 11(4), 227-268.

Durlak, J. A., Weissberg, R. P., Dymnicki, A. B., Taylor, R. D., & Schellinger, K. B. (2011). The impact of enhancing students' social and emotional learning: A meta-analysis of school-based universal interventions. *Child Development*, 82(1), 405-432.

Einstein, A. (1954). *Ideas and opinions.* Crown Publishers.

Frey, C. B., & Osborne, M. A. (2017). The future of employment: How susceptible are jobs to computerisation? *Technological Forecasting and Social Change*, 114, 254-280.

George, J. M. (2000). Emotions and leadership: The role of emotional intelligence. *Human Relations*, 53(8), 1027-1055.

Goleman, D. (1995). *Emotional intelligence: Why it can matter more than IQ*. Bantam Books.

Goleman, D. (1998). *Working with emotional intelligence.* Bantam Books.

Goleman, D. (2013). *Focus: The hidden driver of excellence.* HarperCollins.

Gottman, J. (1999). *The marriage clinic: A scientifically based marital therapy*. Norton.

Goyal, M., Singh, S., Sibinga, E. M., Gould, N. F., Rowland-Seymour, A., Sharma, R., ... & Haythornthwaite, J. A. (2014). Meditation programs for psychological stress and well-being: A systematic review and meta-analysis. *JAMA Internal Medicine*, 174(3), 357-368.

Gross, J. J. (2015). Emotion regulation: Current status and future prospects. *Psychological Inquiry*, 26(1), 1-26.

Heifetz, R. A. (1994). *Leadership without easy answers*. Harvard University Press.

Hunter, J. E., & Schmidt, F. L. (1996). Intelligence and job performance: Economic and social implications. *Psychology, Public Policy, and Law*, 2(3-4), 447-472.

Kubzansky, L. D., & Kawachi, I. (2000). Going to the heart of the matter: Do negative emotions cause coronary heart disease? *Journal of Psychosomatic Research*, 48(4-5), 323-337.

LeDoux, J. (2015). *The emotional brain: The mysterious underpinnings of emotional life*. Simon & Schuster.

Levinson, W., Roter, D. L., Mullooly, J. P., Dull, V. T., & Frankel, R. M. (1997). Physician-patient communication: The relationship with malpractice claims among primary care physicians and surgeons. *JAMA*, 277(7), 553-559.

Livermore, D. (2015). *Leading with cultural intelligence: The real secret to success*. AMACOM.

Mayer, J. D. (2004). What is emotional intelligence? *Implications for educators*. University of New Hampshire.

Mayer, J. D., & Salovey, P. (1997). What is emotional intelligence? In P. Salovey & D. Sluyter (Eds.), *Emotional development and emotional intelligence: Educational implications* (pp. 3-31). Basic Books.

Petrides, K. V. (2009). Psychometric properties of the trait emotional intelligence questionnaire (TEIQue). In C. Stough, D. H. Saklofske, & J. D. Parker (Eds.), *Assessing emotional intelligence* (pp. 85-101). Springer.

Putnam, R. D. (2000). *Bowling alone: The collapse and revival of American community*. Simon & Schuster.

Riggio, R. E., & Reichard, R. J. (2008). The emotional and social intelligences of effective leadership: An emotional and social skill approach. *Journal of Managerial Psychology*, 23(2), 169-185.

Salovey, P., & Mayer, J. D. (1990). Emotional intelligence. *Imagination, Cognition and Personality*, 9(3), 185-211.

Sternberg, R. J. (1985). *Beyond IQ: A triarchic theory of human intelligence*. Cambridge University Press.

Sternberg, R. J. (2003). *Wisdom, intelligence, and creativity synthesized*. Cambridge University Press.

Twenge, J. M. (2017). *iGen: Why today's super-connected kids are growing up less rebellious, more tolerant, less happy—and completely unprepared for adulthood*. Atria Books.

# Chapter 2: The Five Core Components of Emotional Intelligence

## The Architecture of Human Excellence

Within the vast cathedral of human consciousness lies a magnificent quintet—five interconnected chambers of capability that, when harmonised, create something approaching perfection in the art of living. These are not merely academic constructs gathering dust in psychological journals, but living, breathing dimensions of human experience that determine whether we stumble through life reactive and unconscious, or dance with graceful mastery through even its most complex choreographies.

Like the five movements of a Beethoven symphony, each component possesses its own distinct character while contributing to a greater symphonic whole. Yet unlike musical compositions frozen in time, emotional intelligence represents a dynamic, ever-evolving masterpiece that we compose and recompose with every breath, every interaction, every moment of conscious choice.

The architecture we're about to explore isn't theoretical—it's the blueprint of human flourishing, validated by decades of rigorous research and evidenced in the lives of history's most remarkable individuals. From the boardrooms of Fortune 500 companies to the classrooms where tomorrow's leaders are shaped, from the intimate sanctuaries of our most cherished relationships to the global stages where humanity's greatest challenges await resolution, these five components serve as both compass and engine for extraordinary achievement.

# Self-Awareness: The Sacred Mirror of Consciousness

*"Know thyself"*—inscribed upon the ancient Temple of Apollo at Delphi, this timeless injunction represents perhaps humanity's most profound challenge and greatest opportunity. Self-awareness, the foundational cornerstone of emotional intelligence, transcends mere introspection to become a revolutionary act of consciousness itself.

But what does it truly mean to "know oneself" in an age where external distractions multiply exponentially and internal complexity deepens with each passing moment? Self-awareness, in its most sophisticated form, represents the capacity to observe our inner landscape with the clarity of a scientist and the compassion of a loving friend—simultaneously intimate participant and objective witness to the grand theater of our own experience (Goleman, 1998).

## The Neuroscience of Self-Reflection

Modern neuroscience has illuminated the biological foundations of self-awareness with unprecedented precision. The medial prefrontal cortex—our brain's executive boardroom—orchestrates the complex process of self-reflection, integrating emotional information from the limbic system with cognitive analysis from various cortical regions (Northoff et al., 2006). When we engage in genuine self-awareness, we're literally rewiring our neural architecture, strengthening connections between disparate brain regions and creating new pathways for conscious choice.

Research conducted by Dr. Matthew Lieberman at UCLA reveals that the simple act of labelling emotions—what he terms "affect labelling"—reduces activity in the amygdala by up to 50% while simultaneously increasing activity in the prefrontal cortex (Lieberman et al., 2007). This neurological transformation represents more than academic curiosity; it's the biological foundation of emotional mastery itself.

## The Three Pillars of Self-Awareness

**Emotional Self-Awareness:** The capacity to recognise emotions as they arise, understanding their subtle nuances and complex interactions. This isn't merely knowing that you're "angry" or "sad," but perceiving the intricate emotional ecosystem within—the way disappointment mingles with determination, how excitement carries undertones of anxiety, how love and fear often dance together in intimate partnership (Bar-On, 2006).

Consider the executive who notices her shoulders tightening during a challenging board meeting and recognises this physical signal as the early warning system of mounting frustration. Rather than allowing that frustration to escalate into defensive behaviour, she uses this awareness as valuable data, informing her decision to suggest a brief recess or redirect the conversation toward more productive territory.

**Accurate Self-Assessment:** The sophisticated ability to evaluate one's strengths and limitations with neither false humility nor inflated ego, but with the clear-eyed honesty that enables genuine growth (Goleman, 2013). This represents one of the most challenging aspects of self-awareness, requiring us to transcend the psychological defence mechanisms that typically protect our self-concept from uncomfortable truths.

Research by Kruger and Dunning reveals the profound difficulty most individuals face in accurate self-assessment—those with the least competence often demonstrate the greatest confidence in their abilities, while truly skilled individuals tend to underestimate their capabilities (Kruger & Dunning, 1999). Breaking free from these cognitive biases requires sustained commitment to feedback-seeking, reflection, and the humility to acknowledge our perpetual capacity for self-deception.

**Self-Confidence:** Not the brittle bravado that masks insecurity, but the quiet strength that emerges from deep self-knowledge and acceptance. True self-confidence represents an unshakeable trust in one's ability to navigate whatever challenges arise, rooted in accurate understanding of both capabilities and limitations (Bandura, 1997).

## Cultivating the Inner Observer

Developing self-awareness requires the cultivation of what Buddhist psychology terms the "inner observer"—a perspective within consciousness that can witness thoughts, emotions, and reactions without being overwhelmed by them. This isn't about becoming emotionally detached or coldly analytical; rather, it's about developing the capacity for conscious participation in your own experience.

**Mindfulness Meditation:** Extensive research demonstrates that regular mindfulness practice literally reshapes brain structure, increasing gray matter density in areas associated with self-awareness while reducing reactivity in stress-response systems (Hölzel et al., 2011). The practice involves observing thoughts and emotions as they arise without judgment, creating space between stimulus and response where conscious choice becomes possible.

**Emotional Journaling:** The practice of regularly documenting emotional experiences, triggers, and patterns creates a detailed map of your inner landscape. Dr. James Pennebaker's research reveals that expressive writing about emotional experiences produces measurable improvements in physical health, psychological well-being, and immune function (Pennebaker & Chung, 2011).

**360-Degree Feedback:** Actively seeking input from trusted colleagues, friends, and mentors provides external mirrors that illuminate blind spots and validate or challenge self-perceptions. The key lies not in defensive justification but in curious exploration of discrepancies between self-perception and others' observations.

## Self-Regulation: The Alchemy of Emotional Transformation

If self-awareness represents the capacity to see clearly, self-regulation embodies the profound ability to choose consciously. It's the difference between being a victim of circumstance and an architect of response—between reactive existence and creative living.

Self-regulation doesn't mean emotional suppression or the cultivation of stoic indifference. Rather, it represents the sophisticated ability to experience emotions fully while maintaining the executive function necessary for wise action (Gross, 2015). It's emotional jujitsu—using the force of feeling to generate appropriate response rather than being overwhelmed by emotional intensity.

### The Neuroplasticity of Emotional Control

The human brain's remarkable capacity for change—neuroplasticity—reaches its most dramatic expression in the domain of emotional regulation. The prefrontal cortex can literally strengthen its influence over the limbic system through practice, creating what neuroscientists term "top-down regulation" (Davidson & McEwen, 2012).

Dr. Richard Davidson's ground-breaking research with Tibetan monks reveals that extensive meditation practice produces extraordinary changes in brain structure and function. Long-term practitioners demonstrate gamma wave activity—associated with heightened awareness and cognitive function—that's 700% higher than control groups, even during rest states (Lutz et al., 2004). These aren't genetic anomalies but evidence of human potential activated through conscious practice.

## The Five Domains of Self-Regulation

**Emotional Self-Control:** The ability to manage disruptive emotions without suppression, channelling emotional energy constructively rather than destructively. This involves what psychologists term "emotional granularity"—the capacity to distinguish between subtle emotional states and respond appropriately to each (Barrett, 2017).

Consider the leader who feels frustration building during a team meeting but recognises this emotion as valuable information about unaddressed concerns rather than a signal to become defensive or critical. Instead of reacting impulsively, she uses the frustration as motivation to explore underlying issues and facilitate productive problem-solving.

**Adaptability:** The flexibility to adjust strategies, perspectives, and behaviours in response to changing circumstances without losing core values or sense of identity (Martin et al., 2013). In our rapidly evolving world, adaptability has become perhaps the most crucial survival skill—not mere accommodation to change but the ability to thrive within uncertainty.

**Achievement Orientation:** The drive for continuous improvement and excellence that transcends external rewards, rooted in internal standards and intrinsic motivation (McClelland, 1987). This represents the difference between performance for recognition and performance for mastery—between external validation and internal fulfilment.

**Positive Outlook:** The tendency to see opportunities within challenges, to maintain hope during difficulty, and to approach problems with solution-focused thinking rather than deficit-focused rumination (Seligman, 2011). Research demonstrates that optimistic individuals not only experience greater life satisfaction but also demonstrate superior problem-solving capabilities and resilience.

### The Technology of Transformation

Developing self-regulation requires both understanding and practice—cognitive insight combined with embodied skill-building that gradually rewires automatic response patterns.

**Cognitive Reappraisal:** The practice of consciously reframing situations to generate more empowering emotional responses. Dr. Kevin Ochsner's research reveals that cognitive reappraisal activates prefrontal regions while down-regulating amygdala activity, creating the neurological foundation for emotional mastery (Ochsner & Gross, 2005).

**Somatic Awareness:** Learning to recognise the physical manifestations of emotional states—muscle tension, breathing patterns, heart rate changes—provides early warning systems that enable intervention before emotional overwhelm occurs (Van der Kolk, 2014).

**Values Clarification:** Developing crystal-clear understanding of personal values creates an internal compass that guides decision-making even under pressure. Research demonstrates that values-based decision-making activates reward centres in the brain, generating intrinsic motivation that sustains behaviour change (Hare et al., 2009).

## Motivation: The Sacred Fire of Human Achievement

True motivation transcends the superficial rewards that society dangles before us—money, status, recognition—to touch something deeper and more sustaining. It represents the alignment between our deepest values and our daily actions, the harmony between who we are and what we do, the integration of passion and purpose that transforms work into calling and existence into meaning.

Daniel Pink's revolutionary research reveals that traditional carrot-and-stick motivation actually impairs performance on complex, creative tasks—precisely the kind of work that defines our modern economy (Pink, 2011). Instead, intrinsic motivation—driven by autonomy, mastery, and purpose—generates not only superior performance but also greater satisfaction and psychological well-being.

## The Neuroscience of Intrinsic Drive

The neurotransmitter dopamine, long misunderstood as simply a "pleasure chemical," actually functions as the biological foundation of motivation itself. Dr. Wolfram Schultz's pioneering research reveals that dopamine neurons fire not when we receive rewards but when we anticipate them—and more specifically, when we expect to make progress toward meaningful goals (Schultz, 2015).

This neurological insight illuminates why lottery winners often return to baseline happiness levels while individuals engaged in meaningful work report sustained fulfilment. The brain is designed not for the achievement of static happiness but for the pursuit of valued objectives—what psychologists term "eudaimonic well-being" (Ryan & Deci, 2000).

## The Four Pillars of Emotional Motivation

**Achievement Drive:** The internal compulsion toward excellence that persists regardless of external recognition or reward. This represents what Csikszentmihalyi terms "flow"—the state of complete absorption in challenging activities that utilise our highest skills (Csikszentmihalyi, 1990).

**Commitment:** The ability to align personal goals with larger purposes, finding meaning in contribution to something beyond immediate self-interest. Research demonstrates that individuals with strong commitment experience greater resilience during adversity and maintain motivation through extended periods without external reinforcement (Meyer & Allen, 1991).

**Initiative:** The proactive tendency to identify opportunities and take action without waiting for permission or explicit direction. Initiative represents the entrepreneurial spirit applied to any domain—the willingness to create value rather than merely consume it (Frese & Fay, 2001).

**Optimism:** Not naive positivity but realistic hope based on accurate assessment of challenges combined with confidence in one's ability to develop necessary capabilities. Dr. Martin Seligman's research reveals that optimistic individuals demonstrate superior performance across virtually every domain while maintaining better physical and mental health (Seligman, 2011).

## Cultivating Sustainable Motivation

**Purpose Alignment:** The practice of regularly connecting daily activities to larger meanings and values. Research by Dr. Adam Grant demonstrates that even small reminders of purpose can dramatically increase performance and satisfaction (Grant, 2013).

**Mastery Orientation:** Focusing on skill development and learning rather than performance outcomes creates sustainable motivation that persists through setbacks and failures. Carol Dweck's research on growth mindset reveals that individuals who view abilities as developable demonstrate greater resilience and achievement than those who view them as fixed (Dweck, 2006).

**Progress Tracking:** The regular measurement and celebration of advancement toward meaningful goals activates the brain's reward systems and maintains motivation over extended periods. Teresa Amabile's research reveals that the single most important factor in workplace motivation is the experience of making meaningful progress (Amabile & Kramer, 2011).

# Empathy: The Bridge to Sacred Connection

In an age of increasing polarisation and fragmentation, empathy emerges as perhaps our most essential capacity—the bridge that connects us across differences of culture, experience, and belief. Yet empathy represents far more than mere emotional contagion or sympathetic feeling; it embodies a sophisticated form of social intelligence that enables us to understand, resonate with, and respond appropriately to others' inner experiences.

## The Neuroscience of Human Connection

The discovery of mirror neurons—brain cells that fire both when we perform actions and when we observe others performing the same actions—has revolutionised our understanding of empathy's biological foundations (Rizzolatti & Craighero, 2004). These specialised neurons create the neurological basis for our capacity to "feel with" others, to experience resonance that transcends the boundaries of individual consciousness.

Dr. Tania Singer's ground-breaking research using functional magnetic resonance imaging reveals that when we witness others' pain, our own pain centres activate—demonstrating that empathy isn't merely cognitive understanding but embodied experience (Singer & Lamm, 2009). This neurological mirroring provides the foundation for moral behaviour, social cooperation, and the bonds that hold communities together.

## The Three Dimensions of Empathic Understanding

**Cognitive Empathy:** The intellectual ability to understand others' perspectives, motivations, and mental states—what psychologists term "theory of mind." This represents the capacity to step outside our own experience and accurately model others' inner worlds (Baron-Cohen, 2011).

**Affective Empathy:** The emotional capacity to feel what others feel, to experience genuine resonance with their emotional states. This isn't emotional overwhelm but appropriate "attunement"—sharing feelings without losing individual boundaries (Hoffman, 2000).

**Compassionate Empathy:** The motivated concern for others' welfare that moves us from understanding and feeling to helpful action. Research demonstrates that compassionate empathy activates reward centres in the brain, generating positive feelings that reinforce prosocial behaviour (Klimecki et al., 2013).

## Developing Empathic Mastery

**Perspective-Taking Exercises:** Regularly practicing the mental exercise of viewing situations from others' standpoints develops the cognitive flexibility essential for accurate empathy. Research demonstrates that perspective-taking training improves not only empathic accuracy but also reduces prejudice and increases cooperation (Galinsky & Moskowitz, 2000).

**Emotional Vocabulary Development:** Expanding our repertoire of emotional words increases our capacity to recognise and understand subtle emotional states in ourselves and others. Dr. Lisa Feldman Barrett's research reveals that individuals with greater emotional granularity demonstrate superior emotional regulation and social understanding (Barrett, 2017).

**Active Listening Practice:** The discipline of listening not to respond but to understand creates the psychological safety necessary for authentic empathic connection. Carl Rogers' research demonstrates that feeling truly heard and understood produces measurable improvements in psychological well-being and relationship satisfaction (Rogers, 1961).

# Social Skills: The Artistry of Human

# Influence

If empathy provides the capacity to understand others' inner worlds, social skills represent the sophisticated ability to navigate and influence interpersonal dynamics. These aren't manipulative techniques for getting what we want, but authentic expressions of emotional intelligence that create mutual benefit and shared success.

Social skills encompass the entire spectrum of interpersonal effectiveness—from the intimate one-on-one conversations that build trust to the large-group presentations that inspire collective action. They represent emotional intelligence made manifest in the social world, the bridge between internal awareness and external impact.

## The Neuroscience of Social Influence

Recent neuroscientific research reveals that social influence operates through multiple brain systems simultaneously. The anterior cingulate cortex processes social pain and rejection as intensely as physical pain, explaining why social skills that create inclusion and belonging have such profound impact on others' well-being (Eisenberger, 2012).

Meanwhile, the release of oxytocin—often called the "bonding hormone"—during positive social interactions creates neurochemical foundations for trust, cooperation, and mutual support. Dr. Paul Zak's research demonstrates that leaders who generate oxytocin release in their team members achieve superior performance and loyalty (Zak, 2017).

## The Seven Competencies of Social Mastery

**Influence:** The ability to persuade and motivate others through authentic connection rather than manipulation or coercion. Robert Cialdini's research identifies six principles of ethical influence:

reciprocity, commitment, social proof, authority, liking, and scarcity (Cialdini, 2009).

**Coach and Mentor:** The capacity to develop others' capabilities through guidance, feedback, and support. Research demonstrates that effective mentoring relationships produce benefits for both mentors and mentees, creating cycles of growth and development (Kram, 1985).

**Conflict Management:** The sophisticated ability to navigate disagreements constructively, transforming potential destruction into creative problem-solving opportunities. Fisher and Ury's research on principled negotiation provides frameworks for win-win outcomes that preserve relationships while achieving objectives (Fisher & Ury, 1991).

**Team Leadership:** The capacity to inspire and guide groups toward shared objectives while honouring individual contributions and maintaining group cohesion. Jim Collins' research on exceptional leaders reveals that the most effective individuals combine personal humility with professional will (Collins, 2001).

**Inspirational Leadership:** The ability to articulate compelling visions that motivate others toward extraordinary effort and achievement. Transformational leadership research demonstrates that leaders who inspire through meaning and purpose achieve superior results compared to those who rely solely on transactional relationships (Bass & Riggio, 2006).

## The Integration of Excellence

These five components of emotional intelligence don't operate in isolation but function as an integrated system of human capability. Self-awareness provides the foundation for self-regulation, which enables authentic motivation. Empathy deepens our understanding of others, while social skills translate that understanding into effective action.

The synergy created when all five components operate harmoniously produces what researchers term "resonant leadership"—the capacity to create positive emotional climates that bring out the best in individuals and groups (Boyatzis & McKee, 2005). Such leaders don't merely manage emotions; they orchestrate them, creating symphonies of human potential that achieve outcomes previously thought impossible.

The journey toward emotional mastery requires patience, persistence, and profound commitment to growth. Yet the rewards—for ourselves and for all those whose lives we touch—justify every effort invested in this most human of endeavours. In the chapters that follow, we'll explore each component in greater depth, providing the insights and tools necessary for your own transformation into an emotionally masterful human being.

---

**References:**

Amabile, T., & Kramer, S. (2011). *The progress principle: Using small wins to ignite joy, engagement, and creativity at work*. Harvard Business Review Press.

Bandura, A. (1997). *Self-efficacy: The exercise of control.* W.H. Freeman.

Bar-On, R. (2006). The Bar-On model of emotional-social intelligence (ESI). *Psicothema*, 18, 13-25.

Baron-Cohen, S. (2011). *The Science of Evil: On Empathy and the Origins of Cruelty*. Basic Books.

Barrett, L. F. (2017). *How emotions are made: The secret life of the brain*. Houghton Mifflin Harcourt.

Bass, B. M., & Riggio, R. E. (2006). *Transformational leadership.* Lawrence Erlbaum Associates.

Boyatzis, R., & McKee, A. (2005). *Resonant leadership: Renewing yourself and connecting with others through mindfulness, hope, and compassion*. Harvard Business Review Press.

Cialdini, R. B. (2009). *Influence: Science and practice.* Pearson.

Collins, J. (2001). *Good to great: Why some companies make the leap... and others don't.* HarperBusiness.

Csikszentmihalyi, M. (1990). *Flow: The psychology of optimal experience.* Harper & Row.

Davidson, R. J., & McEwen, B. S. (2012). Social influences on neuroplasticity: Stress and interventions to promote well-being. *Nature Neuroscience,* 15(5), 689-695.

Dweck, C. S. (2006). *Mindset: The new psychology of success.* Random House.

Eisenberger, N. I. (2012). The pain of social disconnection: Examining the shared neural underpinnings of physical and social pain. *Nature Reviews Neuroscience,* 13(6), 421-434.

Fisher, R., & Ury, W. (1991). *Getting to yes: Negotiating agreement without giving in.* Penguin Books.

Frese, M., & Fay, D. (2001). Personal initiative: An active performance concept for work in the 21st century. *Research in Organizational behaviour,* 23, 133-187.

Galinsky, A. D., & Moskowitz, G. B. (2000). Perspective-taking: Decreasing stereotype expression, stereotype accessibility, and in-group favoritism. *Journal of Personality and Social Psychology,* 78(4), 708-724.

Goleman, D. (1998). *Working with emotional intelligence.* Bantam Books.

Goleman, D. (2013). *Focus: The hidden driver of excellence.* HarperCollins.

Grant, A. (2013). *Give and take: Why helping others drives our success.* Penguin Books.

Gross, J. J. (2015). Emotion regulation: Current status and future prospects. *Psychological Inquiry,* 26(1), 1-26.

Hare, T. A., Camerer, C. F., Knoepfle, D. T., O'Doherty, J. P., & Rangel, A. (2009). Value computations in ventral medial prefrontal cortex during charitable decision making incorporate input from regions involved in social cognition. *Journal of Neuroscience*, 29(4), 1058-1066.

Hoffman, M. L. (2000). *Empathy and moral development: Implications for caring and justice*. Cambridge University Press.

Hölzel, B. K., Carmody, J., Vangel, M., Congleton, C., Yerramsetti, S. M., Gard, T., & Lazar, S. W. (2011). Mindfulness practice leads to increases in regional brain gray matter density. *Psychiatry Research: Neuroimaging*, 191(1), 36-43.

Klimecki, O. M., Leiberg, S., Ricard, M., & Singer, T. (2013). Differential pattern of functional brain plasticity after compassion and empathy training. *Social Cognitive and Affective Neuroscience*, 9(6), 873-879.

Kram, K. E. (1985). *Mentoring at work: Developmental relationships in organizational life*. Scott Foresman.

Kruger, J., & Dunning, D. (1999). Unskilled and unaware of it: How difficulties in recognizing one's own incompetence lead to inflated self-assessments. *Journal of Personality and Social Psychology*, 77(6), 1121-1134.

Lieberman, M. D., Eisenberger, N. I., Crockett, M. J., Tom, S. M., Pfeifer, J. H., & Way, B. M. (2007). Putting feelings into words: Affect labelling disrupts amygdala activity in response to affective stimuli. *Psychological Science*, 18(5), 421-428.

Lutz, A., Greischar, L. L., Rawlings, N. B., Ricard, M., & Davidson, R. J. (2004). Long-term meditators self-induce high-amplitude gamma synchrony during mental practice. *Proceedings of the National Academy of Sciences*, 101(46), 16369-16373.

Martin, A. J., Nejad, H., Colmar, S., & Liem, G. A. D. (2013). Adaptability: How students' responses to uncertainty and novelty predict their academic and non-academic outcomes. *Journal of Educational Psychology*, 105(3), 728-746.

McClelland, D. C. (1987). *Human motivation.* Cambridge University Press.

Meyer, J. P., & Allen, N. J. (1991). A three-component conceptualization of organizational commitment. *Human Resource Management Review*, 1(1), 61-89.

Northoff, G., Heinzel, A., de Greck, M., Bermpohl, F., Dobrowolny, H., & Panksepp, J. (2006). Self-referential processing in our brain—a meta-analysis of imaging studies on the self. *NeuroImage*, 31(1), 440-457.

Ochsner, K. N., & Gross, J. J. (2005). The cognitive control of emotion. *Trends in Cognitive Sciences*, 9(5), 242-249.

Pennebaker, J. W., & Chung, C. K. (2011). Expressive writing: Connections to physical and mental health. *Oxford handbook of health psychology*, 417-437.

Pink, D. H. (2011). *Drive: The surprising truth about what motivates us*. Riverhead Books.

Rizzolatti, G., & Craighero, L. (2004). The mirror-neuron system. *Annual Review of Neuroscience*, 27, 169-192.

Rogers, C. R. (1961). *On becoming a person: A therapist's view of psychotherapy*. Houghton Mifflin.

Ryan, R. M., & Deci, E. L. (2000). Self-determination theory and the facilitation of intrinsic motivation, social development, and well-being. *American Psychologist*, 55(1), 68-78.

Schultz, W. (2015). Neuronal reward and decision signals: From theories to data. *Physiological Reviews*, 95(3), 853-951.

Seligman, M. E. (2011). *Flourish: A visionary new understanding of happiness and well-being*. Free Press.

Singer, T., & Lamm, C. (2009). The social neuroscience of empathy. *Annals of the New York Academy of Sciences*, 1156(1), 81-96.

Van der Kolk, B. A. (2014). *The body keeps the score: Brain, mind, and body in the healing of trauma*. Viking.

Zak, P. J. (2017). *Trust factor: The science of creating high-performance companies*. AMACOM.

# Chapter 3: The Neuroscience Behind Emotional Intelligence

## Introduction: Peering into the Cathedral of Consciousness

Within the confines of our skulls lies perhaps the most remarkable creation in the known universe—a three-pound mass of neural tissue that orchestrates every thought, every feeling, every moment of human experience. This extraordinary organ, the brain, does not merely house our consciousness; it *is* our consciousness, sculpting reality through intricate networks of neurons that fire in patterns so complex they humble our greatest supercomputers.

Understanding emotional intelligence on a practical level is empowering, yet venturing into its biological foundations reveals a universe of staggering complexity and beauty. Neuroscience—the study of the brain and nervous system—offers us a window into the very machinery of human experience, showing us that emotions are not chaotic storms that sweep through our minds without warning. Rather, they are the products of exquisitely orchestrated neural symphonies, governed by ancient evolutionary imperatives and shaped by the unique geography of our individual neural landscapes (Damasio, 2005).

The neuroscientific exploration of emotional intelligence represents one of the most thrilling frontiers in contemporary research. It bridges the gap between the subjective experience of feeling and the objective reality of neural activation, between the poetry of human emotion and the precision of scientific inquiry. As we delve deeper into this realm, we discover that emotional responses follow structured patterns involving intricate brain systems—systems that govern everything from the lightning-fast reflexes of fear to the nuanced recognition of subtle social cues, from the iron grip of impulse control to the warm embrace of empathy.

This chapter will serve as your guide through the labyrinthine corridors of the emotional brain. We shall explore the ancient structures that pulse with primal emotion, the sophisticated regions that temper and refine our responses, and the chemical messengers that carry emotional information throughout our bodies. Most importantly, we will uncover the revolutionary truth that has emerged from decades of neuroscientific research: the brain's capacity for change, its ability to rewire itself in response to our conscious efforts to develop emotional intelligence (Goleman, 2005; Davidson & Lutz, 2008).

## The Brain's Emotional Architecture: A Cartographer's Dream

The human brain, in all its baroque complexity, represents the culmination of millions of years of evolutionary refinement. It is simultaneously our oldest inheritance and our newest creation—ancient structures buried deep within its core speak to our reptilian past, while the outer layers of cortex represent the flowering of consciousness that makes us uniquely human.

When we speak of emotions and their neural substrates, we must first acknowledge that no single brain region operates in isolation. Instead, we find ourselves mapping an interconnected web of structures, each contributing its unique voice to the grand chorus of emotional experience. These neural networks have evolved not merely to make us feel, but to ensure our survival, to bind us together in social groups, and to navigate the bewildering complexity of human relationships (LeDoux, 2003).

## The Limbic System: The Ancient Heart of Feeling

Deep within the brain's temporal lobes lies what neuroscientists have long called the "emotional brain"—the limbic system. This collection of evolutionarily ancient structures forms the very foundation of our emotional lives, processing the raw data of experience and transforming it into the feelings that colour every moment of our existence.

The limbic system encompasses several critical structures, each playing its part in the emotional orchestra. The hippocampus, named for its resemblance to a seahorse, serves as our brain's librarian, cataloguing memories and linking them inextricably with the emotions that accompanied their formation. It is here that we find the neurobiological basis for the profound truth that memories are never neutral—they are always tinged with feeling, always carrying the emotional signature of their birth (Squire & Kandel, 2009).

The hypothalamus, though small, wields enormous power over our emotional and physical states. This tiny cluster of neurons serves as the body's master regulator, controlling everything from our circadian rhythms to our stress responses. When we speak of emotions as embodied experiences—the racing heart of anxiety, the warm flush of embarrassment, the leaden weight of sadness—we are witnessing the hypothalamus at work, translating psychological states into physiological realities (Saper, 2002).

## The Amygdala: Sentinel of Survival

Among all the structures in the emotional brain, perhaps none has captured the scientific imagination quite like the amygdala. These two almond-shaped clusters of neurons, one nestled in each temporal lobe, serve as our brain's early warning system, constantly scanning the environment for signs of threat or opportunity.

The amygdala's response time is breathtakingly fast—it can trigger an emotional reaction in as little as twelve milliseconds, faster than conscious thought itself. This speed comes at a cost, however. The amygdala operates on pattern recognition and emotional associations rather than careful logical analysis. It asks not "What is this?" but rather "Is this dangerous? Have I encountered something like this before?" (LeDoux, 1996).

This ancient sentinel has served our species well throughout its evolutionary journey. When our ancestors faced the sudden appearance of a predator, those milliseconds of reaction time could mean the difference between life and death. The amygdala's rapid-fire assessment—friend or foe, approach or avoid, fight or flee—kept our forebears alive long enough to pass their genes to the next generation.

Yet in our modern world, the amygdala's hair-trigger sensitivity can become a liability. The same neural circuits that once protected us from sabre-toothed tigers now fire in response to a critical email from our boss, a disapproving look from a colleague, or a challenging question during a presentation. The amygdala cannot distinguish between a physical threat and a social one—it responds to both with the same primal urgency (Öhman & Mineka, 2001).

## The Prefrontal Cortex: The Executive's Suite

If the amygdala represents our brain's most ancient wisdom, the prefrontal cortex embodies its newest evolutionary achievement. Located just behind the forehead, this region of the brain is uniquely developed in human beings, accounting for a larger proportion of our neural real estate than in any other species.

The prefrontal cortex serves as the brain's executive centre, the seat of higher-order thinking, planning, and decision-making. But perhaps most crucially for our discussion of emotional intelligence, it functions as the brain's emotional regulator, capable of modulating and refining the raw emotional impulses generated by the limbic system (Miller & Cohen, 2001).

This remarkable brain region can be thought of as having several specialised subdivisions, each contributing to our emotional intelligence in unique ways. The dorsolateral prefrontal cortex excels at working memory and cognitive control, allowing us to hold multiple pieces of information in mind while making complex decisions. The ventromedial prefrontal cortex specialises in value-based decision-making and emotional regulation, helping us weigh the emotional significance of different choices. The orbitofrontal cortex processes reward and punishment signals, enabling us to learn from our emotional experiences and adjust our behaviour accordingly (Rolls, 2004).

## The Anterior Cingulate Cortex: The Conflict Monitor

Nestled between the prefrontal cortex and the limbic system lies a structure of particular importance to emotional intelligence—the anterior cingulate cortex (ACC). This region serves as a crucial bridge between emotion and cognition, monitoring for conflicts between different neural systems and coordinating appropriate responses.

The ACC plays a vital role in what neuroscientists call "error detection"—the ability to recognise when our emotional responses may be inappropriate or counterproductive. It also contributes to emotional regulation, helping us manage our reactions to challenging situations. Perhaps most intriguingly, the ACC is involved in empathy and social cognition, allowing us to understand and share the emotional experiences of others (Bush et al., 2000).

## The Insula: The Gateway to Self-Awareness

Hidden deep within the brain's lateral sulcus lies one of the most fascinating structures in the emotional brain—the insula. This region serves as a crucial interface between our internal bodily states and our conscious awareness, translating the subtle signals of our autonomic nervous system into the felt sense of emotion.

The insula allows us to perceive our own heartbeat, to feel the flutter of anxiety in our stomach, to experience the warm glow of contentment that spreads through our chest. It is intimately involved in what neuroscientists call "interoception"—the awareness of internal bodily signals that forms the foundation of self-awareness and emotional intelligence (Craig, 2009).

Research has shown that individuals with larger, more active insulae tend to score higher on measures of emotional intelligence and empathy. They are better able to recognise their own emotional states and more skilled at reading the emotional cues of others. The insula, it seems, serves as a crucial gateway between the body's wisdom and the mind's understanding (Critchley et al., 2004).

## The Amygdala Hijack: When Ancient Circuits Override Modern Wisdom

In the pantheon of concepts that have shaped our understanding of emotional intelligence, few have been as influential as Daniel Goleman's notion of the "amygdala hijack." This vivid metaphor captures a fundamental challenge of human emotional life—the tendency for our ancient emotional circuits to override our more recently evolved rational faculties in moments of perceived threat or intense activation.

The amygdala hijack represents a neural coup d'état, a moment when the brain's alarm system seizes control of our behaviour before the prefrontal cortex can mount an effective response. It is the neurobiological explanation for those moments when we find ourselves saying or doing things we later regret, when our emotional reactions seem disproportionate to the actual circumstances we face.

Consider this scenario: You're presenting a crucial proposal to your company's executive team. Months of preparation have gone into this moment. As you begin to speak, the CEO interrupts with a sharp criticism of your opening statement. In that instant, your amygdala processes the interruption not as constructive feedback but as a threat to your professional standing, your competence, your very identity.

The amygdala's response is swift and decisive. Stress hormones flood your system. Your heart rate spikes. Blood flow is redirected away from the prefrontal cortex—the very region you need most for clear thinking—and toward the muscles needed for fight or flight. Before your rational mind can assess the situation, you find yourself responding defensively, perhaps even aggressively, turning what could have been a productive exchange into a career-limiting moment.

This hijacking occurs because the amygdala receives sensory information along two pathways. The first, which neuroscientist Joseph LeDoux calls the "low road," carries information directly from the sensory organs to the amygdala in just 12 milliseconds. This pathway is fast but crude, capable of detecting only the most basic features of a stimulus. The second pathway, the "high road," routes information through the sensory cortex and other brain regions before reaching the amygdala. This pathway provides much more detailed and accurate information, but it takes 24 milliseconds—twice as long (LeDoux, 1996).

In those critical 12 milliseconds of difference, the amygdala can trigger a full-blown emotional response based on incomplete information. By the time the more accurate assessment arrives via the high road, the damage may already be done. The stress hormones have been released, the defensive posture has been assumed, the harsh words have been spoken.

## The Evolutionary Logic of Rapid Response

Understanding the amygdala hijack requires appreciating its evolutionary logic. For our ancestors, the cost of a false alarm—mistaking a shadow for a predator—was relatively minor compared to the cost of failing to detect a real threat. Natural selection favoured individuals whose amygdalae were sensitive to potential dangers, even if this sensitivity occasionally led to unnecessary alarm responses.

This hair-trigger reactivity served our species well in environments where physical threats were common and immediate responses meant the difference between survival and death. The amygdala's rapid-fire assessment—based on stored emotional memories and pattern recognition rather than careful analysis—allowed our forebears to leap away from striking snakes, flee from approaching predators, and band together against rival groups.

But the modern world presents us with a paradox. While our brains retain these ancient response patterns, the nature of the threats we face has changed dramatically. Today's challenges are predominantly social and psychological rather than physical. They require nuanced responses, careful consideration of long-term consequences, and the ability to manage complex interpersonal dynamics. The very neural circuits that once ensured our survival can now undermine our success in contemporary environments (Sapolsky, 2004).

## Emotional Intelligence as Amygdala Management

The development of emotional intelligence can be understood, in large part, as the cultivation of more sophisticated amygdala management skills. Emotionally intelligent individuals are not immune to amygdala activation—they experience the same rapid emotional responses as everyone else. However, they have developed several crucial capabilities that allow them to work with their emotional reactions rather than being controlled by them.

First, they possess enhanced emotional self-awareness. Through years of mindful attention to their internal states, they have learned to recognise the early warning signs of amygdala activation—the subtle shift in breathing, the tightening in the chest, the change in their internal dialogue. This early detection system provides them with a crucial window of opportunity to engage their prefrontal cortex before the hijack becomes complete.

Second, they have developed what might be called "emotional meta-cognition"—the ability to think about their thinking, to observe their emotional responses with a degree of detachment. This capacity allows them to recognise when they are experiencing an amygdala hijack and to consciously choose their response rather than simply reacting automatically.

Third, they have cultivated a repertoire of regulation strategies that can help them regain emotional equilibrium once an amygdala hijack has begun. These might include deep breathing techniques that activate the parasympathetic nervous system, cognitive reappraisal strategies that help them reframe challenging situations, or simple physical interventions like taking a brief walk or counting to ten.

## Neuroplasticity: The Brain's Magnificent Capacity for Change

Perhaps no discovery in neuroscience has been more revolutionary—or more hopeful—than the recognition of the brain's extraordinary capacity for change throughout our entire lives. For much of the 20th century, scientists believed that the adult brain was essentially fixed, that neural development ended in early adulthood, and that we were forever bound by the neural patterns established in our youth.

This view has been utterly transformed by decades of research into neuroplasticity—the brain's ability to reorganise itself by forming new neural connections, strengthening existing pathways, and even generating new neurons throughout our lives. This discovery has profound implications for our understanding of emotional intelligence, suggesting that our capacity for emotional growth and development is far greater than previously imagined (Doidge, 2007).

## The Mechanisms of Neural Change

Neuroplasticity operates through several distinct but interconnected mechanisms. At the most basic level, synaptic plasticity involves changes in the strength of connections between neurons. When we repeatedly engage in specific behaviours or thought patterns, the synapses involved in those activities become stronger and more efficient. This is the neurobiological basis for the old adage that "neurons that fire together, wire together" (Hebb, 1949).

Structural plasticity involves more dramatic changes to the brain's architecture. New dendrites can sprout from existing neurons, creating additional connection points. The myelin sheaths that insulate neural pathways can thicken, speeding the transmission of electrical signals. In some brain regions, entirely new neurons can be born throughout our lives, a phenomenon known as neurogenesis that was once thought impossible in adult brains (Kempermann, 2019).

Perhaps most remarkably, functional plasticity allows the brain to reassign functions from damaged areas to healthy regions. This extraordinary adaptability is what enables stroke patients to recover lost abilities and allows individuals to develop entirely new skills well into their later years.

## Emotional Intelligence and Neural Sculpting

The implications of neuroplasticity for emotional intelligence are profound. Every time we choose to respond thoughtfully rather than react impulsively, we are literally reshaping our brains. Each moment of mindful awareness, each act of empathy, each instance of emotional regulation creates new neural pathways and strengthens existing ones.

Research has shown that individuals who engage in regular mindfulness meditation develop measurable changes in brain structure. The prefrontal cortex—crucial for emotional regulation—becomes thicker and more active. The amygdala, while retaining its capacity for rapid threat detection, becomes less reactive to non-threatening stimuli. The insula, important for self-awareness and empathy, shows increased gray matter density (Lutz et al., 2004).

These changes are not merely cosmetic. They translate into real-world improvements in emotional intelligence. Individuals who engage in contemplative practices show enhanced emotional regulation, increased empathy, improved attention, and greater resilience in the face of stress. They become literally different people, with different neural architectures supporting different patterns of thought, feeling, and behaviour.

## The Practice-Dependent Nature of Change

Understanding neuroplasticity reveals that developing emotional intelligence is fundamentally similar to developing any other skill. Just as musicians develop enhanced auditory processing through years of practice, and athletes develop improved motor control through repetitive training, individuals can develop greater emotional intelligence through dedicated practice of emotional skills.

This practice-dependent change follows certain principles that are crucial to understand. Repetition is essential—occasional attempts at emotional regulation will produce minimal neural change, while consistent daily practice can create profound transformations. Attention and intention matter enormously; mindful, deliberate practice is far more effective than unconscious repetition. Challenge and progression are important; the brain adapts most readily when we push ourselves slightly beyond our current comfort zone.

The time scales involved in neuroplastic change vary depending on the type of adaptation. Some changes, such as alterations in synaptic strength, can occur within hours or days. Others, such as structural modifications to neural architecture, may require weeks or months of consistent practice. The most profound transformations—the development of entirely new patterns of emotional responding—may require years of dedicated effort.

## The Mirror Neuron System: The Neural Basis of Human Connection

Among the most remarkable discoveries in neuroscience has been the identification of mirror neurons—specialised brain cells that activate both when we perform an action and when we observe someone else performing the same action. These extraordinary neurons, first discovered in macaque monkeys by Italian neuroscientist Giacomo Rizzolatti and his colleagues, have revolutionised our understanding of empathy, social learning, and human connection (Rizzolatti & Craighero, 2004).

Mirror neurons represent nature's solution to one of the most fundamental challenges of social existence: how to understand the minds of others. Without direct access to another person's thoughts and feelings, we must somehow infer their mental states from their observable behaviour. Mirror neurons provide a direct neural pathway for this inference, allowing us to literally experience a shadow of what others are experiencing.

## The Discovery That Changed Everything

The discovery of mirror neurons was serendipitous, as many great scientific discoveries are. Researchers in Rizzolatti's laboratory were studying neurons in the premotor cortex of macaque monkeys, attempting to understand how these cells controlled hand movements. They had implanted electrodes that would fire whenever a monkey grasped an object, producing a characteristic sound.

One day, as the story goes, a researcher reached for a piece of food while a monkey was connected to the recording equipment. To everyone's amazement, the neurons fired just as strongly when the monkey observed the human grasping the food as when the monkey performed the action itself. The brain cells seemed to be "mirroring" the observed action, creating an internal simulation of what they were witnessing.

This initial observation launched decades of research that has revealed the extraordinary scope and importance of the mirror neuron system. These neurons are found not only in motor areas but throughout the brain, including regions involved in emotion, sensation, and social cognition. They respond not only to actions but to intentions, emotions, and even the sensory experiences of others.

## The Empathy Engine

The mirror neuron system provides the neural foundation for empathy—our ability to understand and share the emotional experiences of others. When we observe someone experiencing joy, sadness, fear, or anger, our mirror neurons fire in patterns that partially recreate those emotions within our own neural networks.

We don't just think about what others are feeling; we actually feel a diluted version of their emotions ourselves.

This neural mirroring explains many phenomena that have long puzzled psychologists. Why do we wince when we see someone else get hurt? Why do we find ourselves smiling when we see others smile? Why can emotions spread through a crowd like wildfire? The mirror neuron system provides the biological basis for these experiences, revealing that empathy is not just a learned social skill but a fundamental feature of how our brains are wired.

Research has shown that individuals with more active mirror neuron systems tend to score higher on measures of empathy and emotional intelligence. They are better able to recognise emotions in others, more skilled at perspective-taking, and more successful in their social relationships. Their enhanced mirror neuron activity allows them to create more accurate internal models of others' emotional states (Shamay-Tsoory, 2011).

## Cultural Learning and Social Transmission

Mirror neurons also play a crucial role in cultural learning and the transmission of social norms. Much of what we learn about appropriate emotional expression, social behaviour, and cultural values comes not from explicit instruction but from observing and unconsciously imitating others. Mirror neurons provide the neural mechanism for this social learning, allowing us to absorb the emotional and behavioural patterns of our cultural environment.

This process begins in infancy and continues throughout our lives. Babies learn to smile by mirroring their caregivers' expressions. Children learn emotional regulation by observing how adults handle frustration, disappointment, and stress. Adolescents develop their social identities by mirroring the behaviours and attitudes of their peers. Adults continue to refine their emotional intelligence by unconsciously imitating the emotional patterns of those they admire.

### The Dark Side of Mirroring

While the mirror neuron system enables empathy and social connection, it can also create challenges for emotional intelligence. The same neural circuits that allow us to share others' positive emotions also make us vulnerable to "emotional contagion"—the unconscious absorption of negative emotions from our environment.

If we work in a toxic organisational culture, our mirror neurons will constantly fire in response to the stress, anger, and dysfunction around us. Over time, this can reshape our own emotional patterns, making us more stressed, more negative, and less emotionally intelligent. We become, quite literally, what we repeatedly observe and mirror.

Understanding this vulnerability is crucial for developing emotional intelligence. It highlights the importance of choosing our social environments carefully, surrounding ourselves with individuals whose emotional patterns we want to emulate. It also suggests the value of developing what might be called "selective mirroring"—the ability to consciously choose which emotional patterns we allow ourselves to absorb from others.

## Hormones and Neurotransmitters: The Chemical Symphony of Emotion

Emotions are not merely electrical phenomena occurring within neural networks; they are also profoundly chemical experiences. The brain's extensive network of hormones and neurotransmitters creates the biochemical foundation upon which all emotional experience rests. Understanding this chemical dimension of emotion provides crucial insights into how emotional intelligence operates at the most fundamental level.

## Cortisol: The Stress Hormone's Double-Edged Sword

Perhaps no hormone has received more attention in discussions of emotional intelligence than cortisol, often dubbed the "stress hormone." Released by the adrenal glands in response to activation of the hypothalamic-pituitary-adrenal (HPA) axis, cortisol serves as the body's primary chemical messenger during times of perceived threat or challenge.

In acute situations, cortisol is a lifesaver. It mobilises energy reserves, sharpens attention, suppresses non-essential functions like digestion and reproduction, and prepares the body for vigorous action. This stress response system evolved to handle the brief, intense challenges our ancestors faced—escaping from predators, defending territory, or surviving natural disasters.

However, chronic elevation of cortisol—the result of persistent stress in modern life—can wreak havoc on both physical health and emotional intelligence. High cortisol levels impair the function of the prefrontal cortex, the very brain region we depend upon for emotional regulation, decision-making, and social judgment. They also enlarge the amygdala, making us more reactive to perceived threats and less capable of nuanced emotional responses (Sapolsky, 2004).

Individuals with high emotional intelligence tend to have more balanced cortisol patterns. They show appropriate cortisol responses to acute stressors but return to baseline more quickly. Their enhanced emotional regulation skills help them avoid the chronic stress that leads to persistent cortisol elevation, creating a positive feedback loop that supports both psychological well-being and physical health.

## Oxytocin: The Molecule of Connection

At the opposite end of the emotional spectrum from cortisol lies oxytocin, often called the "love hormone" or "bonding hormone."

This neuropeptide, produced in the hypothalamus and released by the posterior pituitary, plays a crucial role in social bonding, trust, empathy, and prosocial behaviour.

Oxytocin levels rise during positive social interactions—hugging, laughing with friends, caring for children, engaging in acts of kindness. These elevated oxytocin levels, in turn, make us more generous, more trusting, more empathetic, and more socially engaged. We become caught in a virtuous cycle where positive social behaviours increase oxytocin, which motivates more positive social behaviours.

Research has shown that individuals with higher baseline oxytocin levels tend to be more emotionally intelligent. They are better at reading social cues, more skilled at building relationships, and more effective at resolving interpersonal conflicts. They also show greater resilience in the face of social stress and recover more quickly from relationship difficulties (Zak, 2012).

Interestingly, oxytocin's effects are not uniformly positive. While it increases trust and cooperation within our social groups, it can also increase suspicion and hostility toward outsiders. This dual nature reflects oxytocin's evolutionary origins as a hormone that promoted survival through group cohesion and defence against external threats.

## Dopamine: The Motivation Molecule

Dopamine, often mischaracterised as the "pleasure hormone," actually serves a more complex and crucial function in emotional intelligence. Rather than simply signalling pleasure, dopamine is primarily involved in motivation, goal-seeking behaviour, and the prediction of rewards. It is the neurochemical that drives us to pursue objectives, learn from experience, and maintain effort in the face of challenges.

The dopamine system consists of several pathways, each serving different functions. The mesolimbic pathway, connecting the ventral tegmental area to the nucleus accumbens, is involved in reward processing and motivation. The mesocortical pathway, projecting to the prefrontal cortex, plays a crucial role in cognitive control and emotional regulation. Dysfunction in these dopamine pathways is associated with various mental health conditions, including depression, ADHD, and addiction.

Individuals with well-functioning dopamine systems tend to be more emotionally resilient, more motivated to pursue long-term goals, and better able to delay gratification. They experience appropriate levels of motivation and reward sensitivity, neither becoming paralysed by perfectionism nor overwhelmed by impulsive desires. Their balanced dopamine function supports the sustained effort required to develop emotional intelligence skills (Schultz, 2016).

## Serotonin: The Mood Stabiliser

Serotonin, perhaps the most famous of the neurotransmitters due to its connection with depression and antidepressant medications, plays a crucial role in mood regulation, emotional stability, and social behaviour. Approximately 90% of the body's serotonin is produced in the gut, highlighting the intimate connection between physical and emotional well-being.

Adequate serotonin levels are associated with stable mood, emotional resilience, impulse control, and social confidence. Low serotonin, conversely, is linked with depression, anxiety, aggression, and poor impulse control. The relationship between serotonin and emotional intelligence is complex and bidirectional—balanced serotonin supports the emotional stability necessary for developing EI skills, while practices that enhance emotional intelligence can help maintain healthy serotonin levels.

Research has shown that activities known to boost emotional intelligence—such as regular exercise, mindfulness meditation, gratitude practice, and positive social interaction—also tend to increase serotonin production. This suggests that developing emotional intelligence and maintaining neurochemical balance are mutually reinforcing processes (Young, 2007).

## Emotional Regulation and the Prefrontal Cortex: The Executive's Challenge

The prefrontal cortex, that uniquely human region of the brain that sits just behind our foreheads, faces perhaps the most challenging task in all of neuroscience: modulating and regulating the powerful emotional signals generated by our ancient limbic system. This neural David must somehow control the Goliath of our emotional responses, transforming raw feeling into appropriate action.

### The Anatomy of Control

The prefrontal cortex is not a uniform structure but rather a collection of specialised regions, each contributing unique capabilities to emotional regulation. The dorsolateral prefrontal cortex (dlPFC) serves as the brain's CEO, maintaining working memory, directing attention, and implementing cognitive control strategies. When we consciously decide to reframe a negative situation or deliberately shift our attention away from troubling thoughts, we are engaging the dlPFC.

The ventromedial prefrontal cortex (vmPFC) specialises in value-based decision-making and emotional evaluation. It helps us assess the emotional significance of different options and integrate emotional information into our decision-making processes. Damage to this region can leave individuals technically capable of logical reasoning but unable to make good decisions because they cannot properly weigh the emotional consequences of their choices.

The orbitofrontal cortex (OFC) processes reward and punishment signals, enabling us to learn from our emotional experiences. It creates predictions about the emotional outcomes of different actions, allowing us to anticipate how we might feel if we choose one course of action over another. This predictive capacity is crucial for emotional intelligence, as it enables us to make choices that support our long-term emotional well-being rather than simply pursuing immediate gratification.

## The Regulation Toolkit

Emotionally intelligent individuals have developed a sophisticated toolkit of regulation strategies, each involving different prefrontal circuits and serving different purposes. Cognitive reappraisal—the ability to reframe situations in more positive or realistic terms—relies heavily on the dlPFC's capacity for cognitive control. When we tell ourselves that a criticism is actually valuable feedback or that a setback is an opportunity for growth, we are using cognitive reappraisal to transform our emotional experience.

Attention regulation involves consciously directing our focus toward or away from emotional stimuli. This might involve choosing to concentrate on solutions rather than problems, focusing on what we can control rather than what we cannot, or deliberately attending to positive aspects of our experience. These attention-based strategies engage networks connecting the prefrontal cortex with parietal attention systems.

Emotion suppression—while sometimes necessary—is generally a less effective and more effortful regulation strategy. It involves using prefrontal control to inhibit the expression of emotion without necessarily changing the underlying emotional experience. While suppression can be useful in certain social situations, chronic use of this strategy is associated with increased stress and reduced well-being.

Response modulation involves changing our behavioural responses to emotions without necessarily changing the emotions themselves. This might involve taking deep breaths when anxious, going for a walk when angry, or engaging in physical exercise when stressed. These strategies work by engaging the body's natural regulatory systems, particularly the parasympathetic nervous system, which promotes calm and recovery.

## The Development of Regulatory Capacity

The prefrontal cortex is among the last brain regions to mature, with some areas not reaching full development until the mid-twenties. This extended developmental timeline has profound implications for emotional intelligence. Children and adolescents are literally working with incomplete regulatory systems, making them more vulnerable to emotional hijacks and less capable of sophisticated emotional regulation.

However, this extended plasticity also creates tremendous opportunities for growth. The regulatory circuits of the prefrontal cortex remain malleable throughout our lives, capable of strengthening and refining through appropriate practice. Individuals who engage in regular emotional intelligence training—whether through formal programmes, contemplative practices, or simply mindful attention to their emotional responses—can continue developing these capacities well into adulthood.

# The Neuroscience of Habit Formation in Emotional Intelligence

The transformation of emotional intelligence from an effortful skill into an automatic capacity depends fundamentally on the brain's extraordinary ability to create and strengthen habitual patterns of response. Understanding the neuroscience of habit formation reveals why some emotional intelligence interventions succeed while others fail, and provides a roadmap for creating lasting change in our emotional lives.

## The Habit Loop in Neural Terms

Every habit, whether behavioural or emotional, follows a predictable neural pattern that researchers call the "habit loop." This loop consists of three components: a cue (the trigger that initiates the habitual response), a routine (the automatic behaviour or emotional response), and a reward (the positive outcome that reinforces the pattern).

In neural terms, this loop involves a complex interaction between several brain systems. The basal ganglia, particularly the striatum, serves as the brain's habit centre, storing automatic behavioural patterns and emotional responses. The prefrontal cortex initially guides the formation of new habits through conscious decision-making and effortful control. However, as habits become more established, control shifts from the prefrontal cortex to the basal ganglia, making the responses more automatic and less effortful (Graybiel, 2008).

## Creating Emotional Habits

Consider the process of developing greater emotional resilience in the face of criticism. Initially, when faced with negative feedback, an individual might naturally experience an amygdala hijack—feeling defensive, angry, or hurt. Developing resilience requires creating a new emotional habit loop.

The cue remains the same: receiving criticism. However, the individual must consciously choose a new routine: taking a deep breath, pausing to consider the validity of the feedback, and responding thoughtfully rather than reactively. The reward—maintaining relationships, learning and growing, feeling proud of their mature response—reinforces this new pattern.

Initially, this new response requires enormous prefrontal effort. The individual must consciously override their natural defensive reactions and deliberately choose a more constructive response. However, with repetition, the neural pathways supporting this new pattern become stronger and more automatic. The basal ganglia begins to store this pattern as a habit, reducing the cognitive effort required and making resilient responses more natural and spontaneous.

## The Time Course of Neural Change

The transformation of emotional intelligence skills into habits follows a predictable timeline that reflects underlying neural changes. In the first stage, lasting roughly 3-4 weeks, individuals must rely heavily on conscious effort and prefrontal control. During this period, the new behaviours feel effortful and unnatural, and there's a high risk of reverting to old patterns under stress.

The second stage, lasting approximately 2-3 months, sees a gradual shift from prefrontal control to basal ganglia automation. The new emotional responses begin to feel more natural, requiring less conscious effort. However, they remain vulnerable to disruption during times of high stress or emotional activation.

The third stage, which may take 6 months to several years depending on the complexity of the pattern, involves full habituation. The new emotional responses become truly automatic, operating even under conditions of stress or distraction. Neural imaging studies show that by this stage, activation has shifted from prefrontal regions to the basal ganglia, indicating that the responses have become truly habitual (Lally et al., 2010).

### Environmental Design for Emotional Habits

Understanding the neuroscience of habit formation highlights the crucial importance of environmental design in developing emotional intelligence. Our brains are constantly shaped by the environmental cues around us, and creating supportive environments can dramatically accelerate the development of emotionally intelligent habits.

This environmental influence operates through what neuroscientists call "contextual cueing." The brain associates specific environments, people, and situations with particular emotional patterns. If we consistently practice emotional regulation in certain contexts, those contexts become cues that automatically trigger more regulated responses. Conversely, environments associated with emotional reactivity can become triggers for less intelligent emotional patterns.

Successful development of emotional intelligence requires careful attention to these environmental factors. This might involve creating physical spaces that support reflection and calm responses, choosing social environments that model emotional intelligence, or developing routines that regularly cue emotionally intelligent behaviours. The brain's habit systems are remarkably sensitive to these contextual factors, making environmental design a powerful tool for emotional development (Wood & Neal, 2007).

## The Social Brain: Networks of Connection and Understanding

Human beings are fundamentally social creatures, and our brains have evolved elaborate neural networks dedicated to understanding, predicting, and responding to the behaviour of others. These social brain networks form the neurobiological foundation for many aspects of emotional intelligence, including empathy, social awareness, and relationship management.

## The Default Mode Network and Social Cognition

One of the most significant discoveries in neuroscience over the past two decades has been the identification of the default mode network (DMN)—a collection of brain regions that becomes active when we're not focused on specific tasks but instead engaged in internally directed cognition. Remarkably, much of this default mental activity involves social thinking: remembering past social interactions, imagining future social scenarios, considering others' perspectives, and reflecting on our own social relationships (Buckner et al., 2008).

The DMN includes several key regions: the medial prefrontal cortex, which is involved in thinking about mental states; the posterior cingulate cortex, which contributes to self-referential thinking; the angular gyrus, which helps integrate information from different sources; and the temporal poles, which are involved in social semantic knowledge. The extensive overlap between the DMN and social cognition networks suggests that social thinking is so fundamental to human experience that it represents our brain's "default" mode of operation.

This has profound implications for emotional intelligence. Individuals with more active and well-connected default mode networks tend to be more socially aware, better at perspective-taking, and more skilled at navigating complex social situations. They spend more time naturally reflecting on social dynamics, anticipating others' reactions, and considering the social implications of their actions.

## Theory of Mind and Mentalising

One of the most sophisticated capabilities of the social brain is theory of mind—the ability to understand that others have beliefs, desires, intentions, and emotions that may differ from our own. This capacity, which typically develops around age 4 in humans, requires the coordination of multiple brain networks and represents one of the pinnacles of human cognitive evolution.

The neural networks supporting theory of mind include the medial prefrontal cortex, the temporoparietal junction, the superior temporal sulcus, and the temporal poles. These regions work together to create what neuroscientists call the "mentalising network"—a system dedicated to understanding the mental states of others (Frith & Frith, 2003).

Advanced theory of mind abilities is crucial for emotional intelligence. They enable us to recognise when others are experiencing emotions different from our own, to understand the complex motivations behind people's behaviour, and to predict how others might react to different social situations. Individuals with enhanced mentalising abilities are typically more successful in leadership roles, more effective at resolving conflicts, and more skilled at building and maintaining relationships.

## The Neurobiology of Social Emotions

Beyond basic emotions like fear, anger, and joy, humans experience a rich array of social emotions—guilt, shame, pride, embarrassment, envy, and gratitude—that evolved specifically to navigate the complexities of group living. These social emotions involve neural circuits that extend beyond the basic emotional systems, incorporating regions involved in social cognition, moral reasoning, and self-evaluation.

Pride, for example, involves not only the positive affect systems associated with dopamine and reward but also regions involved in self-evaluation and social status assessment. Guilt and shame engage networks involved in moral reasoning and social norm violation detection, as well as systems that motivate prosocial repair behaviours. These complex emotional experiences require the integration of multiple neural systems and represent some of the most sophisticated forms of emotional processing (Tangney & Dearing, 2002).

Understanding the neurobiology of social emotions reveals why emotional intelligence involves more than simply managing basic emotional reactions. It requires the development of sophisticated neural networks that can integrate emotional, social, and moral information to generate appropriate responses to complex interpersonal situations.

## Stress, Resilience, and the Emotionally Intelligent Brain

The relationship between stress and emotional intelligence represents one of the most practically important aspects of emotional neuroscience. Chronic stress can undermine virtually every aspect of emotional intelligence, while well-developed emotional intelligence skills can provide remarkable protection against the harmful effects of stress.

### The Neurobiology of Stress Response

When faced with a stressor, the brain initiates a cascade of responses designed to mobilise energy and attention for dealing with the challenge. The sympathetic nervous system triggers the rapid release of adrenaline and noradrenaline, creating the immediate "fight or flight" response. Simultaneously, the hypothalamic-pituitary-adrenal (HPA) axis begins producing cortisol, which sustains the stress response over longer periods.

These stress responses are adaptive in the short term, enhancing performance and survival in genuinely threatening situations. However, chronic activation of these systems can have devastating effects on brain function and emotional intelligence. Prolonged cortisol exposure damages neurons in the hippocampus, impairing memory formation and retrieval. It also reduces the volume and functionality of the prefrontal cortex, undermining cognitive control and emotional regulation (McEwen, 2007).

Perhaps most troubling, chronic stress enlarges the amygdala and increases its reactivity. This creates a vicious cycle where stressed individuals become more sensitive to potential threats, leading to more frequent stress responses and further neural changes. Over time, chronically stressed individuals may find themselves trapped in patterns of emotional reactivity that seem impossible to break.

## The Resilience Factor

Resilience—the ability to bounce back from adversity and maintain psychological well-being in the face of stress—appears to have distinct neural signatures. Resilient individuals show several characteristic brain patterns that distinguish them from those who are more vulnerable to stress-related difficulties.

First, resilient individuals tend to have stronger prefrontal-limbic connections, allowing for better top-down regulation of emotional responses. Their prefrontal cortex remains more active during stress, enabling them to maintain cognitive control and emotional regulation even under challenging circumstances.

Second, they show more balanced activity in the autonomic nervous system, with better parasympathetic recovery following stress activation. This means they not only respond appropriately to stressors but also return to baseline more quickly, preventing the chronic activation that leads to stress-related health problems.

Third, resilient individuals often show enhanced activity in brain regions associated with meaning-making and positive reappraisal. They are neurobiologically equipped to find meaning in adversity, to learn from challenging experiences, and to maintain optimistic perspectives even during difficult periods (Southwick & Charney, 2012).

### Building Resilience Through Emotional Intelligence

The good news is that resilience is not simply a fixed trait but a capacity that can be developed through appropriate training and practice. Many of the interventions that enhance emotional intelligence also build resilience by strengthening the neural circuits involved in stress regulation and emotional control.

Mindfulness practices, for example, have been shown to reduce amygdala reactivity while strengthening prefrontal control networks. Regular meditation literally rewires the brain for greater emotional balance and stress resilience. Similarly, cognitive-behavioural interventions that teach individuals to identify and challenge negative thought patterns strengthen the prefrontal circuits involved in cognitive reappraisal and emotional regulation.

Physical exercise represents another powerful intervention for building both emotional intelligence and resilience. Regular aerobic exercise promotes the growth of new neurons in the hippocampus, enhances prefrontal function, and increases the production of brain-derived neurotrophic factor (BDNF), a protein that supports neural growth and plasticity (Ratey & Hagerman, 2008).

## The Developing Emotional Brain: A Lifelong Journey

Understanding the developmental trajectory of emotional intelligence requires appreciating that different brain regions mature at different rates and that the capacity for emotional growth continues throughout our entire lives. This developmental perspective has profound implications for how we approach emotional intelligence training and support across the lifespan.

## The Adolescent Brain and Emotional Development

Perhaps no period of life presents greater challenges for emotional intelligence than adolescence. During these tumultuous years, the brain undergoes dramatic changes that create a perfect storm of emotional intensity and regulatory difficulty. The limbic system, including the amygdala, reaches adult levels of activation during early adolescence, creating intense emotional experiences. However, the prefrontal cortex—crucial for emotional regulation—doesn't fully mature until the mid-twenties (Steinberg, 2013).

This developmental mismatch explains many of the characteristics we associate with adolescence: emotional intensity, risk-taking behaviour, peer influence, and difficulty with long-term planning. Adolescents are literally working with adult-level emotional systems but child-level regulatory capacity. Understanding this neurobiological reality can help parents, educators, and adolescents themselves approach this developmental period with greater compassion and more appropriate expectations.

The extended plasticity of the adolescent brain also creates remarkable opportunities for emotional development. The neural circuits being established during these years can be shaped by experience, making adolescence a critical period for developing emotional intelligence skills. Programs that teach mindfulness, emotional regulation, and social skills during adolescence can have profound and lasting effects on emotional development.

## Adult Neuroplasticity and Emotional Growth

While the brain's capacity for change is greatest during childhood and adolescence, neuroplasticity continues throughout our entire lives, offering hope for continued emotional growth and development. Adult brains retain the ability to form new neural connections, strengthen existing pathways, and even generate new neurons in certain regions.

This continued plasticity means that adults can develop new emotional intelligence skills, overcome limiting emotional patterns, and create more satisfying relationships at any stage of life. However, adult learning follows somewhat different principles than childhood development. Adult emotional learning tends to be more effortful and requires more conscious intention and practice. It also tends to be more vulnerable to interference from existing neural patterns and habitual responses.

Successful adult emotional development often requires what psychologists call "unlearning"—the weakening of maladaptive neural patterns that were established earlier in life. This process can be challenging and may require professional support, particularly when dealing with trauma-related emotional patterns or deeply ingrained defensive responses.

## The Aging Brain and Emotional Wisdom

Contrary to stereotypes about aging and cognitive decline, research has revealed that certain aspects of emotional intelligence actually improve with age. Older adults often show enhanced emotional regulation, greater emotional stability, and improved social judgment compared to younger individuals. This pattern has been termed "emotional wisdom" and appears to reflect the cumulative effects of life experience combined with age-related changes in brain function (Carstensen et al., 2011).

Several neural changes contribute to this emotional wisdom. The aging brain shows increased activity in prefrontal regions during emotional processing, suggesting enhanced regulatory capacity. There's also evidence of increased bilateral brain activation, which may reflect the recruitment of additional neural resources to maintain emotional functioning.

However, aging also brings challenges for emotional intelligence. Processing speed declines, working memory capacity decreases, and some individuals may experience difficulties with emotional flexibility. Understanding these age-related changes can help older adults adapt their emotional intelligence strategies and maintain high levels of emotional functioning throughout their later years.

## Implications for Training and Development

The neuroscientific understanding of emotional intelligence has profound implications for how we approach emotional development and training. Rather than treating emotional intelligence as an abstract concept, we can now design interventions based on what we know about how the brain actually learns and changes.

### Evidence-Based Interventions

Several training approaches have been validated through neuroscientific research. Mindfulness-based interventions consistently show positive effects on brain structure and function, enhancing prefrontal control while reducing amygdala reactivity. These programmes work by training individuals to observe their thoughts and emotions without immediately reacting, strengthening the neural circuits involved in emotional awareness and regulation.

Cognitive-behavioural approaches that focus on identifying and challenging maladaptive thought patterns also show clear neural effects. These interventions strengthen prefrontal regions involved in cognitive control and reappraisal while reducing activation in emotional processing centres during negative emotional states.

Social and emotional learning (SEL) programmes, particularly those implemented during childhood and adolescence, can have lasting effects on brain development. These programmes work by providing repeated practice in emotional recognition, regulation, and social skills during critical periods of neural plasticity.

### The Importance of Practice and Repetition

Understanding neuroplasticity reveals why emotional intelligence development requires sustained practice rather than simply intellectual understanding. Knowledge about emotions is processed primarily in the brain's cognitive systems, while emotional responses involve limbic and subcortical regions that learn through repetition and experience rather than instruction.

This means that effective emotional intelligence training must provide opportunities for experiential learning and repeated practice. Role-playing exercises, mindfulness practices, real-world application opportunities, and guided reflection all provide the kind of experiential learning that can create lasting neural changes.

### Individual Differences and Personalised Approaches

Neuroscientific research has also revealed significant individual differences in brain structure and function that affect how people learn emotional intelligence skills. Some individuals naturally have stronger prefrontal-limbic connections, making emotional regulation easier. Others may have more reactive amygdalae, requiring different training approaches.

These individual differences suggest the value of personalised approaches to emotional intelligence development. Rather than using one-size-fits-all programmes, the most effective interventions may need to be adapted to individual neural profiles, learning styles, and developmental needs.

## Conclusion: The Promise of Neuroscientific

## Understanding

The neuroscience of emotional intelligence reveals a remarkable truth that should inspire hope in anyone seeking to develop greater emotional wisdom: the brain's capacity for change far exceeds what we previously imagined. We are not prisoners of our genetics, our early experiences, or our current emotional patterns. Instead, we possess neural architectures of extraordinary plasticity, capable of transformation throughout our entire lives.

This scientific understanding liberates us from limiting beliefs about emotional intelligence being a fixed trait that some people possess and others lack. It reveals instead that emotional intelligence is more like physical fitness—a capacity that can be developed through appropriate training, sustained through regular practice, and enhanced throughout our lives.

The journey toward greater emotional intelligence is fundamentally a journey of neural transformation. Each moment of mindful awareness creates new synaptic connections. Every act of empathy strengthens mirror neuron networks. Each instance of emotional regulation builds prefrontal control circuits. We are, quite literally, sculpting our brains with every choice we make about how to respond to the emotional challenges of life.

Yet this understanding also reveals the profound responsibility we bear for our own emotional development. The brain's plasticity is not automatic—it requires conscious intention, sustained effort, and the willingness to persist through the often-uncomfortable process of change. Developing emotional intelligence is not simply a matter of learning new techniques; it requires the courage to rewire fundamental patterns of thinking, feeling, and responding that may have been established over decades.

The neuroscience of emotional intelligence also illuminates the interconnected nature of personal and social transformation. As we develop greater emotional intelligence, we don't just change ourselves—we change the neural environments of everyone around us. Our enhanced empathy activates others' mirror neuron systems. Our emotional regulation models healthier patterns for our children, colleagues, and communities. Our increased social awareness creates more positive interpersonal dynamics that benefit everyone involved.

Perhaps most importantly, this scientific understanding reveals that emotional intelligence is not a luxury reserved for the privileged few but a fundamental capacity that every human being can develop. The neural substrates for empathy, self-awareness, emotional regulation, and social skill exist in every healthy brain. What varies is not the potential for emotional intelligence but the degree to which that potential has been developed and expressed.

As we stand on the threshold of even greater understanding—with new neuroscientific techniques revealing ever more detail about the brain's emotional architecture—we can be confident that the extraordinary hidden power of emotional intelligence lies not in some mystical or intangible realm, but in the very substance of our neural networks. We carry within our skulls the capacity for profound emotional wisdom, extraordinary social connection, and remarkable psychological resilience.

The question is not whether we possess this capacity—neuroscience has conclusively demonstrated that we do. The question is whether we will have the courage, commitment, and compassion to undertake the sacred work of developing it. The brain we shape through our daily choices about how to respond to life's emotional challenges becomes the foundation for everything else we hope to achieve in our relationships, our work, and our contributions to the world.

In the next chapter, we will explore how this neurologically-grounded emotional intelligence translates into tangible success across every domain of human experience—from career advancement to relationship satisfaction, from physical health to psychological well-being. We will see how the ancient circuits of emotion, when properly understood and skilfully developed, become the foundation for a life of meaning, connection, and extraordinary achievement.

---

## References

Buckner, R. L., Andrews-Hanna, J. R., & Schacter, D. L. (2008). The brain's default network: Anatomy, function, and relevance to disease. *Annals of the New York Academy of Sciences*, 1124(1), 1-38.

Bush, G., Luu, P., & Posner, M. I. (2000). Cognitive and emotional influences in anterior cingulate cortex. *Trends in Cognitive Sciences*, 4(6), 215-222.

Carstensen, L. L., Turan, B., Scheibe, S., Ram, N., Ersner-Hershfield, H., Samanez-Larkin, G. R., ... & Nesselroade, J. R. (2011). Emotional experience improves with age: Evidence based on over 10 years of experience sampling. *Psychology and Aging*, 26(1), 21-33.

Craig, A. D. (2009). How do you feel—now? The anterior insula and human awareness. *Nature Reviews Neuroscience*, 10(1), 59-70.

Critchley, H. D., Wiens, S., Rotshtein, P., Öhman, A., & Dolan, R. J. (2004). Neural systems supporting interoceptive awareness. *Nature Neuroscience*, 7(2), 189-195.

Damasio, A. (2005). *Descartes' error: Emotion, reason, and the human brain*. Penguin Books.

Davidson, R. J., & Lutz, A. (2008). Buddha's brain: Neuroplasticity and meditation. *IEEE Signal Processing Magazine*, 25(6), 176-188.

Doidge, N. (2007). *The brain that changes itself: Stories of personal triumph from the frontiers of brain science*. Penguin Books.

Frith, U., & Frith, C. D. (2003). Development and neurophysiology of mentalizing. *Philosophical Transactions of the Royal Society B*, 358(1431), 459-473.

Goleman, D. (2005). *Emotional intelligence: Why it matters more than IQ*. Bantam Books.

Graybiel, A. M. (2008). Habits, rituals, and the evaluative brain. *Annual Review of Neuroscience*, 31, 359-387.

Hebb, D. O. (1949). *The organization of behaviour: A neuropsychological theory*. Wiley.

Kempermann, G. (2019). Environmental enrichment, new neurons and the neurobiology of individuality. *Nature Reviews Neuroscience*, 20(4), 235-245.

Lally, P., Van Jaarsveld, C. H., Potts, H. W., & Wardle, J. (2010). How are habits formed: Modelling habit formation in the real world. *European Journal of Social Psychology*, 40(6), 998-1009.

LeDoux, J. (1996). *The emotional brain: The mysterious underpinnings of emotional life*. Simon & Schuster.

LeDoux, J. (2003). The emotional brain, fear, and the amygdala. *Cellular and Molecular Neurobiology*, 23(4), 727-738.

Lutz, A., Slagter, H. A., Dunne, J. D., & Davidson, R. J. (2008). Attention regulation and monitoring in meditation. *Trends in Cognitive Sciences*, 12(4), 163-169.

McEwen, B. S. (2007). Physiology and neurobiology of stress and adaptation: Central role of the brain. *Physiological Reviews*, 87(3), 873-904.

Miller, E. K., & Cohen, J. D. (2001). An integrative theory of prefrontal cortex function. *Annual Review of Neuroscience*, 24(1), 167-202.

Öhman, A., & Mineka, S. (2001). Fears, phobias, and preparedness: Toward an evolved module of fear and fear learning. *Psychological Review*, 108(3), 483-522.

Ratey, J. J., & Hagerman, E. (2008). *Spark: The revolutionary new science of exercise and the brain*. Little, Brown and Company.

Rizzolatti, G., & Craighero, L. (2004). The mirror-neuron system. *Annual Review of Neuroscience*, 27, 169-192.

Rolls, E. T. (2004). The functions of the orbitofrontal cortex. *Brain and Cognition*, 55(1), 11-29.

Saper, C. B. (2002). The central autonomic nervous system: Conscious visceral perception and autonomic pattern generation. *Annual Review of Neuroscience*, 25(1), 433-469.

Sapolsky, R. M. (2004). *Why zebras don't get ulcers: The acclaimed guide to stress, stress-related diseases, and coping*. Henry Holt and Company.

Schultz, W. (2016). Dopamine reward prediction error coding. *Dialogues in Clinical Neuroscience*, 18(1), 23-32.

Shamay-Tsoory, S. G. (2011). The neural bases for empathy. *The Neuroscientist*, 17(1), 18-24.

Southwick, S. M., & Charney, D. S. (2012). *Resilience: The science of mastering life's greatest challenges*. Cambridge University Press.

Squire, L. R., & Kandel, E. R. (2009). *Memory: From mind to molecules*. Scientific American Library.

Steinberg, L. (2013). The influence of neuroscience on US Supreme Court decisions about adolescents' criminal culpability. *Nature Reviews Neuroscience*, 14(7), 513-518.

Tangney, J. P., & Dearing, R. L. (2002). *Shame and guilt*. Guilford Press.

Wood, W., & Neal, D. T. (2007). A new look at habits and the habit-goal interface. *Psychological Review*, 114(4), 843-863.

Young, S. N. (2007). How to increase serotonin in the human brain without drugs. *Journal of Psychiatry & Neuroscience*, 32(6), 394-399.

Zak, P. J. (2012). *The moral molecule: How trust works.* Penguin Books.

# Chapter 4: Emotional Intelligence and Personal Success

*The Metamorphosis of Human Potential Through Emotional Mastery*

## Introduction: The Silent Revolution of Success

In the labyrinthine corridors of human achievement, where aspirations collide with reality and dreams wrestle with circumstance, a profound revelation has emerged from decades of rigorous research and lived experience. Success—that elusive, multifaceted jewel that has captivated humanity since time immemorial—is not merely the offspring of intellectual prowess or technical acumen. Rather, it is the progeny of something far more nuanced, far more intimate: emotional intelligence.

The contemporary landscape of achievement has undergone a seismic shift. Gone are the days when raw intellect alone could guarantee a trajectory toward excellence. Today's hyper-competitive, digitally interconnected, and perpetually evolving world demands a different kind of intelligence—one that navigates the complex terrain of human emotion, interpersonal dynamics, and psychological resilience (Goleman, 2006). This intelligence, known as emotional quotient (EQ), has emerged as the silent architect of extraordinary success stories, the invisible hand that guides visionaries toward their destinies.

Consider, for a moment, the profound irony of our educational systems and societal structures. We invest countless hours perfecting mathematical equations, memorising historical dates, and mastering scientific principles—all admirable pursuits—yet we remain woefully underprepared for the emotional complexities that define our professional trajectories and personal fulfilment (Bar-On,

2006). It is as if we have been teaching individuals to construct magnificent buildings while neglecting to provide them with the foundational blueprints of emotional architecture.

The research is unequivocal, staggering in its implications. According to Bradberry and Greaves (2009), emotional intelligence accounts for a remarkable 58% of performance across all job categories—a statistic that should fundamentally reshape how we conceptualise human potential. Furthermore, the financial implications are equally compelling: individuals with elevated emotional intelligence earn, on average, $29,000 more annually than their emotionally less sophisticated counterparts (TalentSmart, 2021).

But these numbers, impressive as they may be, barely scratch the surface of emotional intelligence's transformative power. The true magic lies not in statistics but in the profound metamorphosis that occurs when individuals master the art of emotional navigation. It is the difference between merely existing and truly living, between achieving hollow victories and creating meaningful legacies.

In this chapter, we embark on an exploratory journey through the interconnected realms where emotional intelligence exerts its profound influence: career advancement, relationship mastery, mental health optimisation, leadership excellence, and ultimate life satisfaction. Each domain reveals new dimensions of EQ's extraordinary power to reshape human experience, offering insights that can fundamentally alter the trajectory of one's existence.

## The Career Catalyst: How Emotional Intelligence Redefines Professional Success

The modern workplace resembles a complex ecosystem where technical competence represents merely the entry fee, not the guarantee of advancement. In this environment, emotional intelligence emerges as the ultimate differentiator, the secret weapon that transforms good employees into exceptional leaders and ordinary careers into extraordinary journeys.

The research conducted by TalentSmart reveals a truth that should revolutionise our understanding of professional development: while IQ might secure an initial interview, it is emotional intelligence that determines long-term career trajectory, salary progression, and leadership potential (Bradberry & Greaves, 2009). This finding challenges the conventional wisdom that has dominated corporate culture for generations.

## The Adaptability Advantage

In an era characterised by unprecedented technological disruption, market volatility, and organisational restructuring, adaptability has become the paramount survival skill. Emotionally intelligent professionals possess an innate ability to embrace change, viewing disruption not as a threat but as an opportunity for growth and innovation (Mayer & Salovey, 1997). They demonstrate remarkable resilience when faced with shifting priorities, technological upheavals, or organisational restructuring.

Consider the pharmaceutical executive who, upon learning that her division would be eliminated due to patent expirations, channelled her initial disappointment into strategic action. Rather than succumbing to anxiety or resentment, she leveraged her emotional intelligence to identify transferable skills, build cross-functional relationships, and ultimately secure a more senior position in a different division. Her ability to regulate emotional responses while maintaining strategic thinking exemplifies the adaptability advantage that EQ provides.

## Decision-Making Under Pressure

The corporate landscape is littered with cautionary tales of brilliant individuals whose careers derailed due to poor decision-making under emotional duress. High-pressure situations have a tendency to hijack rational thinking, leading to impulsive choices that can have devastating consequences (Goleman, 2013). Emotionally intelligent professionals, however, possess the remarkable ability to maintain cognitive clarity even in the midst of emotional storms.

This capacity manifests in various ways: the marketing director who resists the temptation to launch a defensive campaign after negative publicity, instead taking time to analyse the situation and develop a thoughtful response; the project manager who, when faced with an impossible deadline, acknowledges the emotional stress while methodically evaluating options and communicating transparently with stakeholders.

## The Art of Constructive Conflict Resolution

Workplace conflicts are inevitable—they arise from diverse perspectives, competing priorities, and human ego. However, emotionally intelligent individuals transform these potential disasters into opportunities for strengthening relationships and improving processes (Thomas & Kilmann, 2014). They understand that conflict, when managed skilfully, can lead to innovation, clarity, and deeper understanding.

The emotionally intelligent approach to conflict involves several sophisticated elements: active listening that seeks to understand rather than to be understood, empathy that acknowledges the legitimate concerns of all parties, and creative problem-solving that transcends zero-sum thinking. These individuals rarely engage in blame games or power struggles; instead, they focus on collaborative solutions that address underlying needs while preserving professional relationships.

### Leadership Magnetism

Perhaps the most compelling evidence of emotional intelligence's career impact lies in its relationship to leadership emergence. Research consistently demonstrates that individuals with high EQ are more likely to be promoted to leadership positions, regardless of their initial technical competence (Goleman, Boyatzis & McKee, 2013). This phenomenon occurs because emotionally intelligent individuals naturally inspire trust, facilitate collaboration, and create environments where others can thrive.

The transformation from individual contributor to effective leader requires a fundamental shift in focus—from personal achievement to team empowerment, from technical problem-solving to emotional navigation. Those who make this transition successfully invariably possess high levels of emotional intelligence, enabling them to motivate diverse personalities, manage competing egos, and maintain team cohesion during challenging periods.

## Relationship Mastery: The Emotional Intelligence Advantage in Human Connection

Human beings are fundamentally social creatures, wired for connection and interdependence. Yet paradoxically, many individuals struggle to build meaningful, lasting relationships despite their technical competence and intellectual capabilities (Gottman, 2015). The missing ingredient, more often than not, is emotional intelligence—the sophisticated ability to navigate the complex emotional landscape of human interaction.

## Self-Awareness: The Foundation of Authentic Connection

The journey toward relationship mastery begins with a profound understanding of one's own emotional patterns, triggers, and behavioural tendencies. This self-awareness serves as the cornerstone of authentic connection, enabling individuals to show up fully in relationships without projecting unresolved issues onto others (Brown, 2012).

Consider the professional who recognises her tendency toward perfectionism and how it manifests in criticism of others. Through self-awareness, she can catch herself before making cutting remarks, instead channelling her high standards into constructive feedback that helps rather than hurts. This internal shift transforms her from a dreaded micromanager into a respected mentor whose guidance is actively sought.

Self-awareness also involves understanding one's emotional needs and communicating them effectively rather than expecting others to intuitively fulfil unspoken expectations. The husband who recognises his need for appreciation learns to express this directly rather than growing resentful when his efforts go unacknowledged. This clarity eliminates the guesswork that often leads to relationship friction.

## Self-Regulation: Responding Rather Than Reacting

The space between emotional stimulus and response represents one of the most crucial battlegrounds in relationship dynamics. Individuals with high emotional intelligence have mastered the art of self-regulation—the ability to pause, process, and choose their response rather than being hijacked by immediate emotional impulses (Goleman, 2006).

This skill proves invaluable in countless scenarios: the parent who takes a deep breath before responding to a teenager's provocative comment, the spouse who chooses curiosity over defensiveness when receiving criticism, the friend who offers support rather than advice when someone shares a struggle. In each case, self-regulation transforms potentially destructive interactions into opportunities for deeper connection.

The neurobiological basis of self-regulation involves strengthening the prefrontal cortex's ability to override the amygdala's fight-or-flight responses (Siegel, 2012). This process requires practice and intentionality, but the results are transformative: relationships characterised by safety, trust, and mutual respect rather than volatility and defensiveness.

## Empathy: The Bridge to Understanding

True empathy transcends mere sympathy or intellectual understanding—it involves the sophisticated ability to sense and appreciate others' emotional experiences while maintaining appropriate boundaries (Davis, 2018). This capacity enables emotionally intelligent individuals to build bridges across differences, resolve conflicts constructively, and create spaces where others feel truly seen and valued.

The empathetic response involves several components: emotional recognition (accurately identifying others' feelings), perspective-taking (understanding situations from others' viewpoints), and compassionate response (acting in ways that acknowledge and address others' emotional needs). This multifaceted skill transforms interactions from transactional exchanges into meaningful connections.

## Social Skills: The Art of Emotional Navigation

The culmination of emotional intelligence in relationships manifests through sophisticated social skills that facilitate smooth, productive, and enjoyable interactions. These skills include active listening that makes others feel heard, conflict resolution that preserves dignity while addressing issues, and communication that builds rather than erodes connection (Carnegie, 2016).

Emotionally intelligent individuals possess an intuitive understanding of social dynamics—they know when to speak and when to listen, when to offer solutions and when to provide support, when to challenge and when to comfort. This social agility enables them to navigate complex group dynamics, build coalitions, and create environments where collaboration flourishes.

## Mental Health: The Internal Foundation of External Success

The relationship between emotional intelligence and mental health represents one of the most profound and personally transformative aspects of EQ development. While society often focuses on external achievements and visible successes, the internal landscape of emotional well-being serves as the foundation upon which all other accomplishments rest (Seligman, 2011).

### Anxiety and Depression: The EQ Shield

Modern life presents unprecedented levels of stress, uncertainty, and emotional complexity. The rates of anxiety and depression continue to climb, particularly among high-achieving individuals who face constant pressure to perform and compete (American Psychological Association, 2022). However, research demonstrates that individuals with high emotional intelligence possess natural defences against these mental health challenges.

The protective mechanisms of emotional intelligence operate on multiple levels. Self-awareness enables early recognition of emotional patterns that might spiral into anxiety or depression, allowing for proactive intervention. Self-regulation provides tools for managing stress responses and preventing emotional overwhelm. Social skills facilitate the creation of support networks that provide resilience during difficult periods (Brackett, 2019).

Consider the graduate student who recognises the early signs of perfectionism-induced anxiety. Rather than pushing through with increasingly frantic effort, she pauses to examine her emotional state, adjusts her expectations to more realistic levels, and reaches out to trusted friends for perspective and support. This emotionally intelligent response prevents a minor stress situation from escalating into a major mental health crisis.

## Resilience: Bouncing Back with Grace

Life inevitably presents challenges, setbacks, and disappointments. The differentiating factor between those who thrive despite adversity and those who become overwhelmed lies largely in emotional intelligence—specifically, the capacity for resilience (Reivich & Shatte, 2002). Resilient individuals don't avoid difficulties; rather, they navigate them with emotional sophistication and emerge stronger.

The components of emotional resilience include: realistic optimism (maintaining hope while acknowledging challenges), cognitive flexibility (reframing setbacks as learning opportunities), emotional regulation (managing stress responses effectively), and social connection (drawing strength from relationships during difficult periods). These skills, when developed and practiced, create an internal foundation that can weather virtually any external storm.

## Healthy Coping Strategies: The EQ Advantage

One of the most dangerous aspects of low emotional intelligence lies in its tendency to drive individuals toward destructive coping mechanisms. When people lack the skills to process emotions effectively, they often turn to substances, compulsive behaviours, or other harmful strategies to manage emotional pain (Substance Abuse and Mental Health Services Administration, 2021).

Emotionally intelligent individuals, by contrast, naturally gravitate toward healthy coping strategies. They seek social support when needed, engage in physical activities that release stress, practice mindfulness or meditation, and pursue creative outlets that provide emotional expression. These positive coping mechanisms create an upward spiral of emotional health rather than the downward spiral associated with destructive behaviours.

### Optimism and Emotional Flexibility

Perhaps the most beautiful aspect of high emotional intelligence lies in its capacity to foster genuine optimism—not the naive kind that ignores reality, but the sophisticated optimism that acknowledges challenges while maintaining faith in human capacity for growth and positive change (Fredrickson, 2013). This optimism is coupled with emotional flexibility—the ability to adapt emotional responses to changing circumstances rather than being locked into rigid patterns.

This combination of optimism and flexibility enables individuals to maintain hope during difficult periods, celebrate successes without becoming arrogant, learn from failures without becoming defeated, and approach new situations with curiosity rather than fear. The result is a mental health foundation that supports sustained high performance while maintaining inner peace and joy.

## Leadership Excellence: The Emotional Intelligence Imperative

The landscape of leadership has undergone a revolutionary transformation in recent decades. The command-and-control models that once dominated organisational structures have given way to more sophisticated approaches that recognise the centrality of emotional dynamics in human motivation and performance (Kouzes & Posner, 2017). In this new paradigm, emotional intelligence emerges not as a useful addition to leadership competence but as its very essence.

## Vision and Emotional Resonance

Great leaders understand that vision is not merely about strategy or goals—it's about creating emotional resonance that inspires collective action. The most compelling visions tap into deep human needs for meaning, purpose, and contribution, speaking to both rational analysis and emotional aspiration (Kotter, 2012). Leaders with high emotional intelligence possess the sophisticated ability to craft and communicate visions that ignite passion and sustain motivation even during challenging periods.

Consider the technology CEO who, faced with declining market share and increasing competition, could have focused solely on financial metrics and operational efficiency. Instead, she reframed the company's mission around democratising technology access for underserved communities, creating an emotional narrative that energised employees and attracted top talent despite the challenging business environment. Her emotional intelligence enabled her to understand what would truly motivate her team beyond mere profit maximisation.

## Trust: The Currency of Influence

Leadership authority ultimately derives from trust, and trust emerges from the complex interplay of competence, character, and emotional connection (Covey, 2006). Leaders with high emotional intelligence naturally inspire trust through their authenticity, empathy, and emotional consistency. They create psychological safety that enables team members to take risks, admit mistakes, and contribute their best thinking without fear of judgment or retribution.

The building of trust requires emotional intelligence on multiple levels: self-awareness to maintain consistency between values and actions, empathy to understand and address team members' concerns, and social skills to communicate in ways that build rather than erode confidence. This trust becomes the foundation for all other leadership activities, enabling influence that extends far beyond formal authority.

## Communication: The Art of Emotional Translation

Effective leadership communication transcends the mere transmission of information—it involves the sophisticated art of emotional translation, ensuring that messages not only inform but also inspire, motivate, and guide (Heath & Heath, 2007). Leaders with high emotional intelligence intuitively adjust their communication style to match their audience's emotional state, cultural background, and individual preferences.

This adaptive communication manifests in various ways: the executive who frames difficult news in terms of opportunities rather than threats, the manager who recognises when team members need encouragement versus challenge, the leader who knows when to communicate with data and when to tell stories that capture hearts as well as minds. This emotional attunement to communication enables leaders to maintain engagement and motivation even during difficult periods.

## Conflict Transformation: From Problem to Opportunity

Traditional leadership approaches often view conflict as a problem to be eliminated or controlled. Leaders with high emotional intelligence, however, understand conflict as a natural and potentially valuable aspect of human interaction—one that, when managed skilfully, can lead to innovation, clarity, and stronger relationships (Lencioni, 2002).

The emotionally intelligent approach to conflict involves several sophisticated elements: creating safe spaces for honest dialogue, facilitating perspective-taking that enables mutual understanding, and guiding groups toward solutions that address underlying needs rather than surface positions. These leaders don't avoid difficult conversations; instead, they create frameworks that enable productive engagement with disagreement and tension.

### Change Leadership: Navigating Emotional Turbulence

Organisational change invariably creates emotional turbulence—fear, uncertainty, resistance, and grief for what is being left behind. Leaders with high emotional intelligence understand that successful change management is fundamentally about emotional management (Bridges, 2017). They recognise that rational arguments alone are insufficient to overcome the emotional barriers that prevent adaptation and growth.

The emotionally intelligent approach to change leadership involves acknowledging and validating emotional responses while providing hope and direction for the future. These leaders communicate transparently about challenges while maintaining optimism about possibilities. They create support systems that help individuals process change-related emotions while building the skills necessary for success in new circumstances.

## Life Satisfaction: The Ultimate Measure of Success

While society often measures success through external metrics—wealth, status, recognition, achievements—the most profound indicator of a life well-lived lies in the internal experience of satisfaction, fulfilment, and meaning (Lyubomirsky, 2007). Research consistently demonstrates that individuals with high emotional intelligence experience greater life satisfaction across virtually every domain of human experience.

## Authentic Happiness: Beyond Hedonic Adaptation

The pursuit of happiness has captivated human attention throughout history, yet many individuals find themselves trapped in cycles of achievement and acquisition that provide only temporary satisfaction. The psychological phenomenon of hedonic adaptation ensures that external successes provide diminishing returns in terms of genuine happiness (Kahneman, 2011). Emotionally intelligent individuals, however, discover more sustainable sources of well-being.

These sustainable sources include: deep relationships characterised by mutual understanding and support, meaningful work that aligns with personal values and contributes to something larger than self-interest, personal growth that provides ongoing challenges and learning opportunities, and moments of transcendence that connect individuals to something greater than their immediate concerns (Csikszentmihalyi, 2014).

## Values-Aligned Living: The Compass of Authenticity

One of the most powerful aspects of emotional intelligence lies in its capacity to clarify personal values and guide decision-making that aligns with these deeply held principles. Individuals with high EQ possess greater self-awareness regarding what truly matters to them, enabling them to make choices that create genuine satisfaction rather than hollow achievements (Rokeach, 1973).

This values alignment manifests in career choices that prioritise meaning over mere financial reward, relationship decisions that emphasise compatibility over convenience, and lifestyle choices that support long-term well-being over short-term pleasure. The result is a life characterised by authenticity and integrity—a sense that one's external actions reflect internal truths.

## Purpose and Meaning: The Transcendent Dimension

Research in positive psychology demonstrates that individuals who experience a sense of purpose and meaning report higher levels of life satisfaction, greater resilience during difficult periods, and even improved physical health outcomes (Duckworth, 2016). Emotional intelligence facilitates the discovery and pursuit of purpose by enabling individuals to understand their unique gifts, recognise opportunities for contribution, and maintain motivation during challenging periods.

The sense of purpose often emerges from the intersection of personal strengths, world needs, and emotional passion. Emotionally intelligent individuals possess the self-awareness to identify their strengths, the empathy to recognise world needs, and the motivation to persist in pursuing their calling despite obstacles and setbacks.

## Integration and Wholeness: The EQ Promise

Perhaps the most beautiful aspect of high emotional intelligence lies in its capacity to create integration and wholeness in human experience. Rather than fragmenting life into disconnected compartments—work versus personal, rational versus emotional, individual versus collective—emotional intelligence enables a more integrated approach that honours the full spectrum of human experience (Wilber, 2000).

This integration manifests as leaders who bring authenticity to their professional roles, parents who model emotional intelligence for their children, friends who show up fully in relationships, and individuals who pursue goals that reflect their deepest values and aspirations. The result is a life characterised not by perfection but by authenticity, growth, and meaningful contribution.

## Case Studies: Emotional Intelligence in Action

The theoretical understanding of emotional intelligence gains profound depth and credibility when examined through the lens of real-world application. The following case studies illuminate how emotional intelligence manifests in extraordinary human achievements and transformative leadership.

### Oprah Winfrey: The Empathy Revolution

Oprah Winfrey's journey from poverty and trauma to global influence represents one of the most compelling examples of emotional intelligence in action. Her childhood experiences of abuse and discrimination could have created lasting emotional wounds that limited her potential. Instead, she developed sophisticated emotional intelligence that became the foundation for unprecedented success in media, business, and philanthropy (Winfrey, 2014).

Winfrey's emotional intelligence manifests in multiple dimensions: her ability to create emotional safety for interview subjects that enables them to share their deepest truths, her capacity to connect authentically with diverse audiences across cultural and socioeconomic boundaries, and her skill in transforming personal pain into universal wisdom that helps others heal and grow.

The business implications of her emotional intelligence are staggering. Her media empire generates billions in revenue precisely because audiences trust her emotional authenticity and benefit from her empathetic approach to human stories. She has demonstrated that emotional intelligence is not merely a personal development tool but a powerful business strategy that creates value for all stakeholders.

## Nelson Mandela: Transforming Anger into Wisdom

Nelson Mandela's leadership during South Africa's transition from apartheid represents perhaps the most extraordinary example of emotional intelligence applied to historical transformation. His 27 years of imprisonment could have fostered bitterness, hatred, and desire for revenge—understandable responses to profound injustice. Instead, Mandela developed the emotional sophistication necessary to transcend personal pain in service of national healing (Mandela, 2013).

Mandela's emotional intelligence enabled him to separate individuals from systems, understanding that former oppressors could become allies in building a new society. His capacity for empathy allowed him to appreciate the fears and concerns of white South Africans while maintaining commitment to justice and equality. His self-regulation prevented emotional reactions that could have plunged the country into civil war.

The global impact of Mandela's emotional intelligence extends far beyond South Africa's borders. His example demonstrates that transformative leadership requires not only strategic vision but also emotional mastery that can inspire former enemies to become collaborators in creating a better future.

## Satya Nadella: The Empathy-Driven Transformation

When Satya Nadella assumed the role of CEO at Microsoft in 2014, the company faced significant challenges including declining relevance in mobile technology, cultural rigidity, and employee disengagement. Rather than pursuing a traditional turnaround strategy focused solely on operational efficiency and cost reduction,

Nadella prioritised cultural transformation rooted in emotional intelligence (Nadella, 2017).

Nadella's approach emphasised empathy as a core business competency, encouraging employees to understand and address customer needs more effectively. He replaced Microsoft's historically competitive internal culture with collaborative approaches that leveraged collective intelligence. His growth mindset philosophy encouraged experimentation and learning from failure rather than perfectionist paralysis.

The results speak volumes about the business value of emotional intelligence: Microsoft's market capitalisation increased dramatically under Nadella's leadership, employee engagement scores improved significantly, and the company regained its position as a technology innovator. This transformation demonstrates that emotional intelligence is not merely a "soft skill" but a fundamental driver of business performance.

## Contemporary Examples: EQ in Modern Leadership

Beyond these iconic examples, contemporary leaders across various industries demonstrate the continuing relevance of emotional intelligence in achieving extraordinary results. The healthcare administrator who transformed hospital culture by prioritising empathy and communication, resulting in improved patient outcomes and employee satisfaction. The technology start-up founder whose emotional intelligence enabled her to maintain team cohesion during multiple pivots and eventually achieve successful acquisition. The educational leader whose empathetic approach to student development created unprecedented college acceptance rates in an underserved community.

Each of these examples reinforces the fundamental truth that emotional intelligence serves as a force multiplier for human potential, enabling individuals to achieve results that transcend what might be expected based solely on technical competence or intellectual capability.

## The Future of Emotional Intelligence: Implications and Applications

As we advance deeper into the 21st century, the relevance of emotional intelligence continues to expand rather than diminish. Technological advancement, globalisation, and social complexity create new challenges that require sophisticated emotional navigation. The leaders, professionals, and individuals who thrive in this environment will be those who have mastered the art of emotional intelligence.

The integration of artificial intelligence and human intelligence presents particularly interesting implications for emotional intelligence development. As machines become increasingly capable of handling routine cognitive tasks, uniquely human capabilities—creativity, empathy, complex problem-solving, and emotional navigation—become more valuable rather than less relevant (Pink, 2018).

Educational systems are beginning to recognise the importance of emotional intelligence development, integrating social-emotional learning into curricula from elementary through graduate levels. Organisations are investing in emotional intelligence assessment and development programmes, recognising their impact on performance, retention, and innovation.

The future belongs to those who can navigate complexity with emotional sophistication, build bridges across differences with empathy and understanding, and create meaning and purpose in an increasingly uncertain world. Emotional intelligence provides the foundation for thriving in this future rather than merely surviving it.

## Conclusion: The Transformation Imperative

Emotional intelligence represents far more than a useful skill set or desirable personal quality—it constitutes a fundamental requirement for thriving in the modern world. The research is clear, the examples are compelling, and the implications are profound: individuals who develop sophisticated emotional intelligence gain access to levels of success, satisfaction, and contribution that remain elusive to those who rely solely on traditional forms of intelligence.

The journey toward emotional intelligence mastery requires commitment, practice, and often the guidance of skilled mentors or coaches. It involves honest self-examination, vulnerability in relationships, and the courage to change longstanding patterns that no longer serve growth and effectiveness. Yet the rewards of this journey extend far beyond personal benefit—they create ripple effects that improve families, organisations, communities, and ultimately, the world.

The hidden power of emotional intelligence lies not in its secrecy but in its subtlety. Unlike technical skills that produce immediate and visible results, emotional intelligence works through influence, inspiration, and gradual transformation of human systems. Its effects compound over time, creating legacies that extend far beyond individual lifespans.

As we conclude this exploration of emotional intelligence and personal success, the invitation becomes clear: to embark upon or deepen the journey of emotional development, not merely for personal gain but for the broader contribution that such development enables. The world needs emotionally intelligent leaders, partners, parents, and citizens who can navigate complexity with wisdom, bridge differences with empathy, and create futures that honour the full spectrum of human potential.

In the next chapter, we will delve deeper into the specific applications of emotional intelligence in leadership and management contexts, exploring practical strategies for developing and applying these capabilities in organisational settings. The transformation continues, and the possibilities remain limitless for those willing to embrace the journey of emotional mastery.

## References


American Psychological Association. (2022). *Stress in America: The state of our nation*. Washington, DC: APA Publications.

Bar-On, R. (2006). The Bar-On model of emotional-social intelligence (ESI). *Psicothema*, 18, 13-25.

Brackett, M. (2019). *Permission to feel: Unlocking the power of emotions to help our kids, ourselves, and our society thrive*. New York: Celadon Books.

Bradberry, T., & Greaves, J. (2009). *Emotional intelligence 2.0*. San Diego: TalentSmart.

Bridges, W. (2017). *Managing transitions: Making the most of change* (4th ed.). Boston: Da Capo Press.

Brown, B. (2012). *Daring greatly: How the courage to be vulnerable transforms the way we live, love, parent, and lead*. New York: Gotham Books.

Carnegie, D. (2016). *How to win friends and influence people* (Revised ed.). New York: Simon & Schuster.

Covey, S. R. (2006). *The speed of trust: The one thing that changes everything*. New York: Free Press.

Csikszentmihalyi, M. (2014). *Flow and the foundations of positive psychology*. New York: Springer.

Davis, M. H. (2018). *Empathy: A social psychological approach*. New York: Routledge.

Duckworth, A. (2016). *Grit: The power of passion and perseverance*. New York: Scribner.

Fredrickson, B. L. (2013). *Love 2.0: Finding happiness and health in moments of connection*. New York: Hudson Street Press.

Goleman, D. (2006). *Emotional intelligence: Why it matters more than IQ* (10th ed.). New York: Bantam Books.

Goleman, D. (2013). *Focus: The hidden driver of excellence*. New York: HarperCollins.

Goleman, D., Boyatzis, R., & McKee, A. (2013). *Primal leadership: Realizing the power of emotional intelligence*. Boston: Harvard Business Review Press.

Gottman, J. (2015). *The seven principles for making marriage work* (Revised ed.). New York: Harmony Books.

Heath, C., & Heath, D. (2007). *Made to stick: Why some ideas survive and others die*. New York: Random House.

Kahneman, D. (2011). *Thinking, fast and slow*. New York: Farrar, Straus and Giroux.

Kotter, J. P. (2012). *Leading change* (Revised ed.). Boston: Harvard Business Review Press.

Kouzes, J. M., & Posner, B. Z. (2017). *The leadership challenge: How to make extraordinary things happen in organizations* (6th ed.). San Francisco: Jossey-Bass.

Lencioni, P. (2002). *The five dysfunctions of a team: A leadership fable*. San Francisco: Jossey-Bass.

Lyubomirsky, S. (2007). *The how of happiness: A scientific approach to getting the life you want*. New York: Penguin Books.

Mandela, N. (2013). *Long walk to freedom: The autobiography of Nelson Mandela*. Boston: Back Bay Books.

Mayer, J. D., & Salovey, P. (1997). What is emotional intelligence? In P. Salovey & D. Sluyter (Eds.), *Emotional development and emotional intelligence: Educational implications* (pp. 3-31). New York: Basic Books.

Nadella, S. (2017). *Hit refresh: The quest to rediscover Microsoft's soul and imagine a better future for everyone.* New York: HarperBusiness.

Pink, D. H. (2018). *A whole new mind: Why right-brainers will rule the future* (Updated ed.). New York: Riverhead Books.

Reivich, K., & Shatte, A. (2002). *The resilience factor: 7 keys to finding your inner strength and overcoming life's hurdles.* New York: Broadway Books.

Rokeach, M. (1973). *The nature of human values.* New York: Free Press.

Seligman, M. E. P. (2011). *Flourish: A visionary new understanding of happiness and well-being.* New York: Free Press.

Siegel, D. J. (2012). *The developing mind: How relationships and the brain interact to shape who we are* (2nd ed.). New York: Guilford Press.

Substance Abuse and Mental Health Services Administration. (2021). *Key substance use and mental health indicators in the United States.* Rockville, MD: SAMHSA.

TalentSmart. (2021). *Emotional intelligence research report.* San Diego: TalentSmart Publications.

Thomas, K. W., & Kilmann, R. H. (2014). *Thomas-Kilmann conflict mode instrument.* Tuxedo, NY: Xicom.

Wilber, K. (2000). *Integral psychology: Consciousness, spirit, psychology, therapy.* Boston: Shambhala Publications.

Winfrey, O. (2014). *What I know for sure.* New York: Flatiron Books.

# Chapter 5: Emotional Intelligence in Leadership and Management

*The Alchemy of Human Transformation Through Emotionally Intelligent Leadership*

## Introduction: The Great Leadership Renaissance

In the grand theatre of organisational evolution, we stand witness to a profound metamorphosis—a renaissance that challenges every fundamental assumption about the nature of leadership itself. The traditional bastions of command and control, once deemed immutable pillars of organisational structure, crumble beneath the weight of a new paradigm that recognises the primacy of emotional intelligence in human achievement (Goleman, Boyatzis & McKee, 2013).

This transformation represents far more than a mere shift in management philosophy; it constitutes nothing less than a revolution in our understanding of human potential and organisational possibility. The sterile corridors of corporate hierarchies, once echoing with the hollow commands of positional authority, now resonate with the authentic voices of leaders who understand that true power flows not from titles or organisational charts, but from the profound capacity to connect, inspire, and elevate the human spirit.

The evidence for this transformation is overwhelming in its consistency and compelling in its implications. Research conducted by the Harvard Business Review demonstrates that companies led by emotionally intelligent executives outperform their competitors by margins that would have been deemed impossible under traditional leadership models (Goleman, 2013). The correlation between emotional intelligence and organisational performance is not merely statistically significant—it is transformationally decisive.

Yet this revolution extends beyond mere performance metrics. It touches the very essence of what it means to be human in an organisational context. Where once employees were viewed as interchangeable resources to be managed and controlled, they are now recognised as complex emotional beings whose engagement, creativity, and commitment can only be unlocked through leaders who possess the emotional sophistication to honour their full humanity (Pink, 2018).

The global business landscape bears witness to this transformation daily. Organisations that cling to outdated command-and-control structures find themselves haemorrhaging talent to competitors who understand the new rules of engagement. The most sought-after professionals—the creative innovators, the strategic thinkers, the collaborative catalysts—gravitate toward leaders who demonstrate emotional intelligence because they recognise that such environments offer not merely employment, but the opportunity for authentic self-expression and meaningful contribution (Deci & Ryan, 2017).

In this chapter, we embark upon a comprehensive exploration of how emotional intelligence manifests in leadership contexts, transforming not only individual careers but entire organisational cultures. We will examine the intricate mechanisms through which emotionally intelligent leaders create environments of trust, innovation, and extraordinary performance. More importantly, we will uncover the profound human impact of such leadership—the way it elevates not only business outcomes but the very quality of human experience within organisational settings.

## The Evolutionary Imperative: From Command to Connection

The history of organisational leadership reads like a chronicle of humanity's evolving understanding of motivation, performance, and human potential. The industrial age birthed management philosophies rooted in mechanistic thinking—Frederick Taylor's scientific management, Henri Fayol's administrative principles, Max Weber's bureaucratic structures—all predicated on the assumption that human beings could be managed like machines through systems of control, measurement, and reward (Taylor, 1911; Fayol, 1949; Weber, 1947).

These models served their historical purpose, enabling the coordination of large-scale industrial enterprises and the standardisation of processes that drove economic growth. However, they were founded upon a fundamentally limited understanding of human nature—one that viewed emotion as interference rather than intelligence, creativity as deviation rather than asset, and autonomy as threat rather than opportunity.

The transition from industrial to knowledge-based economies has rendered these assumptions not merely outdated but counterproductive. Today's most valuable organisational assets—innovation, adaptation, collaboration, and creative problem-solving—cannot be commanded into existence. They emerge only within environments that honour the full spectrum of human intelligence, including and especially emotional intelligence (Drucker, 2006).

### The Neuroscience of Leadership Transformation

Contemporary neuroscience provides compelling evidence for the superiority of emotionally intelligent leadership approaches. Research conducted by Matthew Lieberman at the "University of

California, Los Angeles" (UCLA) demonstrates that the human brain is fundamentally social in its architecture, with neural networks dedicated specifically to understanding and responding to social and emotional cues (Lieberman, 2013). This "social brain" operates with remarkable sophistication, processing emotional information at speeds that far exceed conscious analysis.

Leaders who operate primarily through traditional command-and-control mechanisms inadvertently trigger threat responses in these social brain networks, activating fight-or-flight responses that inhibit creativity, collaboration, and higher-order thinking. Conversely, emotionally intelligent leaders who demonstrate empathy, authenticity, and genuine care activate reward networks that enhance cognitive function, promote psychological safety, and enable peak performance (Rock, 2008).

The implications of this neurobiological reality are profound. Leadership effectiveness is not merely a matter of strategic thinking or operational competence—it is fundamentally about creating neural conditions that enable others to access their highest capabilities. This requires a level of emotional sophistication that traditional leadership models never contemplated.

## The Cultural Imperative

The generational shift in workforce demographics has accelerated the demand for emotionally intelligent leadership. Millennials and Generation Z professionals, who now constitute the majority of the global workforce, demonstrate markedly different expectations regarding workplace relationships, purpose-driven work, and authentic leadership (Gallup, 2020). These generations have grown up in an era of unprecedented connectivity and emotional expression, and they bring these expectations into organisational contexts.

Traditional authoritarian leadership styles not only fail to inspire these emerging professionals—they actively repel them. The most talented individuals from these generations actively seek out organisations and leaders who demonstrate emotional intelligence because they recognise that such environments offer opportunities for growth, meaning, and authentic self-expression that are unavailable under more traditional models (Deloitte, 2021).

This cultural shift represents both challenge and opportunity for organisational leaders. Those who adapt to meet these evolving expectations gain access to unprecedented levels of engagement, creativity, and commitment. Those who resist find themselves increasingly isolated in a competitive landscape where talent represents the ultimate competitive advantage.

## The Architecture of Emotionally Intelligent Leadership

The manifestation of emotional intelligence in leadership contexts involves a sophisticated integration of self-awareness, interpersonal skill, and strategic thinking that creates what we might call "emotional architecture"—the invisible structures that shape organisational climate, culture, and performance (Boyatzis & McKee, 2005).

### Self-Awareness: The Foundation of Authentic Leadership

The journey toward emotionally intelligent leadership begins with profound self-awareness—not the superficial self-knowledge that comes from personality assessments or 360-degree feedback, but the deep, continuous, and sometimes uncomfortable process of understanding one's emotional patterns, triggers, biases, and impact on others (Cashman, 2008).

This level of self-awareness manifests in multiple dimensions. Emotional self-awareness involves the ability to recognise and understand one's emotional states as they arise, distinguishing between different emotional experiences and understanding their origins. The executive who notices her irritation during budget meetings and recognises it stems from feeling micromanaged by the board demonstrates this capacity.

Values awareness requires clarity about one's deepest principles and the courage to align actions with these values even when it involves personal or professional risk. The pharmaceutical CEO who refuses to engage in aggressive pricing practices despite analyst pressure exemplifies this dimension of self-awareness.

Impact awareness involves understanding how one's emotional states, communication style, and behavioural patterns affect others. The team leader who recognises that his perfectionist tendencies create anxiety in his direct reports and consciously modifies his approach demonstrates sophisticated impact awareness.

Perhaps most challenging is shadow awareness—the recognition and integration of those aspects of personality that individuals typically suppress or deny. Carl Jung's concept of the shadow suggests that unacknowledged aspects of personality inevitably manifest in unconscious ways that can undermine leadership effectiveness (Jung, 1969). Leaders who engage in honest shadow work—acknowledging their competitive drives, need for control, or fear of vulnerability—paradoxically become more effective because they can channel these energies consciously rather than being controlled by them.

## Self-Regulation: The Art of Conscious Response

While self-awareness provides the foundation for emotionally intelligent leadership, self-regulation represents its active expression—the ability to choose responses rather than being hijacked by automatic reactions. This capacity proves particularly crucial in leadership contexts where decisions made under emotional duress can have far-reaching consequences for individuals, teams, and organisations (Goleman, 2013).

Emotional self-regulation in leadership involves several sophisticated capabilities. Impulse control enables leaders to pause between stimulus and response, creating space for thoughtful decision-making even under intense pressure. The start-up founder who resists the urge to respond defensively to harsh investor feedback and instead seeks to understand the underlying concerns demonstrates this capacity.

Stress tolerance allows leaders to maintain clarity and effectiveness even when facing significant challenges or uncertainty. This doesn't mean suppressing stress responses but rather developing resilience that enables continued high performance despite difficult circumstances. The hospital administrator who maintains calm decisiveness during a crisis while providing emotional support to staff exemplifies this dimension.

Emotional flexibility involves the ability to adapt emotional responses to changing circumstances rather than being locked into rigid patterns. The sales manager who adjusts her motivational approach based on individual team member needs—offering encouragement to some, challenge to others, and autonomy to still others—demonstrates this sophisticated capability.

Perhaps most importantly, values-based decision-making ensures that choices remain aligned with core principles even when external pressures might suggest otherwise. This requires not only clarity about values but also the courage to act on them when doing so involves personal or professional risk.

## Motivation: The Engine of Transformational Leadership

The motivational dimension of emotional intelligence in leadership transcends simple goal-setting or performance management. It involves the cultivation of intrinsic motivation—the deep, sustainable drive that emerges from alignment between personal values, organisational purpose, and meaningful contribution (Deci & Ryan, 2017).

Transformational leaders demonstrate several distinctive motivational characteristics. Achievement orientation focuses not merely on personal success but on creating value for all stakeholders—employees, customers, communities, and society. The technology executive who measures success not only by financial metrics but also by employee development, customer satisfaction, and social impact exemplifies this expanded achievement orientation.

Optimism in leadership involves the sophisticated ability to maintain hope and possibility-thinking even during difficult periods, while remaining grounded in reality. This isn't naive positivity but rather the mature capacity to acknowledge challenges while maintaining faith in human capability and potential for positive change. The non-profit director who inspires continued effort during funding crises by focusing on mission impact demonstrates this quality.

Initiative involves the proactive pursuit of opportunities and solutions rather than merely responding to problems. Emotionally intelligent leaders demonstrate entrepreneurial thinking that seeks to create value and solve problems before they become crises. The manufacturing manager who anticipates supply chain disruptions and develops alternative strategies exemplifies this proactive orientation.

Commitment to continuous learning reflects the understanding that leadership effectiveness requires ongoing development and adaptation. This involves not only technical skill development but also emotional and interpersonal growth. Leaders who actively seek feedback, engage in coaching relationships, and pursue challenging assignments demonstrate this commitment to growth.

## Empathy: The Bridge to Human Connection

Empathy represents perhaps the most distinctive characteristic of emotionally intelligent leadership—the capacity to understand, appreciate, and respond appropriately to others' emotional experiences while maintaining appropriate boundaries and perspective (Baron-Cohen, 2011). This capability enables leaders to build the trust, rapport, and psychological safety that form the foundation of high-performance teams.

Cognitive empathy involves the intellectual understanding of others' perspectives, emotions, and motivations. This includes the ability to see situations from multiple viewpoints and appreciate the complexity of human experience. The merger integration leader who understands the anxiety and identity concerns of employees from both organisations demonstrates this capacity.

Emotional empathy involves the ability to sense and resonate with others' emotional states without becoming overwhelmed or losing objectivity. This enables leaders to provide appropriate support and guidance while maintaining the emotional stability necessary for effective decision-making. The crisis counsellor who feels genuine compassion for trauma survivors while maintaining the emotional regulation necessary to provide effective support exemplifies this balance.

Compassionate action represents the behavioural expression of empathy—the willingness to take action that supports others' well-being and development even when it involves personal cost or inconvenience. The executive who restructures her own role to create development opportunities for high-potential employees demonstrates this dimension.

Cultural empathy involves the ability to understand and appreciate different cultural perspectives, values, and communication styles. In increasingly diverse and global organisations, this capability proves essential for building inclusive environments where all individuals can contribute their best work. The international project manager who adapts her leadership style to honour different cultural approaches to hierarchy, communication, and decision-making demonstrates sophisticated cultural empathy.

## Social Skills: The Orchestration of Human Systems

The social skills dimension of emotionally intelligent leadership involves the sophisticated ability to influence, inspire, and coordinate human systems toward shared objectives. This transcends simple communication competence to encompass the complex art of social architecture—creating environments where individuals and teams can achieve extraordinary results (Cialdini, 2016).

Influential communication involves the ability to convey messages in ways that inspire understanding, commitment, and action. This requires not only clarity of expression but also emotional attunement to audience needs, concerns, and motivations. The change management leader who frames organisational transformation in terms of individual growth opportunities rather than merely operational efficiency demonstrates this capability.

Conflict resolution represents one of the most critical social skills for leaders, involving the ability to navigate disagreements and tensions in ways that strengthen rather than damage relationships. Emotionally intelligent leaders approach conflict as an opportunity for deeper understanding, creative problem-solving, and relationship building rather than viewing it as a threat to be eliminated. The department head who facilitates difficult conversations between competing functional areas and helps them discover collaborative solutions exemplifies this approach.

Team building involves creating psychological and emotional conditions that enable groups to achieve synergistic performance—results that exceed the sum of individual contributions. This requires understanding group dynamics, individual motivations, and the complex interplay between task focus and relationship maintenance. The project leader who develops team rituals, communication protocols, and decision-making processes that honour both efficiency and inclusion demonstrates sophisticated team building capability.

Network building extends beyond simple relationship management to encompass the strategic cultivation of mutually beneficial connections that serve organisational objectives while supporting individual development. The business development executive who creates industry partnerships that provide learning opportunities for employees while advancing company goals exemplifies this sophisticated networking approach.

## The Emotional Climate: The Invisible Architecture of Performance

Every leader, whether consciously or unconsciously, creates an emotional climate within their sphere of influence—an invisible but powerful atmosphere that shapes how people think, feel, and perform (Goleman, 2013). This climate represents one of the most significant yet underappreciated factors in organisational success, influencing everything from creativity and innovation to retention and customer satisfaction.

## The Neurobiology of Emotional Contagion

Research in social neuroscience reveals that emotions are literally contagious, spreading through organisations via mirror neuron systems that cause individuals to unconsciously mimic and internalise the emotional states of those around them (Hatfield, Cacioppo & Rapson, 2019). Leaders, by virtue of their visibility and influence, serve as emotional pacesetters whose moods and attitudes ripple throughout their organisations with remarkable speed and intensity.

This emotional contagion operates below the threshold of conscious awareness, making it particularly powerful in shaping organisational culture. The anxious leader who constantly expresses concern about potential problems inadvertently creates a culture of fear and risk aversion. Conversely, the leader who demonstrates calm confidence during uncertainty helps others maintain clarity and creativity even in challenging circumstances.

The implications for leadership practice are profound. Leaders cannot compartmentalise their emotional states—their internal experiences inevitably become shared organisational experiences. This places a significant responsibility on leaders to develop emotional self-regulation not merely for personal effectiveness but as an act of service to their organisations.

## Psychological Safety: The Foundation of Innovation

Harvard Business School professor Amy Edmondson's ground-breaking research on psychological safety reveals it as the most significant predictor of team performance across diverse organisational contexts (Edmondson, 2019). Psychological safety—the belief that one can speak up, ask questions, admit mistakes, and propose ideas without risk of punishment or humiliation—creates conditions where innovation, learning, and adaptation can flourish.

Emotionally intelligent leaders create psychological safety through several mechanisms. Vulnerability modelling involves leaders demonstrating their own fallibility, uncertainty, and learning processes, thereby giving others permission to be human rather than perfect. The CEO who openly discusses strategic mistakes and lessons learned creates space for others to engage in honest reflection and course correction.

Curiosity cultivation involves approaching problems and disagreements with genuine interest in understanding rather than immediate judgment or solution-providing. The research director who responds to failed experiments by asking "What did we learn?" rather than "Who is responsible?" creates an environment where innovation can thrive despite inevitable setbacks.

Inclusive decision-making ensures that diverse perspectives are not only welcomed but actively sought and integrated into important decisions. This requires leaders to overcome their own biases and preferences in service of broader organisational wisdom. The marketing leader who deliberately seeks input from introverted team members and junior staff demonstrates this commitment to inclusive leadership.

## The Performance Amplification Effect

Organisations led by emotionally intelligent leaders demonstrate measurable performance advantages across multiple dimensions. Employee engagement scores consistently exceed industry averages, reflecting higher levels of emotional connection, motivation, and discretionary effort (Gallup, 2020). Customer satisfaction metrics improve as engaged employees provide superior service experiences. Innovation metrics increase as psychological safety enables creative risk-taking and cross-functional collaboration.

Perhaps most significantly, these organisations demonstrate superior adaptability during periods of change and uncertainty.

Because employees trust their leaders and feel psychologically safe, they more readily embrace new directions, learn new skills, and support organisational transformation initiatives. This adaptability represents a crucial competitive advantage in rapidly evolving business environments.

The financial implications are equally compelling. Research by the Corporate Leadership Council reveals that organisations with engaged employees achieve 2.3 times higher revenue growth than those with disengaged workforces (Corporate Executive Board, 2018). While multiple factors contribute to engagement, leadership emotional intelligence consistently emerges as the most significant predictor of these positive outcomes.

## Conflict Transformation: The Emotionally Intelligent Approach

Traditional approaches to organisational conflict typically focus on resolution—eliminating disagreement and restoring harmony as quickly as possible. Emotionally intelligent leaders, however, understand conflict as a natural and potentially valuable aspect of organisational life that, when managed skilfully, can lead to innovation, stronger relationships, and improved decision-making (Lencioni, 2002).

### The Reframe: From Problem to Opportunity

The emotionally intelligent approach to conflict begins with a fundamental reframe. Rather than viewing disagreement as evidence of dysfunction or failure, these leaders understand conflict as information—feedback about misaligned expectations, unmet needs, or opportunities for creative problem-solving. This reframe changes everything about how conflicts are approached and managed.

The technology start-up founder who interprets heated debates between engineering and marketing teams as evidence of passion and commitment rather than interpersonal dysfunction exemplifies this reframe. By normalising disagreement and establishing processes for productive dialogue, she enables these debates to drive innovation rather than create organisational toxicity.

## The Skills of Conflict Transformation

Emotionally intelligent conflict management involves several sophisticated capabilities. Active listening transcends simple acknowledgment to encompass deep understanding of underlying needs, concerns, and emotions. This requires leaders to suspend their own agendas temporarily and genuinely seek to understand all perspectives before proposing solutions.

Emotional regulation during conflict involves maintaining clarity and objectivity even when others become reactive or emotional. This doesn't mean suppressing emotions but rather using emotional information wisely while avoiding emotional hijacking that could escalate tensions. The department head who remains calm during budget disputes while acknowledging the legitimate concerns of all parties demonstrates this capability.

Facilitation rather than arbitration involves helping conflicting parties discover their own solutions rather than imposing external judgments. This approach builds ownership, develops problem-solving capabilities, and strengthens relationships rather than creating winners and losers. The project manager who guides competing teams through structured dialogue processes exemplifies this facilitative approach.

Systems thinking enables leaders to understand conflicts within broader organisational contexts rather than treating them as isolated interpersonal issues. This involves recognising how organisational structures, processes, and incentives might contribute to disagreements and addressing root causes rather than merely symptoms.

### The Transformational Outcomes

When managed through emotionally intelligent approaches, organisational conflicts can produce extraordinary positive outcomes. Innovation often emerges from the creative tension between different perspectives, as individuals are challenged to transcend their initial positions and discover novel solutions. The pharmaceutical research team that transformed their debate about drug development priorities into a breakthrough multi-indication strategy exemplifies this transformational potential.

Relationship strengthening represents another counterintuitive outcome of skilfully managed conflict. Individuals who successfully navigate disagreements together often develop deeper trust and respect than those who never experience conflict. The joint venture partners who worked through cultural misunderstandings to create innovative collaboration processes demonstrate this possibility.

Organisational learning occurs when conflicts reveal systemic issues that require attention. The manufacturing company that used inter-departmental tensions to identify and resolve supply chain inefficiencies exemplifies how conflict can drive organisational improvement when approached with emotional intelligence.

## Case Studies: Masters of Emotionally Intelligent Leadership

The theoretical understanding of emotionally intelligent leadership gains profound depth and credibility when examined through the lens of real-world application. The following case studies illuminate how emotional intelligence manifests in extraordinary leadership achievements across diverse contexts and challenges.

## Satya Nadella: The Cultural Alchemist

When Satya Nadella assumed the role of Microsoft CEO in 2014, he inherited an organisation struggling with cultural rigidity, internal competition, and declining relevance in mobile and cloud computing. Rather than pursuing a traditional turnaround strategy focused primarily on cost reduction and restructuring, Nadella embarked on a profound cultural transformation rooted in emotional intelligence principles (Nadella, 2017).

Nadella's approach demonstrated sophisticated self-awareness. He recognised that his own leadership style needed to evolve from the command-and-control patterns that had historically characterised Microsoft leadership. Through extensive coaching and reflection, he developed a more collaborative, empathetic approach that honoured diverse perspectives and encouraged experimentation.

His emphasis on empathy as a core business competency represented a radical departure from Microsoft's historically competitive culture. Nadella consistently communicated that understanding customer needs, partner perspectives, and employee experiences was not merely good human relations but essential business strategy. This empathetic orientation drove product innovations that better served user needs and market opportunities.

The growth mindset philosophy that Nadella championed throughout the organisation reflected sophisticated motivational leadership. Rather than punishing failures or mistakes, the new culture celebrated learning, experimentation, and continuous improvement. This shift unlocked innovation and risk-taking that had been suppressed under previous cultural norms.

The results speak volumes about the business impact of emotionally intelligent leadership. Microsoft's market capitalisation increased dramatically during Nadella's tenure, employee engagement scores improved significantly, and the company regained its position as a premier technology innovator. This transformation demonstrates that emotional intelligence represents not merely a "soft skill" but a fundamental driver of business performance.

## Jacinda Ardern: The Empathetic Statesman

Jacinda Ardern's leadership as Prime Minister of New Zealand provided compelling evidence of emotional intelligence in action during times of crisis. Her responses to the Christchurch mosque shootings and the COVID-19 pandemic demonstrated how empathy, authenticity, and emotional regulation can serve as powerful tools of effective governance (Ardern, 2021).

Following the Christchurch tragedy, Ardern's immediate response demonstrated remarkable empathy and emotional intelligence. Rather than focusing primarily on policy implications or political messaging, she led with genuine human compassion, visiting victims' families, wearing a hijab in solidarity, and speaking directly to the nation's grief and pain. This authentic emotional response created space for national healing while building trust and unity.

Her COVID-19 leadership exemplified the power of clear, empathetic communication during uncertainty. Ardern's regular press conferences combined factual information with emotional acknowledgment of citizens' fears, frustrations, and sacrifices. Her "team of five million" messaging created a sense of collective purpose and shared responsibility that enabled New Zealand to achieve remarkable public health outcomes.

The emotional regulation Ardern demonstrated during these crises proved equally important. Despite facing enormous pressure and criticism, she maintained composure, clarity, and focus on serving the public good rather than political self-interest. This emotional stability enabled effective decision-making during periods when many leaders might have become reactive or defensive.

While Ardern's tenure ended earlier than many expected, her leadership legacy demonstrates how emotional intelligence can enable extraordinary results even in the most challenging circumstances. Her example has influenced political leaders worldwide and redefined expectations for authentic, empathetic leadership in public service.

## Howard Schultz: The Relationship Revolutionary

Howard Schultz's leadership of Starbucks represents one of the most compelling examples of emotionally intelligent business building in modern corporate history. His vision of creating a "third place" between home and work required deep understanding of human emotional needs and the ability to translate these insights into business strategy (Schultz & Yang, 2019).

Schultz's approach to employee relationships demonstrated sophisticated empathy and social intelligence. His decision to provide healthcare benefits and stock options to part-time employees reflected understanding that emotional engagement and financial security were interconnected. This insight drove customer service excellence that became Starbucks' primary competitive advantage.

The emphasis on store atmosphere and customer experience required remarkable cultural empathy—understanding how different communities wanted to experience coffee, conversation, and connection. Schultz's ability to create consistent emotional experiences across diverse geographic and cultural contexts while maintaining local relevance demonstrates sophisticated emotional intelligence application.

During the 2008 financial crisis, Schultz's return as CEO and his focus on rekindling the emotional connection between employees, customers, and the brand exemplified emotionally intelligent crisis leadership. Rather than focusing solely on cost reduction, he invested in employee training, store renovation, and customer experience improvements that restored the emotional foundations of the business.

The global impact of Schultz's emotionally intelligent leadership extends beyond business results to social influence. Starbucks' commitment to social responsibility, employee development, and community engagement has influenced countless other organisations to recognise the business value of emotional and social intelligence.

## Contemporary Examples: EQ Leadership in Action

Beyond these iconic examples, contemporary leaders across various industries continue to demonstrate the transformative power of emotional intelligence in leadership contexts. The healthcare system CEO who transformed hospital culture by prioritising empathy and communication training, resulting in improved patient outcomes and employee satisfaction. The technology start-up founder whose emotional intelligence enabled her to maintain team cohesion through multiple pivots and eventually achieve successful acquisition. The educational leader whose empathetic approach to student and faculty development created unprecedented college acceptance rates and research achievements in an underserved community.

Each of these examples reinforces the fundamental truth that emotional intelligence serves as a force multiplier for leadership effectiveness, enabling individuals to achieve results that transcend what might be expected based solely on technical competence or strategic thinking.

## The Development Imperative: Cultivating

# Emotionally Intelligent Leadership

The recognition of emotional intelligence as essential for leadership effectiveness raises crucial questions about development—how can aspiring and current leaders cultivate these sophisticated capabilities? The journey toward emotionally intelligent leadership requires commitment, practice, and often the guidance of skilled mentors or coaches (Boyatzis, 2006).

## The Foundation: Self-Reflection and Awareness

The development of emotionally intelligent leadership begins with rigorous self-reflection—honest examination of one's emotional patterns, leadership behaviours, and impact on others. This process often requires overcoming the natural human tendency toward self-deception and social desirability bias that can obscure accurate self-perception.

Structured reflection practices prove invaluable in this development process. Regular journaling about leadership experiences, emotional responses, and lessons learned creates space for deeper self-understanding. The executive who spends fifteen minutes each evening reflecting on her interactions, decisions, and emotional states develops awareness that enables conscious improvement over time.

Multi-source feedback processes, when conducted with skill and sensitivity, provide external perspectives that can illuminate blind spots and confirm areas of strength. The 360-degree feedback process that includes not only supervisors and peers but also direct reports and even customers provides comprehensive insight into leadership impact.

Executive coaching relationships create safe spaces for honest self-examination and skill development. The most effective coaching relationships combine challenge with support, enabling leaders to examine difficult aspects of their behaviour while developing practical strategies for improvement. The manufacturing director who worked with a coach to address his tendency toward micromanagement discovered more effective ways to maintain quality standards while empowering his team.

## The Practice: Mindful Leadership Development

The cultivation of emotional intelligence requires moving beyond intellectual understanding to embodied practice. Mindfulness practices prove particularly valuable in developing the self-awareness and self-regulation capabilities essential for emotionally intelligent leadership (Kabat-Zinn, 2018).

Mindful communication involves bringing full attention and presence to interactions with others. This means setting aside distractions, truly listening to understand rather than to respond, and noticing one's own emotional reactions during conversations. The project manager who practices mindful listening during team meetings discovers previously hidden sources of tension and creative potential.

Emotional regulation practices help leaders develop the capacity to choose responses rather than being hijacked by automatic reactions. Simple techniques such as the "pause and breathe" practice—taking three conscious breaths before responding to challenging situations—can create space for more thoughtful and effective leadership responses.

Empathy development involves consciously practicing perspective-taking and emotional attunement. The sales leader who makes a point of understanding each team member's personal motivations, challenges, and aspirations develops the empathetic intelligence necessary for individualised motivation and support.

## The Integration: Systems-Level Development

The most effective emotionally intelligent leadership development occurs at systems levels rather than merely individual levels. Organisations that commit to developing emotional intelligence throughout their leadership ranks achieve sustainable cultural transformation that extends far beyond individual improvement (Cherniss & Goleman, 2001).

Leadership development programmes that emphasise emotional intelligence create shared language, expectations, and practices that reinforce individual development efforts. The technology company that integrated emotional intelligence assessment and development into all leadership roles created cultural norms that supported continued growth and application.

Mentoring relationships between emotionally intelligent senior leaders and developing managers provide real-world learning opportunities that accelerate development. The pharmaceutical executive who mentored emerging leaders by modelling vulnerable leadership and providing feedback on emotional intelligence demonstrated how development can occur through relationship rather than merely training.

Organisational systems and processes that reward and recognise emotionally intelligent leadership behaviours create incentives for continued development and application. The consulting firm that included emotional intelligence metrics in performance evaluations and promotion decisions signalled the importance of these capabilities while encouraging continued growth.

# The Future of Leadership: Emotional Intelligence in a Digital Age

As we advance deeper into the digital age, the relevance of emotional intelligence in leadership contexts continues to expand rather than diminish. Technological advancement, artificial intelligence, and remote work capabilities create new challenges that require sophisticated emotional navigation rather than merely technical competence (Schwab, 2017).

## The Human-Technology Interface

The integration of artificial intelligence and human intelligence in organisational contexts presents particular opportunities for emotionally intelligent leadership. As machines become increasingly capable of handling routine cognitive tasks, uniquely human capabilities—creativity, empathy, complex problem-solving, and emotional navigation—become more valuable rather than less relevant.

Leaders who understand how to leverage technology while preserving human connection gain significant competitive advantages. The global project manager who uses digital collaboration tools to maintain team cohesion across time zones while ensuring that virtual interactions preserve emotional connection and trust demonstrates this integration.

The ethical implications of artificial intelligence and automation require emotionally intelligent leadership to navigate. Decisions about job displacement, privacy, and algorithmic bias involve complex human considerations that require empathy, ethical reasoning, and stakeholder engagement rather than merely technical analysis.

## The Remote Leadership Challenge

The shift toward remote and hybrid work arrangements has intensified the importance of emotional intelligence in leadership. Building trust, maintaining engagement, and fostering collaboration without face-to-face interaction requires sophisticated emotional and social skills that many leaders are still developing (Ferrazzi, 2020).

Virtual emotional intelligence involves adapting traditional emotional intelligence capabilities to digital mediums. This includes recognising emotional cues through video calls, creating psychological safety in virtual meetings, and maintaining individual connections despite physical distance. The start-up CEO who schedules regular one-on-one virtual coffee chats with team members demonstrates this adaptation.

Digital empathy requires understanding how technology mediums can both facilitate and inhibit emotional connection. The department head who recognises that certain sensitive conversations require video calls rather than email demonstrates sophisticated understanding of digital communication dynamics.

## The Global Leadership Imperative

Increasing globalisation and cultural diversity in organisational contexts require leaders who possess sophisticated cultural and emotional intelligence. The ability to understand, appreciate, and bridge different cultural approaches to hierarchy, communication, and decision-making becomes essential for effective leadership in multinational contexts (Livermore, 2015).

Cross-cultural emotional intelligence involves recognising that emotional expression, communication styles, and relationship expectations vary significantly across cultures. The international business leader who adapts her leadership approach to honour different cultural norms while maintaining consistent values demonstrates this sophisticated capability.

Global empathy requires understanding how different historical, economic, and social contexts shape individual and collective experiences. The non-profit director who successfully coordinates disaster relief efforts across multiple countries demonstrates how cultural and emotional intelligence enable effective global leadership.

## Conclusion: The Leadership Legacy of Emotional Intelligence

As we conclude this comprehensive exploration of emotional intelligence in leadership and management, the evidence becomes overwhelming: the future belongs to leaders who can navigate complexity with emotional sophistication, build bridges across differences with empathy and understanding, and create environments where human potential can flourish.

The transformation from traditional command-and-control leadership to emotionally intelligent leadership represents more than an evolution in management practice—it constitutes a fundamental shift in our understanding of human potential and organisational possibility. Leaders who embrace this transformation gain access to levels of influence, impact, and fulfilment that remain elusive to those who rely solely on positional authority or technical expertise.

The ripple effects of emotionally intelligent leadership extend far beyond immediate organisational boundaries. These leaders create cultures that develop other leaders, establish standards that influence entire industries, and model possibilities that inspire societal transformation. Their legacy lies not merely in business results but in the elevation of human experience within organisational contexts.

The journey toward emotionally intelligent leadership requires courage—the willingness to examine oneself honestly, to be vulnerable in service of authentic connection, and to choose long-term relationship building over short-term task completion. It demands commitment to continuous learning, practice, and refinement of capabilities that can always be improved but never perfected.

Yet the rewards of this journey extend far beyond professional success. Leaders who develop emotional intelligence discover that their enhanced capabilities improve every aspect of their lives—their relationships become deeper, their decision-making becomes wiser, their resilience becomes stronger, and their sense of purpose becomes clearer.

In our next chapter, we will explore how emotional intelligence shapes our most intimate human connections—examining how these same capabilities that transform organisational cultures can revolutionise personal relationships, family dynamics, and romantic partnerships. The journey of emotional intelligence continues, and its potential for human transformation remains limitless.

## References

Ardern, J. (2021) *They Are Us: The New Zealand Response to the March 15 Christchurch Terrorist Attack.* Auckland: Auckland University Press.

Baron-Cohen, S. (2011) *The Science of Evil: On Empathy and the Origins of Cruelty*. New York: Basic Books.

Boyatzis, R. (2006) *Resonant Leadership: Renewing Yourself and Connecting with Others Through Mindfulness, Hope, and Compassion.* Boston: Harvard Business Review Press.

Boyatzis, R. and McKee, A. (2005) *Resonant Leadership.* Boston: Harvard Business School Press.

Cashman, K. (2008) *Leadership from the Inside Out: Becoming a Leader for Life.* 2nd edn. San Francisco: Berrett-Koehler Publishers.

Cherniss, C. and Goleman, D. (2001) *The Emotionally Intelligent Workplace: How to Select for, Measure, and Improve Emotional Intelligence in Individuals, Groups, and Organizations.* San Francisco: Jossey-Bass.

Cialdini, R. (2016) *Pre-Suasion: A Revolutionary Way to Influence and Persuade*. New York: Simon & Schuster.

Corporate Executive Board (2018) *Driving Performance and Retention Through Employee Engagement*. Arlington: CEB Corporate Leadership Council.

Deci, E.L. and Ryan, R.M. (2017) *Self-Determination Theory: Basic Psychological Needs in Motivation, Development, and Wellness*. New York: Guilford Publications.

Deloitte (2021) *The Social Enterprise at Work: Paradox as a Path Forward - 2021 Deloitte Global Human Capital Trends*. London: Deloitte Insights.

Drucker, P. (2006) *The Effective Executive: The Definitive Guide to Getting the Right Things Done*. New York: HarperBusiness.

Edmondson, A. (2019) *The Fearless Organization: Creating Psychological Safety for Learning, Innovation, and Growth*. Hoboken: John Wiley & Sons.

Fayol, H. (1949) *General and Industrial Management*. London: Pitman Publishing.

Ferrazzi, K. (2020) *Leading Without Authority: How to Create Change When No One Listens*. New York: Currency.

Gallup (2020) *State of the Global Workplace*. Washington, D.C.: Gallup Press.

Goleman, D. (2013) *Focus: The Hidden Driver of Excellence*. New York: HarperCollins.

Goleman, D., Boyatzis, R. and McKee, A. (2013) *Primal Leadership: Realizing the Power of Emotional Intelligence*. Boston: Harvard Business Review Press.

Hatfield, E., Cacioppo, J.T. and Rapson, R.L. (2019) *Emotional Contagion*. Cambridge: Cambridge University Press.

Jung, C.G. (1969) *The Archetypes and the Collective Unconscious*. 2nd edn. Princeton: Princeton University Press.

Kabat-Zinn, J. (2018) *Wherever You Go, There You Are: Mindfulness Meditation in Everyday Life*. New York: Hachette Books.

Lencioni, P. (2002) *The Five Dysfunctions of a Team: A Leadership Fable*. San Francisco: Jossey-Bass.

Lieberman, M. (2013) *Social: Why Our Brains Are Wired to Connect*. New York: Crown Publishers.

Livermore, D. (2015) *Leading with Cultural Intelligence: The Real Secret to Success*. 2nd edn. New York: AMACOM.

Nadella, S. (2017) *Hit Refresh: The Quest to Rediscover the Soul of Microsoft*. New York: HarperBusiness.

Pink, D.H. (2018) *Drive: The Surprising Truth About What Motivates Us*. Edinburgh: Canongate Books.

Rock, D. (2008) *SCARF: A Brain-Based Model for Collaborating with and Influencing Others*. NeuroLeadership Journal, 1(1), pp. 44-52.

Schultz, H. and Yang, D.J. (2019) *From the Ground Up: A Journey to Reimagine the Promise of America*. New York: Random House.

Schwab, K. (2017) *The Fourth Industrial Revolution*. Geneva: World Economic Forum.

Taylor, F.W. (1911) *The Principles of Scientific Management*. New York: Harper & Brothers.

Weber, M. (1947) *The Theory of Social and Economic Organization*. New York: Oxford University Press.

# Chapter 6: How Emotional Intelligence Shapes Relationships

*The Sacred Architecture of Human Connection*

## Introduction: The Eternal Dance of Hearts and Minds

In the vast cosmos of human experience, where individual consciousness meets the collective tapestry of existence, relationships emerge as the fundamental organising principle of our earthly journey. They are not mere social constructs or evolutionary conveniences, but rather the sacred architecture through which we discover ourselves, transcend our limitations, and touch the infinite mystery of what it means to be truly alive (Buber, 1970).

Every relationship—whether fleeting or eternal, joyous or challenging, intimate or professional—carries within it the seeds of transformation. These connections serve as mirrors that reflect our deepest truths, catalysts that accelerate our growth, and crucibles that forge our character. Yet paradoxically, while we are born with an innate capacity for connection, the art of relationship mastery remains one of humanity's most elusive achievements (Bowlby, 1988).

The statistics paint a sobering picture of our collective relationship struggles. Divorce rates hover around fifty percent in many developed nations, workplace conflict costs organisations billions annually in lost productivity, and loneliness has reached epidemic proportions despite unprecedented digital connectivity (Cacioppo & Patrick, 2008). These numbers represent more than mere social metrics—they reflect the profound gap between our yearning for authentic connection and our capacity to create and sustain meaningful bonds.

At the heart of this paradox lies a fundamental truth that psychology, neuroscience, and human wisdom traditions have converged upon: the quality of our relationships is inextricably linked to our emotional intelligence. This connection is not merely correlational but causal—emotional intelligence serves as the invisible architecture that determines whether our relationships become sources of joy or suffering, growth or stagnation, healing or harm (Gottman, 2015).

The research is unequivocal in its findings. Studies spanning decades and cultures demonstrate that individuals with higher emotional intelligence experience more satisfying relationships, lower divorce rates, stronger friendships, better family dynamics, and more effective professional collaborations (Bar-On, 2006). These are not modest improvements but transformational differences that reshape the entire trajectory of human experience.

Yet emotional intelligence in relationships transcends simple skill acquisition or behavioural modification. It represents a fundamental shift in consciousness—from viewing relationships as transactions to experiencing them as transformations, from seeking to be understood to prioritising understanding, from defending positions to exploring possibilities (Siegel, 2012).

In this chapter, we embark upon a comprehensive exploration of how emotional intelligence weaves its transformative magic through every dimension of human relationship. We will examine the invisible forces that create trust or suspicion, intimacy or distance, harmony or conflict. More importantly, we will discover how the cultivation of emotional intelligence can transform our most challenging relationships into our greatest teachers and our most cherished bonds into sources of mutual flourishing.

# The Alchemy of Connection: Understanding Relationship Fundamentals

Human relationships operate according to laws as precise and predictable as those governing the physical universe, yet far subtler and more complex. These relational laws are not written in physics textbooks but encoded in the deep structures of human psychology, neurobiology, and consciousness itself (Fisher, 2016).

## The Neurobiological Foundation of Connection

Contemporary neuroscience reveals that human beings are literally wired for connection. The discovery of mirror neurons—brain cells that fire both when we perform an action and when we observe others performing the same action—provides compelling evidence that empathy and emotional attunement are not learned behaviours but fundamental aspects of human neurological architecture (Rizzolatti & Craighero, 2004).

This neurobiological capacity for connection operates through multiple sophisticated systems. The vagus nerve, often called the "nerve of compassion," regulates our capacity for social engagement, emotional regulation, and empathetic response (Porges, 2011). When activated through positive social connection, it enhances physical health, emotional well-being, and relational satisfaction. Conversely, chronic relationship stress dysregulates this system, leading to anxiety, depression, and physical illness.

The attachment system, first identified by John Bowlby and Mary Ainsworth, governs how we approach relationships throughout our lives based on early caregiving experiences (Ainsworth et al., 1978). This system operates largely outside conscious awareness, yet profoundly influences our expectations, behaviours, and emotional responses in relationships.

Understanding and working with attachment patterns becomes crucial for developing emotionally intelligent relationships.

Oxytocin and vasopressin, often called "bonding hormones," facilitate trust, empathy, and long-term pair bonding (Carter, 2014). These neurochemicals are released through positive social interactions, physical touch, and emotional intimacy, creating biological reinforcement for relationship behaviours that promote connection and cooperation.

## The Energetic Dynamics of Relationship

Beyond neurobiological mechanisms, relationships operate through more subtle energetic dynamics that ancient wisdom traditions have long recognised and modern physics is beginning to validate. The phenomenon of emotional contagion demonstrates that emotions literally spread between individuals through unconscious mimicry and energetic resonance (Hatfield, Cacioppo & Rapson, 2019).

This energetic dimension of relationship explains why some individuals drain our energy while others restore it, why certain conversations leave us feeling depleted while others energise us, and why the "chemistry" between people can be felt immediately despite lacking rational explanation. Emotionally intelligent individuals develop sensitivity to these energetic dynamics and learn to consciously influence them through their presence, attention, and emotional regulation.

The concept of resonance—borrowed from physics but applicable to human relationships—describes how individuals can synchronise their emotional and energetic states, creating amplified positive experiences or, conversely, escalating negative spirals (Goleman, 2006). Couples who achieve emotional resonance report experiences of deep intimacy, mutual understanding, and shared consciousness that transcend ordinary relational interaction.

## The Five Pillars of Emotionally Intelligent Relationships

The architecture of emotionally intelligent relationships rests upon five fundamental pillars, each requiring sophisticated emotional and social capabilities. These pillars operate synergistically—weakness in one area undermines the entire relational structure, while strength in all areas creates relationships of extraordinary resilience and beauty.

### Pillar One: Trust - The Foundation of Vulnerability

Trust represents the fundamental currency of all meaningful relationships. It is simultaneously the most precious and most fragile aspect of human connection—built slowly through countless small interactions yet capable of destruction through a single betrayal (Covey, 2006). Trust operates on multiple levels: competence trust (believing others can do what they say they will do), character trust (believing others have good intentions), and care trust (believing others genuinely value our well-being).

Emotional intelligence contributes to trust-building through several mechanisms. Self-awareness enables individuals to make realistic commitments and acknowledge their limitations honestly rather than making promises they cannot keep. The executive who admits uncertainty about project timelines rather than offering false reassurances demonstrates this trust-building self-awareness.

Self-regulation enables consistency between internal states and external behaviours, creating the predictability that trust requires. Individuals who can manage their emotional reactions maintain steady, reliable responses that others can depend upon. The parent who responds calmly to teenage provocations rather than escalating emotionally creates an environment where trust can flourish.

Empathy builds trust by demonstrating genuine care for others' experiences and well-being. When people feel truly seen and understood, they naturally extend trust. The friend who remembers important details about our struggles and celebrates our victories without prompting demonstrates the empathetic attention that deepens trust.

Social skills enable the delicate dance of vulnerability that trust requires. Building trust involves gradually increasing levels of self-disclosure and emotional intimacy, carefully calibrated to match the developing capacity of the relationship. The colleague who shares professional challenges appropriately while maintaining necessary boundaries demonstrates sophisticated trust-building social skills.

The violation of trust represents one of the most challenging tests of emotional intelligence in relationships. Research by John Gottman reveals that successful relationship repair following trust violations requires specific emotional intelligence capabilities: genuine remorse, empathetic understanding of impact, and sustained behavioural change over time (Gottman, 2015). The capacity to rebuild trust often proves more valuable than never breaking it in the first place.

## Pillar Two: Communication - The Bridge Between Inner Worlds

Communication in emotionally intelligent relationships transcends the mere exchange of information to become a sacred act of mutual revelation and understanding. It involves not only speaking truthfully but creating space for others to do the same, not only expressing ourselves clearly but listening with such depth that others feel truly heard and valued (Rogers, 1961).

The most sophisticated aspect of emotionally intelligent communication lies in its multi-dimensional nature. Verbal communication involves not only the words chosen but their timing, tone, and emotional resonance. The apology that arrives too late or too early often fails despite containing all the right words. The compliment delivered with emotional distance may be received as manipulation rather than appreciation.

Nonverbal communication carries even greater relational significance. Research suggests that 55% of communication impact comes from body language, 38% from vocal tone, and only 7% from actual words (Mehrabian, 1971). Emotionally intelligent individuals develop exquisite sensitivity to these nonverbal channels, both in receiving others' messages and in managing their own nonverbal expression.

The practice of empathetic listening represents perhaps the highest form of communicative art. It involves temporarily setting aside one's own agenda, assumptions, and need to respond in order to truly understand another's experience. This level of listening requires emotional regulation to manage the discomfort of uncertainty and the impulse to fix or advise. The therapist who sits with a client's pain without rushing to solutions demonstrates this sophisticated capability.

Meta-communication—communication about communication—becomes essential for navigating relationship challenges. The couple who can discuss their communication patterns, emotional triggers, and differing styles demonstrates the sophisticated awareness necessary for relationship growth. "I notice I get defensive when you use that tone—can we find a different way to discuss this?" exemplifies this meta-communicative skill.

Digital communication presents new challenges and opportunities for emotionally intelligent interaction. The absence of nonverbal cues in text-based communication requires heightened awareness and intentionality. The manager who recognises that sensitive feedback requires a phone call rather than email demonstrates adaptation of emotional intelligence to digital mediums.

## Pillar Three: Empathy - The Gateway to Intimacy

Empathy stands as perhaps the most transformative capacity within emotional intelligence, enabling the profound experience of shared consciousness that forms the heart of intimate relationship. Yet true empathy involves far more than emotional sensitivity or sympathetic response—it requires the sophisticated ability to understand others' experiences while maintaining healthy boundaries and perspective (Davis, 2018).

Cognitive empathy involves intellectually understanding others' thoughts, motivations, and perspectives. This includes the capacity to see situations from multiple viewpoints simultaneously, appreciating the complexity and validity of different experiences. The mediator who can articulate both parties' positions with equal clarity and compassion demonstrates sophisticated cognitive empathy.

Emotional empathy involves the ability to sense and resonate with others' emotional states without becoming overwhelmed or losing one's own emotional centre. This requires exquisite emotional regulation—the capacity to feel with others while maintaining the stability necessary to provide support. The emergency room physician who connects emotionally with patients' fear while maintaining the clarity needed for effective treatment exemplifies this balance.

Compassionate empathy represents the behavioural expression of empathetic understanding—the willingness to take action that serves others' well-being even when it involves personal cost or inconvenience. This level of empathy transforms relationships from transactional exchanges into opportunities for mutual service and growth.

Cultural empathy becomes increasingly important in our interconnected world, involving the ability to understand and appreciate different cultural approaches to relationship, communication, and emotional expression. The international business leader who adapts her interaction style to honour different cultural norms while maintaining authentic connection demonstrates sophisticated cultural empathy.

The shadow side of empathy—emotional overwhelm, boundary confusion, and empathetic burnout—requires careful attention in relationship contexts. Individuals who absorb others' emotions without discrimination often become depleted and resentful. The helping professional who maintains compassionate engagement while protecting her emotional well-being demonstrates healthy empathetic boundaries.

## Pillar Four: Respect and Boundaries - The Framework of Freedom

Respect in emotionally intelligent relationships involves the recognition and honouring of others' fundamental autonomy, dignity, and inherent worth. It transcends mere politeness or social convention to encompass a deep appreciation for the mystery and complexity of other human beings (Kant, 1785). Respect creates the psychological safety necessary for authentic self-expression and vulnerable connection.

Boundary setting represents one of the most sophisticated aspects of relational emotional intelligence. Healthy boundaries require clarity about one's own needs, values, and limits while respecting others' autonomy to make their own choices. The parent who maintains loving connection while allowing teenage children to experience the consequences of their decisions demonstrates sophisticated boundary management.

The communication of boundaries involves expressing personal limits clearly and kindly without demanding that others change their behaviour to accommodate these limits. "I'm not available for conversations that involve criticism of my family, though I'd love to talk about other topics" demonstrates clear boundary communication that preserves relationship while protecting personal well-being.

Boundary flexibility enables adaptation to changing circumstances and relationship dynamics while maintaining core principles. The employee who adjusts her availability during crisis periods while maintaining work-life balance demonstrates this adaptive boundary management.

Respecting others' boundaries requires an empathetic understanding of their needs and limitations even when these differ from our own preferences. The friend who accepts that others need more alone time without taking it personally demonstrates mature boundary respect.

The violation of boundaries—whether intentional or unconscious—requires skillful repair processes that acknowledge impact while rebuilding trust. The ability to recognise boundary violations, take responsibility, and adjust behaviour demonstrates the emotional intelligence necessary for relationship sustainability.

## Pillar Five: Emotional Safety - The Sanctuary of Authentic Expression

Emotional safety represents the crown jewel of emotionally intelligent relationships—the creation of an interpersonal environment where vulnerability becomes possible, authenticity is valued, and growth is celebrated rather than criticised (Brown, 2012). This safety is not given but co-created through consistent, caring interactions that demonstrate trustworthiness and acceptance.

The creation of emotional safety requires sophisticated emotional regulation from all parties. Individuals must manage their own reactive patterns to avoid triggering others' defensiveness while also developing resilience to remain open despite inevitable relationship challenges. The couple who can discuss their deepest fears without judgment or criticism creates the emotional safety necessary for profound intimacy.

Vulnerability in emotionally safe relationships becomes a source of connection rather than risk. The sharing of fears, dreams, mistakes, and insecurities deepens bonds rather than creating ammunition for future conflicts. This requires not only the courage to be vulnerable but the wisdom to receive others' vulnerability with honour and care.

Emotional repair processes become essential for maintaining safety when interactions go awry. The ability to recognise emotional injuries, offer authentic apologies, and rebuild trust demonstrates the sophisticated skills necessary for relationship sustainability. "I can see that my comment hurt you, and I'm sorry. Help me understand how I can handle similar situations differently in the future" exemplifies this repair capability.

The celebration of growth and change within emotionally safe relationships enables individuals to evolve without fear of losing connection. Partners who encourage each other's development rather than feeling threatened by change create dynamic relationships that strengthen over time rather than stagnating.

## The Landscape of Relationships: How EQ Transforms Different Connection Types

Human relationships exist across a vast spectrum of intimacy, purpose, and duration. Each type presents unique opportunities and challenges for the application of emotional intelligence. Understanding these differences enables more skilful navigation of our complex relational world.

## Romantic Relationships: The Crucible of Intimate Connection

Romantic relationships represent perhaps the most intensive laboratory for emotional intelligence development. The combination of physical attraction, emotional intimacy, and life partnership creates conditions where emotional intelligence capabilities are both essential and continuously challenged (Fisher, 2017).

The neurobiological basis of romantic attraction involves complex interactions between brain chemistry, attachment patterns, and emotional resonance. The initial phase of romantic attraction—characterised by dopamine and norepinephrine activation—creates heightened emotional states that can either enhance or impair emotional intelligence functioning. Couples who navigate this phase successfully learn to maintain emotional regulation while allowing themselves to experience the full intensity of romantic connection.

Attachment theory provides crucial insights into romantic relationship dynamics. Individuals with secure attachment styles naturally demonstrate many emotional intelligence capabilities—they trust easily, communicate directly, and provide support without losing their sense of self. Those with insecure attachment patterns may struggle with jealousy, emotional regulation, or intimacy, yet these patterns can be transformed through conscious emotional intelligence development and secure relationship experiences (Johnson, 2019).

The concept of "emotional attunement" in romantic relationships involves the sophisticated ability to sense and respond to a partner's emotional states, needs, and rhythms. This goes beyond mere empathy to encompass a kind of emotional dance where partners synchronise their energies and responses. Couples who achieve consistent attunement report experiences of deep intimacy and mutual understanding that transcend ordinary relational interaction.

Conflict in romantic relationships provides opportunities for deepening intimacy when navigated with emotional intelligence. Research by John Gottman identifies specific patterns that predict relationship success or failure: successful couples avoid criticism, contempt, defensiveness, and stonewalling while demonstrating repair behaviours, emotional regulation, and genuine interest in understanding each other's perspectives (Gottman, 2015).

The development of mature love—beyond initial attraction and infatuation—requires emotional intelligence capabilities that enable long-term partnership despite inevitable challenges. This involves accepting partners fully while continuing to grow individually, maintaining passion while building security, and navigating life transitions while preserving connection.

Sexual intimacy in emotionally intelligent relationships becomes an expression of emotional connection rather than merely physical gratification. The vulnerability, communication, and attunement required for satisfying sexual relationships parallel and reinforce other dimensions of emotional intelligence.

## Friendships: The Gardens of Mutual Growth

Friendships occupy a unique position in the relationship ecosystem—they are chosen rather than assigned, voluntary rather than obligated, and often endure longer than romantic partnerships while requiring different forms of commitment and intimacy (Aristotle, 350 BCE).

The formation of meaningful friendships requires sophisticated social and emotional intelligence. The ability to recognise potential compatibility, initiate connection, and develop intimacy gradually demands skills in reading social cues, managing vulnerability, and creating mutual benefit. The capacity to move relationships from acquaintance to friendship involves emotional intelligence capabilities that many individuals struggle to develop.

Friendship maintenance presents ongoing challenges that test emotional intelligence in subtle ways. The ability to maintain connection despite geographical distance, life changes, and competing priorities requires intentionality and emotional skill. Friends who remain close through decades of change demonstrate sophisticated relationship intelligence.

The navigation of friendship conflicts requires particular emotional intelligence because friendships lack the formal structures and expectations that govern family or romantic relationships. Friends must create their own processes for addressing disagreements, disappointments, and changing needs. The friends who can discuss hurt feelings directly and work toward resolution demonstrate mature emotional and social capabilities.

Friendship boundaries present unique challenges because the voluntary nature of these relationships can make limit-setting feel like rejection. The friend who can maintain personal boundaries while preserving affection demonstrates sophisticated emotional intelligence. "I care about you deeply and I'm not available to discuss your marriage problems every day" exemplifies this skilful boundary communication.

The celebration of friends' successes without envy or competitiveness requires emotional maturity and security. The capacity to feel genuine joy for others' achievements while managing one's own comparative feelings demonstrates sophisticated emotional regulation and empathetic capability.

Different types of friendships—from casual social connections to soul-mate level intimacy—require different emotional intelligence applications. The wisdom to recognise and honour these differences while not demanding more intimacy than relationships can sustainably provide demonstrates mature social intelligence.

## Family Relationships: The Complex Tapestry of Unconditional Love

Family relationships present perhaps the most complex emotional intelligence challenges because they combine involuntary assignment, intense emotional history, multi-generational dynamics, and often lifetime duration (McGoldrick, Gerson & Petry, 2008). These relationships serve as both our first teachers in emotional intelligence and our most enduring testing grounds.

Parent-child relationships involve profound power imbalances and developmental responsibilities that require extraordinary emotional intelligence from parents. The capacity to provide guidance and structure while honouring children's developing autonomy demands sophisticated emotional regulation, empathy, and social skills. Parents who can maintain authority while treating children with respect model emotional intelligence capabilities that children internalise and carry forward.

Sibling relationships often involve complex dynamics of competition, comparison, and shared history that can either strengthen or undermine emotional intelligence development. Siblings who learn to navigate jealousy, support each other's growth, and maintain connection despite different life paths demonstrate sophisticated relational capabilities.

Intergenerational relationships—between parents and adult children, grandparents and grandchildren—require emotional intelligence adaptations as roles, needs, and capacities change over time. The adult child who can provide care for aging parents while maintaining appropriate boundaries demonstrates mature emotional intelligence.

Extended family relationships—aunts, uncles, cousins, in-laws—present opportunities for practicing emotional intelligence skills in lower-stakes environments while potentially providing additional sources of support and connection.

Family cultural dynamics add additional complexity, as families transmit not only individual emotional patterns but also cultural values, communication styles, and relationship expectations. Individuals who can honour family cultural heritage while developing their own emotional intelligence demonstrate sophisticated integration capabilities.

The healing of family emotional wounds—whether from childhood trauma, ongoing conflicts, or intergenerational patterns—often requires the highest levels of emotional intelligence application. Family members who can acknowledge past hurts while working toward repair and growth demonstrate extraordinary emotional courage and skill.

## Workplace Relationships: The Professional Practice of Human Connection

Workplace relationships present unique emotional intelligence challenges because they combine professional objectives with human needs, formal hierarchies with interpersonal dynamics, and diverse personalities with shared goals (Goleman, 2013). Success in professional contexts increasingly depends on emotional and social intelligence rather than merely technical competence.

Colleague relationships require the ability to collaborate effectively with individuals who may have very different working styles, communication preferences, and professional priorities. The capacity to find common ground, appreciate diverse perspectives, and create synergistic outcomes demonstrates sophisticated workplace emotional intelligence.

Manager-subordinate relationships involve complex power dynamics that require emotional intelligence from both parties. Effective managers must provide guidance and feedback while maintaining psychological safety and supporting development. Effective subordinates must communicate needs and concerns while respecting organisational hierarchies and demonstrating professional maturity.

Customer and client relationships demand the ability to understand and respond to diverse needs, manage difficult interactions with professionalism, and create positive experiences that serve both individual and organisational objectives. Service professionals who consistently create positive customer experiences demonstrate sophisticated emotional intelligence application.

Team dynamics in professional settings require individuals to balance personal recognition with collective success, manage conflicts constructively, and maintain motivation during challenging projects. Teams that function with high emotional intelligence achieve superior results while maintaining positive working relationships.

Organisational culture both shapes and is shaped by the collective emotional intelligence of its members. organisations with high emotional intelligence cultures demonstrate greater innovation, employee engagement, customer satisfaction, and financial performance. Individuals who contribute positively to organisational emotional intelligence serve both their own career development and broader organisational success.

Professional networking requires sophisticated social intelligence—the ability to build mutually beneficial relationships, offer value to others, and maintain connections over time without appearing opportunistic or manipulative. Professionals who excel at networking demonstrate authentic interest in others' success while clearly communicating their own values and objectives.

# The Transformative Power of Conflict: EQ in Challenging Moments

Conflict represents one of the most crucial testing grounds for emotional intelligence in relationships. While often viewed as something to be avoided or resolved as quickly as possible, conflict actually provides opportunities for deepening understanding, strengthening bonds, and fostering individual growth when approached with emotional intelligence (Lencioni, 2002).

## Reframing Conflict as Opportunity

The emotionally intelligent approach to conflict begins with a fundamental reframe—viewing disagreements, tensions, and even arguments as information rather than threats. This perspective shift changes everything about how conflicts are approached and resolved. Instead of seeking to win or to end the conflict as quickly as possible, emotionally intelligent individuals seek to understand what the conflict reveals about underlying needs, values, and perspectives.

The marketing executive who interprets heated debates between team members as evidence of passion and investment rather than interpersonal dysfunction exemplifies this reframe. By normalising disagreement and creating structures for productive dialogue, she enables these debates to drive innovation rather than create team toxicity.

## The Neurobiology of Conflict Response

Understanding the neurobiological basis of conflict responses provides crucial insights for emotionally intelligent conflict navigation. When individuals perceive threat or disagreement, the amygdala activates fight-or-flight responses that can hijack rational thinking and empathetic capacity (LeDoux, 2015). Emotionally intelligent individuals learn to recognise these activation patterns and develop strategies for maintaining access to higher-order thinking even during conflicts.

Breathing techniques, mindfulness practices, and conscious pausing can help maintain prefrontal cortex function during conflicts, enabling more thoughtful and effective responses. The couple who agrees to take breaks during heated discussions when either person becomes overwhelmed demonstrates this sophisticated self-regulation capability.

## The Skills of Emotionally Intelligent Conflict Resolution

Effective conflict resolution requires several sophisticated emotional intelligence capabilities working in coordination. Active listening during conflict involves setting aside defensive responses and genuinely seeking to understand others' perspectives, even when those perspectives feel threatening or invalid. This requires emotional regulation to manage discomfort and curiosity to explore different viewpoints.

Emotional validation during conflict involves acknowledging others' feelings and experiences without necessarily agreeing with their conclusions or demands. "I can see that you're really frustrated about this situation, and I'd like to understand what would help" demonstrates validation while maintaining space for dialogue.

Perspective-taking during conflict requires the cognitive and emotional flexibility to see situations from multiple viewpoints simultaneously. This doesn't mean abandoning one's own perspective but rather expanding to encompass additional viewpoints that might inform creative solutions.

Collaborative problem-solving focuses on identifying underlying needs and interests rather than defending positions. The divorce mediation process that helps couples identify their shared interest in children's well-being despite their disagreement about custody arrangements exemplifies this approach.

Repair and reconciliation following conflicts require sophisticated emotional intelligence to acknowledge injuries, offer authentic apologies, and rebuild trust. The ability to separate impact from intention, take responsibility for one's part in conflicts, and make behavioural changes to prevent future similar issues demonstrates mature conflict resolution capability.

### Conflict as Intimacy Deepener

When navigated skilfully, conflicts can actually deepen relationships by creating opportunities for greater understanding, authenticity, and trust. Partners who successfully work through disagreements often report feeling closer and more understood than before the conflict arose. This counterintuitive outcome occurs when conflicts are approached as collaborative challenges rather than competitive battles.

The vulnerability required to share one's deepest concerns, fears, and needs during conflicts can create profound intimacy when received with empathy and care. The couple who can discuss their different financial values without judgment creates deeper understanding and more sustainable solutions than those who avoid such conversations.

## Emotional Intelligence Through Life's Seasons: Relationships in Transition

Relationships do not exist in static states but rather evolve continuously through various seasons of growth, challenge, stability, and change. Emotional intelligence becomes particularly crucial during transition periods when established patterns must be renegotiated and new ways of relating must be developed (Bridges, 2017).

## Relationship Beginnings: The Art of Conscious Connection

The formation of new relationships requires sophisticated emotional intelligence to navigate the complex dance of gradual intimacy development. This involves calibrating vulnerability levels appropriately, reading and responding to others' comfort levels, and building trust through consistent, caring interactions.

The early stages of relationship development require particular emotional intelligence because individuals must balance authenticity with appropriate boundaries, enthusiasm with realistic expectations, and investment with self-protection. The dating process that allows individuals to reveal themselves gradually while assessing compatibility demonstrates sophisticated emotional and social intelligence.

Online relationship formation presents new challenges and opportunities for emotional intelligence application. The absence of nonverbal cues in digital communication requires heightened verbal emotional intelligence, while the abundance of potential connections requires sophisticated discernment and decision-making capabilities.

## Relationship Deepening: The Courage of Increasing Intimacy

As relationships deepen, emotional intelligence requirements become more sophisticated. The willingness to be increasingly vulnerable requires trust in both self and others, while the capacity to receive others' vulnerability requires empathy and emotional regulation. Couples who successfully navigate this deepening process report feeling both seen and accepted at profound levels.

The integration of individual lives into shared experiences requires emotional intelligence to balance autonomy with connection, personal growth with relationship stability, and individual needs with partnership requirements. The couple who can maintain their individual friendships while building shared friendships demonstrates this sophisticated balance.

Sexual intimacy in deepening relationships requires emotional intelligence to communicate desires and boundaries, navigate differences in preferences and needs, and maintain connection during inevitable challenges. Couples who can discuss sexual concerns openly while maintaining emotional safety create the foundation for lifelong intimate connection.

## Relationship Challenges: Growing Through Adversity

Every significant relationship encounters periods of challenge—whether from external stressors, internal conflicts, or life transitions. These challenges test and potentially strengthen emotional intelligence capabilities while providing opportunities for relationship growth and deepening.

Health crises within relationships require emotional intelligence to provide appropriate support while maintaining personal well-being, to navigate changing roles and capabilities, and to find meaning and connection despite suffering. Couples who successfully navigate serious illness often report that the experience deepened their appreciation and connection.

Financial stress tests relationships by activating fears, triggering different coping mechanisms, and potentially creating conflicts over values and priorities. Partners who can discuss financial concerns openly while supporting each other emotionally demonstrate sophisticated emotional intelligence under pressure.

Career transitions—whether voluntary or involuntary—require emotional intelligence to manage identity changes, support each other's growth, and adapt relationship dynamics to new circumstances. The couple who can celebrate one partner's career advancement while supporting the other through job loss demonstrates mature emotional intelligence.

Family crises—such as aging parents, teenage struggles, or extended family conflicts—require emotional intelligence to manage competing loyalties, provide appropriate support, and maintain partnership strength despite external pressures.

## Relationship Endings: The Wisdom of Conscious Completion

Not all relationships are meant to continue indefinitely, and emotional intelligence includes the wisdom to recognise when relationships have reached natural completion points or when they have become harmful rather than beneficial. The process of relationship ending requires sophisticated emotional intelligence to navigate grief, anger, disappointment, and practical concerns.

Friendship endings often lack clear protocols, requiring individuals to recognise when relationships are no longer serving both parties and to create conscious completion processes. The friend who can acknowledge that their lives have grown in different directions while expressing gratitude for shared experiences demonstrates mature emotional intelligence.

Romantic relationship endings require emotional intelligence to separate shared lives while maintaining dignity and respect, to manage complex emotions while making practical decisions, and to learn from the relationship experience while remaining open to future connection. The divorcing couple who can prioritise their children's well-being while processing their own grief demonstrates extraordinary emotional intelligence.

Professional relationship endings—whether due to job changes, retirement, or organisational restructuring—require emotional intelligence to maintain connections that serve both parties while adapting to new circumstances. The colleague who can maintain friendship after leaving a shared workplace demonstrates sophisticated social intelligence.

## The Cultivation of Relational Emotional Intelligence: Practical Pathways to Mastery

The development of emotional intelligence in relationship contexts requires intentional practice, honest self-examination, and often the support of mentors, coaches, or therapists who can provide guidance and feedback. This development is not merely skill acquisition but personal transformation that affects every aspect of one's relational life.

### The Foundation: Self-Knowledge and Self-Regulation

The development of relational emotional intelligence begins with profound self-knowledge—understanding one's emotional patterns, triggers, attachment style, and impact on others. This self-awareness provides the foundation for conscious choice rather than automatic reaction in relationship situations.

Regular self-reflection practices help develop this awareness. Journaling about relationship experiences, emotional responses, and lessons learned creates space for deeper understanding. The individual who spends time each week reflecting on her relationship interactions and identifying patterns develops sophisticated self-awareness over time.

Mindfulness practices enhance emotional awareness and regulation capabilities. The ability to notice emotional states as they arise, observe them without judgment, and choose responses rather than being controlled by reactions represents sophisticated emotional intelligence application. The parent who can notice his frustration rising during homework time and consciously choose a supportive response demonstrates this capability.

Feedback from trusted others provides external perspectives that can illuminate blind spots and confirm areas of strength. The willingness to seek and receive honest feedback about one's relational patterns demonstrates the humility and growth orientation necessary for emotional intelligence development.

## The Practice: Conscious Relationship Skills Development

The development of specific relationship skills requires conscious practice and often involves stepping outside comfort zones. Communication skills can be developed through practicing active listening, learning to express emotions clearly, and developing facility with difficult conversations.

Empathy development involves consciously practicing perspective-taking, asking curious questions about others' experiences, and developing sensitivity to emotional and energetic cues. The manager who makes a point of understanding each team member's individual motivations and challenges develops sophisticated empathetic intelligence.

Conflict resolution skills can be developed through studying effective approaches, practicing new behaviours in low-stakes situations, and gradually applying new capabilities to more challenging relationship issues. The couple who takes a communication workshop and practices new skills together demonstrates commitment to relationship growth.

Boundary setting and maintenance requires developing clarity about personal values and limits, learning to communicate boundaries clearly, and developing the emotional regulation necessary to maintain boundaries despite pressure or guilt. The helping professional who learns to provide excellent service while maintaining personal well-being demonstrates healthy boundary management.

### The Integration: Holistic Relationship Transformation

The highest levels of relational emotional intelligence involve integration of all capabilities into a coherent way of being that naturally creates positive relationship experiences. This integration transcends skill application to become an authentic expression of one's mature personality.

This integration often requires healing previous relationship wounds that may interfere with current connection capabilities. The individual who addresses childhood attachment issues through therapy becomes more available for secure adult relationships. The couple who works through trust violations creates a stronger foundation than they had before the crisis.

Spiritual and philosophical development often accompanies advanced emotional intelligence development, as individuals recognise the profound interconnectedness of human experience and their responsibility to contribute positively to the relational world. The leader who sees her role as serving others' growth and well-being demonstrates this integrated approach to relationship.

## Conclusion: The Infinite Potential of Conscious Relationship

As we conclude this comprehensive exploration of how emotional intelligence shapes relationships, we arrive at a profound recognition: our capacity for connection represents perhaps the most significant factor in determining the quality of our human experience. The relationships we create and maintain serve as both the context for our growth and the legacy of our existence.

The research is clear, the examples are compelling, and the implications are profound: individuals who develop sophisticated emotional intelligence capabilities gain access to levels of relational satisfaction, intimacy, and mutual support that remain elusive to those who rely solely on intuition or social convention. These capabilities can be developed at any age and stage of life, offering hope for transformation even in the most challenging relationship circumstances.

The journey toward relational emotional intelligence mastery requires courage—the willingness to examine ourselves honestly, to be vulnerable in service of authentic connection, and to choose growth over comfort when relationships challenge us to become better versions of ourselves. It demands commitment to continuous learning, practice, and refinement of capabilities that can always be improved but never perfected.

Yet the rewards of this journey extend far beyond personal satisfaction. Individuals who develop sophisticated relational emotional intelligence become catalysts for positive change in their families, communities, and organisations. They model possibilities that inspire others to develop their own capabilities. They create ripple effects of healing, understanding, and connection that extend far beyond their immediate relationships.

The ancient wisdom traditions speak of love as the fundamental force of the universe—not merely romantic love, but the deeper love that recognises the interconnectedness of all existence and seeks to serve the highest good of all beings. Emotional intelligence provides practical pathways for expressing this love through our relationships, transforming theoretical understanding into lived experience.

In our next chapter, we will explore the foundation of all emotional intelligence—self-awareness—examining how the journey inward creates the capacity for authentic connection with others. The adventure continues, and the potential for transformation remains limitless for those willing to embrace the courage and commitment that conscious relationship requires.

The sacred architecture of human connection awaits our conscious participation. Through the application of emotional intelligence, we become both architects and inhabitants of relationships that honour the full mystery and potential of human experience. In this way, our relationships become not merely sources of personal satisfaction but contributions to the collective evolution of human consciousness itself.

---

## References

Ainsworth, M. D. S., Blehar, M. C., Waters, E., & Wall, S. (1978). *Patterns of attachment: A psychological study of the strange situation.* Hillsdale, NJ: Lawrence Erlbaum.

Aristotle. (350 BCE). *Nicomachean ethics* (T. Irwin, Trans.). Indianapolis: Hackett Publishing. (Original work published 350 BCE)

Bar-On, R. (2006). The Bar-On model of emotional-social intelligence (ESI). *Psicothema*, 18, 13-25.

Bowlby, J. (1988). *A secure base: Parent-child attachment and healthy human development.* New York: Basic Books.

Bridges, W. (2017). *Transitions: Making sense of life's changes* (40th anniversary ed.). Boston: Da Capo Press.

Brown, B. (2012). *Daring greatly: How the courage to be vulnerable transforms the way we live, love, parent, and lead.* New York: Gotham Books.

Buber, M. (1970). *I and thou* (W. Kaufmann, Trans.). Edinburgh: T&T Clark. (Original work published 1923)

Cacioppo, J. T., & Patrick, W. (2008). *Loneliness: Human nature and the need for social connection*. New York: W. W. Norton & Company.

Carter, C. S. (2014). Oxytocin pathways and the evolution of human behaviour. *Annual Review of Psychology*, 65, 17-39.

Covey, S. R. (2006). *The speed of trust: The one thing that changes everything*. New York: Free Press.

Davis, M. H. (2018). *Empathy: A social psychological approach*. New York: Routledge.

Fisher, H. (2016). *Anatomy of love: A natural history of mating, marriage, and why we stray* (Completely revised and updated ed.). New York: W. W. Norton & Company.

Fisher, H. (2017). *The tyranny of love: Love addiction, codependency, and attachment theory*. Psychology Today, 48(3), 34-41.

Goleman, D. (2006). *Social intelligence: The new science of human relationships*. New York: Bantam Dell.

Goleman, D. (2013). *Focus: The hidden driver of excellence*. New York: HarperCollins.

Gottman, J. M. (2015). *The seven principles for making marriage work* (2nd ed.). New York: Harmony Books.

Hatfield, E., Cacioppo, J. T., & Rapson, R. L. (2019). *Emotional contagion: Studies in emotion and social interaction*. Cambridge: Cambridge University Press.

Johnson, S. M. (2019). *Attachment in psychotherapy*. New York: Guilford Publications.

Jung, C. G. (1969). *The archetypes and the collective unconscious* (R. F. C. Hull, Trans.). Princeton: Princeton University Press. (Original work published 1959)

Kant, I. (1785). *Groundwork for the metaphysics of morals* (M. Gregor, Trans.). Cambridge: Cambridge University Press.

LeDoux, J. (2015). *Anxious: Using the brain to understand and treat fear and anxiety*. New York: Viking.

Lencioni, P. (2002). *The five dysfunctions of a team: A leadership fable*. San Francisco: Jossey-Bass.

Lieberman, M. D. (2013). *Social: Why our brains are wired to connect*. New York: Crown Publishers.

McGoldrick, M., Gerson, R., & Petry, S. (2008). *Genograms: Assessment and intervention* (3rd ed.). New York: W. W. Norton & Company.

Mehrabian, A. (1971). *Silent messages: Implicit communication of emotions and attitudes*. Belmont, CA: Wadsworth.

Pink, D. H. (2018). *Drive: The surprising truth about what motivates us* (Updated ed.). New York: Riverhead Books.

Porges, S. W. (2011). *The polyvagal theory: Neurophysiological foundations of emotions, attachment, communication, and self-regulation*. New York: W. W. Norton & Company.

Rizzolatti, G., & Craighero, L. (2004). The mirror-neuron system. *Annual Review of Neuroscience*, 27, 169-192.

Rogers, C. R. (1961). *On becoming a person: A therapist's view of psychotherapy*. Boston: Houghton Mifflin.

Siegel, D. J. (2012). *The developing mind: How relationships and the brain interact to shape who we are* (2nd ed.). New York: Guilford Press.

# Chapter 7: Building Emotional Self-Awareness

*The Sacred Architecture of Inner Knowing*

## Introduction: The Cartography of the Heart

In the labyrinthine corridors of human consciousness, where thoughts cascade like waterfalls and emotions surge like underground rivers, lies a singular chamber—the observatory of self-awareness. Here, in this sacred space, we become both the astronomer and the constellation, the cartographer and the terrain itself (Goleman, 2006). Emotional intelligence, that most elusive yet essential of human capacities, finds its genesis not in grand gestures or dramatic revelations, but in the quiet, persistent act of turning our gaze inward with the precision of a surgeon and the tenderness of a mother.

The ancient Greeks inscribed "Know thyself" upon the Temple of Apollo at Delphi, yet they could scarcely have imagined the neurological symphony that accompanies this deceptively simple directive. Today, we understand that emotional self-awareness is not merely philosophical wisdom—it is the fundamental architecture upon which every other aspect of emotional intelligence is constructed (Bar-On, 2006). Without this cornerstone, emotional regulation becomes as futile as attempting to conduct an orchestra while blindfolded; empathy remains as shallow as a puddle reflecting only our own projections; and social skills crumble like ancient parchment exposed to harsh light.

But what does it truly mean to know oneself emotionally? The answer unfolds like a Russian nesting doll, revealing layers of complexity that extend far beyond the superficial recognition of happiness or sadness. True emotional self-awareness is a multidimensional phenomenon that encompasses the immediate recognition of emotional states, the understanding of their origins and trajectories, and the profound insight into how these internal weather patterns shape our interactions with the external world (Mayer & Salovey, 1997).

Consider, for a moment, the difference between a novice sailor and a master mariner facing an approaching storm. The novice sees only the darkening sky and feels only fear. The master, however, reads the subtle signs—the particular quality of the wind's whistle, the specific pattern of wave formations, the almost imperceptible shift in atmospheric pressure. This is the difference between basic emotional awareness and the sophisticated emotional literacy we seek to cultivate.

## The Anatomy of Emotional Self-Awareness: A Multifaceted Jewel

Emotional self-awareness reveals itself as a complex, multifaceted phenomenon that operates simultaneously across multiple dimensions of human experience. Like a prism refracting white light into its constituent colours, this capacity breaks down into distinct yet interconnected components, each contributing to our overall emotional literacy (Boyatzis, Goleman & Rhee, 2000).

### Moment-to-Moment Awareness: The Art of Emotional Presence

The first dimension involves what researchers term "online awareness"—the ability to recognise and identify emotions as they arise in the present moment, before they crystallise into automatic behaviours or entrenched patterns (Feldman-Barrett, 2017). This is akin to becoming a meteorologist of your own inner climate, capable of detecting the earliest signs of an approaching emotional front.

Imagine Sarah, a marketing executive, sitting in a budget meeting. As her colleague dismisses her proposal with a casual wave of his hand, she notices—in real-time—the heat rising in her chest, the tightening of her jaw, the subtle acceleration of her heartbeat. Rather than allowing these physiological signals to cascade into an explosive response, her moment-to-moment awareness creates what psychologists call "response flexibility"—a precious pause between stimulus and reaction (Siegel, 2010).

This immediate awareness operates through what neuroscientist Antonio Damasio (2018) describes as "somatic markers"—the body's emotional wisdom speaking through sensation. The tremor in your hands before a presentation, the knot in your stomach when facing a difficult conversation, the lightness in your chest when encountering unexpected kindness—these are not mere physiological accidents but sophisticated emotional intelligence systems that evolved over millennia to guide our navigation through complex social landscapes.

## Deeper Insight: Archaeological Excavation of the Emotional Self

The second dimension transcends immediate recognition to encompass what we might call "emotional archaeology"—the patient excavation of the deeper sources, patterns, and meanings that give rise to our emotional experiences (Pennebaker, 1997). This involves understanding the intricate web of past experiences, core values, unconscious beliefs, and existential aspirations that serve as the substrate from which our emotions emerge.

Consider Marcus, a successful attorney who finds himself inexplicably anxious whenever his teenage daughter expresses interest in creative pursuits. Through deeper self-examination, he begins to recognise that his anxiety stems not from concern about her future financial security, but from his own abandoned dreams of becoming a musician—dreams sacrificed on the altar of parental expectations and societal pressure. His daughter's artistic enthusiasm triggers a complex emotional cocktail of vicarious longing, protective fear, and unresolved grief for his younger self's abandoned aspirations.

This archaeological dimension requires what psychologist Carl Jung (1968) termed "active imagination"—the willingness to engage with the symbolic and metaphorical dimensions of our emotional lives. It demands that we become detective, therapist, and witness to our own internal drama, tracing the golden threads that connect present emotional responses to their historical origins and future implications.

## The Temporal Dimension: Emotions as Dynamic Systems

Emotional self-awareness also encompasses what systems theorists call "temporal sensitivity"—the recognition that emotions are not static states but dynamic processes that unfold across time with their own rhythms, intensities, and natural lifecycles (Frijda, 2007). Like weather systems, emotions have beginnings, peaks, and natural dissipations. Understanding these temporal patterns allows us to work with our emotions rather than against them.

Research in affective neuroscience reveals that most emotional states, left undisturbed by our attempts to amplify or suppress them, follow predictable temporal arcs lasting between 90 seconds and several minutes (Taylor, 2008). This knowledge transforms our relationship with difficult emotions from one of resistance to one of informed patience—we can weather the storm because we understand its meteorology.

## Self-Awareness vs. Self-Consciousness: The Crucial Distinction

One of the most common misconceptions in emotional development involves confusing self-awareness with self-consciousness—a distinction as crucial as the difference between a clear mirror and a funhouse distortion (Duval & Wicklund, 1972). This confusion has led countless individuals down paths of paralysis rather than empowerment, self-flagellation rather than self-understanding.

Self-awareness operates like a wise, compassionate observer—curious rather than judgmental, interested rather than alarmed. It maintains what Buddhists call "beginner's mind," approaching each emotional experience with fresh eyes and open heart (Suzuki, 1970). When self-aware, we might notice: "Ah, there's anger arising. I wonder what this might be teaching me about my boundaries or values?"

Self-consciousness, by contrast, functions like a harsh internal critic, turning our attention toward ourselves but through a lens of evaluation, comparison, and often shame. It asks not "What is this emotion telling me?" but rather "What does this emotion say about me as a person? How am I appearing to others? Am I handling this correctly?" The self-conscious individual becomes trapped in recursive loops of meta-emotion—feeling bad about feeling bad, becoming anxious about being anxious.

The neuroscientist Matthew Lieberman (2013) has identified distinct neural networks associated with these different forms of self-attention. Self-awareness activates regions associated with interoception (awareness of internal bodily signals) and reflective cognition, while self-consciousness tends to activate areas associated with social threat detection and self-referential rumination.

This distinction has profound practical implications. Self-awareness enhances emotional regulation and decision-making capacity, while self-consciousness often impairs both. The self-aware person can use emotions as information; the self-conscious person becomes imprisoned by them.

## The Profound Stakes: Why Emotional Self-Awareness Matters

To understand why emotional self-awareness deserves such focused attention, we must examine both its absence and its presence—the shadow and the light it casts across the landscape of human experience.

### The Cost of Emotional Blindness

Without emotional self-awareness, we become what psychologists term "alexithymic"—literally "without words for feelings" (Sifneos, 1973). But the condition extends beyond vocabulary to encompass a fundamental disconnection from our emotional guidance system. The consequences ripple through every domain of human experience like stones thrown into still water.

In our professional lives, emotional blindness manifests as reactive leadership, impulsive decision-making, and the inability to read the emotional undercurrents that often determine the success or failure of collaborative endeavours (Cherniss, 2010). The emotionally unaware manager might puzzle over why their team seems disengaged, never recognising how their own anxiety creates an atmosphere of tension, or how their unacknowledged need for control stifles creativity and initiative.

In our intimate relationships, emotional blindness creates what attachment theorists call "earned insecurity"—patterns of disconnection that persist despite our best conscious intentions (Main, 1996). We project unresolved emotions onto our partners, react to present situations based on past wounds, and remain mystified by recurring conflicts that seem to arise from nowhere yet follow depressingly familiar scripts.

Perhaps most tragically, emotional blindness cuts us off from our own authentic desires and values, leaving us vulnerable to what the philosopher Charles Taylor (1991) calls "the malaise of modernity"—a profound sense of meaninglessness and disconnection despite external success. We may achieve conventional markers of success while remaining strangers to ourselves, wondering why accomplishments feel hollow and victories taste like ash.

## The Gifts of Emotional Lucidity

Conversely, emotional self-awareness opens doorways to experiences that transform the quality of human existence itself. Research consistently demonstrates that individuals with higher emotional self-awareness exhibit greater life satisfaction, more resilient stress responses, and more authentic relationships (Schutte et al., 2007).

In leadership contexts, emotionally self-aware individuals create what researchers call "positive emotional contagion"—their emotional regulation and authenticity inspire similar qualities in others (Hatfield, Cacioppo & Rapson, 1994). They make decisions from a place of clarity rather than reactivity, navigate conflict with grace rather than defensiveness, and inspire trust through their consistent alignment between inner experience and outer expression.

In intimate relationships, emotional self-awareness enables what psychologist John Gottman (1999) identifies as one of the strongest predictors of relationship longevity: the ability to repair emotional ruptures quickly and effectively. When we understand our own emotional patterns, we can take responsibility for our contributions to conflict, communicate our needs clearly, and respond to our partners from a place of choice rather than compulsion.

Most profoundly, emotional self-awareness serves as a compass for authentic living—helping us distinguish between desires that arise from our deepest values and those that stem from social conditioning, fear, or unhealed wounds. It enables what the psychologist Rollo May (1975) called "authentic choosing"—decisions that align with our genuine nature rather than external expectations or internal compulsions.

## The Neuroscience of Emotional Self-Awareness: Mapping the Brain's Emotional Intelligence

Recent advances in neuroscience have illuminated the biological substrates of emotional self-awareness with unprecedented clarity, revealing it to be not merely a psychological skill but a fundamental reorganisation of brain function itself (Damasio, 2018). This neurological perspective transforms our understanding of emotional development from wishful thinking to evidence-based practice.

### The Prefrontal Revolution

The prefrontal cortex, that evolutionarily recent addition to the human brain, serves as the command centre for emotional self-awareness. Within this region, specific areas have been identified as crucial for different aspects of emotional intelligence (Ochsner & Gross, 2005).

The ventromedial prefrontal cortex (vmPFC) acts as the brain's emotional integration centre, weaving together sensory information, memory, and emotional significance into coherent narratives of experience. When this region is active, we experience what researchers call "affective labelling"—the ability to recognise and name our emotional states with precision and nuance (Lieberman et al., 2007).

The anterior cingulate cortex (ACC) functions as an emotional conflict monitor, alerting us when our current emotional state conflicts with our goals or values. This region enables what psychologists call "cognitive control"—the ability to recognise when our emotions might be leading us astray and to consciously choose alternative responses (Botvinick, Cohen & Carter, 2004).

The dorsolateral prefrontal cortex (dlPFC) serves as the brain's executive editor, capable of stepping back from immediate emotional experience to evaluate patterns, consider consequences, and implement strategic responses. This region is particularly crucial for what researchers term "meta-cognitive awareness"—thinking about our thinking, including our emotional thinking (Fernandez-Duque, Baird & Posner, 2000).

## The Amygdala Hijack and Its Prevention

The amygdala, often called the brain's "alarm system," serves crucial protective functions but can overwhelm higher-order thinking when it perceives threat—a phenomenon psychologist Daniel Goleman (1995) termed "amygdala hijack." Understanding this neurological process illuminates both the challenge and the opportunity of emotional self-awareness.

During amygdala activation, stress hormones like cortisol and adrenaline flood the system, creating physiological changes designed for immediate action: increased heart rate, heightened muscle tension, narrowed attention, and decreased access to complex reasoning (LeDoux, 2015). While adaptive in genuine emergencies, these responses can be counterproductive in modern contexts where the "threats" are often social, psychological, or symbolic rather than physical.

Emotional self-awareness serves as a neurological intervention in this process. When we recognise the early signs of amygdala activation—the racing heart, the tightening chest, the tunnel vision—we can consciously engage the prefrontal cortex through techniques like cognitive reappraisal, deep breathing, or mindful observation (Gross, 2015). This creates what neuroscientist Rick Hanson (2013) calls "top-down regulation"—the higher brain centres calming and directing the more primitive emotional centres.

### The Neuroplasticity Advantage

Perhaps most encouragingly, research demonstrates that the neural networks underlying emotional self-awareness exhibit remarkable plasticity throughout the lifespan. Regular practice of mindfulness meditation, for example, has been shown to increase gray matter density in regions associated with emotional regulation while decreasing reactivity in the amygdala (Lutz et al., 2004).

This neuroplasticity means that emotional self-awareness is not a fixed trait but a capacity that can be developed through intentional practice. Each time we pause to notice our emotions, each moment we choose awareness over reactivity, we literally rewire our brains for greater emotional intelligence.

## Common Barriers to Self-Awareness: The Internal Resistance

Despite its obvious benefits, developing emotional self-awareness often encounters significant internal resistance. These barriers, rooted in evolutionary psychology, cultural conditioning, and personal history, require understanding and compassion rather than judgment and force (Kegan & Lahey, 2009).

### The Evolutionary Bias Toward Action

From an evolutionary perspective, our ancestors survived not by contemplating their emotions but by acting upon them quickly. Fear of predators demanded immediate flight; anger at rivals required swift aggression; attraction to potential mates called for rapid approach. This "action bias" remains embedded in our neural architecture, making the pause required for emotional self-awareness feel unnatural or even dangerous (Gilbert, 2009).

Modern life, however, presents challenges that require sophistication rather than speed. The colleague who criticises our work is not a sabre-toothed tiger; the traffic jam that makes us late is not a life-threatening emergency; the rejection we experience in dating is not exile from the tribe. Yet our emotional systems often respond as if these modern stressors carried ancient stakes.

Developing emotional self-awareness requires what psychologist Steven Hayes (2019) calls "psychological flexibility"—the ability to stay present with our emotions long enough to understand them, even when every instinct screams for immediate action.

## Cultural Conditioning and Emotional Suppression

Most cultures develop implicit rules about which emotions are acceptable to feel and express, often along lines of gender, class, profession, or social role (Hochschild, 1983). These "feeling rules" become so deeply internalised that we may lose awareness of emotions that fall outside acceptable parameters.

Men in many cultures learn to suppress vulnerability, sadness, or fear, developing what psychologist Terrence Real (1997) calls "covert depression"—emotional numbness masquerading as strength. Women may learn to suppress anger or ambition, experiencing these natural emotions as guilt or self-doubt rather than recognising them as valid responses to challenging situations.

Professional environments often have their own emotional codes. Healthcare workers may suppress grief to maintain clinical objectivity; business leaders may suppress uncertainty to project confidence; teachers may suppress frustration to maintain classroom control. While these suppressions may serve short-term functional purposes, they can gradually erode our connection to our authentic emotional experience.

### The Fear of Emotional Overwhelm

Many individuals avoid developing emotional self-awareness from a well-founded fear that paying attention to their emotions will intensify them beyond manageable levels. This fear often stems from past experiences of emotional overwhelm or from growing up in environments where emotions were either dangerous or unwelcome (van der Kolk, 2014).

The paradox is that emotional avoidance often creates the very overwhelm we seek to prevent. Suppressed emotions don't disappear; they accumulate pressure like steam in a sealed container, eventually erupting in ways that feel chaotic and uncontrollable. Emotional self-awareness, by contrast, provides what psychologist Marsha Linehan (2014) calls "emotional regulation"—the ability to experience emotions fully while maintaining our capacity for wise action.

## Practical Strategies for Cultivating Emotional Self-Awareness

Developing emotional self-awareness is both an art and a science, requiring sustained practice across multiple dimensions of experience. The following strategies represent evidence-based approaches that can be adapted to individual preferences and circumstances.

### Mindfulness Meditation: The Foundation Practice

Mindfulness meditation serves as perhaps the most universally effective method for developing emotional self-awareness. Research has consistently demonstrated its effects on emotional regulation, stress reduction, and overall psychological well-being (Goyal et al., 2014).

The practice involves what Buddhist teacher Jon Kabat-Zinn (2003) describes as "paying attention in a particular way: on purpose, in the present moment, and non-judgmentally." For emotional development, this means learning to observe our emotional states with the same neutral curiosity we might bring to watching clouds form and dissolve in the sky.

A basic emotional mindfulness practice might proceed as follows:

**Preparation**: Find a quiet space where you can sit comfortably for 10-20 minutes without interruption. Close your eyes or soften your gaze downward.

**Anchoring**: Begin by focusing attention on your breath, using it as an anchor for present-moment awareness. Notice the natural rhythm of inhalation and exhalation without trying to change it.

**Emotional Scanning**: After several minutes of breath awareness, gently expand your attention to include your emotional state. Ask yourself: "What am I feeling right now?" without trying to change or fix anything.

**Labelling**: When emotions arise, practice gentle labelling: "Ah, anxiety is here," or "I notice sadness," or "There's excitement." The key is to name emotions as temporary visitors rather than permanent residents.

**Bodily Awareness**: Notice where emotions manifest in your body. Does anxiety create tension in your shoulders? Does sadness feel heavy in your chest? Does joy create lightness in your stomach?

**Non-Reactive Witnessing**: Practice observing emotions without immediately trying to understand, change, or act upon them. Simply allow them to be present, knowing that all emotions are temporary and contain information.

## The Emotion Journal: Writing Your Way to Understanding

Expressive writing has been shown to have profound effects on both psychological and physical health, with specific benefits for emotional self-awareness and regulation (Pennebaker & Smyth, 2016). The act of translating emotional experience into words activates the left hemisphere of the brain, which tends to be more analytical and less reactive than the right hemisphere's immediate emotional processing.

Effective emotion journaling involves several key elements:

**Daily Consistency**: Even five minutes of daily writing can be more beneficial than occasional longer sessions. Consistency allows patterns to emerge that might not be visible in sporadic entries.

**Specific Emotional Vocabulary**: Rather than relying on general terms like "good" or "bad," develop precision in emotional description. Was it frustration or disappointment? Excitement or anxiety? Contentment or relief?

**Trigger Identification**: For each significant emotional experience, explore what preceded it. Was it a specific interaction, thought, memory, or environmental factor? Understanding triggers helps predict and prepare for future emotional responses.

**Bodily Sensations**: Include descriptions of how emotions manifested physically. This strengthens the connection between mind and body while developing somatic awareness.

**Values and Needs Exploration**: Ask what each emotion might be telling you about your deeper values or unmet needs. Anger might signal violated boundaries; sadness might indicate loss or disappointment; joy might reveal what matters most to you.

## Somatic Awareness: The Body's Emotional Wisdom

The body serves as a sophisticated emotional processing system, often recognising and responding to emotional information before the conscious mind becomes aware of it (Levine, 2010). Developing somatic awareness—conscious attention to bodily sensations—can dramatically enhance emotional self-awareness.

Regular body scanning practices involve systematically bringing attention to different parts of the body, noticing sensations without trying to change them. Over time, practitioners develop sensitivity to the subtle ways emotions manifest somatically:

- **Anxiety** might appear as chest tightness, shallow breathing, or stomach butterflies

- **Anger** might manifest as heat in the face, tension in the jaw, or clenched fists

- **Sadness** might feel like heaviness in the chest, slumped shoulders, or a lump in the throat

- **Joy** might create lightness in the chest, relaxed muscles, or an expansive feeling throughout the torso

This somatic literacy becomes an early warning system for emotional states, allowing intervention before emotions become overwhelming or problematic.

## Feedback Loops: The Mirror of Relationship

While self-reflection is crucial, we often have blind spots that require external perspective to illuminate. Trusted friends, family members, mentors, or therapists can serve as emotional mirrors, reflecting back patterns we might not see ourselves (Johari, 1955).

Seeking feedback requires vulnerability and courage, but it can accelerate emotional development dramatically. Useful questions for trusted others might include:

- "What emotions do you notice I express most frequently?"
- "How do I tend to respond when I'm stressed or upset?"
- "What emotional patterns do you see in me that I might not be aware of?"
- "How does my emotional state seem to affect our interactions?"

The key is to approach feedback with genuine curiosity rather than defensiveness, recognising that others' perceptions—while subjective—often contain valuable information about our emotional impact.

## The Transformative Promise: Deep Benefits of Emotional Self-Awareness

As emotional self-awareness develops and deepens, it catalyses transformations that extend far beyond simple self-understanding. These changes often surprise practitioners with their scope and profundity, touching every aspect of lived experience.

### Emotional Freedom and Response Flexibility

Perhaps the most immediate benefit involves what psychologist Viktor Frankl (1963) described as the "space between stimulus and response"—the precious pause in which choice becomes possible. Rather than being controlled by emotional reactivity, emotionally self-aware individuals develop what researchers call "response flexibility"—the ability to choose their actions based on conscious values rather than unconscious impulses.

This freedom manifests in countless daily situations: pausing before responding to a provocative email, choosing curiosity over defensiveness when receiving criticism, maintaining equanimity during stressful circumstances, or responding to children's difficult behaviour from wisdom rather than reactivity.

## Authentic Relationships and Emotional Intimacy

Emotional self-awareness transforms relationships by enabling what psychologist Susan Johnson (2019) calls "emotional accessibility and responsiveness." When we understand our own emotional patterns, we can communicate more clearly about our needs, take responsibility for our contributions to conflict, and respond to others from presence rather than projection.

This creates an upward spiral in relationship quality: our emotional authenticity invites others to be more genuine, our emotional regulation helps others feel safe, and our emotional wisdom contributes to better collective decision-making.

## Purposeful Living and Values Alignment

Emotions serve as sophisticated guidance systems, pointing toward what matters most to us. Fear might signal threats to our values; anger might indicate boundary violations; joy might reveal our authentic desires; sadness might honour what we've lost or what we long for (Greenberg, 2015).

Emotional self-awareness enables what the philosopher Charles Taylor (1991) calls "strong evaluation"—the ability to distinguish between desires that align with our deepest values and those that stem from conditioning, compulsion, or external pressure. This capacity is essential for what psychologists call "eudaimonic well-being"—flourishing that comes from living in accordance with our authentic nature rather than merely pursuing pleasure or avoiding pain (Ryff, 2014).

### Resilience and Post-Traumatic Growth

Emotional self-awareness enhances resilience by transforming our relationship with difficult experiences. Rather than being overwhelmed by challenging emotions, we learn to work with them as sources of information and catalysts for growth (Tedeschi & Calhoun, 2004).

This doesn't mean becoming emotionally invulnerable or perpetually positive. Instead, it involves developing what psychologist Kristin Neff (2011) calls "self-compassion"—the ability to meet our emotional pain with the same kindness we would offer a dear friend. This compassionate awareness creates the safety necessary for genuine healing and growth.

## Conclusion: The Ongoing Journey of Emotional Mastery

Emotional self-awareness is not a destination but a lifelong journey of deepening intimacy with the full spectrum of human experience. Like learning to play a musical instrument or mastering a martial art, it requires patient practice, gentle persistence, and compassionate self-forgiveness when we fall short of our aspirations.

The rewards, however, extend far beyond personal benefit. In a world often characterised by emotional reactivity, polarisation, and disconnection, individuals who develop genuine emotional self-awareness become agents of healing and wisdom. Their presence creates spaces of safety where others can explore their own emotional depths; their responses model possibilities for conscious choice rather than unconscious reaction; their authenticity invites others into greater genuineness.

As we conclude this exploration of emotional self-awareness, we prepare to turn our attention to its natural complement: the art of emotional regulation. For awareness without skilful management can become overwhelming, while regulation without awareness remains superficial. In the next chapter, we will explore how to transform emotional understanding into emotional mastery, learning to dance with our emotions rather than being danced by them.

The journey continues, each step deepening our capacity for wisdom, compassion, and authentic living. In developing emotional self-awareness, we gift ourselves not merely better emotion management, but the possibility of becoming fully human—present to the full spectrum of experience, responsive rather than reactive, connected to ourselves and others in ways that honour the profound complexity and beauty of emotional life.

## References

Bar-On, R. (2006). The Bar-On model of emotional-social intelligence (ESI). *Psicothema*, 18, 13-25.

Botvinick, M. M., Cohen, J. D., & Carter, C. S. (2004). Conflict monitoring and anterior cingulate cortex: An update. *Trends in Cognitive Sciences*, 8(12), 539-546.

Boyatzis, R., Goleman, D., & Rhee, K. (2000). Clustering competence in emotional intelligence: Insights from the Emotional Competence Inventory (ECI). *Handbook of Emotional Intelligence*, 343-362.

Cherniss, C. (2010). *Emotional intelligence: New insights and further clarifications*. Industrial and Organizational Psychology, 3(2), 183-191.

Damasio, A. (2018). *The strange order of things: Life, feeling, and the making of cultures*. Pantheon Books.

Duval, S., & Wicklund, R. A. (1972). *A theory of objective self-awareness*. Academic Press.

Feldman-Barrett, L. (2017). *How emotions are made: The secret life of the brain.* Houghton Mifflin Harcourt.

Fernandez-Duque, D., Baird, J. A., & Posner, M. I. (2000). Executive attention and metacognitive regulation. *Consciousness and Cognition*, 9(2), 288-307.

Frankl, V. E. (1963). *Man's search for meaning.* Beacon Press.

Frijda, N. H. (2007). *The laws of emotion.* Lawrence Erlbaum Associates.

Gilbert, P. (2009). *The compassionate mind.* Constable.

Goleman, D. (1995). *Emotional intelligence.* Bantam Books.

Goleman, D. (2006). *Social intelligence: The new science of human relationships.* Bantam Books.

Gottman, J. (1999). *The marriage clinic: A scientifically based marital therapy.* W. W. Norton & Company.

Goyal, M., Singh, S., Sibinga, E. M., Gould, N. F., Rowland-Seymour, A., Sharma, R., ... & Haythornthwaite, J. A. (2014). Meditation programs for psychological stress and well-being: A systematic review and meta-analysis. *JAMA Internal Medicine*, 174(3), 357-368.

Greenberg, L. S. (2015). *Emotion-focused therapy: Coaching clients to work through their feelings.* American Psychological Association.

Gross, J. J. (2015). Emotion regulation: Current status and future prospects. *Psychological Inquiry*, 26(1), 1-26.

Hanson, R. (2013). *Hardwiring happiness: The new brain science of contentment, calm, and confidence.* Harmony Books.

Hatfield, E., Cacioppo, J. T., & Rapson, R. L. (1994). *Emotional contagion.* Cambridge University Press.

Hayes, S. C. (2019). *A liberated mind: How to pivot toward what matters.* Avery.

Hochschild, A. R. (1983). *The managed heart: Commercialization of human feeling.* University of California Press.

Johari, J. (1955). The Johari window, a graphic model of interpersonal awareness. *Proceedings of the Western Training Laboratory in Group Development*, UCLA.

Johnson, S. (2019). *Attachment in psychotherapy*. Guilford Publications.

Jung, C. G. (1968). *Man and his symbols*. Dell Publishing.

Kabat-Zinn, J. (2003). *Mindfulness-based interventions in context: Past, present, and future*. Clinical Psychology: Science and Practice, 10(2), 144-156.

Kegan, R., & Lahey, L. L. (2009). *Immunity to change: How to overcome it and unlock potential in yourself and your organisation*. Harvard Business Review Press.

LeDoux, J. (2015). *Anxious: Using the brain to understand and treat fear and anxiety*. Penguin Books.

Levine, P. A. (2010). *In an unspoken voice: How the body releases trauma and restores goodness*. North Atlantic Books.

Lieberman, M. D. (2013). *Social: Why our brains are wired to connect*. Crown Publishers.

Lieberman, M. D., Eisenberger, N. I., Crockett, M. J., Tom, S. M., Pfeifer, J. H., & Way, B. M. (2007). Putting feelings into words: Affect labeling disrupts amygdala activity in response to affective stimuli. *Psychological Science*, 18(5), 421-428.

Linehan, M. (2014). *DBT Skills Training Manual*. Guilford Publications.

Lutz, A., Slagter, H. A., Dunne, J. D., & Davidson, R. J. (2008). Attention regulation and monitoring in meditation. *Trends in Cognitive Sciences*, 12(4), 163-169.

Main, M. (1996). Introduction to the special section on attachment and psychopathology: 2. Overview of the field of attachment. *Journal of Consulting and Clinical Psychology*, 64(2), 237-243.

May, R. (1975). *The courage to create.* W. W. Norton & Company.

Mayer, J. D., & Salovey, P. (1997). What is emotional intelligence? In P. Salovey & D. Sluyter (Eds.), *Emotional development and emotional intelligence: Educational implications* (pp. 3-31). Basic Books.

Neff, K. (2011). *Self-compassion: The proven power of being kind to yourself.* William Morrow Paperbacks.

Ochsner, K. N., & Gross, J. J. (2005). The cognitive control of emotion. *Trends in Cognitive Sciences*, 9(5), 242-249.

Pennebaker, J. W. (1997). *Opening up: The healing power of expressing emotions*. Guilford Publications.

Pennebaker, J. W., & Smyth, J. M. (2016). *Opening up by writing it down: How expressive writing improves health and eases emotional pain*. Guilford Publications.

Real, T. (1997). *I don't want to talk about it: Overcoming the secret legacy of male depression*. Scribner.

Ryff, C. D. (2014). Psychological well-being revisited: Advances in the science and practice of eudaimonia. *Psychotherapy and Psychosomatics*, 83(1), 10-28.

Schutte, N. S., Malouff, J. M., Thorsteinsson, E. B., Bhullar, N., & Rooke, S. E. (2007). A meta-analytic investigation of the relationship between emotional intelligence and health. *Personality and Individual Differences*, 42(6), 921-933.

Siegel, D. J. (2010). *Mindsight: The new science of personal transformation*. Bantam Books.

Sifneos, P. E. (1973). The prevalence of 'alexithymic' characteristics in psychosomatic patients. *Psychotherapy and Psychosomatics*, 22(2-6), 255-262.

Suzuki, S. (1970). *Zen mind, beginner's mind.* Weatherhill.

Taylor, C. (1991). *The malaise of modernity*. House of Anansi Press.

Taylor, J. B. (2008). *My stroke of insight: A brain scientist's personal journey*. Viking.

Tedeschi, R. G., & Calhoun, L. G. (2004). Posttraumatic growth: Conceptual foundations and empirical evidence. *Psychological Inquiry*, 15(1), 1-18.

van der Kolk, B. (2014). *The body keeps the score: Brain, mind, and body in the healing of trauma*. Viking.

# Chapter 8: Mastering Self-Regulation for Inner Peace

*The Alchemy of Emotional Mastery*

## Introduction: The Sacred Dance Between Feeling and Response

In the vast amphitheatre of human consciousness, where emotions surge like tsunamis and thoughts flutter like autumn leaves, there exists a profound moment—a crystalline pause between the lightning of feeling and the thunder of action. This moment, gossamer-thin yet infinitely powerful, contains within it the entire architecture of human agency, the very foundation upon which we construct lives of meaning rather than mere reaction (Gross, 2015). Here, in this sacred interlude, lies the art and science of emotional self-regulation: not the suppression of our humanity, but its most exquisite expression.

Consider the violinist who, in the midst of a thunderous symphony, maintains perfect pitch despite the chaos surrounding her. Her fingers dance across the strings with precision born not of rigidity, but of disciplined flexibility—responding to the music's demands while never losing her cantered awareness. This is the essence of emotional self-regulation: the capacity to remain authentically responsive to life's emotional symphony while maintaining the clarity and intentionality that allow us to play our part with grace (Baumeister & Vohs, 2007).

Emotions, those primordial forces that have guided human survival for millennia, surge through our neural pathways with the power of ancient rivers. Fear quickens our pulse when danger approaches; love opens our hearts to connection; anger mobilises our energy when boundaries are violated; joy elevates our spirits when life aligns with our deepest values (Ekman, 2003). These emotional currents are not obstacles to overcome but intelligence systems to understand—evolutionary gifts that, when properly channelled, become the very fuel for wisdom, creativity, and authentic living.

Yet in our modern world, where the sabre-toothed tigers of prehistory have been replaced by performance reviews, traffic jams, and social media notifications, our ancient emotional systems often fire with the same intensity as if our physical survival were at stake (Sapolsky, 2017). The challenge we face is not to eliminate these responses—an impossible and undesirable goal—but to develop what neuroscientist Daniel Siegel (2012) calls "response flexibility": the capacity to feel deeply while choosing wisely, to honour our emotional truth while aligning our actions with our highest aspirations.

This is the promise of emotional self-regulation: not the cold detachment of suppression, but the warm wisdom of conscious choice. It is the difference between being a leaf blown about by every emotional wind and being a deeply rooted tree that can bend with the storm while remaining fundamentally stable. It transforms us from passive recipients of our emotional experience into active collaborators with our inner life, co-creators of our own becoming.

## The Architecture of Emotional Self-Regulation: A Multidimensional Framework

Emotional self-regulation reveals itself as a sophisticated cognitive-emotional process that operates across multiple dimensions of human experience simultaneously. Like a master conductor orchestrating a complex symphony, effective regulation requires the coordination of attention, cognition, behaviour, and physiology in service of conscious intention (Gross & Thompson, 2007).

## The Recognition Dimension: The Lighthouse of Awareness

The foundation of all regulation lies in recognition—the ability to detect emotional states as they emerge from the unconscious depths into the light of conscious awareness. This recognition operates like a lighthouse, casting its beam across the often-turbulent waters of inner experience, illuminating what might otherwise remain hidden until it crashes upon the shores of impulsive action (Feldman Barrett, 2017).

Dr. Sarah, an emergency room physician, describes this recognition process with remarkable clarity: "In the middle of a code blue, when a patient is dying and family members are screaming, I can feel my own system starting to flood with stress hormones. But somewhere in my awareness, there's this observer—this part of me that notices, 'Ah, the anxiety is spiking now. The anger at the family's accusations is rising.' This recognition doesn't eliminate the emotions, but it gives me a choice about how to channel them."

This recognition requires what researchers call "emotional granularity"—the ability to distinguish between similar emotional states with precision and nuance (Kashdan, Barrett & McKnight, 2015). Rather than experiencing a generic "feeling bad," emotionally regulated individuals can differentiate between disappointment, frustration, embarrassment, or grief. This specificity is not merely academic; different emotions contain different information and call for different responses.

The cultivation of recognition involves developing what mindfulness teacher Tara Brach (2003) describes as "radical acceptance"—the willingness to turn toward our emotional experience with curiosity rather than judgment, investigation rather than avoidance. This requires courage, for emotions often carry messages we would prefer not to hear: the anger that reveals our violated boundaries, the sadness that acknowledges our losses, the fear that exposes our vulnerabilities.

## The Pause Dimension: The Sacred Space of Choice

Between the recognition of emotion and the selection of response lies what may be the most crucial element of emotional regulation: the pause. This is not mere delay or hesitation, but an active, conscious creation of space—a momentary sanctuary where wisdom can emerge and choice can flourish (Kabat-Zinn, 2003).

Neurologically, the pause activates what researchers call the "cognitive control network," a constellation of brain regions including the prefrontal cortex, anterior cingulate cortex, and parietal cortex that work together to evaluate options, consider consequences, and select appropriate responses (Miller & Cohen, 2001). This network, often called the brain's "executive function," can only operate effectively when given sufficient time and space to engage—precisely what the pause provides.

Master negotiator William Ury (2007) describes the pause as "going to the balcony"—stepping back from the immediate emotional fray to gain perspective on the larger dynamics at play. From this elevated vantage point, we can see not only our own emotional state but also the broader context: the other person's possible motivations, the long-term implications of different responses, the alignment between potential actions and our deeper values.

The pause need not be lengthy to be effective. Research suggests that even a brief moment of conscious breathing can significantly alter the trajectory of an emotional response (Arch & Craske, 2006). The key is intentionality—the deliberate creation of space for reflection rather than the automatic cascade from feeling to action that characterises emotional reactivity.

## The Appraisal Dimension: The Art of Reframing

Perhaps no aspect of emotional regulation is more powerful than our capacity to influence our emotional experience through the conscious modification of our interpretations and evaluations of events. This process, known as cognitive reappraisal, operates on the principle that our emotions are not direct responses to events themselves, but to our interpretations of those events (Lazarus & Folkman, 1984).

Consider Maria, a marketing executive who discovers that her carefully prepared presentation has been moved to a less prominent slot in the conference agenda. Her initial interpretation—"They don't value my contribution. This is a sign of disrespect."—generates feelings of anger, disappointment, and anxiety. However, through conscious reappraisal, she might consider alternative interpretations: "Perhaps they're saving the best for last. Maybe there were scheduling conflicts I'm not aware of. This could be an opportunity to refine my presentation further."

The power of reappraisal lies not in positive thinking or denial of legitimate concerns, but in the recognition that our initial interpretations are often incomplete, biased, or unnecessarily catastrophic (Beck, 2011). By consciously examining our automatic appraisals and considering alternatives, we can often discover more balanced, nuanced, and ultimately more accurate ways of understanding our circumstances.

Effective reappraisal involves several key strategies:

**Perspective-taking**: Imagining how the situation might appear to a neutral observer or considering how it might seem in five years' time.

**Benefit-finding**: Identifying potential positive outcomes or learning opportunities within challenging circumstances.

**Temporal distancing**: recognising that present difficulties are temporary and placing them within the broader context of one's life journey.

**Causal complexity**: Acknowledging that most situations result from multiple factors rather than single causes, reducing the tendency toward blame or oversimplification.

## The Implementation Dimension: From Insight to Action

Recognition, pause, and reappraisal remain merely intellectual exercises unless they culminate in skilful action—responses that align with our values, serve our long-term interests, and contribute to the wellbeing of ourselves and others. This implementation dimension involves translating emotional wisdom into behavioural choice (Mischel, 2014).

Effective implementation requires what psychologist Roy Baumeister (2011) calls "self-control strength"—the capacity to override immediate impulses in service of longer-term goals. This strength operates like a muscle, becoming fatigued with use but also growing stronger through regular exercise. Each time we choose a thoughtful response over an impulsive reaction, we strengthen our capacity for future regulation.

The implementation of emotional regulation often involves what researchers term "emotion regulation strategies"—specific techniques for modulating emotional experience and expression (Webb, Miles & Sheeran, 2012):

**Situation selection**: Proactively choosing environments and interactions that support emotional wellbeing while avoiding unnecessary triggers.

**Situation modification**: Altering aspects of situations to reduce their emotional intensity or change their meaning.

**Attentional deployment**: Consciously directing attention toward or away from particular aspects of emotional experiences.

**Response modulation**: Adjusting the expression or physiological manifestation of emotions once they have been fully experienced.

## The Neuroscientific Symphony: Brain Networks in Emotional Regulation

The capacity for emotional self-regulation emerges from the coordinated activity of multiple brain networks, each contributing distinct capabilities to the overall regulatory process. Understanding this neurological symphony enhances both our appreciation for the complexity of emotional regulation and our ability to strengthen it through targeted practice (Ochsner & Gross, 2014).

### The Prefrontal Conductor: Executive Control and Regulation

The prefrontal cortex, that evolutionarily recent addition to the human brain, serves as the primary conductor of the emotional regulation orchestra. This region, located just behind the forehead, contains several specialised areas that contribute different aspects of regulatory capacity (Miller & Cohen, 2001).

The dorsolateral prefrontal cortex (dlPFC) functions as the brain's strategic planner, maintaining goal representations and implementing cognitive control. When we consciously choose to respond calmly to provocation or to reinterpret a threatening situation more benignly, the dlPFC orchestrates these regulatory efforts.

The ventromedial prefrontal cortex (vmPFC) serves as an integration centre, weaving together emotional, social, and value-based information to guide decision-making. This region helps us consider the broader implications of our emotional responses and align our actions with our deeper values and long-term goals.

The orbitofrontal cortex (OFC) specialises in evaluating the emotional significance of situations and predicting the likely consequences of different responses. It helps us learn from past emotional experiences and adjust our regulatory strategies accordingly.

## The Anterior Cingulate: The Conflict Monitor

The anterior cingulate cortex (ACC) functions as the brain's conflict detection system, alerting us when our current emotional impulses conflict with our goals or values (Botvinick, Cohen & Carter, 2004). This region activates when we experience the tension between wanting to lash out in anger and knowing that such a response would be counterproductive.

The ACC also plays a crucial role in effortful control—the deliberate regulation of attention and behaviour in the face of competing impulses. When we choose to focus on our breathing during a stressful moment or deliberately shift our attention away from anxiety-provoking thoughts, the ACC coordinates these regulatory efforts.

## The Limbic Players: Emotion Generation and Memory

While regulation primarily involves prefrontal regions, the limbic system—including the amygdala, hippocampus, and associated structures—provides the emotional raw material that regulation seeks to modulate (LeDoux, 2015).

The amygdala, often characterised as the brain's "alarm system," rapidly evaluates incoming information for potential threats and triggers appropriate emotional responses. While sometimes portrayed as the antagonist in discussions of emotional regulation, the amygdala actually serves crucial protective and motivational functions. Effective regulation doesn't suppress amygdala activity but rather integrates its emotional intelligence with prefrontal wisdom.

The hippocampus contributes contextual information and episodic memories that help us understand the broader significance of current emotional experiences. It helps us recognise patterns—"This situation reminds me of..."—and apply lessons learned from past regulatory successes and failures.

## The Insula: Interoceptive Awareness and Emotional Insight

The insula, a region buried deep within the lateral sulcus, serves as a crucial bridge between bodily sensations and conscious emotional awareness (Craig, 2009). This region integrates interoceptive information—awareness of heartbeat, breathing, muscle tension, and other internal bodily states—with emotional and cognitive processing.

The insula's role in emotional regulation involves what researchers call "embodied awareness"—the recognition that emotions are not merely psychological phenomena but whole-body experiences. When we notice the tightness in our chest that accompanies anxiety or the heat in our face that signals rising anger, the insula makes this somatic information available to consciousness where it can inform our regulatory choices.

# Common Obstacles to Emotional Regulation: The Shadow Side of Human Nature

Despite our best intentions and growing understanding of regulatory processes, most individuals encounter persistent obstacles that can derail even well-developed emotional regulation skills. These obstacles, rooted in evolutionary history, cultural conditioning, and personal experience, require compassionate understanding rather than harsh judgment (Hayes, Strosahl & Wilson, 2011).

## The Immediacy Bias: When Present Emotions Overwhelm Future Considerations

Human beings possess what psychologists call a "present bias"—a tendency to overweight immediate experiences relative to future consequences (Frederick, Loewenstein & O'Donoghue, 2002). This bias, adaptive in ancestral environments where immediate threats required immediate responses, can undermine emotional regulation in modern contexts where short-term emotional satisfaction often conflicts with long-term wellbeing.

Consider David, a talented software engineer who struggles with anger management. When his code is criticised during team meetings, his immediate emotional experience—feeling attacked, misunderstood, defensive—overwhelms his rational understanding that collaborative feedback improves the final product. Despite knowing that defensive responses damage his professional relationships, the immediate intensity of his emotional experience makes calm, receptive responses feel impossible.

This immediacy bias explains why regulatory strategies often fail precisely when they are needed most: during moments of intense emotional activation. The present-focused emotional brain literally hijacks attention and decision-making resources, making future-oriented considerations feel abstract and irrelevant.

## Emotional Perfectionism: The Tyranny of "Shoulds"

Many individuals approach emotional regulation with perfectionist expectations, believing they should be able to maintain constant emotional equilibrium and never experience "negative" emotions (Hewitt & Flett, 2007). This perfectionist stance, paradoxically, often undermines genuine regulation by creating secondary emotional problems—feeling bad about feeling bad, becoming anxious about anxiety, or getting angry about anger.

Jennifer, a high-achieving medical student, illustrates this pattern clearly. Raised in a family that valued emotional control and rational thinking, she learned to view emotions like sadness, fear, or anger as signs of weakness or failure. When these emotions inevitably arose during the stresses of medical training, she would compound her initial emotional experience with harsh self-criticism and desperate attempts at suppression.

Emotional perfectionism ignores the fundamental reality that emotions are normal, healthy, and often appropriate responses to life circumstances. Effective regulation involves working with emotions rather than against them, accepting their presence while choosing skilful responses to their messages.

## The Suppression Trap: When Avoidance Creates Amplification

One of the most common yet counterproductive approaches to emotional regulation involves suppression—the attempt to eliminate unwanted emotional experiences through force of will (Wegner, 1994). Research consistently demonstrates that thought suppression not only fails to eliminate unwanted thoughts and emotions but often increases their frequency and intensity through what psychologist Daniel Wegner called the "ironic process theory."

The classic demonstration involves instructing someone not to think about a white bear. Inevitably, attempts to suppress the thought of a white bear result in more frequent intrusions of white bear imagery. The same principle applies to emotional suppression: trying not to feel anxious often increases anxiety; attempting to eliminate anger often intensifies it; fighting sadness often prolongs it.

Suppression also exacts what researchers call "regulatory costs"—the cognitive and emotional resources required for suppression are no longer available for other tasks (Muraven & Baumeister, 2000). Individuals who chronically suppress emotions often report feeling emotionally numb, cognitively depleted, and socially disconnected.

## Cultural and Gender Conditioning: The Invisible Constraints on Emotional Expression

Most cultures develop implicit rules about which emotions are acceptable for different groups to experience and express (Matsumoto et al., 2008). These "display rules" become so deeply internalised that we may lose conscious awareness of their influence on our emotional regulation attempts.

Traditional masculine socialisation, for example, often encourages the suppression of vulnerability, sadness, or fear while permitting or even celebrating anger. Men socialised within this framework may struggle to recognise and regulate emotions outside the narrow band of culturally sanctioned feelings, leading to what psychologist Terrence Real (1997) calls "covert depression"—emotional numbness masquerading as strength.

Similarly, traditional feminine socialisation may discourage the direct expression of anger while encouraging the suppression of ambition or competitive feelings. Women may learn to transform anger into self-doubt or to express competitive drives indirectly, creating internal conflicts that complicate straightforward emotional regulation.

Professional environments add additional layers of emotional constraint. Healthcare workers may suppress grief to maintain clinical objectivity; business leaders may suppress uncertainty to project confidence; teachers may suppress frustration to maintain classroom authority. While these suppressions may serve immediate functional purposes, they can gradually erode authentic emotional regulation capacity.

## Advanced Strategies for Emotional Mastery: The Practitioner's Toolkit

Developing sophisticated emotional regulation requires moving beyond basic techniques to embrace more nuanced, flexible, and contextually sensitive approaches. These advanced strategies integrate insights from neuroscience, contemplative traditions, and therapeutic practice to create a comprehensive toolkit for emotional mastery (Siegel, 2012).

### Mindful Awareness: The Foundation of All Regulation

Mindfulness—defined as present-moment awareness characterised by acceptance and non-judgment—serves as the foundational skill underlying all other regulatory capacities (Kabat-Zinn, 2003). Unlike suppression or distraction, mindfulness involves turning toward emotional experience with curiosity and compassion, creating the conditions necessary for genuine understanding and skilful response.

**The RAIN Technique**: Developed by meditation teacher Tara Brach (2003), RAIN provides a structured approach to mindful emotional engagement:

- **Recognition**: Clearly acknowledging what is happening emotionally in the present moment

- **Allowing**: Permitting the experience to be present without immediately trying to fix or change it

- **Investigation**: Exploring the emotion with gentle curiosity—where it's felt in the body, what thoughts accompany it, what it might be communicating

- **Natural awareness**: Resting in spacious awareness that can hold all emotional experiences without being overwhelmed by them

**Body-Based Mindfulness**: Since emotions are fundamentally embodied phenomena, developing somatic awareness enhances regulatory capacity significantly (Levine, 2010). This involves:

- **Progressive body scanning**: Systematically bringing attention to different areas of the body to notice tension, sensations, and emotional holding patterns

- **Breath awareness**: Using the breath as both an anchor for present-moment attention and a tool for physiological regulation

- **Movement practices**: Incorporating gentle movement, yoga, or tai chi to process emotions through the body rather than remaining trapped in cognitive loops

## Cognitive Flexibility: The Art of Perspective Transformation

While mindfulness provides the foundation for emotional awareness, cognitive flexibility enables the transformation of our relationship to emotional experiences through the conscious modification of our interpretative frameworks (Kashdan & Rottenberg, 2010).

**Multiple Perspective Taking**: This involves consciously adopting different viewpoints on challenging situations:

- **Temporal perspectives**: How will this situation appear in a week, month, or year?

- **Stakeholder perspectives**: How might other involved parties be experiencing this situation?

- **Observer perspectives**: How would a wise, compassionate friend view this circumstance?

- **Cultural perspectives**: How might someone from a different cultural background interpret these events?

**Benefit Finding and Post-Traumatic Growth**: Research demonstrates that individuals who can identify meaningful benefits within challenging experiences develop greater resilience and life satisfaction (Tedeschi & Calhoun, 2004). This doesn't involve denial or minimisation of genuine difficulties but rather the cultivation of what psychologist Richard Tedeschi calls "expert companionship" with adversity.

**Values-Based Reframing**: Rather than asking "How can I feel better?" values-based reframing asks "How can I respond in ways that align with who I want to be?" This shift from emotional comfort to values alignment often paradoxically creates greater emotional satisfaction while building character and integrity.

## Physiological Regulation: Working with the Body's Wisdom

Emotions involve complex physiological processes—changes in heart rate, breathing patterns, muscle tension, and hormonal activity (Porges, 2011). Advanced emotional regulation involves working skilfully with these physiological dimensions rather than trying to overcome them through mental effort alone.

**Heart Rate Variability Training**: Research demonstrates that coherent breathing patterns—typically around 5-6 breaths per minute—optimise heart rate variability and enhance emotional regulation capacity (McCraty & Shaffer, 2015). This involves:

- **Coherent breathing**: Establishing slow, rhythmic breathing patterns that synchronise heart rate, respiratory rate, and nervous system activity

- **Heart-focused breathing**: Directing attention to the heart area while maintaining coherent breathing rhythms

- **Positive emotion activation**: Cultivating feelings of appreciation, care, or compassion while maintaining coherent breathing patterns

**Progressive Muscle Relaxation**: This involves systematically tensing and releasing different muscle groups to reduce physical tension and promote emotional calm (Jacobson, 1938). The practice enhances awareness of the connection between emotional states and physical tension while providing concrete tools for physiological regulation.

**Cold Exposure and Stress Inoculation**: Controlled exposure to manageable stressors—such as cold water, intense exercise, or challenging breathing practices—can build resilience and emotional regulation capacity through what researchers call "hormetic stress" (Seery, 2011). These practices strengthen the physiological systems involved in stress recovery and emotional regulation.

## Social and Interpersonal Regulation: The Co-Regulation Dynamic

Human beings are fundamentally social creatures, and our emotional regulation capacities develop and function within interpersonal contexts (Schore, 2003). Advanced regulation involves understanding and skilfully utilising these social dimensions.

**Co-Regulation**: This involves using supportive relationships to enhance individual regulation capacity. Rather than always trying to regulate emotions in isolation, we can:

- **Seek appropriate support**: Reaching out to trusted others when emotional challenges exceed individual capacity

- **Practice emotional transparency**: Sharing emotional experiences in ways that invite support and understanding rather than judgment or advice

- **Offer regulation support**: Providing calm, grounded presence for others during their emotional difficulties

**Boundary Setting and Assertiveness**: Many emotional regulation challenges stem from unclear or porous interpersonal boundaries (Cloud & Townsend, 2017). Developing the capacity to say no, express needs clearly, and maintain appropriate limits often resolves chronic emotional difficulties more effectively than individual regulation techniques.

**Conflict Resolution Skills**: Since many intense emotions arise within interpersonal conflicts, developing sophisticated conflict resolution capabilities enhances overall emotional regulation (Fisher, Ury & Patton, 2011). This includes:

- **Nonviolent communication**: Learning to express needs and feelings without blame or attack
- **Active listening**: Developing the capacity to truly hear others' perspectives, especially during disagreement
- **Collaborative problem-solving**: Moving beyond win-lose thinking to find mutually beneficial solutions

## Integration and Implementation: Building a Personal Regulation Practice

Transforming theoretical understanding into lived emotional mastery requires the development of a personalised, sustainable practice that integrates multiple regulatory approaches while honouring individual temperament, life circumstances, and goals (Siegel, 2012).

### Designing Your Regulation Architecture

Effective emotional regulation develops through what researchers call "deliberate practice"—sustained, focused effort directed toward specific skill development (Ericsson, 2016). This requires moving beyond occasional techniques to create systematic approaches to emotional development.

**Daily Foundation Practices**: These might include:

- Morning mindfulness meditation (10-20 minutes)
- Regular body scanning or somatic awareness practices
- Evening reflection and emotional journaling
- Consistent sleep, exercise, and nutrition routines that support emotional stability

**Situational Regulation Strategies**: Developing specific approaches for predictable challenging situations:

- Workplace stress and conflict
- Family dynamics and intimate relationships
- Performance anxiety and evaluation situations
- Loss, grief, and major life transitions

**Crisis Regulation Protocols**: Having clear, practiced responses for moments of intense emotional activation:

- Immediate grounding techniques (breathing, body awareness, environmental connection)
- Support network activation (who to call, when to seek help)
- Values clarification (remembering what matters most during difficult moments)
- Recovery and learning protocols (how to process and learn from regulatory failures)

### The Long-Term Journey: Emotional Regulation as Spiritual Practice

Ultimately, emotional regulation transcends mere technique to become what contemplative traditions have long recognised as spiritual practice—the ongoing cultivation of wisdom, compassion, and authentic presence (Kornfield, 2000). This perspective transforms regulatory challenges from problems to be solved into opportunities for deepening understanding and expanding capacity for love.

From this view, each difficult emotion becomes a teacher, each regulatory failure becomes a lesson in humility and recommitment, and each moment of skilful response becomes a gift to ourselves and others. The goal shifts from emotional comfort to emotional wisdom, from regulatory control to regulatory grace.

This spiritual dimension of emotional regulation involves recognising that our emotional experiences connect us to the fundamental human condition—the joys and sorrows, hopes and fears that unite us across all apparent differences. Our capacity to meet our own emotions with compassion directly enhances our ability to extend that compassion to others, creating ripples of healing that extend far beyond our individual lives.

## Conclusion: The Ripening of Emotional Wisdom

Mastering emotional self-regulation represents one of humanity's greatest achievements—the capacity to remain deeply feeling while becoming increasingly wise, passionately engaged while maintaining inner peace, authentically responsive while choosing skilful action. It transforms us from victims of our emotional weather into collaborators with our inner climate, from reactive beings into responsive creators of our own experience.

The journey toward emotional mastery is not linear or predictable. It involves seasons of breakthrough and periods of apparent stagnation, moments of crystalline clarity and times of confusing complexity. Yet each step along this path—each moment of choosing awareness over reactivity, each instance of responding from values rather than impulses—contributes to the gradual ripening of emotional wisdom.

As we develop greater regulatory capacity, we discover that the goal was never to eliminate difficult emotions but to transform our relationship with the full spectrum of human feeling. We learn to dance with our emotions rather than being danced by them, to surf the waves of inner experience rather than being overwhelmed by them, to remain cantered in the midst of life's inevitable storms while staying open to its boundless beauty.

In the next chapter, we will explore how this foundation of emotional self-awareness and regulation becomes the launching pad for one of life's most transformative capacities: self-motivation. We will discover how emotionally regulated individuals can tap into sustainable sources of passion and purpose, creating lives of meaning and contribution that extend far beyond personal satisfaction to encompass service to the larger human community.

The journey continues, each chapter building upon the last, each skill enhancing the others, until we find ourselves capable of living with a fullness and authenticity that seemed impossible when we began. This is the promise of emotional intelligence: not perfection, but presence; not invulnerability, but wisdom; not the absence of feeling, but the mastery of response.

# References

Arch, J. J., & Craske, M. G. (2006). Mechanisms of mindfulness: Emotion regulation following a focused breathing induction. *Behaviour Research and Therapy*, 44(12), 1849-1858.

Baumeister, R. F. (2011). *Willpower: Rediscovering the greatest human strength*. Penguin Books.

Baumeister, R. F., & Vohs, K. D. (2007). Self-regulation, ego depletion, and motivation. *Social and Personality Psychology Compass*, 1(1), 115-128.

Beck, A. T. (2011). *Cognitive behaviour therapy: Basics and beyond*. Guilford Press.

Botvinick, M. M., Cohen, J. D., & Carter, C. S. (2004). Conflict monitoring and anterior cingulate cortex: An update. *Trends in Cognitive Sciences*, 8(12), 539-546.

Brach, T. (2003). *Radical acceptance: Embracing your life with the heart of a Buddha*. Bantam Books.

Cloud, H., & Townsend, J. (2017). *Boundaries: When to say yes, how to say no to take control of your life*. Zondervan.

Craig, A. D. (2009). How do you feel—now? The anterior insula and human awareness. *Nature Reviews Neuroscience*, 10(1), 59-70.

Ekman, P. (2003). *Emotions revealed: Recognizing faces and feelings to improve communication and emotional life*. Times Books.

Ericsson, A. (2016). *Peak: Secrets from the new science of expertise*. Houghton Mifflin Harcourt.

Feldman Barrett, L. (2017). *How emotions are made: The secret life of the brain*. Houghton Mifflin Harcourt.

Fisher, R., Ury, W., & Patton, B. (2011). *Getting to yes: Negotiating agreement without giving in*. Penguin Books.

Frederick, S., Loewenstein, G., & O'donoghue, T. (2002). Time discounting and time preference: A critical review. *Journal of Economic Literature*, 40(2), 351-401.

Gross, J. J. (2015). Emotion regulation: Current status and future prospects. *Psychological Inquiry*, 26(1), 1-26.

Gross, J. J., & Thompson, R. A. (2007). Emotion regulation: Conceptual foundations. *Handbook of Emotion Regulation*, 3, 24.

Hayes, S. C., Strosahl, K. D., & Wilson, K. G. (2011). *Acceptance and commitment therapy: The process and practice of mindful change.* Guilford Press.

Hewitt, P. L., & Flett, G. L. (2007). When does conscientiousness become perfectionism? *Current Psychiatry*, 6(7), 49-60.

Jacobson, E. (1938). *Progressive relaxation.* University of Chicago Press.

Kabat-Zinn, J. (2003). Mindfulness-based interventions in context: Past, present, and future. *Clinical Psychology: Science and Practice*, 10(2), 144-156.

Kashdan, T. B., Barrett, L. F., & McKnight, P. E. (2015). Unpacking emotion differentiation: Transforming unpleasant experience by perceiving distinctions in negativity. *Current Directions in Psychological Science*, 24(1), 10-16.

Kashdan, T. B., & Rottenberg, J. (2010). Psychological flexibility as a fundamental aspect of health. *Clinical Psychology Review*, 30(7), 865-878.

Kornfield, J. (2000). *After the ecstasy, the laundry: How the heart grows wise on the spiritual path*. Bantam Books.

Lazarus, R. S., & Folkman, S. (1984). *Stress, appraisal, and coping.* Springer Publishing Company.

LeDoux, J. (2015). *Anxious: Using the brain to understand and treat fear and anxiety*. Penguin Books.

Levine, P. A. (2010). *In an unspoken voice: How the body releases trauma and restores goodness.* North Atlantic Books.

Matsumoto, D., Yoo, S. H., Fontaine, J., Anguas-Wong, A. M., Arriola, M., Ataca, B., ... & Grossi, E. (2008). Mapping expressive differences around the world: The relationship between emotional display rules and individualism versus collectivism. *Journal of Cross-Cultural Psychology*, 39(1), 55-74.

McCraty, R., & Shaffer, F. (2015). Heart rate variability: New perspectives on physiological mechanisms, assessment of self-regulatory capacity, and health risk. *Global Advances in Health and Medicine*, 4(1), 46-61.

Miller, E. K., & Cohen, J. D. (2001). An integrative theory of prefrontal cortex function. *Annual Review of Neuroscience*, 24(1), 167-202.

Mischel, W. (2014). *The marshmallow test: Mastering self-control.* Little, Brown and Company.

Muraven, M., & Baumeister, R. F. (2000). Self-regulation and depletion of limited resources: Does self-control resemble a muscle? *Psychological Bulletin*, 126(2), 247-259.

Ochsner, K. N., & Gross, J. J. (2014). The neural bases of emotion and emotion regulation: A valuation perspective. *Handbook of Emotion Regulation*, 2, 23-42.

Porges, S. W. (2011). *The polyvagal theory: Neurophysiological foundations of emotions, attachment, communication, and self-regulation*. W. W. Norton & Company.

Real, T. (1997). *I don't want to talk about it: Overcoming the secret legacy of male depression*. Scribner.

Sapolsky, R. M. (2017). *Behave: The biology of humans at our best and worst*. Penguin Books.

Schore, A. N. (2003). *Affect dysregulation and disorders of the self.* W. W. Norton & Company.

Seery, M. D. (2011). Resilience: A silver lining to experiencing adverse life events? *Current Directions in Psychological Science*, 20(6), 390-394.

Siegel, D. J. (2012). *The developing mind: How relationships and the brain interact to shape who we are*. Guilford Press.

Tedeschi, R. G., & Calhoun, L. G. (2004). Posttraumatic growth: Conceptual foundations and empirical evidence. *Psychological Inquiry*, 15(1), 1-18.

Ury, W. (2007). *Getting to yes with yourself: And other worthy opponents*. HarperOne.

Webb, T. L., Miles, E., & Sheeran, P. (2012). Dealing with feeling: A meta-analysis of the effectiveness of strategies derived from the process model of emotion regulation. *Psychological Bulletin*, 138(4), 775-808.

Wegner, D. M. (1994). Ironic processes of mental control. *Psychological Review*, 101(1), 34-52.

# Chapter 9: The Art of Self-Motivation: Fuelling Passion and Purpose

*The Alchemical Fire of Human Becoming*

## Introduction: The Sacred Flame Within

In the vast cathedral of human potential, where dreams echo like whispered prayers against the vaulted ceilings of possibility, there burns a flame—ancient, eternal, and uniquely personal. This is the fire of self-motivation: not merely the crude ambition of acquisition or the desperate scramble for external validation, but the refined passion that transforms souls and reshapes worlds (Deci & Ryan, 2017). It is the difference between being pulled by the magnetic force of authentic purpose and being pushed by the whip of circumstance—between creating from the fullness of inner conviction and reacting from the emptiness of external compulsion.

Consider the artist who labours in obscurity for decades, perfecting her craft not for fame or fortune, but because something within her demands expression. Or the scientist who pursues questions that may yield no practical applications, driven by an insatiable curiosity about the nature of reality itself. These individuals have tapped into what psychologist Abraham Maslow (1968) recognised as the wellspring of human excellence: the capacity to be moved by forces deeper than survival, more enduring than pleasure, more compelling than social approval.

Self-motivation, in its most evolved form, represents the marriage of emotional intelligence and existential purpose—the ability to sustain passionate engagement with life even when external rewards are absent, recognition is delayed, and obstacles appear insurmountable (Csikszentmihalyi, 1990). It transforms the harsh landscape of human striving into fertile ground for growth, meaning, and contribution. Where others see burden, the self-motivated individual discovers opportunity; where others retreat in defeat, they find lessons that fuel further progress; where others require constant encouragement from without, they generate renewable energy from within.

This inner engine of motivation does not operate in isolation from our emotional landscape—it is fundamentally dependent upon it. Without emotional self-awareness, we pursue goals that belong to others rather than ourselves, chasing mirages that forever recede as we approach them. Without emotional regulation, we become vulnerable to the inevitable setbacks and frustrations that accompany any meaningful endeavour, abandoning our dreams when they need us most. Yet when emotional intelligence provides the foundation, self-motivation becomes not a desperate striving but a joyful expression of our deepest nature (Goleman, 1995).

The stakes of this internal fire could not be higher. In a world increasingly characterised by external noise, shallow distractions, and manufactured needs, the capacity for authentic self-motivation becomes a form of spiritual resistance—a declaration of independence from the tyranny of circumstance and a commitment to the sovereignty of purpose. It is the difference between living a life of quiet desperation and experiencing what the poet Rainer Maria Rilke called "the deep joy of being absolutely faithful to your own nature."

## The Architecture of Authentic Motivation: Understanding the Inner Landscape

Self-motivation reveals itself as a complex psychological phenomenon that emerges from the intersection of multiple internal systems—cognitive, emotional, neurological, and spiritual. Like a cathedral whose beauty depends upon the harmonious interaction of countless architectural elements, sustainable motivation requires the integration of diverse psychological capacities working in concert toward a unified vision (Bandura, 2006).

## The Foundational Layer: Values and Meaning

At the bedrock of authentic motivation lies what psychologist Viktor Frankl (1963) identified as humanity's primary drive: the search for meaning. Unlike the pleasure principle proposed by Freud or the power principle suggested by Adler, Frankl's "will to meaning" recognises that humans can endure almost any hardship when they understand its significance within a larger framework of purpose.

Dr. Elizabeth Chen, a paediatric oncologist, exemplifies this principle with remarkable clarity. Working in one of the most emotionally demanding fields imaginable, she finds herself energised rather than depleted by her daily encounters with childhood cancer. "Every day brings heartbreak," she reflects, "but also the profound privilege of walking with families through their darkest moments. When I remember that my presence might be the difference between despair and hope for a frightened parent, fatigue transforms into fuel."

This meaning-making capacity involves what researchers call "eudaimonic motivation"—the drive to live in accordance with one's deepest values and to contribute to something greater than oneself (Ryff & Keyes, 1995). Unlike hedonic motivation, which seeks pleasure and avoids pain, eudaimonic motivation finds energy in challenge, growth in adversity, and satisfaction in service. It represents what the ancient Greeks called "arete"—excellence of character expressed through virtuous action.

The cultivation of meaning-based motivation requires what philosopher Charles Taylor (1991) terms "strong evaluation"—the ability to distinguish between desires that align with our authentic values and those that stem from social conditioning, fear, or compulsion. This involves regular introspection, honest self-examination, and the courage to acknowledge when our current pursuits may be leading us away from rather than toward our genuine aspirations.

## The Emotional Substrata: Passion and Purpose in Dynamic Tension

Above the foundational layer of meaning lies the rich emotional terrain where passion and purpose dance their eternal dialogue. Passion provides the heat—the intense emotional energy that makes extraordinary effort feel effortless. Purpose provides the direction—the clear sense of where that passionate energy should be focused for maximum impact and fulfilment (Vallerand, 2015).

Research in positive psychology has revealed that the most sustainably motivated individuals experience what psychologist Robert Vallerand calls "harmonious passion"—deep engagement with activities that align with their identity and values without consuming their entire sense of self. This contrasts with "obsessive passion," which may generate temporary intensity but ultimately leads to burnout, anxiety, and a fragmented sense of identity.

Consider Maria, an environmental scientist whose childhood experiences of pristine wilderness ignited a lifelong passion for conservation. Her motivation stems not from abstract concern about climate change but from visceral memories of morning mist rising from mountain lakes and the profound peace she experienced in nature's embrace. This emotional connection provides renewable energy for the often-tedious work of data collection, grant writing, and policy advocacy. Her purpose—protecting these experiences for future generations—gives her passion coherent direction and social significance.

The integration of passion and purpose requires what psychologist Mihaly Csikszentmihalyi (1990) identified as "flow states"—moments of deep absorption where challenge and skill are perfectly matched, self-consciousness disappears, and action becomes effortless. These experiences provide both immediate reward for sustained effort and glimpses of our highest potential, creating what researchers call "intrinsic motivation loops" that become self-reinforcing over time.

## The Cognitive Architecture: Beliefs, Expectations, and Mental Models

The cognitive dimension of self-motivation involves the complex web of beliefs, expectations, and mental models that shape how we interpret challenges, setbacks, and possibilities. This internal narrative framework determines whether we approach difficulties as threats to be avoided or opportunities for growth and learning (Dweck, 2006).

Central to this cognitive architecture is what psychologist Carol Dweck calls "mindset"—the fundamental beliefs we hold about the nature of ability and intelligence. Individuals with a "fixed mindset" believe that capabilities are static traits that cannot be significantly developed, leading them to avoid challenges that might reveal limitations. Those with a "growth mindset" understand abilities as capacities that can be expanded through effort, strategy, and learning from failure.

The implications for motivation are profound. Fixed mindset individuals must constantly protect their self-image by avoiding situations where they might struggle or fail, leading to what researchers call "defensive pessimism" and ultimately, motivational decline. Growth mindset individuals, by contrast, find energy in challenge and meaning in struggle, viewing setbacks as information rather than indictments of their worth (Yeager & Dweck, 2012).

This cognitive reframing extends to what psychologist Albert Bandura (2006) terms "self-efficacy"—the belief in one's capacity to execute behaviours necessary to produce specific performance attainments. High self-efficacy doesn't require unrealistic optimism about outcomes, but rather realistic confidence in one's ability to learn, adapt, and persist in the face of obstacles.

Dr. James Wright, a surgeon who overcame a learning disability to excel in medical school, illustrates this principle: "I never believed I was the smartest person in the room. But I absolutely believed I could outwork, out-prepare, and out-persist almost anyone. When other students were discouraged by difficult cases, I saw puzzles that would make me a better doctor. That shift in interpretation changed everything."

## The Neurobiological Foundation: The Chemistry of Drive and Determination

Recent advances in neuroscience have illuminated the biological substrates of motivation with unprecedented precision, revealing intricate networks of brain regions and neurotransmitter systems that orchestrate our capacity for sustained effort and goal pursuit (Berridge & Robinson, 2016).

At the heart of motivational neurobiology lies the dopaminergic system, particularly the pathways connecting the ventral tegmental area (VTA) to the nucleus accumbens and prefrontal cortex. Contrary to popular understanding, dopamine is not simply a "pleasure chemical" but rather a "prediction error" signal that fires most intensely when outcomes exceed expectations and helps the brain learn which activities are worth pursuing (Schultz, 2016).

This neurological insight has profound implications for sustainable motivation. The dopamine system responds most strongly to intermittent, unpredictable rewards rather than constant gratification. This explains why the most motivating goals often involve elements of challenge, uncertainty, and progressive mastery rather than simple pleasure-seeking or comfort-maintenance.

The prefrontal cortex, particularly the anterior cingulate cortex (ACC), plays a crucial role in what researchers call "cognitive control"—the ability to maintain goal-directed behaviour despite distractions, setbacks, or competing impulses (Botvinick & Braver, 2015). This region enables what psychologist Angela Duckworth (2016) terms "grit"—the capacity to maintain effort and interest despite failure, adversity, and plateaus in progress.

Neuroplasticity research demonstrates that these motivational circuits can be strengthened through deliberate practice. Meditation, visualisation, goal-setting exercises, and exposure to moderate challenges all enhance the brain's capacity for sustained motivation and resilience (Tang & Posner, 2009).

## The Emotional Intelligence-Motivation Nexus: Where Inner Wisdom Meets Outer Action

The relationship between emotional intelligence and self-motivation represents one of the most elegant examples of psychological synergy—each capacity enhancing and being enhanced by the other in an upward spiral of personal development and effectiveness (Bar-On, 2006).

### Self-Awareness: The Compass of Authentic Striving

Emotional self-awareness serves as the navigational system for motivation, ensuring that our efforts are directed toward goals that genuinely resonate with our authentic nature rather than imposed expectations or social pressures. Without this inner compass, we risk what psychologist Tim Kasser (2002) calls "materialistic value orientation"—pursuing external markers of success that ultimately leave us feeling empty and directionless.

Consider Sarah, a successful corporate lawyer who spent the first decade of her career climbing the partnership ladder, driven by family expectations and social status. Despite achieving conventional success, she found herself increasingly anxious, irritable, and disconnected from her work. Through developing greater self-awareness, she recognised that her true passion lay in environmental advocacy—work that paid less but aligned with her deepest values about sustainability and social justice.

The transition wasn't immediate or easy. "I had to distinguish between the lawyer my parents wanted me to be, the lawyer my peers expected me to be, and the lawyer I actually was," she reflects. "That process of emotional archaeology revealed that my real motivation had been buried under layers of 'should' and 'supposed to.' Once I connected with my authentic passion, energy I didn't know I had become available."

This process of authentic goal selection involves what researchers call "values clarification"—the systematic exploration of what matters most deeply to us, independent of external pressures or expectations (Harris, 2019). It requires the courage to acknowledge when our current pursuits may be serving others' dreams rather than our own, and the wisdom to gradually realign our efforts with our genuine aspirations.

## Self-Regulation: The Sustaining Force of Disciplined Passion

Emotional regulation provides the stability and persistence that transform fleeting inspiration into sustained achievement. Even the most passionate individuals encounter periods of doubt, frustration, boredom, or discouragement. The capacity to navigate these emotional weather patterns without abandoning meaningful goals distinguishes those who achieve lasting success from those whose motivation burns bright but briefly (Mischel, 2014).

Research by psychologist Angela Duckworth (2016) on "grit" reveals that high achievers are characterised not primarily by talent or intelligence, but by the combination of passion and perseverance for long-term goals. This capacity involves what she calls "deliberate practice"—the willingness to engage in activities that are challenging, effortful, and not inherently enjoyable but that contribute to skill development and goal attainment.

The regulation of motivational emotions involves several key strategies:

**Emotional Granularity**: Developing precise vocabulary for describing motivational states. Rather than simply feeling "unmotivated," recognising whether the underlying emotion is boredom (suggesting need for increased challenge), frustration (indicating skill gaps that can be addressed), or fatigue (pointing toward need for rest and renewal).

**Reappraisal Training**: Learning to reinterpret setbacks and challenges through motivational lenses. Research by psychologist Alia Crum demonstrates that individuals who view stress as enhancing rather than debilitating show improved performance and resilience (Crum, Salovey & Achor, 2013).

**Energy Management**: Understanding that motivation fluctuates naturally and developing strategies for working with rather than against these rhythms. This includes recognising peak energy periods for demanding tasks, building in recovery time, and creating systems that maintain momentum during low-energy phases.

## Empathy and Social Motivation: The Ripple Effect of Purpose

While self-motivation might seem inherently individualistic, research consistently demonstrates that the most sustainably motivated individuals are those whose goals extend beyond personal benefit to encompass contribution to others (Grant, 2013). This connection between empathy and motivation creates what psychologists call "prosocial motivation"—the drive to expend effort to benefit other people.

Dr. Paul Farmer, the late physician and global health pioneer, exemplified this principle throughout his extraordinary career. Working in some of the world's most challenging medical contexts, from Haiti to Rwanda, he maintained incredible energy and commitment despite facing seemingly insurmountable obstacles. His motivation stemmed not from personal ambition but from profound empathy for those suffering from preventable diseases and structural inequalities.

"The thing that keeps you going," Farmer once observed, "is not the hope of solving everything, but the knowledge that your efforts might alleviate one person's suffering, might save one life, might restore one family's hope. When you understand that your work is connected to something larger than yourself, fatigue becomes fuel."

This prosocial dimension of motivation involves what researcher Adam Grant calls "relational job crafting"—the ability to perceive how one's work impacts others and to maintain awareness of those connections during challenging periods. Even routine tasks can become sources of sustainable motivation when individuals understand their contribution to larger purposes and human welfare.

## Practical Strategies for Cultivating Unshakeable Motivation

Developing robust self-motivation requires moving beyond inspiration and good intentions to embrace systematic practices that strengthen motivational capacity over time. Like physical fitness, motivational fitness develops through consistent exercise of specific psychological skills and habits (Clear, 2018).

## The Practice of Purpose Archaeology

Most individuals carry within them multiple layers of motivation—some authentic, others acquired through socialisation, expectation, or circumstance. Developing sustainable motivation requires what we might call "purpose archaeology": the patient excavation of genuine passions and values from beneath accumulated layers of external conditioning.

**Values Identification Exercises**: Regular reflection on peak experiences, moments of deep satisfaction, and instances of effortless engagement. What values were being expressed during these times? What needs were being met? What aspects of your authentic nature were finding expression?

**The Deathbed Test**: Imagining yourself at the end of life, looking back on your choices and achievements. What would you regret not pursuing? What would fill you with pride and satisfaction? This exercise, while sobering, can provide remarkable clarity about what truly matters.

**Energy Auditing**: Systematically tracking your energy levels throughout different activities, relationships, and environments. Which pursuits energise you even when they're challenging? Which drain you even when they're easy? This somatic wisdom often reveals authentic motivations more clearly than intellectual analysis.

**The Five Whys Technique**: For any major goal or commitment, asking "why" five times to unearth deeper motivations. The first "why" often reveals surface reasons; the fifth typically uncovers core values and authentic drivers.

## Goal Architecture: Building Motivational Momentum

Effective goals function like well-designed buildings—they provide structure and direction while remaining flexible enough to accommodate changing circumstances and growing understanding.

Research in goal-setting theory reveals specific characteristics that enhance motivational power (Locke & Latham, 2019).

**Hierarchical Goal Systems**: Organising objectives across multiple time horizons and levels of abstraction. Life purpose provides overarching direction; yearly themes translate purpose into actionable domains; quarterly projects create specific focus areas; monthly milestones generate regular achievement experiences; weekly practices maintain daily momentum.

**Process vs. Outcome Focus**: While outcome goals provide direction and inspiration, process goals sustain daily motivation. Rather than focusing solely on "losing 30 pounds," developing habits around "preparing healthy meals" and "enjoying daily movement" creates sustainable behavioural change.

**Challenge Calibration**: Goals that are too easy fail to engage our full capacity; those that are too difficult trigger discouragement and avoidance. The optimal challenge level—what Csikszentmihalyi calls the "flow zone"—stretches current abilities while remaining achievable through sustained effort.

**Implementation Intentions**: Moving beyond general commitments to specific "if-then" plans. Research by psychologist Peter Gollwitzer demonstrates that individuals who specify when, where, and how they will pursue their goals show significantly higher achievement rates than those with general good intentions (Gollwitzer & Sheeran, 2006).

## The Neuroscience of Motivational Maintenance

Understanding the brain's motivational circuits allows for strategic interventions that maintain drive and momentum over extended periods. These practices work with rather than against our neurobiological design.

**Dopamine optimisation**: Since dopamine responds to prediction error and progress, creating systems that provide regular feedback about advancement toward goals maintains motivational chemistry. This might involve progress tracking, skill development metrics, or regular check-ins with mentors or coaches.

**Visualisation Practices**: Mental rehearsal of successful goal achievement activates the same neural networks involved in actual performance. Daily visualisation sessions—imagining not just outcomes but the process of overcoming obstacles and maintaining effort—strengthen motivational circuits and enhance performance (Holmes et al., 2016).

**Micro-Recovery Protocols**: Understanding that motivational resources are finite and require renewal. Building in regular periods of rest, reflection, and restoration prevents the depletion that leads to motivational collapse. This includes both physical practices (sleep, exercise, nutrition) and psychological practices (meditation, nature exposure, creative expression).

**Social Accountability Systems**: Since humans are fundamentally social beings, our motivational systems are designed to respond to group dynamics and social support. Creating accountability partnerships, joining communities of practice, or working with coaches provides external structure that supports internal drive.

## Advanced Motivational Strategies: The Master's Toolkit

As motivational capacity develops, practitioners can embrace more sophisticated approaches that transform challenges into fuel and setbacks into stepping stones.

**Antifragility Training**: Nassim Taleb's concept of "antifragility"—systems that grow stronger under stress—applies powerfully to motivation. Rather than simply enduring difficulties, learning to extract energy and wisdom from challenges creates exponential motivational growth (Taleb, 2012).

**Paradoxical Thinking**: Embracing apparent contradictions rather than resolving them. Being simultaneously ambitious and patient, confident and humble, focused and flexible. This mental agility allows for sustained motivation across diverse circumstances and changing conditions.

**Meta-Motivation**: Developing motivation for motivation itself—finding satisfaction in the process of maintaining drive and commitment regardless of external outcomes. This creates what researchers call "intrinsic motivation loops" that become self-sustaining over time.

**Legacy Consciousness**: Regularly contemplating the impact of your efforts on future generations. What kind of world are you helping to create? How will your contributions ripple forward through time? This temporal expansion of awareness provides renewable energy for challenging work.

## Common Motivational Obstacles and Their Transformation

Even the most naturally motivated individuals encounter predictable challenges that can derail progress or dampen enthusiasm. Understanding these obstacles and developing sophisticated responses transforms potential setbacks into opportunities for deeper development (Duckworth, 2016).

### The Perfectionism Trap: When Excellence Becomes Paralysis

Perfectionism represents one of the most common yet misunderstood obstacles to sustainable motivation. While often disguised as high standards or commitment to excellence, perfectionism actually stems from fear—fear of judgment, fear of failure, fear of not being enough (Brown, 2010).

Dr. Michael Chen, a renowned surgeon, struggled with perfectionist tendencies that nearly ended his career before it began. "In medical school, I would spend hours perfecting assignments that other students completed in half the time. I was terrified of making any mistake, which ironically made me more prone to errors because I was so anxious. I almost failed my surgical rotation because I couldn't make decisive cuts—I kept second-guessing myself."

The transformation came through what he calls "embracing excellence over perfection." This involved several key shifts:

**Process Excellence**: Focusing on giving maximum effort and attention rather than demanding flawless outcomes. This allowed him to maintain high standards while accepting the inevitable learning curves and human limitations.

**Iteration Mindset**: Understanding that excellence emerges through repeated cycles of attempt, feedback, and refinement rather than through single perfect performances. Each surgery became an opportunity to improve rather than a test of worth.

**Compassionate Standards**: Applying the same kindness to himself that he would offer a struggling colleague or patient. This created psychological safety that actually enhanced performance by reducing anxiety and increasing creative problem-solving capacity.

## The Comparison Trap: When Others' Success Diminishes Our Own

In our hyper-connected world, constant exposure to others' achievements can create what researchers call "compare and despair" cycles that erode intrinsic motivation and authentic goal pursuit (Festinger, 1954). Social media amplifies this tendency by providing curated highlights of others' lives while we experience our own struggles in real-time.

The antidote involves what psychologist Rachel Calogero calls "comparison immunity"—the capacity to appreciate others' success without diminishing our own journey or worth. This includes:

**Abundance Mindset**: recognising that others' success doesn't diminish available opportunities for us. In most domains, excellence is not a zero-sum game—one person's achievement often creates possibilities for others.

**Personal Benchmarking**: Measuring progress against our own past performance rather than others' current status. The only meaningful comparison is between who we are today and who we were yesterday.

**Collaborative Perspective**: Viewing successful individuals as teachers and inspirations rather than competitors. What can we learn from their journey? How can their achievements inform our own development?

## The Plateau Effect: When Progress Seems to Stagnate

All meaningful pursuits involve periods where progress feels minimal or absent despite continued effort. These plateaus can trigger what researchers call "learned helplessness"—the belief that our efforts don't matter and that improvement is impossible (Seligman, 2006).

Understanding plateaus as natural and necessary parts of skill development rather than evidence of inadequacy transforms these experiences from motivation killers into motivation sustainers. Research in expertise development reveals that plateaus often precede breakthrough moments as the brain consolidates learning and prepares for the next level of performance (Ericsson, 2016).

**Plateau Navigation Strategies**:

**Process Faith**: Trusting that consistent effort is creating internal changes that aren't yet visible externally. Like strength training, motivational development often involves periods of adaptation that precede observable growth.

**Micro-Progress Recognition**: Developing sensitivity to subtle improvements that might be missed by gross measurements. Enhanced ease, increased creativity, or improved consistency often indicate progress even when headline metrics remain stable.

**Strategic Variation**: Introducing new challenges, perspectives, or approaches that can break through stagnation and reignite growth. Sometimes plateaus indicate the need for different strategies rather than more effort.

## The Ripple Effect: How Self-Motivation Transforms Everything

Authentic self-motivation creates cascading positive changes that extend far beyond individual achievement to influence relationships, communities, and even future generations. This ripple effect represents one of the most profound aspects of motivational development—the way that inner fire illuminates not only our own path but also lights the way for others (Sinek, 2009).

### Personal Transformation: The Alchemy of Sustained Effort

Individuals who develop robust self-motivation often report that the journey toward their goals transforms them more profoundly than achieving the goals themselves. This transformation involves what psychologists call "character development"—the gradual cultivation of virtues like courage, perseverance, integrity, and wisdom through consistent practice under challenging conditions (Peterson & Seligman, 2004).

Dr. Jane Goodall's six-decade study of chimpanzees illustrates this transformative power beautifully. What began as a young woman's fascination with animals evolved into ground-breaking scientific research that revolutionised our understanding of primate behaviour and ultimately sparked a global conservation movement. The daily discipline of patient observation, the courage to challenge established scientific paradigms, and the perseverance to continue despite scepticism transformed not only scientific knowledge but also Goodall herself into one of the world's most influential advocates for environmental protection.

"I didn't set out to become an activist," Goodall reflects. "I was just a young woman who loved animals and wanted to learn about them. But the more I understood about the interconnectedness of all life, the more I felt compelled to act. The chimpanzees taught me not just about their behaviour, but about my own responsibility to protect the natural world. The motivation to study became the motivation to serve."

## Relational Enrichment: How Motivation Inspires Connection

Genuinely motivated individuals often find that their enthusiasm and commitment inspire deeper, more meaningful relationships. This occurs through several mechanisms that psychologists are beginning to understand more clearly (Reis & Shaver, 2018).

**Authenticity Attraction**: When we pursue goals that align with our genuine values and passions, we show up more authentically in relationships. This authenticity attracts others who appreciate genuineness and creates the foundation for deeper connections.

**Energy Contagion**: Motivation, like other emotional states, is contagious. Individuals who are genuinely excited about their pursuits often energise others, creating what researchers call "positive emotional spirals" in their social networks.

**Purpose Magnetism**: People are naturally drawn to those who seem to have found their "why" in life. This magnetism isn't about perfection or constant positivity, but about the attractive quality of someone who is living intentionally and meaningfully.

### Social Impact: Motivation as Service

Perhaps most significantly, authentic self-motivation tends to evolve naturally toward service and contribution. As individuals develop greater capacity for sustained effort and achievement, they often discover that their deepest satisfaction comes not from personal success but from using their abilities to benefit others (Grant, 2013).

This evolution reflects what psychologist Abraham Maslow (1968) identified as "self-actualisation"—the highest level of human motivation, characterised by the drive to fulfil one's potential in service of something greater than oneself. Self-actualised individuals find that their personal growth and social contribution become inseparable—each enhancing the other in an upward spiral of development and service.

Consider Elon Musk, whose companies span electric vehicles, space exploration, neural interfaces, and sustainable energy. While often characterised as driven by personal ambition, Musk consistently frames his motivations in terms of human survival and flourishing: making humanity a multi-planetary species, accelerating the transition to sustainable energy, and enhancing human cognitive capabilities. Whether one agrees with his methods or not, his example illustrates how the highest forms of self-motivation naturally expand to encompass species-level concerns.

## Integration and Daily Practice: Living the Motivated Life

Transforming understanding into lived experience requires the development of daily practices that strengthen motivational capacity while remaining sustainable over time. Like physical fitness, motivational fitness develops through consistent exercise rather than sporadic intense efforts (Clear, 2018).

## The Architecture of Motivated Days

The structure of our daily routines either supports or undermines our motivational capacity. Research in chronobiology reveals that most individuals have predictable patterns of energy, focus, and emotional regulation throughout the day. Aligning important activities with optimal biological rhythms enhances both performance and satisfaction (Roenneberg, 2012).

**Morning Foundation Practices**:

- Gratitude reflection to activate positive emotional circuits
- Intention setting to provide daily direction and focus
- visualisation of successful goal progression
- Physical movement to optimise neurochemistry for motivation

**Midday Maintenance Rituals**:

- Progress check-ins to maintain awareness of advancement
- Energy assessment and adjustment protocols
- Connection with purpose through brief reflection or service actions
- Social interaction with supportive, motivated individuals

**Evening Integration Practices**:

- Daily review of learning and growth experiences
- Celebration of progress, however small

- Planning and preparation for the following day
- Restoration activities that renew motivational resources

## The Seasonal Approach to Motivation

Just as nature operates in cycles of expansion and contraction, planting and harvesting, activity and rest, sustainable motivation requires understanding and working with natural rhythms rather than demanding constant peak performance (Ulrich, 1984).

**Seasonal Motivation Planning**:

**Spring (Growth and Initiation)**: Ideal for beginning new projects, learning new skills, and expanding horizons. Energy is naturally rising and optimism runs high.

**Summer (Peak Performance and Action)**: Perfect for intensive work periods, major pushes toward goals, and maximum output activities. Resources are abundant and capacity is highest.

**Autumn (Harvest and Integration)**: Time for completing projects, integrating learning, and celebrating achievements. Natural energy supports consolidation and preparation.

**Winter (Rest and Reflection)**: Essential for renewal, strategic planning, and inner development. Apparent inactivity actually supports the regeneration necessary for future growth cycles.

## Building Motivational Resilience

The most sustainably motivated individuals develop what researchers call "motivational resilience"—the capacity to maintain commitment and effort despite setbacks, disappointments, and changing circumstances (Bonanno, 2004). This resilience emerges from several key capabilities:

**Flexibility in Methods, Consistency in Vision**: Being willing to adapt strategies and approaches while maintaining commitment to core purposes and values. This prevents the brittleness that comes from being overly attached to specific methods or timelines.

**Emotional Granularity**: Developing sophisticated vocabulary for describing motivational states and their variations. Rather than simply feeling "unmotivated," recognising whether the underlying issue is fatigue (requiring rest), boredom (needing increased challenge), frustration (indicating skill gaps), or discouragement (needing perspective and support).

**Support Network Cultivation**: Building relationships with individuals who understand and support your goals while also being willing to provide honest feedback and accountability. This creates external scaffolding for internal motivation during difficult periods.

**Meaning-Making Capacity**: Developing the ability to find significance and learning in all experiences, including failures and setbacks. This transforms obstacles from motivation killers into motivation sustainers.

## Conclusion: The Eternal Flame of Human Potential

The art of self-motivation ultimately transcends technique and strategy to become a way of being—a fundamental orientation toward life characterised by curiosity, courage, compassion, and commitment. It represents our species' most remarkable capacity: the ability to envision possibilities that don't yet exist and to sustain effort toward their realisation despite uncertainty, setbacks, and criticism.

When we master this art, we discover that motivation is not something we must constantly generate but something we must learn to channel and direct. Like a river whose power comes not from forcing water uphill but from removing obstacles to its natural flow, authentic motivation emerges when we align our efforts with our deepest nature and highest aspirations.

The journey toward motivational mastery is itself a form of service—not only to our own growth and fulfilment but to the collective human project of creating a world worthy of our children's inheritance. Each time we choose persistence over surrender, growth over comfort, contribution over consumption, we add our flame to the great fire of human becoming.

In our next exploration, we will discover how this inner fire of motivation naturally illuminates one of humanity's most beautiful capacities: empathy—the bridge that connects our individual journey of growth to the shared journey of our species toward greater understanding, compassion, and connection.

The flame burns on, and its light reveals that we are never truly alone in our aspirations. We are part of an endless chain of seekers, dreamers, and builders whose combined efforts across time have brought us to this moment of possibility. Our motivation is their gift to us; our achievements will be our gift to those who follow.

---

## References

Bandura, A. (2006). *Guide for constructing self-efficacy scales.* Information Age Publishing.

Bar-On, R. (2006). The Bar-On model of emotional-social intelligence (ESI). *Psicothema*, 18(supl), 13-25.

Berridge, K. C., & Robinson, T. E. (2016). Liking, wanting, and the incentive-sensitization theory of addiction. *American Psychologist*, 71(8), 670-679.

Bonanno, G. A. (2004). Loss, trauma, and human resilience: Have we underestimated the human capacity to thrive after extremely aversive events? *American Psychologist*, 59(1), 20-28.

Botvinick, M., & Braver, T. (2015). Motivation and cognitive control: From behaviour to neural mechanism. *Annual Review of Psychology*, 66, 83-113.

Brown, B. (2010). *The gifts of imperfection: Let go of who you think you're supposed to be and embrace who you are.* Hazelden Publishing.

Clear, J. (2018). *Atomic habits: An easy & proven way to build good habits & break bad ones.* Avery.

Crum, A. J., Salovey, P., & Achor, S. (2013). Rethinking stress: The role of mindsets in determining the stress response. *Journal of Personality and Social Psychology*, 104(4), 716-733.

Csikszentmihalyi, M. (1990). *Flow: The psychology of optimal experience.* Harper & Row.

Deci, E. L., & Ryan, R. M. (2017). *Self-determination theory: Basic psychological needs in motivation, development, and wellness.* Guilford Publications.

Duckworth, A. (2016). *Grit: The power of passion and perseverance.* Scribner.

Dweck, C. (2006). *Mindset: The new psychology of success.* Random House.

Ericsson, A. (2016). *Peak: Secrets from the new science of expertise.* Houghton Mifflin Harcourt.

Festinger, L. (1954). A theory of social comparison processes. *Human Relations*, 7(2), 117-140.

Frankl, V. E. (1963). *Man's search for meaning.* Beacon Press.

Goleman, D. (1995). *Emotional intelligence.* Bantam Books.

Gollwitzer, P. M., & Sheeran, P. (2006). Implementation intentions and goal achievement: A meta-analysis of effects and processes. *Advances in Experimental Social Psychology*, 38, 69-119.

Grant, A. M. (2013). *Give and take: Why helping others drives our success.* Penguin Books.

Harris, R. (2019). *ACT made simple: An easy-to-read primer on acceptance and commitment therapy.* New Harbinger Publications.

Holmes, E. A., Blackwell, S. E., Burnett Heyes, S., Renner, F., & Raes, F. (2016). Mental imagery in depression: Phenomenology, potential mechanisms, and treatment implications. *Annual Review of Clinical Psychology*, 12, 249-280.

Kasser, T. (2002). *The high price of materialism*. MIT Press.

Locke, E. A., & Latham, G. P. (2019). The development of goal setting theory: A half century retrospective. *Motivation Science*, 5(2), 93-105.

Maslow, A. H. (1968). *Toward a psychology of being*. Van Nostrand Reinhold.

Mischel, W. (2014). *The marshmallow test: Mastering self-control*. Little, Brown and Company.

Peterson, C., & Seligman, M. E. P. (2004). *Character strengths and virtues: A handbook and classification*. Oxford University Press.

Reis, H. T., & Shaver, P. (2018). Intimacy as an interpersonal process. In S. Duck & D. F. Hay (Eds.), *Handbook of personal relationships* (pp. 367-389). Wiley.

Roenneberg, T. (2012). *Internal time: Chronotypes, social jet lag, and why you're so tired*. Harvard University Press.

Ryff, C. D., & Keyes, C. L. M. (1995). The structure of psychological well-being revisited. *Journal of Personality and Social Psychology*, 69(4), 719-727.

Schultz, W. (2016). Dopamine reward prediction error coding. *Dialogues in Clinical Neuroscience*, 18(1), 23-32.

Seligman, M. E. P. (2006). *Learned optimism: How to change your mind and your life*. Vintage Books.

Sinek, S. (2009). *Start with why: How great leaders inspire everyone to take action*. Portfolio.

Taleb, N. N. (2012). *Antifragile: Things that gain from disorder*. Random House.

Tang, Y. Y., & Posner, M. I. (2009). Attention training and attention state training. *Trends in Cognitive Sciences*, 13(5), 222-227.

Taylor, C. (1991). *The ethics of authenticity*. Harvard University Press.

Ulrich, R. (1984). View through a window may influence recovery from surgery. *Science*, 224(4647), 420-421.

Vallerand, R. J. (2015). *The psychology of passion: A dualistic model.* Oxford University Press.

Yeager, D. S., & Dweck, C. S. (2012). Mindsets that promote resilience: When students believe that personal characteristics can be developed. *Educational Psychologist*, 47(4), 302-314.

# Chapter 10: Developing Empathy: The Bridge to Deep Connections

## Introduction

In the vast constellation of human emotional capacities, empathy emerges as perhaps the most luminous star—a beacon that guides us through the treacherous waters of interpersonal complexity toward shores of genuine understanding. It is, indeed, the golden thread that weaves the tapestry of human connection, binding together souls across the seemingly insurmountable chasms of cultural difference, experiential diversity, ideological divergence, and emotional variance.

Yet empathy remains one of our most misunderstood virtues. Too often relegated to the realm of mere sentiment—dismissed as "being nice" or reduced to superficial expressions of pity—true empathy transcends these shallow interpretations. It represents nothing less than the courageous act of stepping beyond the fortress of self to inhabit, however briefly, the inner world of another. This is not the passive absorption of others' emotions, nor the patronising gesture of sympathy, but rather the active, deliberate cultivation of understanding that honours the full complexity of human experience.

Baron-Cohen (2011) describes empathy as our "most precious resource," arguing that its presence or absence determines whether societies flourish or fracture. This profound capacity—to recognise, comprehend, and authentically respond to the emotional landscape of others—serves as both the foundation of individual relationships and the cornerstone of civilised society itself.

In our increasingly fragmented world, where digital communication often strips away the nuanced layers of human interaction, the cultivation of empathy becomes not merely advantageous but essential for survival. The ability to bridge differences, to find common ground amidst discord, to create connection where division once reigned—these are the gifts that empathy bestows upon those who dare to develop it.

This chapter will traverse the multifaceted terrain of empathic understanding, exploring its neurological foundations, psychological mechanisms, and practical applications. We shall examine the delicate interplay between cognitive understanding and emotional resonance, investigate the barriers that impede empathic development, and ultimately provide a roadmap for cultivating this most human of capacities.

## The Architecture of Understanding: What Is Empathy?

Empathy, in its fullest expression, represents a sophisticated orchestration of cognitive and emotional processes that enable one human being to access the subjective experience of another. Davis (1994) conceptualises empathy as a multidimensional construct encompassing both cognitive and affective components, each contributing to our capacity for interpersonal understanding.

The cognitive dimension—what researchers term "cognitive empathy" or "perspective-taking"—involves the intellectual ability to understand another's thoughts, motivations, and emotional states without necessarily experiencing them ourselves. This capacity requires the sophisticated mental operation of decentring from one's own perspective to consider alternative viewpoints. Hoffman (2000) describes this as the ability to "put oneself in another's shoes," though such a metaphor hardly captures the neurological complexity involved in this seemingly simple act.

Emotional empathy, by contrast, involves the vicarious experience of another's emotional state. When we witness suffering and feel that suffering within ourselves, when joy observed becomes joy experienced, we engage in emotional empathy. This phenomenon, rooted in our evolutionary heritage as social beings, creates the emotional resonance that binds communities together and motivates prosocial behaviour.

Yet neither cognitive nor emotional empathy alone suffices for meaningful human connection. The third dimension—compassionate empathy—bridges understanding and feeling with action. Goleman (2006) emphasises that this form of empathy moves beyond passive recognition to active engagement, transforming empathic awareness into concrete efforts to alleviate suffering or enhance wellbeing.

Consider the intricate dance that occurs when a skilled therapist encounters a client in distress. The therapist must simultaneously understand the cognitive framework through which the client interprets their experience (cognitive empathy), feel something of the emotional weight carried by the client (emotional empathy), and channel both understanding and feeling into therapeutic interventions designed to promote healing (compassionate empathy). Each dimension enriches and amplifies the others, creating a synergistic whole that transcends the sum of its parts.

This tripartite structure reveals empathy's true sophistication. Far from being a simple emotional reflex, empathy emerges as one of humanity's most complex achievements—a capacity that requires the integration of multiple cognitive and emotional systems, refined through practice and guided by wisdom.

## The Imperative of Connection: Why Empathy Matters

The absence of empathy creates a world both recognisable and terrifying—a landscape populated by isolated individuals, each trapped within the prison of their own perspective, unable to bridge the gulf that separates self from other. In such a world, relationships become mere transactions, devoid of the emotional intimacy that transforms human interaction from economic exchange to meaningful communion.

Research consistently demonstrates empathy's crucial role in relationship satisfaction and stability. Gottman and Levenson (1992) found that couples' ability to empathically respond to each other's emotional bids predicted relationship longevity with remarkable accuracy. When partners consistently failed to recognise and respond to each other's attempts at emotional connection, relationships deteriorated rapidly, often ending in divorce or prolonged dysfunction.

The workplace, too, suffers in empathy's absence. organisations lacking empathic leadership experience higher turnover rates, decreased employee engagement, and reduced innovation (Boyatzis & McKee, 2005). Employees report feeling undervalued, misunderstood, and disconnected from organisational purpose when leaders fail to demonstrate genuine understanding of their experiences and perspectives.

Conversely, the presence of empathy transforms every dimension of human interaction. In romantic partnerships, empathy creates the psychological safety necessary for vulnerability, intimacy, and growth. Partners who feel understood and accepted can risk authentic self-disclosure, knowing their emotional offerings will be received with care rather than judgment.

Friendship, too, deepens through empathic exchange. The bonds that sustain us through life's inevitable challenges are forged in moments of empathic connection—when friends not only hear our words but understand our hearts, when they stand with us in our struggles and celebrate our triumphs as if they were their own.

Family relationships flourish under empathy's gentle guidance. Parents who empathically attune to their children's emotional needs create secure attachment bonds that serve as the foundation for lifelong emotional health (Bowlby, 1988). Children raised in empathic environments develop stronger emotional regulation skills, healthier relationships, and greater resilience in the face of adversity.

Perhaps most significantly, empathy serves as the antidote to humanity's tendency toward tribalism and othering. When we empathically engage with those who differ from us—whether in race, religion, culture, or ideology—we discover the fundamental commonality that underlies surface differences. We recognise that beneath varying expressions of humanity lies the same basic needs for love, acceptance, purpose, and belonging.

## The Neural Symphony: The Neuroscience of Empathy

The human brain, sculpted by millions of years of evolutionary pressure toward social cooperation, contains sophisticated neural networks dedicated to empathic processing. These systems, operating largely below conscious awareness, enable us to automatically and rapidly process others' emotional states, intentions, and needs.

Central to empathic processing are mirror neuron systems, first discovered by Rizzolatti and his colleagues (1996) in macaque monkeys. These remarkable neurons fire both when an individual performs an action and when they observe another performing the same action. In humans, mirror neuron networks extend beyond simple motor mimicry to encompass emotional mirroring—when we observe another's emotional expression, our brains activate neural patterns similar to those we would experience if feeling that emotion ourselves.

This neural mirroring provides the biological foundation for emotional empathy. When we witness another's joy, pain, fear, or anger, our mirror neuron systems create a sort of neural simulation, allowing us to literally experience an echo of their emotional state within our own nervous system. This automatic, unconscious process explains why emotional contagion occurs so readily in human groups—why laughter spreads through crowds, why anxiety ripples through organisations, why one person's mood can influence an entire family system.

The anterior insula and anterior cingulate cortex (ACC) play crucial roles in processing both our own emotional states and those of others. Lamm, Decety, and Singer (2011) demonstrated that these brain regions show increased activation when individuals witness others in physical or emotional pain. Remarkably, the neural signature of observing others' suffering closely resembles the pattern observed when experiencing suffering first-hand, suggesting that empathy involves genuine neural resonance rather than mere intellectual understanding.

The medial prefrontal cortex contributes the cognitive component of empathy, enabling us to consider others' perspectives, intentions, and mental states. This region, highly developed in humans compared to other species, allows us to engage in complex theory of mind operations—to understand that others possess beliefs, desires, and intentions that may differ from our own.

Neuroplasticity research reveals that empathic neural networks can be strengthened through practice. Klimecki and colleagues (2013) found that compassion training increased gray matter density in empathy-related brain regions and enhanced participants' ability to regulate their emotional responses to others' suffering. This finding suggests that empathy, far from being a fixed trait, represents a skill that can be developed throughout life.

The neuroscience of empathy also reveals its potential shadows. Excessive empathic activation can lead to emotional overwhelm and burnout, particularly among helping professionals who regularly encounter others' suffering. The balance between empathic engagement and emotional self-protection represents one of the most crucial skills for maintaining both mental health and helping effectiveness.

## The Spectrum of Understanding: Different Types of Empathy

The multifaceted nature of empathy becomes clearer when we examine its distinct varieties, each serving unique functions in human relationship and each requiring different skills for optimal development.

### Cognitive Empathy: The Mind's Eye

Cognitive empathy represents our capacity to understand another's mental state through intellectual analysis rather than emotional experience. This "cold" form of empathy enables us to predict others' behaviour, understand their motivations, and respond appropriately to their needs without becoming emotionally overwhelmed.

In professional contexts, cognitive empathy proves invaluable. Effective salespeople use cognitive empathy to understand customers' decision-making processes and address their concerns. Skilled negotiators employ it to identify win-win solutions that address all parties' underlying interests. Teachers rely on cognitive empathy to recognise when students are struggling and adapt their instructional approaches accordingly.

The development of cognitive empathy requires what Selman (1980) terms "social perspective-taking"—the ability to simultaneously hold multiple viewpoints in mind and understand how different perspectives might lead to different conclusions. This capacity emerges gradually throughout childhood and continues developing into adulthood, influenced by factors such as social experience, education, and cultural exposure.

However, cognitive empathy alone can feel cold and calculating. When individuals possess high cognitive empathy but lack emotional resonance, their understanding may be accurate but their responses may feel inauthentic or manipulative. The stereotypical "used car salesman" who understands exactly what customers want to hear but feels no genuine concern for their wellbeing exemplifies cognitive empathy divorced from compassion.

## Emotional Empathy: The Heart's Mirror

Emotional empathy involves the automatic, involuntary sharing of others' emotional states. When we witness a child's delight and feel joy bubbling up within ourselves, when we observe suffering and experience genuine distress, we engage in emotional empathy.

This form of empathy emerges early in human development. Infants as young as a few days old show distress responses to other babies' crying, suggesting that emotional contagion represents one of our most fundamental social capacities (Hoffman, 2000). Throughout childhood, emotional empathy continues developing, influenced by factors such as parental modelling, secure attachment, and exposure to diverse emotional experiences.

Emotional empathy serves crucial social functions. It motivates prosocial behaviour by making others' wellbeing personally relevant to us. When we feel others' pain as our own, we become motivated to alleviate that pain. It also facilitates social bonding by creating shared emotional experiences that bind individuals together.

Yet emotional empathy presents unique challenges. Individuals high in emotional empathy may become overwhelmed by others' emotions, leading to empathic distress rather than empathic concern. They may also struggle with emotional boundaries, taking on others' emotions to such an extent that they lose touch with their own authentic feelings.

The key lies in developing what researchers call "empathic regulation"—the ability to feel with others while maintaining enough emotional distance to respond helpfully rather than becoming overwhelmed. This skill enables healthcare workers to provide compassionate care without burning out, allows parents to comfort distressed children without becoming distressed themselves, and helps friends offer support without taking on others' problems as their own.

## Compassionate Empathy: The Bridge to Action

Compassionate empathy represents empathy's highest expression—the integration of understanding and feeling with wise, skilful action. Individuals demonstrating compassionate empathy not only understand others' experiences and feel their emotions but also respond in ways that genuinely help.

This form of empathy requires what Gilbert (2009) terms "empathic wisdom"—the ability to discern when and how to help most effectively. Sometimes compassionate empathy involves offering emotional support; other times it requires practical assistance. Occasionally, it means maintaining boundaries or offering "tough love" when enabling behaviour would ultimately prove harmful.

Compassionate empathy emerges from the integration of multiple capacities: cognitive understanding of others' situations, emotional resonance with their experiences, self-awareness of one's own emotional responses, practical wisdom about effective helping strategies, and the courage to act despite potential personal costs.

Consider the difference between these three responses to a friend's job loss:

- *Cognitive empathy*: "I understand you must be worried about finances and feeling uncertain about the future."
- *Emotional empathy*: Feeling anxious and distressed alongside your friend, sharing their emotional burden.
- *Compassionate empathy*: Understanding their concerns, feeling their distress, and responding with both emotional support ("This must be really difficult for you") and practical assistance ("I'd like to help you review your resume and practice interviewing").

Each form of empathy contributes to human connection, but compassionate empathy transforms understanding into meaningful action that genuinely improves others' lives.

## The Obstacles to Understanding: Barriers to Empathy

Despite empathy's importance, numerous factors can impede its development and expression. Understanding these barriers represents the first step toward overcoming them and cultivating greater empathic capacity.

### The Overwhelm of Feeling: Emotional Flooding

One of empathy's most paradoxical challenges emerges from empathy itself. When individuals become too immersed in others' emotional experiences, they may experience what Hoffman (2000) terms "empathic overarousal"—a state of emotional overwhelm that impairs rather than enhances helping behaviour.

Healthcare professionals frequently encounter this phenomenon. Emergency room physicians who become too emotionally involved in patients' suffering may experience decision paralysis or burnout that ultimately reduces their effectiveness. Similarly, parents who absorb their children's every emotional fluctuation may find themselves unable to provide the stable, calming presence children need during distress.

The solution lies not in reducing empathic sensitivity but in developing what researcher Kristin Neff (2003) calls "empathic regulation"—the ability to feel with others while maintaining enough emotional equilibrium to respond helpfully. This involves learning to create what Buddhist teacher Pema Chödrön describes as "compassionate space"—a loving presence that holds others' pain without becoming consumed by it.

Practical strategies for managing empathic overwhelm include:

- **Mindful awareness**: recognising when you're absorbing others' emotions and consciously distinguishing between your feelings and theirs.

- **Emotional breathing space**: Taking brief pauses to center yourself before responding to others' distress.

- **Self-compassion practices**: Treating yourself with the same kindness you would offer a good friend experiencing difficulty.

- **Professional boundaries**: Maintaining appropriate limits in helping relationships to prevent emotional enmeshment.

## The Prison of Prejudice: Bias and Judgment

Perhaps no factor limits empathic development more powerfully than unconscious bias and prejudicial thinking. When we encounter others through the lens of stereotype and preconception, we see not their full humanity but our projected assumptions about who they are and what they represent.

Implicit bias research reveals the extent to which unconscious prejudices shape empathic responses. Studies consistently show that individuals demonstrate greater empathic concern for in-group members than out-group members, even when group membership is based on arbitrary characteristics (Cikara, Bruneau, & Saxe, 2011). We more readily empathise with those who look like us, share our values, or belong to our social circles.

This bias manifests in subtle but profound ways. Healthcare providers show greater empathic concern for patients who share their racial or ethnic background. Teachers demonstrate more patience and understanding with students from similar socioeconomic backgrounds. Even our capacity for emotional contagion varies based on perceived similarity to others.

Overcoming empathic bias requires what researchers call "perspective-taking interventions"—deliberate practices designed to expand empathic concern beyond natural in-group boundaries. These might include:

- **Imagining detailed personal histories** for individuals from different backgrounds.

- **Engaging in structured intergroup contact** under conditions that promote positive interaction.

- **Practicing loving-kindness meditation** that explicitly includes out-group members.

- **Exposing oneself to diverse narratives** through literature, film, and personal conversations.

The goal is not to eliminate all preferences and distinctions but to ensure that our capacity for empathic understanding extends to all members of the human family.

## The Tyranny of Self: Self-Absorption and Narcissism

In our culture of individualism and self-focus, the capacity for genuine empathy often becomes stunted by excessive self-preoccupation. When individuals become overly consumed with their own needs, desires, and concerns, they lose the ability to genuinely see and respond to others.

Clinical narcissism represents the extreme end of this spectrum, but subtler forms of self-absorption affect many well-intentioned individuals. The parent too focused on their own parenting performance to truly attune to their child's needs. The friend so concerned with their own problems that they can't offer genuine support to others. The leader so invested in their own success that they fail to recognise their team's struggles.

Self-absorption often masks deeper insecurities and unmet needs. Individuals who haven't developed a secure sense of self may become hypervigilant about their own status and safety, leaving little emotional energy for empathic engagement with others. The remedy involves not self-criticism but self-compassion—developing the inner security that allows attention to flow naturally toward others.

Practices for reducing self-absorption include:

- **Daily gratitude practices** that shift attention from what's lacking to what's present.

- **Service activities** that involve helping others without personal benefit.

- **Mindfulness meditation** that reduces rumination and self-focused attention.

- **Perspective-taking exercises** that deliberately shift focus to others' experiences.

The paradox of empathy is that it requires a secure sense of self to truly transcend self. Only when we feel safe and grounded in our own identity can we risk the vulnerability required for genuine empathic connection.

## The Transformation of Relationship: How Empathy Strengthens Connections

When empathy becomes a living reality rather than mere concept, it transforms every dimension of human relationship. The quality of connection shifts from surface interaction to deep communion, from transactional exchange to meaningful encounter.

### Romantic Relationships: The Dance of Intimate Understanding

In romantic partnerships, empathy serves as both foundation and catalyst for lasting love. Research by John Gottman reveals that couples' ability to empathically respond to each other's "emotional bids"—attempts to connect emotionally—predicts relationship success with remarkable accuracy (Gottman & Levenson, 1992).

Consider the seemingly mundane moment when one partner mentions seeing a beautiful sunset on their commute home. This represents an emotional bid—an invitation to share a moment of appreciation and connection. An empathic partner might respond with genuine interest: "That sounds lovely. What made it particularly beautiful?" This response acknowledges not just the content but the emotional invitation, creating a moment of shared appreciation that strengthens the relationship bond.

Empathy in romantic relationships extends far beyond responding to positive bids. When partners face conflict, empathic engagement transforms potential battles into opportunities for deeper understanding. Instead of defensively arguing their position, empathic partners seek to understand their beloved's perspective, even—especially—when that perspective differs from their own.

The practice of empathic communication in intimate relationships involves several key elements:

- **Emotional attunement**: recognising and responding to your partner's emotional state, not just their words.

- **Perspective validation**: Acknowledging that your partner's viewpoint makes sense from their perspective, even if you disagree.

- **Curiosity over certainty**: Approaching conflicts with genuine interest in understanding rather than winning.

- **Emotional holding**: Providing comfort and support during your partner's difficult emotions without trying to fix or change them.

## Friendship: The Garden of Mutual Understanding

Friendship represents perhaps the purest expression of empathic connection, free from the biological imperatives of family or the practical necessities of work relationships. In friendship, we choose to care about another's wellbeing simply because we value them as a person.

Deep friendship requires what philosopher Aristotle termed "philia"—a love based on virtue and mutual respect rather than mere pleasure or utility. This form of love emerges through empathic knowing—truly seeing and appreciating another person's character, struggles, dreams, and growth.

The empathic friend offers what Carl Rogers called "unconditional positive regard"—acceptance and care that doesn't depend on the friend's behaviour or success. This creates the psychological safety necessary for authentic self-disclosure and vulnerability, allowing friendships to deepen beyond superficial interaction.

Research on adult friendship reveals that empathic responsiveness serves as one of the strongest predictors of friendship satisfaction and longevity (Davis & Oathout, 1987). Friends who feel understood, accepted, and emotionally supported report greater life satisfaction and better mental health outcomes than those whose friendships lack empathic depth.

## Family Life: The Crucible of Empathic Development

Family relationships provide both the greatest opportunity and the greatest challenge for empathic development. The intensity and complexity of family dynamics can either nurture empathic growth or create defensive patterns that inhibit emotional connection.

Empathic parenting involves what developmental psychologist Daniel Siegel calls "attunement"—the ability to sense and respond appropriately to children's emotional states (Siegel, 2012). Attuned parents help children develop emotional intelligence by modelling empathic responses and teaching emotion regulation skills.

The empathic parent doesn't try to eliminate children's difficult emotions but instead helps them understand and manage these feelings. When a child experiences frustration, the empathic parent might say, "You seem really upset that your tower fell down. It's disappointing when something we worked hard on doesn't turn out the way we wanted." This response validates the child's emotional experience while providing language for emotional understanding.

Sibling relationships, too, benefit from empathic engagement. When parents model empathy and encourage children to consider each other's perspectives, siblings develop stronger bonds and better conflict resolution skills. Family therapy research consistently shows that families with higher levels of empathic communication experience less dysfunction and greater resilience during stressful periods.

## Professional Relationships: Leading with Heart

In workplace settings, empathy transforms leadership from mere authority into genuine influence. Empathic leaders understand that human beings, not abstract resources, drive organisational success. They recognise that employee engagement, creativity, and productivity flow from feeling valued, understood, and cared for as individuals.

Research on emotional intelligence in leadership consistently identifies empathy as a key differentiator between average and exceptional leaders (Boyatzis & McKee, 2005). Empathic leaders demonstrate several distinctive characteristics:

- **Active listening**: They give full attention to others' perspectives without interrupting or immediately offering solutions.

- **Emotional awareness**: They recognise and acknowledge others' emotional states, even when those emotions aren't explicitly expressed.

- **Perspective-taking**: They consider how decisions and changes will affect different team members and stakeholders.

- **Responsive communication**: They adapt their communication style to meet others' needs and preferences.

- **Supportive challenge**: They provide feedback and guidance in ways that promote growth rather than defensiveness.

The empathic workplace becomes a space where individuals can bring their full selves to work, where diverse perspectives are valued, and where collective success emerges from genuine care for individual wellbeing.

## The Art of Empathic Engagement: Practical Strategies for Cultivation

Developing empathy requires more than good intentions; it demands deliberate practice and skillful cultivation. The following strategies, grounded in research and refined through practice, offer pathways for expanding empathic capacity.

### The Foundation: Active Listening as Sacred Practice

True listening—the kind that transforms both listener and speaker—represents empathy's most fundamental skill. Yet genuine listening has become increasingly rare in our culture of constant distraction and rapid response.

Active listening involves several interconnected elements:

- **Presence**: Bringing full attention to the speaker without mental multitasking or distraction.

- **Suspension of judgment**: Temporarily setting aside your own opinions and reactions to create space for the other's experience.

- **Emotional attunement**: Sensing not just words but the feelings and meanings beneath them.

- **Reflective response**: Offering back what you've heard in ways that demonstrate understanding and invite deeper sharing.

- **Curious inquiry**: Asking questions that explore rather than interrogate, that open rather than close conversational space.

The practice of active listening begins with recognising how rarely we truly listen. Most conversations involve two people taking turns speaking rather than genuine dialogue. We listen partially while simultaneously formulating our response, judging the speaker's words, or thinking about unrelated matters.

Transforming this pattern requires what Buddhist teacher Thich Nhat Hanh calls "deep listening"—listening with the intention to understand and compassionately respond rather than to reply or defend. This involves:

- **Creating physical space** for listening by eliminating distractions and positioning yourself to give full attention.

- **Offering emotional space** by setting aside your own agenda and opening to whatever the speaker needs to share.

- **Providing reflective responses** that demonstrate understanding: "It sounds like you're feeling..." or "What I'm hearing is..."

- **Asking questions that explore meaning**: "What was that experience like for you?" or "How did that affect you?"

## The Practice: Perspective-Taking as Mental Exercise

Perspective-taking—the ability to see situations through others' eyes—represents empathy's cognitive component and can be strengthened through deliberate practice.

Research shows that even brief perspective-taking exercises can increase empathic accuracy and reduce prejudicial thinking. These exercises might include:

- **Imaginary role-playing**: When facing conflict with someone, spend time mentally inhabiting their perspective. What concerns might drive their behaviour? What fears or hopes might influence their actions?

- **Narrative imagination**: Create detailed mental stories about strangers you encounter. What might their day have been like? What challenges might they face? What dreams might they harbour?

- **Historical perspective-taking**: When reading about historical events or social issues, imagine experiencing these situations from different viewpoints—various ethnicities, genders, social classes, or age groups.

- **Literary engagement**: Read fiction from diverse authors representing different backgrounds and experiences. Research shows that reading literary fiction increases empathic accuracy more than reading nonfiction or popular fiction.

The key to effective perspective-taking lies in specificity and imagination. Rather than making general assumptions about others' experiences, create detailed, nuanced pictures of their inner lives. Consider not just their obvious circumstances but their hopes, fears, memories, and dreams.

## The Skill: Managing Emotional Boundaries

One of empathy's greatest challenges involves maintaining appropriate emotional boundaries—feeling with others without becoming overwhelmed by their emotions. This skill, sometimes called "empathic regulation," enables sustained empathic engagement without emotional burnout.

Developing healthy empathic boundaries requires:

- **Self-awareness**: recognising when you're absorbing others' emotions and distinguishing between your feelings and theirs.

- **Grounding practices**: Techniques for returning to your own emotional center when you become overwhelmed by others' experiences.

- **Compassionate detachment**: Caring deeply while maintaining enough emotional distance to respond helpfully rather than reactively.

- **Regular self-care**: Maintaining your own emotional wellbeing through practices that replenish rather than drain your empathic reserves.

Practical boundary-setting strategies include:

- **The emotional pause**: When encountering others' strong emotions, take a brief moment to centre yourself before responding.

- **The loving boundary**: Offering care and support while maintaining your own emotional equilibrium—"I care about you and I'm not going to take on your emotions as my own."

- **The helper's breath**: Using conscious breathing to create space between yourself and others' emotional states.

- **Regular emotional clearing**: Engaging in practices that help release absorbed emotions—meditation, journaling, physical exercise, or time in nature.

## Empathy Embodied: Real-World Examples of Transformative Understanding

The true measure of empathy lies not in theoretical understanding but in lived application. Throughout history, individuals have demonstrated empathy's transformative power through their responses to suffering, injustice, and human need.

### Nelson Mandela: The Alchemy of Empathic Leadership

Perhaps no historical figure better exemplifies empathy's political power than Nelson Mandela. After twenty-seven years of imprisonment, Mandela emerged not with vengeance but with an empathic understanding that transformed a nation.

Mandela's empathy extended even to his former oppressors. He recognised that white South Africans' support for apartheid often stemmed from fear—fear of losing status, security, and identity in a changing world. Rather than dismissing these fears, Mandela acknowledged them while offering a vision of inclusion that addressed underlying needs for safety and belonging.

This empathic approach proved practically as well as morally superior to alternatives. By understanding and addressing white South Africans' fears, Mandela prevented the racial civil war that many predicted. His empathy didn't excuse injustice but created space for reconciliation and healing.

Mandela's example reveals empathy's political dimensions. In leadership, empathy enables the recognition of shared humanity beneath ideological differences. It allows leaders to address not just people's stated positions but their underlying needs and concerns.

## Brené Brown: Vulnerability as Empathic Bridge

Researcher and author Brené Brown has revolutionised our understanding of empathy through her ground-breaking work on vulnerability, shame, and human connection. Brown's research reveals empathy's role in combating isolation and building authentic relationships.

Brown distinguishes between empathy and sympathy, noting that empathy involves feeling with people while sympathy involves feeling sorry for them. Empathy, she argues, requires vulnerability—the willingness to touch our own experiences of pain, fear, or struggle in order to connect with others' similar experiences.

Her work demonstrates empathy's healing power. When individuals feel truly seen and understood in their struggles—not judged, fixed, or pitied—they experience the connection that facilitates growth and resilience. This empathic witnessing transforms shame from an isolating experience into an opportunity for human connection.

Brown's approach to empathy emphasises its bidirectional nature. True empathy requires not just understanding others but allowing ourselves to be understood. This mutual vulnerability creates the authentic connections that sustain us through life's challenges.

## Healthcare Heroes: Compassionate Care in Crisis

Healthcare workers daily demonstrate empathy's practical application in high-stakes environments. During the COVID-19 pandemic, healthcare professionals worldwide exemplified compassionate empathy while facing unprecedented challenges.

Consider the Intensive Care Unit (ICU) nurse who, despite exhaustion and personal risk, takes time to hold a dying patient's hand, knowing the patient's family cannot be present. This action embodies all three dimensions of empathy: cognitive understanding of the patient's fear and loneliness, emotional resonance with their suffering, and compassionate action that provides comfort in their final moments.

Healthcare empathy requires exceptional skill in emotional regulation. Healthcare workers must feel enough to provide genuine compassion while maintaining enough emotional distance to make clear medical decisions. They must balance professional boundaries with human connection, protocol with personalisation.

The pandemic revealed both empathy's necessity and its challenges in healthcare settings. Healthcare workers who maintained empathic engagement reported greater job satisfaction and sense of purpose, while those who became emotionally overwhelmed experienced higher rates of burnout and trauma.

## The Ripple Effect: Empathy's Transformative

# Power

When empathy becomes more than individual skill but cultural value, its effects ripple through communities and societies, creating positive change that extends far beyond personal relationships. Research in social psychology reveals what practitioners have long understood: empathy is contagious (Hatfield, Cacioppo, & Rapson, 1994). When we encounter genuine empathic understanding, we become more likely to offer it to others. The kindness we receive multiplies through our interactions, creating positive feedback loops that strengthen the social fabric of our communities.

This contagion effect operates through multiple mechanisms. Mirror neuron systems ensure that we automatically mimic others' emotional expressions and postures, creating opportunities for emotional resonance. Social learning theory demonstrates that we acquire new behaviours by observing and imitating those around us. When we witness empathic responses, we internalise these patterns and reproduce them in our own relationships.

The workplace provides a compelling example of empathy's contagious nature. organisations with empathic leadership cultures report higher levels of employee engagement, creativity, and collaboration (Dutton & Heaphy, 2003). When leaders model empathic behaviour, it cascades through organisational hierarchies, creating environments where individuals feel safe to be vulnerable, innovative, and authentically themselves.

Healthcare settings similarly demonstrate empathy's ripple effects. When healthcare workers receive empathic support from colleagues and supervisors, they report greater job satisfaction and are better able to provide compassionate care to patients. This creates positive cycles where empathy begets empathy, transforming healthcare environments from sites of technical intervention to spaces of genuine healing.

## The Global Imperative: Empathy in an Interconnected World

In our increasingly interconnected world, empathy becomes not just a personal virtue but a global necessity. Climate change, economic inequality, refugee crises, and pandemics require collective responses that transcend national, cultural, and ideological boundaries. These challenges can only be addressed through the kind of cooperative action that emerges from empathic understanding of our shared humanity and interconnected fate.

The climate crisis provides a compelling example of empathy's global importance. Addressing climate change requires affluent nations to empathically understand how their consumption patterns affect vulnerable populations worldwide. It demands that current generations consider the needs of future generations who will inherit the environmental consequences of today's decisions.

Similarly, addressing global inequality requires empathic engagement with the experiences of individuals whose circumstances differ dramatically from our own. When privileged individuals empathically understand the systemic barriers faced by marginalised communities, they become motivated to support policies and practices that promote greater equity and justice.

The refugee crisis challenges us to extend empathic concern beyond the comfortable boundaries of national identity. When we empathically engage with the experiences of individuals fleeing violence, persecution, and poverty, we recognise our shared humanity and moral obligation to provide assistance and welcome.

These global challenges reveal both empathy's promise and its limitations. While empathy motivates concern and action, it must be coupled with systemic thinking, policy expertise, and sustained commitment to address complex social problems effectively. Empathy provides the emotional foundation for global cooperation, but it requires translation into concrete policies and practices to create meaningful change.

## The Neuroscience of Empathic Development

Recent advances in neuroscience research provide unprecedented insight into how empathy develops and how it can be enhanced throughout the lifespan. This research offers hope for individuals seeking to strengthen their empathic capacities and for societies working to create more compassionate cultures.

Neuroplasticity studies reveal that empathy-related brain regions remain malleable throughout life (Klimecki et al., 2013). Adults who engage in empathy training show measurable changes in brain structure and function, including increased gray matter density in regions associated with emotional processing and perspective-taking.

Meditation practices, particularly loving-kindness meditation, demonstrate remarkable effects on empathic capacity. Participants in loving-kindness training show increased activation in empathy-related brain networks and greater prosocial behaviour in laboratory experiments (Weng et al., 2013). These findings suggest that ancient contemplative practices offer scientifically validated methods for empathic development.

Mindfulness training also enhances empathic capacity by improving emotional regulation and reducing self-focused attention. When individuals develop greater awareness of their own emotional states, they become better able to recognise and respond appropriately to others' emotions.

Virtual reality technology offers innovative approaches to empathy training by allowing individuals to literally experience situations from others' perspectives. Virtual Reality (VR) empathy training has shown promise in reducing prejudice, increasing helping behaviour, and enhancing emotional understanding across group boundaries.

These technological and scientific advances suggest that empathy development need not rely solely on natural talent or fortunate circumstances. Instead, empathy emerges as a skill that can be systematically cultivated through targeted interventions and deliberate practice.

## Restorative Justice: Healing Through Understanding

Restorative justice programmes demonstrate empathy's power to transform criminal justice from punishment-focused to healing-focused approaches. These programmes bring together victims, offenders, and community members to address harm through dialogue and mutual understanding.

The empathic process of restorative justice requires offenders to truly understand the impact of their actions on victims and communities. Rather than simply receiving punishment, offenders must engage empathically with those they've harmed, developing genuine understanding of the pain they've caused.

Victims, too, often benefit from empathic engagement with offenders. Understanding the circumstances and motivations behind crimes doesn't excuse harmful behaviour but can reduce fear and promote healing. Many victims report that face-to-face dialogue with offenders provides closure that traditional criminal justice processes cannot offer.

Research on restorative justice programmes shows reduced recidivism rates and higher victim satisfaction compared to traditional approaches. By centring empathy and understanding, these programmes address not just criminal behaviour but its underlying causes and effects.

## Conflict Resolution: Empathy as Peace-making Tool

In international conflicts, empathy offers pathways to peace that the military might cannot provide. Successful peace processes typically involve helping conflicting parties understand each other's perspectives, fears, and needs.

The Oslo Accords between Israelis and Palestinians, while ultimately incomplete, demonstrated empathy's potential in conflict resolution. Secret negotiations succeeded partly because representatives developed personal relationships and began to see each other as human beings rather than enemies.

Similarly, the Northern Ireland peace process benefited from empathic engagement between former adversaries. When paramilitaries from opposing sides began to understand each other's historical experiences and contemporary concerns, violence gave way to dialogue and eventual agreement.

These examples reveal empathy's political necessity. Lasting peace requires not just cessation of hostilities but transformation of relationships. This transformation occurs through empathic understanding that recognises shared humanity beneath ideological differences.

## Educational Reform: Teaching with Heart

Educational settings increasingly recognise empathy's role in effective teaching and learning. Empathic teachers who understand students' backgrounds, challenges, and learning styles create more inclusive and effective learning environments.

Research consistently shows that students perform better academically when they feel understood and cared for by their teachers. This empathic connection provides the psychological safety necessary for intellectual risk-taking and creative thinking.

Empathy-based educational approaches also address inequality and cultural barriers to learning. When teachers empathically understand the challenges faced by students from different backgrounds, they can adapt their teaching methods and create more equitable learning opportunities.

Social-emotional learning (SEL) programmes that explicitly teach empathy and emotional intelligence show promising results in reducing bullying, improving academic performance, and preparing students for successful adult relationships and careers.

## Practical Wisdom: Advanced Empathic Skills

For individuals committed to deepening their empathic capacities, several advanced practices offer pathways to greater skill and wisdom.

**Somatic empathy** involves developing sensitivity to others' physical and energetic states. Many emotions manifest in bodily sensations before becoming conscious thoughts. Learning to read others' posture, breathing patterns, muscle tension, and energy levels provides valuable information about their emotional states that may not be verbally expressed.

**Cultural empathy** requires understanding how cultural backgrounds shape emotional expression and interpersonal communication. What appears as rudeness in one culture may represent respect in another. Developing cultural empathy involves learning about different cultural norms while remaining open to individuals who may not conform to cultural stereotypes.

**Historical empathy** enables understanding of how past experiences shape present behaviour. Trauma, loss, and significant life events create lasting impacts on individuals' emotional patterns and relational capacities. Empathic individuals learn to recognise these historical influences without using them to excuse harmful behaviour.

**Developmental empathy** involves understanding how different life stages create different needs and capacities. The empathy appropriate for a three-year-old differs from that needed by a teenager or elderly adult. Skilled empaths adjust their responses based on developmental considerations.

**Systems empathy** recognises how larger social, economic, and political systems influence individual experiences. This broader empathy understands that personal struggles often reflect systemic inequities and works to address both individual needs and structural barriers.

These advanced empathic skills require ongoing development and refinement. They represent not destinations but directions for continued growth throughout life.

## The Philosophical Foundations: Why Empathy Matters

Beyond its practical benefits, empathy carries profound philosophical significance that speaks to fundamental questions about human nature, moral obligation, and the meaning of existence. Understanding these deeper dimensions enriches our appreciation of empathy's importance and motivates sustained commitment to its development.

From an existential perspective, empathy represents our response to the fundamental isolation of human consciousness. Each individual exists within the private world of their own subjective experience, unable to directly access others' inner lives. Empathy bridges this existential gap, creating moments of genuine connection that transcend the boundaries of separate selfhood.

Philosopher Emmanuel Levinas argued that ethical responsibility emerges from face-to-face encounters with others (Levinas, 1969). When we truly see another person—not as an object or category but as a unique individual—we experience an ethical call to respond to their needs and vulnerability. Empathy enables this kind of authentic seeing that transforms strangers into neighbours and creates moral obligations that extend beyond self-interest.

Religious and spiritual traditions across cultures recognise empathy's sacred dimensions. Buddhism emphasises compassion as one of its core virtues, arguing that genuine happiness emerges from concern for others' wellbeing. Christianity centres love of neighbour as fundamental to spiritual development. Judaism emphasises the obligation to "repair the world" through acts of justice and compassion. Islam highlights mercy and compassion as divine qualities that humans are called to embody.

These convergent wisdom traditions suggest that empathy represents more than psychological capacity or social skill—it reflects something essential about what it means to be fully human. The development of empathy becomes not just personal growth but spiritual evolution, not just social improvement but moral transformation.

## The Shadow Side: When Empathy Goes Awry

Yet empathy, like any powerful capacity, carries potential for distortion and misuse. Understanding these shadow aspects proves crucial for healthy empathic development and prevents the burnout, manipulation, and boundary violations that can result from empathy's misapplication.

**Empathic distress** occurs when individuals become so overwhelmed by others' emotions that they lose the capacity for helpful response. Instead of feeling with others in ways that motivate supportive action, they become paralysed by emotional overwhelm. This phenomenon frequently affects highly sensitive individuals who lack skills for emotional regulation and boundary-setting.

**False empathy** emerges when individuals claim empathic understanding while actually projecting their own experiences and assumptions onto others. This pseudo-empathy often manifests in statements like "I know exactly how you feel" or premature advice-giving that reflects the helper's needs rather than the recipient's actual experience.

**Manipulative empathy** represents empathy's darkest expression—the use of empathic understanding to exploit others' vulnerabilities. Con artists, abusive partners, and unethical leaders often demonstrate sophisticated empathic skills that they employ for selfish purposes rather than genuine care.

**Empathic bias** limits empathic concern to in-group members while withholding understanding from out-group individuals. This selective empathy reinforces existing prejudices and social divisions rather than bridging them.

Preventing these empathic distortions requires ongoing self-reflection, skill development, and ethical commitment. The empathic individual must continuously examine their motivations, maintain appropriate boundaries, and ensure that their empathic responses serve others' genuine needs rather than their own psychological satisfaction.

## The Future of Empathy: Challenges and Opportunities

As we look toward the future, empathy faces both unprecedented challenges and remarkable opportunities. Understanding these trends helps us prepare for the empathic requirements of tomorrow's world.

**Digital technology** presents complex challenges for empathic development. Social media and digital communication can reduce opportunities for face-to-face interaction while creating new forms of connection and understanding. The key lies in using technology to enhance rather than replace genuine human connection.

**Artificial intelligence** raises profound questions about the nature of empathy and emotional understanding. As AI systems become more sophisticated at recognising and responding to human emotions, we must consider what authentic empathy requires and how to maintain genuine human connection in an increasingly automated world.

**Global migration** creates unprecedented opportunities for cross-cultural empathic engagement while also generating anxiety and resistance in many communities. The future will require empathic skills that bridge not just individual differences but cultural and linguistic barriers.

**Climate change** will likely create new forms of suffering and displacement that will test our empathic capacities and require new forms of global cooperation and understanding.

**Generational change** brings both hope and concern for empathy's future. Younger generations demonstrate greater concern for social justice and global issues while also facing challenges related to digital communication and social media's impact on relationship skills.

These trends suggest that empathy will become increasingly important while also requiring new skills and applications. The future belongs to individuals and societies that can maintain genuine human connection while navigating technological change and global complexity.

## A Personal Commitment: Your Empathic Journey

As this exploration of empathy draws to a close, the real work begins—the daily practice of empathic living that transforms understanding into action and knowledge into wisdom. Your empathic journey is uniquely yours, shaped by your experiences, relationships, and chosen commitments.

This journey requires patience with yourself and others. Empathy develops gradually through practice and reflection, not through sudden insight or transformation. There will be moments of profound connection and periods of struggle, times when empathy flows naturally and occasions when it requires great effort.

The empathic path also demands courage—the courage to feel deeply in a world that often encourages emotional numbing, the courage to remain open when experiences tempt us toward defensiveness, the courage to act compassionately even when such action requires personal sacrifice.

Yet this courage brings rewards beyond measure: the joy of genuine connection, the satisfaction of contributing to others' wellbeing, the peace that comes from living in alignment with our deepest values, and the sense of meaning that emerges from participating in something larger than ourselves.

Your empathic development serves not only your own growth but the healing of our world. Each moment of genuine understanding, each act of compassionate response, each bridge built across difference contributes to the great work of creating a more empathic, connected, and peaceful world.

The invitation is before you: to develop empathy not as an abstract ideal but as lived reality, not as an occasional gesture but as a way of being, not as personal achievement but as a gift to the world. The choice—and the journey—is yours.

## Conclusion: The Courage to Connect

Empathy emerges not as mere niceness or sentimental feeling but as one of humanity's greatest achievements—a capacity that requires courage, skill, and wisdom to develop fully. It asks us to venture beyond the familiar territory of our own experience to explore the vast, uncharted landscapes of others' inner lives.

This journey demands everything we have to offer: our attention, our emotional availability, our willingness to be changed by what we discover. It requires the humility to acknowledge that others' experiences may differ radically from our own, the patience to truly listen without rushing to judgment or solution, and the strength to feel deeply without being overwhelmed.

Yet the rewards of this journey extend far beyond individual benefit. When we develop genuine empathy, we contribute to the healing of our fractured world. We become agents of connection in an age of division, builders of bridges across chasms of difference, healers of wounds that separate us from one another.

The empathic individual transforms every interaction into an opportunity for deeper understanding. In boardrooms and bedrooms, classrooms and emergency rooms, the presence of genuine empathy shifts the quality of human exchange from mechanical transaction to meaningful encounter. Conflicts become conversations, strangers become neighbours, and enemies discover their shared humanity.

This transformation radiates outward in ever-widening circles. The parent who empathically attunes to their child's emotional needs raises a more emotionally intelligent human being who will, in turn, create more empathic relationships throughout their life. The teacher who sees beyond students' behaviour to their underlying needs cultivates not just academic learning but emotional wisdom that students carry into their future relationships and careers.

The leader who empathically understands their team members' perspectives creates organisational cultures where innovation flourishes, where diversity becomes strength, and where collective success emerges from genuine care for individual wellbeing. The friend who offers empathic presence during times of struggle provides not just momentary comfort but a model of relationship that inspires others to love more deeply and connect more authentically.

In the next chapter, we will explore Social Skills and Influence: Leading with Heart—examining how emotional intelligence shapes our capacity to communicate effectively, build meaningful relationships, and inspire positive change in the world around us. The empathic foundation we have built here will serve as the bedrock for developing these more external expressions of emotional wisdom.

## References

Baron-Cohen, S. (2011). *The Science of Evil: On Empathy and the Origins of Cruelty*. Basic Books.

Bowlby, J. (1988). *A Secure Base: Parent-Child Attachment and Healthy Human Development*. Basic Books.

Boyatzis, R., & McKee, A. (2005). *Resonant Leadership: Renewing Yourself and Connecting with Others Through Mindfulness, Hope, and Compassion*. Harvard Business Review Press.

Cikara, M., Bruneau, E. G., & Saxe, R. R. (2011). Us and them: Intergroup failures of empathy. *Current Directions in Psychological Science*, 20(3), 149-153.

Davis, M. H. (1994). *Empathy: A Social Psychological Approach*. Brown & Benchmark.

Davis, M. H., & Oathout, H. A. (1987). Maintenance of satisfaction in romantic relationships: Empathy and relational competence. *Journal of Personality and Social Psychology*, 53(2), 397-410.

Dutton, J. E., & Heaphy, E. D. (2003). The power of high-quality connections. In K. S. Cameron, J. E. Dutton, & R. E. Quinn (Eds.), *Positive Organizational Scholarship: Foundations of a New Discipline* (pp. 263-278). Berrett-Koehler Publishers.

Gilbert, P. (2009). *The Compassionate Mind: A New Approach to Life's Challenges*. Constable.

Goleman, D. (2006). *Emotional Intelligence: Why It Matters More Than IQ*. Bantam Books.

Gottman, J. M., & Levenson, R. W. (1992). Marital processes predictive of later dissolution: behaviour, physiology, and health. *Journal of Personality and Social Psychology*, 63(2), 221-233.

Hatfield, E., Cacioppo, J. T., & Rapson, R. L. (1994). *Emotional Contagion*. Cambridge University Press.

Hoffman, M. L. (2000). *Empathy and Moral Development: Implications for Caring and Justice*. Cambridge University Press.

Klimecki, O. M., Leiberg, S., Lamm, C., & Singer, T. (2013). Functional neural plasticity and associated changes in positive affect after compassion training. *Cerebral Cortex*, 23(7), 1552-1561.

Lamm, C., Decety, J., & Singer, T. (2011). Meta-analytic evidence for common and distinct neural networks associated with directly experienced pain and empathy for pain. *NeuroImage*, 54(3), 2492-2502.

Levinas, E. (1969). *Totality and Infinity: An Essay on Exteriority*. Duquesne University Press.

Neff, K. D. (2003). Self-compassion: An alternative conceptualization of a healthy attitude toward oneself. *Self and Identity*, 2(2), 85-101.

Rizzolatti, G., Fadiga, L., Gallese, V., & Fogassi, L. (1996). Premotor cortex and the recognition of motor actions. *Cognitive Brain Research*, 3(2), 131-141.

Selman, R. L. (1980). *The Growth of Interpersonal Understanding: Developmental and Clinical Analyses*. Academic Press.

Siegel, D. J. (2012). *The Developing Mind: How Relationships and the Brain Interact to Shape Who We Are*. Guilford Press.

Weng, H. Y., Fox, A. S., Shackman, A. J., Stodola, D. E., Caldwell, J. Z., Olson, M. C., Rogers, G. M., & Davidson, R. J. (2013). Compassion training alters altruism and neural responses to suffering. *Psychological Science*, 24(7), 1171-1180.

# Chapter 11: Social Skills and Influence: Leading with Heart

## Introduction

Within the magnificent architecture of emotional intelligence, social skills represent the cathedral's spire—the soaring apex where all foundational elements converge into visible, transformative action. Here, the interior work of self-awareness crystallises into external impact; the disciplined cultivation of self-regulation manifests as grace under pressure; the fires of motivation ignite others' passion; and the bridges of empathy become highways for collective endeavour.

Yet social skills remain perhaps the most misunderstood dimension of emotional intelligence. Too often reduced to superficial networking or manipulative charm, genuine social competence transcends these hollow facades. True social mastery emerges from the intersection of authentic self-expression and profound attunement to others—a dynamic dance between revealing one's deepest truths and creating space for others to do the same.

Goleman (2006) describes social skills as "the culmination of emotional intelligence," arguing that without the ability to translate internal awareness into effective relationship management, all other emotional competencies remain merely potential rather than power. This external expression of emotional wisdom transforms individuals from passive recipients of social dynamics into active architects of human connection and positive change.

In our hyperconnected yet increasingly fragmented world, the capacity for genuine social influence becomes not merely advantageous but essential for survival and flourishing. The leader who can inspire rather than coerce, the colleague who can collaborate rather than compete, the friend who can comfort rather than merely commiserate—these individuals possess the social skills that create the bonds holding civilisation together.

The profound irony of our digital age lies in its simultaneous expansion and contraction of social possibilities. While technology enables unprecedented connection across geographical boundaries, it often diminishes the quality of interpersonal engagement that builds trust, inspires loyalty, and fosters genuine collaboration. Surface-level interactions proliferate while deep relationships wither, creating what sociologist Robert Putnam (2000) termed "bowling alone"—the paradox of connection without community.

This chapter will explore the multifaceted terrain of social competence, examining its neurological foundations, psychological mechanisms, and practical applications. We shall investigate how authentic influence differs from manipulation, how leadership emerges from service rather than dominance, and how the heart's wisdom can guide social action toward outcomes that elevate rather than exploit human potential.

## The Orchestration of Connection: Understanding Social Skills

Social skills, in their most sophisticated expression, represent the art of human orchestration—the capacity to conduct complex interpersonal symphonies where diverse individuals contribute their unique talents toward harmonious collective achievement. This orchestration requires not the authoritarian baton of command but the gentle guidance of invitation, not the rigid structure of hierarchy but the flexible responsiveness of jazz improvisation.

Bar-On (2006) conceptualises social skills as comprising multiple interconnected competencies: interpersonal relationships, social responsibility, and reality testing. Each component contributes to our overall capacity for effective social functioning, yet their integration creates something greater than the sum of their parts—the ability to create positive social change through conscious relationship management.

Consider the complexity involved in a single meaningful conversation. The socially skilled individual must simultaneously monitor their own emotional state, accurately read the other person's verbal and nonverbal communications, adjust their communication style to match the relational context, manage any conflicts or tensions that arise, and guide the interaction toward mutually beneficial outcomes. This requires what researchers call "social intelligence"—a sophisticated form of problem-solving applied to the realm of human relationships (Thorndike, 1920).

The development of social skills follows a predictable yet highly individual trajectory. Children begin with basic social awareness—recognising that others have different perspectives and needs. They gradually develop more sophisticated capacities for cooperation, negotiation, and leadership. Yet this development never truly ends; even experienced adults continue refining their social competencies throughout life as they encounter new relationships, cultures, and contexts.

Research reveals significant individual differences in social skill development, influenced by factors such as temperament, family dynamics, cultural background, and educational experiences. Some individuals appear naturally gifted in social contexts, effortlessly reading interpersonal dynamics and responding appropriately. Others must consciously develop these competencies through deliberate practice and reflection. Yet regardless of starting point, social skills remain learnable capacities that can be strengthened through commitment and effort.

The neuroscience of social skills reveals their deep biological foundations. Social cognition involves multiple brain networks working in concert: the mirror neuron system for understanding others' actions and intentions, the theory of mind network for perspective-taking, the empathy network for emotional resonance, and the executive control network for managing one's own responses (Baron-Cohen, 2011). This neural complexity explains both the sophistication of human social behaviour and the challenges many individuals face in developing social competence.

## The Imperative of Connection: Why Social Skills Transform Everything

The absence of social skills creates a world both familiar and devastating—organisations plagued by miscommunication and mistrust, families fractured by unresolved conflicts, communities divided by inability to find common ground. Without social competence, human potential remains isolated and ineffective, like individual instruments attempting to create music without coordination or harmony.

Research consistently demonstrates social skills' crucial role in virtually every domain of human functioning. In educational settings, students with strong social skills achieve better academic outcomes, experience fewer behavioural problems, and develop healthier peer relationships (Durlak et al., 2011). Teachers with advanced social competencies create more engaging learning environments and experience greater job satisfaction and effectiveness.

The workplace reveals social skills' economic implications with particular clarity. Organisations with emotionally intelligent leadership demonstrate higher employee engagement, reduced turnover, increased innovation, and improved financial performance (Boyatzis & McKee, 2005). Leaders who possess strong social skills create cultures of trust and collaboration that enable teams to achieve extraordinary results while maintaining high levels of job satisfaction and personal wellbeing.

Healthcare environments showcase social skills' life-and-death significance. Physicians with strong communication abilities achieve better patient compliance, experience fewer malpractice claims, and report greater professional satisfaction (Levinson et al., 1997). Nurses who demonstrate empathic communication skills provide more effective patient care and experience lower rates of burnout and compassion fatigue.

Family relationships, too, flourish or founder based on social competencies. Parents with advanced social skills raise children with better emotional regulation, stronger social relationships, and greater resilience in facing life's challenges. Spouses who communicate effectively and manage conflicts constructively report higher relationship satisfaction and greater longevity in their partnerships.

Perhaps most significantly, social skills serve as the foundation for societal progress and democratic governance. Communities with citizens skilled in dialogue, negotiation, and collaborative problem-solving address collective challenges more effectively and maintain social cohesion during times of stress and change. Nations with leaders who demonstrate authentic social competence build stronger international relationships and contribute more effectively to global cooperation.

The ripple effects of social competence extend far beyond immediate relationships. When individuals develop genuine social skills, they become catalysts for positive change that radiates through their networks, organisations, and communities. The teacher who inspires students creates educators for the next generation. The leader who empowers employees develops future leaders. The parent who models emotional intelligence raises children who will build healthier relationships throughout their lives.

## The Alchemy of Authentic Influence

Influence—genuine, lasting, transformative influence—emerges not from power over others but from power with others. It flows not from the ability to command compliance but from the capacity to inspire commitment. This distinction represents one of social skills' most profound insights: that sustainable influence arises from service rather than self-interest, from empowerment rather than control.

Cialdini (2006) identifies six principles of influence that reveal its psychological foundations: reciprocity, commitment and consistency, social proof, authority, liking, and scarcity. Yet when these principles are employed manipulatively—as tools for personal advantage rather than mutual benefit—they create temporary compliance that ultimately breeds resentment and resistance. Authentic influence transcends these tactical approaches by addressing not just people's decision-making processes but their deepest needs for meaning, connection, and contribution.

Consider the difference between transactional and transformational leadership styles. Transactional leaders focus on exchanges—rewards for performance, punishments for failure, clear expectations and consequences. This approach can achieve short-term results but rarely inspires extraordinary effort or loyalty. Transformational leaders, by contrast, inspire others by connecting work to larger purposes, developing individual capabilities, and creating shared visions that elevate everyone involved (Bass & Riggio, 2006).

The transformational approach requires sophisticated social skills: the ability to understand what truly motivates different individuals, to communicate visions that resonate emotionally as well as intellectually, to provide supportive challenge that promotes growth, and to model the values and behaviours one seeks to inspire in others. This form of leadership creates what researchers call "discretionary effort"—the additional energy and creativity that people contribute when they feel genuinely engaged and valued.

Authentic influence also requires what might be termed "emotional courage"—the willingness to be vulnerable, to admit mistakes, to share struggles as well as successes. This transparency creates psychological safety that enables others to bring their full selves to relationships and collaborations. When leaders demonstrate genuine humanity, they give permission for others to do the same, creating environments where innovation, creativity, and authentic connection can flourish.

The neuroscience of influence reveals its basis in mirror neuron systems and emotional contagion processes. When we observe someone expressing genuine passion, commitment, or joy, our brains automatically activate similar neural patterns, creating resonance that can inspire similar feelings and motivations (Hatfield et al., 1994). This suggests that authentic influence works primarily through modelling and emotional transmission rather than logical persuasion alone.

Yet influence carries significant ethical responsibilities. The same social skills that can inspire positive change can also be used to manipulate and exploit others. The difference lies not in technique but in intention and outcome. Ethical influence seeks win-win solutions that benefit all parties involved, respects others' autonomy and dignity, and contributes to collective wellbeing rather than merely personal advantage.

## The Neural Symphony of Social Connection

The human brain's capacity for social connection represents one of evolution's most sophisticated achievements—a complex network of neural systems that enable us to understand others' minds, share their emotions, coordinate group activities, and build the cooperative relationships that have enabled our species' remarkable success.

Central to social competence are mirror neuron systems, first discovered by Rizzolatti and colleagues (1996) in macaque monkeys and later identified in humans. These remarkable cells fire both when we perform actions and when we observe others performing similar actions, creating the neural foundation for imitation, empathy, and social learning. Mirror neurons enable us to understand others' intentions, predict their behaviours, and respond appropriately to social situations.

The superior temporal sulcus plays a crucial role in processing social information, particularly in interpreting others' eye gaze, facial expressions, and body language. This region helps us understand where others are looking, what they might be thinking, and how they might be feeling based on nonverbal cues. Damage to this area can significantly impair social functioning, highlighting its importance for effective interpersonal interaction.

The medial prefrontal cortex enables theory of mind—our capacity to understand that others have beliefs, desires, and intentions that may differ from our own. This region allows us to engage in complex perspective-taking, predict others' behaviours based on their mental states, and adjust our own actions accordingly. The development of theory of mind represents a crucial milestone in children's social development and continues refining throughout life.

Oxytocin and vasopressin, often called the "bonding hormones," facilitate social connection and trust. These neuropeptides are released during positive social interactions—touching, eye contact, shared activities, acts of kindness—and reinforce the neural pathways associated with social bonding (Carter, 2014). They create the biological foundation for attachment, loyalty, and cooperative behaviour that makes complex social relationships possible.

The vagus nerve, connecting the brain to various organ systems, plays a crucial role in social engagement through what researcher Stephen Porges calls the "social engagement system" (Porges, 2011).

When this system is activated, we experience feelings of safety and connection that enable authentic social interaction. When it's suppressed due to stress or threat, we become defensive and less capable of genuine social engagement.

Recent research reveals that social skills training can actually change brain structure and function. Individuals who participate in empathy training show increased gray matter density in regions associated with emotional processing and perspective-taking. Meditation practices focused on loving-kindness increase activation in empathy-related brain networks and enhance prosocial behaviour.

These findings suggest that social competence is not fixed at birth but remains malleable throughout life. The brain's neuroplasticity enables us to continue developing social skills through deliberate practice, mindful attention to interpersonal dynamics, and exposure to diverse social experiences.

## The Architecture of Social Mastery: Core Competencies

Social skills encompass multiple interrelated competencies, each contributing to our overall capacity for effective relationship management. Understanding these components enables targeted development efforts and helps identify areas for growth and refinement.

### The Art of Authentic Listening

Deep listening—the kind that transforms both listener and speaker—represents perhaps the most fundamental social skill. Yet genuine listening has become increasingly rare in our culture of constant stimulation and rapid response. Most conversations involve two people taking turns speaking rather than authentic dialogue where understanding and connection develop progressively.

Active listening involves several interconnected elements that together create space for genuine communication. **Presence** requires bringing full attention to the speaker without mental multitasking or distraction. This means setting aside devices, internal preoccupations, and the urge to formulate responses while others are speaking.

**Empathic attunement** involves sensing not just words but the emotions and meanings beneath them. Skilled listeners notice changes in tone, pace, and energy that reveal feelings not explicitly expressed. They attend to nonverbal communications—body language, facial expressions, breathing patterns—that often convey more information than verbal content.

**Reflective responding** demonstrates understanding while inviting deeper sharing. This might involve paraphrasing what was heard ("It sounds like you're feeling..."), asking clarifying questions ("What was that experience like for you?"), or simply offering supportive presence during emotional moments.

Research reveals active listening's profound effects on both relationships and individual wellbeing. When people feel truly heard and understood, they experience reduced stress, increased self-esteem, and greater willingness to be vulnerable and authentic (Rogers, 1961). For listeners, the practice develops empathy, reduces judgment, and creates deeper connections with others.

## The Craft of Conscious Communication

Effective communication transcends the mere transmission of information to become an art form that bridges differences, builds understanding, and inspires action. Conscious communicators understand that the message received often differs significantly from the message intended, requiring careful attention to both content and context.

**Audience awareness** involves understanding who you're communicating with and adjusting your message accordingly. This includes considering others' backgrounds, values, communication preferences, and current emotional states. The same information might need to be presented very differently to different audiences to achieve understanding and engagement.

**Emotional intelligence in communication** requires recognising and addressing the emotional dimensions of interaction. This means acknowledging others' feelings, managing your own emotional responses, and creating emotional safety that enables authentic dialogue. Emotionally intelligent communicators understand that people must feel heard and respected before they can fully receive new information or perspectives.

**Clarity and precision** involve expressing ideas in ways that minimise misunderstanding while maximising impact. This requires organising thoughts logically, using appropriate language and examples, and checking for understanding rather than assuming successful communication. Clear communicators take responsibility for ensuring their messages are received as intended.

**Timing and context** significantly influence communication effectiveness. The same message delivered at different times or in different settings can produce completely different results. Skilled communicators develop sensitivity to situational factors and choose optimal timing and context for important conversations.

## The Discipline of Constructive Conflict Management

Conflict—the inevitable friction that arises when different perspectives, needs, or interests collide—represents one of social interaction's greatest challenges and opportunities. Most people approach conflict with fight, flight, or freeze responses that escalate tensions rather than resolving underlying issues. Emotionally intelligent conflict management transforms these destructive patterns into opportunities for deeper understanding and stronger relationships.

**Early intervention** involves recognising and addressing tensions before they escalate into destructive conflicts. This requires sensitivity to subtle signs of disagreement or dissatisfaction and the courage to initiate difficult conversations rather than hoping problems will resolve themselves.

**Interest-based negotiation** focuses on underlying needs rather than stated positions (Fisher & Ury, 1991). When people argue about positions—what they want—conflicts often become zero-sum battles where one person's gain requires another's loss. When conflicts focus on interests—why people want what they want—creative solutions often emerge that address everyone's core needs.

**Emotional regulation during conflict** requires managing one's own emotional responses while remaining empathically connected to others' experiences. This involves recognising when emotions are escalating, taking breaks when necessary, and returning to dialogue with renewed perspective and commitment to resolution.

**Collaborative problem-solving** transforms conflicts from adversarial battles into joint efforts to find mutually beneficial solutions. This requires shifting from "me versus you" thinking to "us versus the problem" approaches that preserve relationships while addressing substantive issues.

## The Foundation of Trust and Rapport Building

Trust—the invisible foundation upon which all meaningful relationships rest—cannot be demanded or manufactured but must be earned through consistent, authentic action over time. Trust building requires aligning words with actions, demonstrating genuine care for others' wellbeing, and maintaining reliability even when it requires personal sacrifice.

**Consistency** involves demonstrating predictable behaviour patterns that others can rely upon. This doesn't mean rigidity but rather dependable integrity—doing what you say you'll do, showing up when expected, and maintaining your values under pressure. Inconsistency erodes trust more quickly than almost any other factor.

**Vulnerability and authenticity** paradoxically build trust by demonstrating humanity and fallibility. When leaders admit mistakes, share struggles, and acknowledge limitations, they create psychological safety that enables others to be equally authentic. This mutual vulnerability creates bonds stronger than those based purely on competence or authority.

**Active concern for others' wellbeing** transforms relationships from transactional exchanges to genuine partnerships. This involves remembering personal details, inquiring about others' lives and challenges, and offering support during difficult times. When people feel genuinely cared for, they become more willing to extend trust and loyalty.

**Competence and reliability** provide the practical foundation for trust in professional contexts. While emotional connection matters, trust also requires confidence in others' abilities to deliver results and fulfill commitments. Building trust requires demonstrating both heart and competence.

## The Practice of Inspirational Leadership

Leadership—authentic leadership that inspires rather than coerces—emerges not from position or authority but from the ability to articulate compelling visions, develop others' capabilities, and model the qualities one seeks to inspire. This form of leadership creates followership through attraction rather than obligation.

**Vision communication** involves articulating futures that resonate emotionally as well as intellectually. Inspiring leaders help others see not just what needs to be done but why it matters, how it connects to larger purposes, and what role each person plays in creating positive outcomes. They translate abstract goals into concrete images that motivate action.

**Individual development** transforms leadership from directing others to developing their capabilities. This requires understanding each person's strengths, growth areas, and aspirations, then providing opportunities, challenges, and support that enable their flourishing. Leaders who develop others create loyalty and engagement that far exceeds what authority alone can achieve.

**Modelling and integrity** demonstrate that leaders hold themselves to the same standards they expect from others. This involves "walking the talk"—embodying the values, behaviours, and commitment levels one seeks to inspire. Authentic leaders understand that their actions speak louder than their words and that modelling creates influence more powerfully than preaching.

**Empowerment and delegation** involve sharing power and responsibility rather than hoarding them. This requires trusting others with important decisions, providing support while allowing autonomy, and celebrating others' successes rather than claiming credit. Empowering leaders create cultures where initiative and innovation flourish.

## The Laboratory of Social Excellence: Practical Development Strategies

Developing sophisticated social skills requires more than theoretical understanding; it demands deliberate practice, mindful attention to interpersonal dynamics, and willingness to learn from both successes and failures. The following strategies provide pathways for continuous growth in social competence.

## The Practice of Mindful Social Awareness

Social mindfulness involves bringing conscious attention to interpersonal dynamics as they unfold, noticing both your own internal responses and others' verbal and nonverbal communications. This awareness enables real-time adjustments that improve interaction quality and outcomes.

**Internal monitoring** requires developing sensitivity to your own emotional states, triggers, and reaction patterns during social interactions. This involves noticing when you become defensive, judgmental, or disconnected, then making conscious choices about how to respond rather than reacting automatically.

**External observation** involves attending carefully to others' communications, both verbal and nonverbal. This includes noticing changes in tone, energy, body language, and engagement levels that might indicate emotions or needs not directly expressed. Skilled observers pick up subtle cues that enable more effective responses.

**Dynamic adjustment** involves modifying your communication style, energy level, and approach based on real-time feedback from social situations. This might mean slowing down when others seem overwhelmed, increasing energy when groups feel flat, or shifting topics when conversations become unproductive.

## The Discipline of Feedback Integration

Feedback—both giving and receiving it effectively—accelerates social skill development by providing information about impact that might otherwise remain hidden. Yet most people struggle with feedback due to fear of conflict, concerns about others' reactions, or difficulty receiving criticism without defensiveness.

**Seeking feedback actively** involves regularly asking others about your communication effectiveness, leadership impact, and relationship management skills. This requires overcoming ego defensiveness and creating safety for others to share honest observations. Questions might include: "How did that conversation feel for you?" or "What could I do differently to be more effective?"

**Receiving feedback gracefully** requires managing emotional reactions while extracting useful information for growth. This involves listening without defensiveness, asking clarifying questions, and expressing appreciation for others' willingness to share observations. The goal is learning rather than defending or justifying current approaches.

**Giving feedback skilfully** involves sharing observations in ways that promote growth rather than defensiveness. This requires focusing on specific behaviours rather than character judgments, sharing impact rather than assumptions about intent, and offering suggestions for improvement rather than just criticism.

## The Art of Social Experimentation

Social skill development benefits from conscious experimentation with new approaches, communication styles, and relationship strategies. This involves trying new behaviours in safe contexts, observing results, and refining approaches based on outcomes and feedback.

**Communication style flexibility** might involve experimenting with different levels of directness, emotional expression, or formal versus informal approaches. Notice how different styles affect others' responses and relationship dynamics.

**Conflict approach variations** could include trying interest-based negotiation, collaborative problem-solving, or empathic listening during disagreements. Observe which approaches produce better outcomes and stronger relationships.

**Leadership style exploration** might involve experimenting with different levels of direction versus empowerment, task focus versus relationship focus, or individual versus team-oriented approaches.

Notice which styles bring out the best in different people and situations.

### The Foundation of Self-Care and Emotional Management

Social skills require significant emotional energy and can be depleted through overuse or stressful interactions. Maintaining social effectiveness requires attention to your own emotional wellbeing and energy management.

**Emotional regulation practices** help maintain equilibrium during challenging social situations. This might include breathing techniques, brief mindfulness practices, or cognitive reframing strategies that enable remaining centred under pressure.

**Energy management** involves recognising your social energy patterns and planning accordingly. Some people are energised by social interaction while others find it draining. Understanding your patterns enables better planning and self-care.

**Boundary setting** protects your emotional wellbeing while maintaining relationship effectiveness. This might involve limiting exposure to particularly difficult people, taking breaks during intense social periods, or saying no to commitments that would compromise your ability to show up authentically.

## Exemplars of Heart-Centred Leadership

Throughout history, certain leaders have demonstrated the transformative power of combining social competence with authentic care for others' wellbeing. These examples provide models for how social skills can be employed in service of higher purposes.

## Jacinda Ardern: Empathy in Political Leadership

New Zealand's former Prime Minister Jacinda Ardern redefined political leadership by demonstrating that strength and compassion could coexist in governance. Her response to national tragedies—the Christchurch shooting, the White Island volcanic eruption, the COVID-19 pandemic—exemplified emotionally intelligent leadership that prioritised human welfare over political calculation.

Ardern's social skills manifested in several distinctive ways. Her **communication style** combined clarity with empathy, delivering difficult messages with genuine concern for their impact on citizens' lives. Rather than hiding behind political rhetoric, she spoke directly and authentically about challenges facing the nation.

Her **crisis leadership** demonstrated how emotional intelligence enhances rather than undermines effective decision-making. During the COVID-19 pandemic, Ardern balanced public health requirements with economic concerns while maintaining consistent, compassionate communication that helped citizens understand and comply with necessary restrictions.

**Inclusive governance** characterised Ardern's approach to leadership, actively seeking diverse perspectives and creating space for marginalised voices in policy discussions. Her coalition government demonstrated how leaders with strong social skills can build bridges across ideological differences to achieve shared goals.

Ardern's resignation speech revealed perhaps her greatest social skill—self-awareness about her own limitations and the courage to step aside when she could no longer serve effectively. This demonstrated the kind of ego-transcendent leadership that puts collective wellbeing ahead of personal ambition.

## Mahatma Gandhi: The Power of Nonviolent Influence

Gandhi's transformation of Indian independence movements from violent resistance to nonviolent civil disobedience demonstrates social skills' power to create systemic change through moral influence rather than physical force. His approach required a sophisticated understanding of human psychology, cultural dynamics, and the mechanics of social transformation.

**Empathic understanding** enabled Gandhi to recognise the fears and concerns of both British colonisers and Indian citizens, crafting strategies that addressed underlying needs rather than simply opposing positions. He understood that lasting change required transformation of hearts and minds, not just political structures.

**Moral authority** emerged from Gandhi's alignment of personal behaviour with his stated values. His willingness to endure suffering, live simply, and sacrifice personally for his principles created the credibility necessary for sustained influence. People followed him because his life embodied his message.

**Strategic communication** involved using symbols, stories, and actions that resonated across cultural and educational boundaries. The salt march, the spinning wheel, fasting—these symbolic acts communicated complex political messages in ways that illiterate peasants and educated professionals could both understand and support.

**Inclusive mobilisation** brought together diverse groups—Hindus and Muslims, urban and rural populations, different castes and classes—around shared goals of independence and dignity. Gandhi's social skills enabled him to build coalitions that transcended traditional divisions and created unified movements for change.

## Fred Rogers: Transformative Communication with

### Children

Fred Rogers' television programme "Mister Rogers' Neighbourhood" demonstrated how authentic communication could nurture children's emotional development and social competence. His approach provides a model for how social skills can be employed to create safe spaces where vulnerability and growth can flourish.

**Authentic presence** characterised every interaction Rogers had with children. He spoke to them as fully human beings worthy of respect and understanding, never talking down or oversimplifying complex emotions. This authentic regard created trust that enabled children to share their deepest concerns and fears.

**Emotional validation** involved acknowledging children's feelings without judgment or immediate attempts to fix or change them. Rogers understood that being heard and accepted represented the first step toward emotional growth and resilience.

**Clear boundaries with warmth** demonstrated how limits could be set with love rather than punishment. Rogers consistently maintained appropriate boundaries while communicating genuine care and acceptance for each child as an individual.

**Hope and resilience messaging** helped children understand that difficulties were temporary and that they possessed inner resources for coping with challenges. Rather than minimising problems, Rogers helped children develop confidence in their ability to grow through difficulties.

## The Ripple Effects of Social Mastery: Creating Positive Change

When individuals develop genuine social competence, the effects extend far beyond personal success to create positive change that ripples through relationships, organisations, communities, and cultures. Understanding these ripple effects reveals social skills' profound importance for collective human flourishing.

## Personal Relationships and Family Systems

Individuals with advanced social skills create family environments characterised by emotional safety, open communication, and mutual support. These healthy family dynamics produce children who develop stronger emotional intelligence, better social relationships, and greater resilience throughout their lives.

**Generational healing** occurs when individuals use their social skills to break cycles of dysfunction, abuse, or emotional neglect that may have characterised their family histories. By learning healthier communication patterns and relationship skills, they create new family legacies that benefit future generations.

**Community building** extends beyond family to include friends, neighbours, and broader social networks. Socially skilled individuals often become connectors who bring people together, facilitate friendships, and create supportive communities that enhance everyone's quality of life.

## Organisational Culture and Performance

Leaders with exceptional social skills create organisational cultures that enable human potential to flourish while achieving extraordinary results. These cultures demonstrate how social competence directly impacts organisational effectiveness and sustainability. These leaders understand that sustainable success emerges from engaged, empowered employees rather than fearful, compliant workers.

**Employee engagement** increases dramatically when workers feel understood, valued, and empowered by their leaders. Research consistently shows that engaged employees demonstrate higher productivity, creativity, and loyalty while experiencing better physical and mental health outcomes.

**Psychological safety** enables innovation and creativity by creating environments where people feel safe to take risks, share ideas, and admit mistakes without fear of punishment or ridicule (Edmondson, 1999). Leaders with strong social skills foster this safety through their own vulnerability, consistent support for learning, and responses to failure that focus on growth rather than blame.

**Innovation and creativity** flourish in psychologically safe environments where people feel free to share ideas, take risks, and learn from failures. Leaders with strong social skills create these conditions through their responses to new ideas, handling of mistakes, and support for experimentation.

**Talent retention and development** improve significantly in organisations with emotionally intelligent leadership. People want to work for leaders who see their potential, provide growth opportunities, and create positive work environments where they can thrive personally and professionally. Talent development transforms organisations from places where people work to places where people grow. Leaders with advanced social skills recognise and nurture others' potential, providing opportunities, feedback, and support that enable career advancement and personal fulfilment.

**Collaborative decision-making** leverages diverse perspectives and expertise to achieve better outcomes than any individual could accomplish alone. This requires social skills for managing group dynamics, facilitating productive discussions, and building consensus around shared goals.

## Community Building

Social skills enable the creation of communities characterised by mutual support, shared purpose, and collective resilience. These communities demonstrate how individual social competence contributes to broader social capital and civic engagement.

**Bridge-building** across differences requires social skills for finding common ground among diverse populations, managing conflicts constructively, and creating inclusive environments where all voices are heard and valued.

**Volunteer mobilisation** depends on leaders who can inspire others to contribute time and energy to collective causes. This requires understanding what motivates different people and communicating visions that resonate with diverse audiences.

**Crisis response coordination** reveals social skills' practical importance during emergencies when communities must work together rapidly and effectively. Leaders with strong social competence can organise resources, coordinate efforts, and maintain morale during difficult times.

## Cultural Evolution

Throughout history, individuals with exceptional social skills have served as catalysts for cultural transformation, challenging existing norms and inspiring new ways of thinking about human relationships and social organisation.

**Social movement leadership** requires ability to articulate compelling visions, build coalitions across diverse groups, and sustain momentum over the extended periods necessary for systemic change. Social movements succeed when they combine moral clarity with sophisticated understanding of human motivation and group dynamics.

**Institution building** involves creating new organisations, policies, and social structures that embody more enlightened approaches to human relationship and collective action. This requires social skills for engaging diverse stakeholders, building consensus around shared goals, and maintaining organisational cultures that reflect desired values.

**Institutional reform** often depends on leaders who can work within existing systems while advocating for necessary changes. This requires political skill, relationship building, and the ability to find win-win solutions that address reform needs while minimising resistance.

**Bridge building** across racial, religious, political, and cultural divides requires exceptional social skills for finding common ground, managing difficult conversations, and creating relationships that transcend traditional boundaries. These bridge-builders often become trusted voices who can facilitate dialogue between groups in conflict.

**Intergenerational wisdom transmission** involves passing knowledge, values, and skills from older to younger generations in ways that inspire rather than impose. This requires understanding how different generations communicate and learn most effectively.

## The Shadow Side: When Social Skills Go Astray

Like any powerful capacity, social skills can be distorted or misused in ways that harm rather than help human relationships and social functioning. Understanding these shadow aspects helps prevent their emergence and enables more ethical application of social competencies.

### Manipulation Versus Influence

The line between authentic influence and manipulative control can be subtle yet crucial. Both involve understanding human psychology and using that understanding to shape others' behaviour. The difference lies in intention, process, and outcome.

**Manipulative approaches** prioritise the influencer's benefit over others' wellbeing, use deception or coercion to achieve compliance, and create relationships based on exploitation rather than mutual benefit. Manipulators may possess sophisticated social skills but employ them without ethical consideration for others' autonomy and dignity.

**Authentic influence** seeks win-win outcomes that benefit all parties, respects others' right to make independent decisions, and builds relationships based on trust and mutual respect. Authentic influencers use their social skills to create value for others while achieving their own legitimate goals.

The key difference often lies in transparency and reciprocity. Authentic influencers are willing to explain their intentions and methods, while manipulators rely on deception and hidden agendas. Ethical influence creates relationships that strengthen over time, while manipulation typically produces short-term compliance followed by resentment and resistance.

## Charismatic Leadership Versus Authentic Leadership

Charismatic leaders possess exceptional social skills that enable them to inspire strong emotional responses and devoted followership. Yet charisma can serve either constructive or destructive purposes, depending on the leader's character and intentions.

**Destructive charismatic leaders** use their social skills to serve their own ego needs and power drives rather than followers' or organisations' best interests. They may create cultures of dependency where followers lose their own judgment and agency. History provides numerous examples of charismatic leaders who used their influence to promote harmful ideologies or personal aggrandisement.

**Authentic charismatic leaders** employ their social skills to serve purposes larger than themselves, develop others' capabilities rather than creating dependency, and remain accountable to ethical principles and collective wellbeing. They use their influence to empower rather than control others.

The difference often becomes apparent in how leaders respond to criticism, share credit for successes, handle failures, and treat those with less power. Authentic leaders demonstrate humility, accountability, and genuine concern for others' growth and wellbeing.

## Social Skill Deficits and Their Consequences

While much attention focuses on developing social skills, it's equally important to understand the consequences of social skill deficits and how they can be addressed.

**Communication difficulties** can create persistent misunderstandings, conflict escalation, and relationship breakdown. Individuals who struggle with clear expression or empathic listening often experience frustration and isolation that compounds their social challenges.

**Conflict avoidance** may seem like a social skill but often reflects inability to manage disagreement constructively. People who avoid necessary conflicts often allow problems to escalate until they become much more difficult to resolve.

**Boundary issues** can manifest as either excessive rigidity that prevents intimacy or inadequate boundaries that lead to emotional overwhelm and exploitation. Both extremes reflect underdeveloped social skills that require targeted attention and practice.

**Cultural insensitivity** in our increasingly diverse world can severely limit social effectiveness and create unintended harm. Developing cultural competence represents an essential component of modern social skill development.

# The Future of Social Connection

As we navigate a rapidly changing world characterised by technological advancement, global interconnection, and social transformation, social skills face both unprecedented challenges and remarkable opportunities. Understanding these trends helps prepare for the social competencies needed in tomorrow's world.

## Digital Communication and Social Skills

Technology continues reshaping how humans connect and communicate, creating both opportunities for broader connection and challenges for deep relationship building.

**Digital literacy** increasingly includes not just technical skills but emotional intelligence applied to online interactions. This involves understanding how digital communication affects relationship dynamics, managing the emotional impacts of social media, and maintaining authentic connection through technological mediation.

**Hybrid communication competence** requires facility with both face-to-face and digital interaction, understanding when different modalities are most appropriate, and seamlessly transitioning between them. Future social competence will require mastery of multiple communication channels and platforms.

**Virtual relationship building** presents unique challenges and opportunities as remote work, online education, and digital social interaction become increasingly common. Developing trust, empathy, and collaboration through screens requires adapted social skills that many are still learning to navigate.

## Global Social Competence

Our interconnected world requires social skills that transcend cultural, linguistic, and national boundaries while respecting local customs and values.

**Cultural intelligence** involves understanding how cultural backgrounds shape communication styles, relationship patterns, and decision-making processes. This requires both knowledge about different cultures and flexibility in adapting one's own communication style to work effectively across cultural boundaries.

**Language sensitivity** includes not just multilingual capability but understanding how language shapes thought and relationship patterns. Even within shared languages, regional differences, generational variations, and professional vocabularies can create communication barriers that require social skill to navigate.

**Global citizenship** requires social skills for engaging constructively with global challenges that require international cooperation. This includes ability to find common ground across national interests, communicate effectively with diverse stakeholders, and build coalitions for addressing shared problems.

## Intergenerational Social Dynamics

Different generations bring distinct communication preferences, technology usage patterns, and social values that require adaptive social competence to bridge effectively.

**Generational communication differences** reflect varying experiences with technology, social change, and cultural evolution. Baby Boomers may prefer face-to-face or phone communication, while Generation Z gravitates toward text-based digital platforms. Effective social skills require understanding and adapting to these preferences rather than imposing one's own communication style.

**Value system navigation** involves recognising how different generations prioritise work-life balance, authority relationships, social justice issues, and environmental concerns. Social competence requires finding shared values while respecting generational differences in priorities and approaches.

**Mentorship and reverse-mentorship dynamics** require social skills for learning from both older and younger colleagues. Traditional mentorship involves older individuals sharing wisdom with younger ones, while reverse mentorship enables younger people to share technological expertise and contemporary perspectives with older colleagues.

**Knowledge transfer facilitation** becomes crucial as experienced workers retire and new generations enter the workforce. This requires social skills for creating learning environments where tacit knowledge can be shared effectively across generational boundaries.

## The Personal Journey: Developing Your Social Mastery

The development of sophisticated social skills represents a lifelong journey of growth, reflection, and practice. Unlike technical skills that can be mastered through study and repetition, social competence requires ongoing refinement as we encounter new relationships, contexts, and challenges throughout life.

### Self-Assessment and Awareness Building

The foundation of social skill development lies in honest self-assessment of current competencies and growth areas. This requires the courage to examine both strengths and limitations without defensiveness or harsh self-judgment.

**360-degree feedback** involves gathering input from supervisors, peers, direct reports, family members, and friends about your social effectiveness. This comprehensive perspective reveals blind spots and patterns that might not be apparent from self-reflection alone. Questions might explore communication clarity, listening effectiveness, conflict management skills, and leadership impact.

**Social situation analysis** involves reflecting on specific interpersonal interactions to identify what worked well and what could be improved. This might include examining successful collaborations to understand contributing factors or analysing difficult conversations to identify alternative approaches that might have produced better outcomes.

**Emotional pattern recognition** requires developing awareness of your typical emotional responses in social situations. Do you become defensive when criticised? Do you withdraw during conflicts? Do you dominate conversations when nervous? Understanding these patterns enables conscious choice rather than automatic reaction.

**Values clarification** helps ensure that social skills serve authentic purposes rather than mere social manipulation. What do you hope to achieve through improved social competence? How do you want others to feel after interacting with you? What kind of relationships and communities do you want to create?

## Skill-Building Through Deliberate Practice

Social skills improve through intentional practice rather than passive experience. This requires identifying specific competencies to develop and creating opportunities for focused skill building.

**Communication experiments** might involve trying new approaches to difficult conversations, practicing different levels of directness or emotional expression, or experimenting with various listening techniques. The key is conscious experimentation followed by reflection on outcomes and refinement of approaches.

**Role-playing and simulation** provide safe environments for practicing challenging social situations. This might include rehearsing difficult conversations with trusted friends, participating in leadership development programmes that include interpersonal skill building, or joining groups like Toastmasters that focus on communication effectiveness.

**Mentorship and coaching** accelerate social skill development by providing expert guidance and feedback. This might involve working with a professional coach who specialises in interpersonal effectiveness, finding mentors who demonstrate exceptional social competence, or participating in peer coaching relationships that provide mutual support and accountability.

**Cross-cultural exposure** develops cultural intelligence and communication flexibility by providing opportunities to interact with people from different backgrounds. This might include travel, volunteering with diverse populations, participating in interfaith or multicultural organisations, or simply making conscious efforts to engage with people who differ from you in age, race, religion, or socioeconomic background.

## Integration and Sustainable Growth

The ultimate goal of social skill development is integration—making empathic communication, authentic leadership, and collaborative relationship building natural expressions of who you are rather than techniques you consciously employ.

**Regular reflection practices** help consolidate learning and maintain awareness of social dynamics. This might include journaling about interpersonal experiences, discussing relationship challenges with trusted friends or counsellors, or participating in personal growth groups that focus on interpersonal effectiveness.

**Continuous learning mindset** recognises that social competence requires ongoing development as we encounter new people, contexts, and challenges throughout life. This involves remaining curious about others' perspectives, seeking feedback on social effectiveness, and staying open to new approaches and insights.

**Service orientation** ensures that developing social skills serves purposes larger than personal advancement. When social competence is employed in service of others' wellbeing and collective flourishing, it becomes a source of meaning and fulfilment rather than merely instrumental success.

**Authentic expression** involves using social skills to reveal rather than hide your true self. The most powerful social competence emerges when individuals develop the confidence to be genuinely themselves while remaining sensitively attuned to others' needs and perspectives.

## The Transformation of Leadership: From Authority to Authenticity

The evolution of leadership thinking over the past century reveals a fundamental shift from authority-based to relationship-based approaches. This transformation reflects a growing understanding of human motivation, organisational dynamics, and the social skills required for sustainable influence.

### The Old Paradigm: Command and Control

Traditional leadership models emphasised hierarchy, control, and compliance. Leaders were expected to have all the answers, make decisions independently, and ensure subordinate compliance through rewards and punishments. This approach worked reasonably well in stable, predictable environments with routine tasks and homogeneous workforces.

Yet command-and-control leadership proved increasingly ineffective as work became more complex, creative, and collaborative. Knowledge workers require autonomy and meaning rather than merely direction and supervision. Global organisations need local adaptation rather than rigid standardisation. Innovation demands psychological safety rather than fearful compliance.

The limitations of authoritarian leadership became particularly apparent during times of rapid change or crisis. Leaders who relied primarily on position power found themselves unable to inspire the extraordinary effort, creativity, and resilience required to navigate unprecedented challenges successfully.

## The New Paradigm: Authentic and Empowering Leadership

Contemporary leadership models emphasise relationship building, empowerment, and shared purpose. Modern leaders serve as coaches, facilitators, and vision communicators rather than directors and controllers. This approach requires sophisticated social skills for building trust, inspiring commitment, and coordinating collective action.

**Servant leadership**, popularised by Robert Greenleaf (1977), positions leaders as servants first—individuals who lead because they want to serve others rather than because they desire power or status. This approach requires genuine humility, authentic care for others' development, and willingness to share power rather than hoarding it.

**Transformational leadership** focuses on inspiring others to transcend self-interest for collective purposes (Burns, 1978). Transformational leaders articulate compelling visions, provide individual consideration for followers' needs, offer intellectual stimulation that challenges assumptions, and model the values they seek to inspire.

**Authentic leadership** emphasises self-awareness, relational transparency, balanced processing of information, and moral perspective (Avolio & Gardner, 2005). Authentic leaders understand their own values, strengths, and limitations; they build relationships based on trust and openness; they seek diverse input before making decisions; and they act according to ethical principles rather than mere expedience.

**Distributed leadership** recognises that leadership can emerge from anywhere in organisations and communities rather than being confined to formal positions. This approach requires social skills for recognising others' leadership potential, creating opportunities for leadership development, and coordinating multiple leaders working toward shared goals.

## The Skills of Heart-Centred Leadership

Leading with heart requires specific social competencies that enable authentic connection while achieving collective purposes. These skills differ significantly from traditional management techniques yet prove more effective for inspiring sustained high performance and organisational health.

**Emotional attunement** involves recognising and responding appropriately to others' emotional states, both individually and collectively. Heart-centred leaders notice when team energy is flagging, when individuals are struggling with personal challenges, or when group dynamics are becoming dysfunctional. They respond with appropriate support, encouragement, or intervention.

**Vision communication that inspires** goes beyond strategic planning to create shared meaning and purpose. This requires understanding what motivates different people and connecting organisational goals to individual values and aspirations. Inspiring leaders help others see how their work contributes to something meaningful and worthwhile.

**Difficult conversation mastery** enables leaders to address performance issues, conflicts, and organisational challenges directly yet compassionately. This requires courage to initiate difficult discussions, skill to navigate emotional reactions, and wisdom to find solutions that address problems while preserving relationships and dignity.

**Culture creation and maintenance** involves consciously shaping organisational environments that bring out the best in people. This requires understanding how values, norms, rituals, and practices influence behaviour, then deliberately creating cultures that support both individual flourishing and collective success.

**Change leadership** requires special social skills for helping people navigate uncertainty, loss, and transformation. Effective change leaders acknowledge the emotional dimensions of change, provide stability amid uncertainty, and help people find meaning and opportunity within disruption.

## The Global Imperative: Social Skills for Collective Challenges

The challenges facing humanity in the 21st century—climate change, inequality, technological disruption, political polarisation—require unprecedented levels of cooperation across traditional boundaries. These collective challenges can only be addressed through the kind of collaborative action that emerges from sophisticated social competence applied at scale.

### Climate Change and Environmental Stewardship

Addressing climate change requires coordinated action across nations, industries, and communities with different interests, capabilities, and priorities. This coordination depends on social skills for building trust, finding common ground, and inspiring collective action despite competing short-term interests.

**Stakeholder engagement** requires the ability to communicate with diverse audiences—scientists, policymakers, business leaders, community members—in ways that resonate with their values and concerns. Environmental leaders must translate complex scientific information into compelling narratives that motivate action across different populations.

**Negotiation and compromise** become essential for crafting policies and agreements that address environmental needs while respecting economic and social constraints. This requires understanding different parties' underlying interests and finding creative solutions that meet everyone's core needs.

**Behaviour change facilitation** involves understanding what motivates individuals and communities to adopt more sustainable practices. This requires insights into human psychology, social influence processes, and cultural change dynamics.

## Social Justice and Inequality

Addressing persistent inequalities requires social skills for building bridges across racial, economic, and cultural divides while advocating for necessary systemic changes.

**Cross-cultural dialogue** enables productive conversations across differences that build understanding rather than defensiveness. This requires skills for managing difficult emotions, acknowledging different perspectives, and finding shared values despite different experiences.

**Advocacy and activism** require ability to communicate injustices compellingly while building coalitions for change. Effective advocates understand how to engage both hearts and minds, mobilise diverse constituencies, and maintain momentum over extended periods required for systemic change.

**Healing and reconciliation** processes require sophisticated social skills for addressing historical trauma, building trust across groups that have experienced conflict, and creating new relationships based on mutual respect and understanding.

### Technology and Human Connection

As artificial intelligence and automation reshape work and society, social skills become increasingly important for maintaining human connection and ensuring technology serves human flourishing rather than replacing human relationships.

**Human-AI collaboration** requires understanding how to work effectively with artificial intelligence systems while maintaining the uniquely human capacities for empathy, creativity, and ethical reasoning that technology cannot replicate.

**Digital wisdom** involves using technology to enhance rather than replace authentic human connection. This includes understanding when face-to-face interaction is necessary, how to maintain empathy through digital mediums, and how to protect human relationships from technological disruption.

**Ethical technology leadership** requires social skills for engaging diverse stakeholders in conversations about how technology should be developed and deployed to benefit humanity while minimising harmful consequences.

## Conclusion: The Call to Social Leadership

As we stand at the threshold of unprecedented global challenges and opportunities, the development of social skills emerges not as an optional enhancement but as a moral imperative. The future belongs to individuals and societies capable of creating authentic connections across differences, building trust in the face of uncertainty, and inspiring collaborative action toward shared goals.

The journey toward social mastery requires everything we have to offer: our willingness to see ourselves clearly, our courage to remain open when circumstances invite defensiveness, our commitment to serve purposes larger than personal advancement, and our faith that genuine human connection can transcend even the most daunting obstacles.

This journey transforms not only our relationships but our very understanding of what it means to be human in relationship with others. We discover that our individual flourishing depends inextricably on collective wellbeing, that our personal growth serves purposes beyond self-improvement, and that our capacity for authentic connection represents perhaps our species' greatest evolutionary achievement.

The invitation before us is profound: to develop social skills not as techniques for personal advantage but as expressions of our deepest humanity, not as strategies for getting what we want but as pathways for creating what the world needs, not as tools for individual success but as gifts for collective healing and transformation.

The world awaits leaders who can inspire rather than coerce, who can build bridges rather than walls, who can create trust rather than fear, who can foster hope rather than despair. These leaders emerge not from positions of authority but from depths of authentic care for human flourishing. They lead not because they seek power but because they cannot bear to see human potential wasted or human dignity diminished.

Your social skills—developed with consciousness, employed with integrity, and offered in service of collective wellbeing—represent your contribution to this great work of creating a more connected, compassionate, and collaborative world. The choice to undertake this development seriously represents both personal commitment and social responsibility.

In our next chapter, we will explore how these social competencies become even more crucial during times of crisis and change, when emotional intelligence provides the foundation for resilience, adaptation, and renewed hope in the face of uncertainty and challenge.

The future calls for leaders with heart—individuals who understand that true strength lies not in domination but in connection, not in having all the answers but in asking better questions, not in avoiding difficulty but in facing it together with courage, compassion, and unwavering commitment to human dignity and flourishing.

---

## References


Avolio, B. J., & Gardner, W. L. (2005). Authentic leadership development: Getting to the root of positive forms of leadership. *The Leadership Quarterly*, 16(3), 315-338.

Bar-On, R. (2006). The Bar-On model of emotional-social intelligence (ESI). *Psicothema*, 18, 13-25.

Baron-Cohen, S. (2011). *The Science of Evil: On Empathy and the Origins of Cruelty*. Basic Books.

Bass, B. M., & Riggio, R. E. (2006). *Transformational Leadership* (2nd ed.). Lawrence Erlbaum Associates.

Boyatzis, R., & McKee, A. (2005). *Resonant Leadership: Renewing Yourself and Connecting with Others Through Mindfulness, Hope, and Compassion*. Harvard Business Review Press.

Burns, J. M. (1978). *Leadership*. Harper & Row.

Carter, C. S. (2014). Oxytocin pathways and the evolution of human behaviour. *Annual Review of Psychology*, 65, 17-39.

Cialdini, R. B. (2006). *Influence: The Psychology of Persuasion* (Revised ed.). Harper Business.

Durlak, J. A., Weissberg, R. P., Dymnicki, A. B., Taylor, R. D., & Schellinger, K. B. (2011). The impact of enhancing students' social and emotional learning: A meta-analysis of school-based universal interventions. *Child Development*, 82(1), 405-432.

Edmondson, A. (1999). Psychological safety and learning behaviour in work teams. *Administrative Science Quarterly*, 44(2), 350-383.

Fisher, R., & Ury, W. (1991). *Getting to Yes: Negotiating Agreement Without Giving In*. Penguin Books.

Goleman, D. (2006). *Emotional Intelligence: Why It Matters More Than IQ*. Bantam Books.

Greenleaf, R. K. (1977). *Servant Leadership: A Journey into the Nature of Legitimate Power and Greatness*. Paulist Press.

Hatfield, E., Cacioppo, J. T., & Rapson, R. L. (1994). *Emotional Contagion*. Cambridge University Press.

Levinson, W., Roter, D. L., Mullooly, J. P., Dull, V. T., & Frankel, R. M. (1997). Physician-patient communication: The relationship with malpractice claims among primary care physicians and surgeons. *JAMA*, 277(7), 553-559.

Porges, S. W. (2011). *The Polyvagal Theory: Neurophysiological Foundations of Emotions, Attachment, Communication, and Self-regulation*. W. W. Norton & Company.

Putnam, R. D. (2000). *Bowling Alone: The Collapse and Revival of American Community*. Simon & Schuster.

Rizzolatti, G., Fadiga, L., Gallese, V., & Fogassi, L. (1996). Premotor cortex and the recognition of motor actions. *Cognitive Brain Research*, 3(2), 131-141.

Rogers, C. R. (1961). *On Becoming a Person: A Therapist's View of Psychotherapy*. Houghton Mifflin.

Thorndike, E. L. (1920). Intelligence and its uses. *Harper's Magazine*, 140, 227-235.

# Chapter 12: Emotional Intelligence in Times of Crisis and Change

## Introduction: The Crucible of Human Resilience

Life, in its relentless choreography of unpredictability, presents us with moments that shatter the comfortable illusions of stability we so desperately construct. These moments—sudden, jarring, transformative—arrive like lightning strikes across the landscape of our existence, illuminating truths we had previously hidden from ourselves in the shadows of routine and complacency. From the intimate devastation of personal upheavals—job loss that strips away identity, illness that confronts mortality, relationship breakdowns that leave us questioning the very nature of love—to the sweeping cataclysms of global crises such as pandemics that reshape civilisation, political instability that undermines social fabric, and economic downturns that expose systemic vulnerabilities, change and crisis represent the fundamental constants in an otherwise variable human experience (Goleman, 2006).

Yet here lies a paradox worthy of profound contemplation: while our technological prowess has reached unprecedented heights, while our analytical capabilities have been honed to razor-sharp precision, and while our access to information has expanded exponentially, we find ourselves paradoxically ill-equipped to navigate the turbulent waters of emotional upheaval that crisis inevitably brings. Technical skills, those measurable competencies we celebrate in boardrooms and academic institutions, crumble like ancient parchment when confronted with the raw, primal forces of human emotion unleashed during times of crisis (Bar-On, 2006).

It is in these crucible moments that emotional intelligence—that mysterious alchemy of self-awareness, empathy, and social grace—emerges not merely as a desirable trait but as the fundamental architecture upon which resilience, adaptability, authentic leadership, and meaningful recovery are constructed. This chapter ventures into the complex terrain where human emotion intersects with crisis, where vulnerability becomes strength, and where the capacity to understand and navigate our inner emotional landscape determines not merely survival, but the possibility of transformation and growth (Mayer & Salovey, 1997).

## The Existential Nature of Crisis and the Architecture of Disruption

Crisis, etymologically derived from the Greek word 'krisis' meaning decision or judgment, represents far more than mere disruption—it constitutes a fundamental rupture in the narrative coherence of existence. When crisis strikes, it doesn't simply interrupt our daily routines; it demolishes the very foundational assumptions upon which we have constructed our understanding of reality, identity, and future possibility (Caplan, 1964). The comfortable predictability that allows us to function with automaticity suddenly evaporates, leaving us suspended in a liminal space where past certainties no longer apply and future outcomes remain shrouded in uncertainty.

Consider the profound psychological dimensions of this disruption. The human psyche, evolutionarily designed to seek patterns, predict outcomes, and maintain homeostasis, finds itself confronted with chaos that defies comprehension (Lazarus & Folkman, 1984). Our carefully constructed mental models of how the world operates—those cognitive frameworks that Daniel Kahneman (2011) describes as System 1 thinking—suddenly prove inadequate to process the complexity and unpredictability of crisis situations.

The emotional responses that emerge during such periods reflect the depth of this existential disruption. Fear, that most primal of emotions, surges not merely as a response to immediate threat but as a recognition of our fundamental vulnerability and the illusory nature of control we believed we possessed. Anxiety manifests as the mind's desperate attempt to predict and prepare for unpredictable futures, creating elaborate scenarios of potential catastrophe that often exceed the actual reality of the situation (Beck, 1976).

Grief emerges not only in response to tangible losses but as a mourning for the death of our previous worldview, the comfortable assumptions that crisis has rendered obsolete. This anticipatory grief, as Elisabeth Kübler-Ross and David Kessler (2005) observed, represents a profound psychological process of letting go of who we were in order to discover who we might become.

Anger, perhaps the most misunderstood crisis emotion, often serves as a protective mechanism—a fierce assertion of agency in the face of circumstances that threaten to overwhelm our sense of personal power and autonomy. Yet beneath anger's aggressive surface lies a deeper vulnerability, a fear of helplessness that strikes at the core of human dignity (Tavris, 1989).

The sensation of helplessness that pervades crisis experiences reflects our confrontation with the fundamental limitations of individual control in a complex, interconnected world. This learned helplessness, as Martin Seligman (1972) demonstrated, can either paralyse us in despair or, paradoxically, liberate us to discover new sources of strength and resilience we never knew we possessed.

Finally, confusion—that disorienting fog that settles over our cognitive processes during crisis—represents the mind's honest acknowledgment that our existing knowledge systems are insufficient to navigate unprecedented circumstances. This confusion, while deeply uncomfortable, creates the psychological space necessary for learning, adaptation, and growth (Festinger, 1957).

## The Transformative Power of Emotional Intelligence in Crisis Navigation

When emotional intelligence is absent during crisis, these intense emotional responses can overwhelm our rational faculties, leading to a cascade of destructive outcomes: impulsive decisions made in the grip of panic, relationships fractured by misdirected anger, mental health deterioration due to unprocessed trauma, and opportunities for growth squandered in the chaos of unmanaged emotion (Brackett, 2019).

However, when emotional intelligence serves as our compass during these turbulent times, crisis transforms from a destructive force into a catalyst for unprecedented growth, innovation, and the forging of deeper, more authentic human connections. This transformation doesn't occur through the denial or suppression of difficult emotions, but through their skilful navigation and integration (Siegel, 2012).

## The Neuroscientific Foundation of Crisis Response and Emotional Regulation

To understand how emotional intelligence functions during crisis, we must first examine the remarkable neurobiological processes that unfold when we encounter a threat or significant change. The human brain, sculpted by millions of years of evolution, contains sophisticated alarm systems designed to ensure survival in dangerous environments (LeDoux, 2015).

When a crisis strikes, the amygdala—those twin almond-shaped structures nestled deep within the limbic system—instantly evaluates incoming sensory information for potential threats. Upon detecting danger, real or perceived, the amygdala triggers the sympathetic nervous system, flooding the body with stress hormones including cortisol, adrenaline, and norepinephrine. This neurochemical cascade, known as the "fight, flight, or freeze" response, represents one of nature's most ancient and effective survival mechanisms (Sapolsky, 2004).

In the short term, this stress response provides remarkable advantages: heightened alertness, increased physical strength, enhanced focus on immediate threats, and accelerated decision-making capabilities. However, when this system remains chronically activated—as often occurs during prolonged crises—it begins to impair the very cognitive functions we most need for effective crisis navigation (McEwen, 2007).

The prefrontal cortex, that magnificent region responsible for executive functions such as strategic planning, emotional regulation, moral reasoning, and complex problem-solving, becomes compromised under sustained stress. This neurological hijacking explains why intelligent, capable individuals often make poor decisions during crisis periods, why emotional reactions become disproportionate to actual circumstances, and why long-term thinking becomes nearly impossible (Arnsten, 2009).

Emotional intelligence interventions work by reactivating the prefrontal cortex through specific practices that engage higher-order cognitive functions. Mindfulness meditation, for example, strengthens the connections between the prefrontal cortex and the amygdala, essentially creating a neural pathway that allows rational thought to modulate emotional reactivity (Davidson & Lutz, 2008). Cognitive reframing techniques help individuals restructure their interpretation of crisis events, reducing the amygdala's threat detection sensitivity and allowing for more nuanced, strategic responses (Beck, 2011).

# The Five Pillars of Crisis-Resilient Emotional Intelligence

## 1. Self-Awareness: The Foundation of Emotional Mastery

Self-awareness during crisis transcends simple emotion recognition; it requires the development of what we might call "meta-emotional awareness"—the capacity to observe our emotional processes with the detached curiosity of a scientist studying a fascinating phenomenon (Mayer & Stevens, 1994). This involves recognising not only what we are feeling but understanding the complex web of thoughts, memories, physical sensations, and environmental triggers that contribute to our emotional experience.

Consider the profound difference between these two internal monologues during a crisis situation:

Unconscious reaction: "I'm losing control. Everything is falling apart. I can't handle this."

Self-aware observation: "I notice fear arising in my chest, along with a familiar pattern of catastrophic thinking that often emerges when I feel uncertain about the future. My breathing has become shallow, and I'm experiencing the physical sensations I associate with anxiety. These are understandable responses to a genuinely challenging situation."

This shift from identification with emotion to observation of emotion creates what psychologists call "emotional granularity"—the ability to make fine-grained distinctions between different emotional states (Barrett, 2017). Research demonstrates that individuals with higher emotional granularity show greater resilience during stressful periods, better decision-making under pressure, and more effective emotional regulation strategies.

The practice of naming emotions, rooted in ancient contemplative traditions and validated by contemporary neuroscience, literally changes the brain's response to emotional stimuli. When we label an emotion, we activate the prefrontal cortex's language centres, which then send inhibitory signals to the amygdala, reducing its reactivity (Lieberman et al., 2007). This process, termed "affect labelling," represents one of the most powerful and immediate emotional intelligence interventions available during crisis.

## 2. Self-Regulation: The Art of Emotional Alchemy

Self-regulation during crisis resembles the ancient alchemist's quest to transform base metals into gold—it involves the skilful transformation of potentially destructive emotional energy into constructive action and wise response. This doesn't mean suppressing or denying difficult emotions, which research shows can actually intensify their impact and lead to psychological and physical health problems (Gross, 2002). Instead, self-regulation involves accepting emotions while choosing how to express and channel them.

The physiological dimension of self-regulation centres on breath awareness and regulation. During crisis, our breathing often becomes rapid and shallow, reinforcing the body's stress response and perpetuating feelings of panic and overwhelm. Conscious breathing practices—from simple deep breathing to sophisticated techniques like box breathing or alternate nostril breathing—activate the parasympathetic nervous system, triggering the body's relaxation response and creating space for thoughtful action (Brown & Gerbarg, 2012).

Cognitive self-regulation involves what cognitive behavioural therapists call "cognitive restructuring"—the process of examining and challenging the automatic thoughts and interpretations that fuel emotional distress. During crisis, our minds often engage in cognitive distortions such as catastrophising (imagining the worst possible outcomes), all-or-nothing thinking (seeing situations in extreme terms), or mental filtering (focusing exclusively on negative aspects while ignoring positive elements) (Burns, 1999).

The practice of self-regulation also includes what we might term "energy management"—the strategic allocation of our limited emotional and physical resources during demanding periods. This involves recognising that crisis periods require us to make conscious choices about where to direct our attention and energy, prioritising essential activities while temporarily releasing non-essential commitments.

## 3. Motivation: The Sacred Fire of Purpose

Motivation during crisis transcends simple goal-setting or positive thinking; it involves connecting with what Viktor Frankl (1946) called our "why"—the deeper purpose and meaning that can sustain us through even the most challenging circumstances. Frankl's observations from his experiences in Nazi concentration camps revealed that individuals who maintained a sense of purpose and meaning were significantly more likely to survive extreme adversity than those who lost connection to their deeper motivations.

This intrinsic motivation emerges from what psychologists call "eudaimonic well-being"—a form of fulfilment that comes from living in accordance with our deepest values and contributing to something larger than ourselves (Ryan & Deci, 2000). During crises, when external rewards and recognition may disappear, when familiar sources of validation evaporate, and when future outcomes remain uncertain, this connection to intrinsic purpose becomes our psychological anchor.

The cultivation of crisis-resilient motivation requires regular reflection on questions such as: What values do I want to embody regardless of external circumstances? How can I contribute meaningfully even within current limitations? What legacy do I want to create through my response to this challenge? What would I regret not attempting if this crisis continued indefinitely?

Research in positive psychology demonstrates that individuals who maintain what is called a "benefit-finding" orientation during crises—the ability to identify growth opportunities, strengthened relationships, or clarified priorities within difficult circumstances—show greater psychological resilience and post-traumatic growth (Tedeschi & Calhoun, 2004).

## 4. Empathy: The Bridge of Shared Humanity

Empathy during crises operates on multiple dimensions, each requiring distinct skills and awareness. Cognitive empathy involves intellectually understanding others' perspectives and emotional experiences, while affective empathy involves actually feeling resonance with others' emotions. Compassionate empathy goes further, motivating us to take action to help alleviate others' suffering (Goleman, 2006).

During crisis periods, empathy becomes particularly complex because everyone's emotional capacity is stretched thin. The tendency toward emotional contagion—unconsciously absorbing others' anxiety, fear, or despair—can overwhelm sensitive individuals and reduce their effectiveness in providing support (Hatfield et al., 1994). Skilled empathy during crises requires what we might call "boundaried compassion"—the ability to remain emotionally available to others while maintaining enough emotional regulation to avoid becoming overwhelmed by their distress.

This sophisticated form of empathy also involves recognising that people respond to crises in dramatically different ways based on their personal history, cultural background, available resources, and psychological makeup. What appears as strength in one person may mask profound struggle, while what looks like weakness in another may represent their most courageous effort. Empathy calls us to suspend judgment and offer our presence as a gift of shared humanity.

The neuroscience of empathy reveals that our capacity for empathic response is enhanced when we ourselves feel emotionally regulated and secure (Decety & Jackson, 2004). This creates what might seem like a paradox: to be most helpful to others during crises, we must first ensure our own emotional stability. Like the airline instruction to put on our own oxygen mask before helping others, emotional self-care becomes an act of service to our community.

## 5. Social Skills: The Art of Human Connection in Turbulent Times

Social skills during crises extend far beyond basic communication techniques; they encompass the sophisticated ability to create psychological safety, foster collaboration, and maintain human connection despite external chaos and uncertainty. These skills become particularly crucial because crisis often triggers our most primitive social responses—the tendency to withdraw, blame, compete for limited resources, or form in-groups that exclude others (Taylor, 2006).

Effective crisis communication requires what Marshall Rosenberg (2003) termed "nonviolent communication"—a way of speaking and listening that fosters connection rather than defensiveness. This involves expressing our own needs and emotions clearly while remaining curious about others' experiences rather than making assumptions or judgments.

The social skill of "holding space" becomes particularly important during crises. This involves creating an emotional container where others can experience and express difficult emotions without feeling the need to fix, change, or improve their emotional state. Holding space requires tremendous restraint—resisting the urge to offer premature solutions, platitudes, or reassurances that may actually invalidate others' legitimate concerns and feelings.

Leadership during crises demands an additional layer of social skills that we might call "inspirational realism"—the ability to acknowledge difficult realities honestly while maintaining hope and vision for positive outcomes. This requires walking the delicate balance between truth-telling and despair-inducing, between optimism and denial.

## Advanced Strategies for Building Emotional Resilience During Crises

### The Practice of Radical Acceptance

Radical acceptance, a concept drawn from Dialectical behaviour Therapy, involves fully accepting reality as it is rather than fighting against circumstances we cannot change (Linehan, 1993). This doesn't mean passive resignation or approval of negative circumstances; rather, it represents a strategic allocation of energy toward what we can influence rather than exhausting ourselves in futile battles against unchangeable realities.

The practice of radical acceptance often begins with a simple but profound phrase: "This is what is happening right now." This statement helps ground us in present-moment reality rather than getting lost in regrets about the past or anxiety about the future. From this foundation of acceptance, we can begin to ask more productive questions: "Given that this is the current reality, what are my options? What can I learn from this situation? How can I respond in a way that aligns with my values?"

## Cognitive Flexibility and Perspective-Taking

Crisis often triggers what psychologists call "cognitive rigidity"—the tendency to become stuck in particular ways of thinking or problem-solving that may no longer be effective given changed circumstances (Kashdan & Rottenberg, 2010). Developing cognitive flexibility involves deliberately practicing multiple perspectives on challenging situations.

One powerful technique involves what we might call "temporal perspective-taking"—imagining how we might view the current crisis from different points in time. How might we understand this situation one year from now? Five years from now? How might we view it from the perspective of our 80-year-old self? This practice helps us recognise that our current intense emotional reactions, while valid, represent just one possible way of interpreting and responding to circumstances.

## The Cultivation of Post-Traumatic Growth

Research in psychology has revealed that many individuals don't simply return to their pre-crisis functioning following traumatic or challenging experiences; instead, they experience what researchers call "post-traumatic growth"—actual improvements in psychological functioning, relationships, life philosophy, and personal strength (Tedeschi & Calhoun, 2004).

Post-traumatic growth isn't automatic; it requires intentional cultivation through practices such as meaning-making (finding purpose or lessons within difficult experiences), relationship deepening (using crisis as an opportunity to develop more authentic connections with others), and spiritual development (exploring existential questions about life's meaning and our place in the larger cosmos).

## Building Antifragility Through Controlled Stress

### Exposure

Nassim Taleb's concept of "antifragility" describes systems that become stronger through stress rather than simply surviving it (Taleb, 2012). We can cultivate emotional antifragility by gradually exposing ourselves to manageable challenges that build our capacity to handle larger stressors when they inevitably arise.

This might involve deliberately practicing discomfort through activities like cold exposure, challenging physical exercise, public speaking, or engaging in difficult conversations. The key is ensuring that these challenges remain within our "zone of proximal development"—difficult enough to promote growth but not so overwhelming as to trigger trauma responses.

## Leadership in Crisis: The Emotionally Intelligent Response

Crisis leadership requires a sophisticated integration of all emotional intelligence components, manifested through what we might call "adaptive leadership"—the ability to help individuals and organisations navigate unfamiliar challenges for which there are no predetermined solutions (Heifetz et al., 2009).

Emotionally intelligent crisis leaders understand that their primary role isn't to have all the answers or to project invulnerability; instead, their role is to maintain what Ronald Heifetz calls "the holding environment"—a psychological space where people can grapple with difficult realities, experiment with new approaches, and develop collective solutions to unprecedented challenges.

This type of leadership requires remarkable emotional regulation on the part of the leader, who must remain centered and clear-thinking while surrounded by others who may be experiencing panic, anger, or despair. It also requires the sophisticated social skill of managing what researchers call "group emotional norms"—the unspoken rules about which emotions are acceptable to express and how they should be managed within the organisational or community context (Barsade & Gibson, 2007).

## Conclusion: Crisis as the Crucible of Transformation

Crisis and change represent the ultimate proving ground for emotional intelligence—the arena where our capacity for self-awareness, regulation, empathy, motivation, and social connection faces its most rigorous testing. Yet it is precisely in these moments of maximum challenge that we discover our greatest potential for growth, connection, and contribution.

The individuals and communities that emerge from crisis not merely intact but transformed share certain characteristics: they have learned to dance with uncertainty rather than demanding certainty; they have developed the capacity to hold multiple perspectives simultaneously rather than clinging to single narratives; they have cultivated what we might call "wise hope"—a form of optimism that acknowledges difficulty while maintaining faith in human resilience and creativity.

As we prepare to explore the practical tools and techniques for developing emotional intelligence in our next chapter, we carry with us this fundamental understanding: crisis is not the enemy of human flourishing but rather its catalyst. Through the skilful cultivation of emotional intelligence, we transform ourselves from victims of circumstance into conscious participants in the ongoing creation of a more resilient, compassionate, and connected world.

In the words of the poet Rainer Maria Rilke (1903), "The only journey is the one within." Crisis strips away external securities and forces us to undertake this inner journey with unprecedented urgency and authenticity. Those who travel this path with emotional intelligence as their compass discover not only their own resilience but their capacity to light the way for others navigating similar darkness.

The question that remains is not whether we will face a crisis—we will. The question is whether we will meet it with the full depth of our emotional intelligence, transforming challenge into growth, isolation into connection, and fear into the fierce compassion that recognises our shared humanity in the face of uncertainty.

---

## References


Arnsten, A. F. T. (2009). Stress signalling pathways that impair prefrontal cortex structure and function. *Nature Reviews Neuroscience*, 10(6), 410-422.

Bar-On, R. (2006). The Bar-On model of emotional-social intelligence (ESI). *Psicothema*, 18, 13-25.

Barrett, L. F. (2017). *How emotions are made: The secret life of the brain*. Houghton Mifflin Harcourt.

Barsade, S. G., & Gibson, D. E. (2007). Why does affect matter in organizations? *Academy of Management Perspectives*, 21(1), 36-59.

Beck, A. T. (1976). *Cognitive therapy and the emotional disorders.* International Universities Press.

Beck, J. S. (2011). *Cognitive behaviour therapy: Basics and beyond* (2nd ed.). Guilford Press.

Brackett, M. (2019). *Permission to feel: Unlocking the power of emotions to help our kids, ourselves, and our society thrive.* Celadon Books.

Brown, R. P., & Gerbarg, P. L. (2012). The healing power of the breath: Simple techniques to reduce stress and anxiety, enhance concentration, and balance your emotions. Shambhala Publications.

Burns, D. D. (1999). *Feeling good: The new mood therapy.* Harper.

Caplan, G. (1964). *Principles of preventive psychiatry.* Basic Books.

Davidson, R. J., & Lutz, A. (2008). Buddha's brain: Neuroplasticity and meditation. *IEEE Signal Processing Magazine,* 25(6), 176-188.

Decety, J., & Jackson, P. L. (2004). The functional architecture of human empathy. *behavioural and Cognitive Neuroscience Reviews,* 3(2), 71-100.

Festinger, L. (1957). *A theory of cognitive dissonance.* Stanford University Press.

Frankl, V. E. (1946). *Man's search for meaning.* Beacon Press.

Goleman, D. (2006). *Emotional intelligence: Why it matters more than IQ.* Bantam Books.

Gross, J. J. (2002). Emotion regulation: Affective, cognitive, and social consequences. *Psychophysiology,* 39(3), 281-291.

Hatfield, E., Cacioppo, J. T., & Rapson, R. L. (1994). *Emotional contagion.* Cambridge University Press.

Heifetz, R., Grashow, A., & Linsky, M. (2009). *The practice of adaptive leadership: Tools and tactics for changing your organization and the world.* Harvard Business Press.

Kahneman, D. (2011). *Thinking, fast and slow.* Farrar, Straus and Giroux.

Kashdan, T. B., & Rottenberg, J. (2010). Psychological flexibility as a fundamental aspect of health. *Clinical Psychology Review,* 30(7), 865-878.

Kübler-Ross, E., & Kessler, D. (2005). *On grief and grieving: Finding the meaning of grief through the five stages of loss.* Scribner.

Lazarus, R. S., & Folkman, S. (1984). *Stress, appraisal, and coping.* Springer.

LeDoux, J. (2015). *Anxious: Using the brain to understand and treat fear and anxiety.* Viking.

Lieberman, M. D., Eisenberger, N. I., Crockett, M. J., Tom, S. M., Pfeifer, J. H., & Way, B. M. (2007). Putting feelings into words: Affect labeling disrupts amygdala activity in response to affective stimuli. *Psychological Science,* 18(5), 421-428.

Linehan, M. M. (1993). *Cognitive-behavioural treatment of borderline personality disorder.* Guilford Press.

Mayer, J. D., & Salovey, P. (1997). What is emotional intelligence? In P. Salovey & D. J. Sluyter (Eds.), *Emotional development and emotional intelligence: Educational implications* (pp. 3-34). Harper Collins.

Mayer, J. D., & Stevens, A. A. (1994). An emerging understanding of the reflective (meta-) experience of mood. *Journal of Research in Personality,* 28(3), 351-373.

McEwen, B. S. (2007). Physiology and neurobiology of stress and adaptation: Central role of the brain. *Physiological Reviews,* 87(3), 873-904.

Rilke, R. M. (1903). *Letters to a young poet.* Nórton.

Rosenberg, M. B. (2003). *Nonviolent communication: A language of life.* PuddleDancer Press.

Ryan, R. M., & Deci, E. L. (2000). Self-determination theory and the facilitation of intrinsic motivation, social development, and well-being. *American Psychologist,* 55(1), 68-78.

Sapolsky, R. M. (2004). *Why zebras don't get ulcers: The acclaimed guide to stress, stress-related diseases, and coping* (3rd ed.). Henry Holt.

Seligman, M. E. P. (1972). Learned helplessness: Annual review of medicine. *Annual Review of Medicine,* 23(1), 407-412.

Siegel, D. J. (2012). *The developing mind: How relationships and the brain interact to shape who we are* (2nd ed.). Guilford Press.

Taleb, N. N. (2012). *Antifragile: Things that gain from disorder*. Random House.

Tavris, C. (1989). *Anger: The misunderstood emotion*. Simon & Schuster.

Taylor, S. E. (2006). Tend and befriend: Biobehavioural bases of affiliation under stress. *Current Directions in Psychological Science*, 15(6), 273-277.

Tedeschi, R. G., & Calhoun, L. G. (2004). Posttraumatic growth: Conceptual foundations and empirical evidence. *Psychological Inquiry*, 15(1), 1-18.

# Chapter 13: Training Your Emotional Intelligence: Tools and Techniques for Transformational Growth

## Introduction: The Architecture of Emotional Mastery

In the labyrinthine corridors of human consciousness, where reason wrestles with passion and logic dances with intuition, lies perhaps the most profound capacity we possess: emotional intelligence. Unlike the static monuments of traditional intelligence—those crystalline structures of analytical prowess and computational ability—emotional intelligence emerges as a living, breathing ecosystem of skills that can be cultivated, nurtured, and transformed through deliberate practice (Goleman, 1995).

This is not merely another self-help platitude. The neuroplasticity revolution in neuroscience has fundamentally altered our understanding of human potential. Dr. Norman Doidge's ground-breaking research reveals that our brains remain malleable throughout our lives, capable of rewiring themselves in response to new experiences and deliberate practice (Doidge, 2007). When we speak of training emotional intelligence, we are literally speaking of reshaping the neural pathways that govern our emotional responses, our social interactions, and our capacity for resilience.

Yet here we encounter a paradox that would have delighted the ancient philosophers: the very emotions we seek to master are the same forces that can either propel us toward growth or ensnare us in cycles of reactivity. As the Stoic philosopher Epictetus observed, "It's not what happens to you, but how you react to it that matters" (Epictetus, circa 100 CE). This wisdom, echoing across millennia, finds remarkable validation in contemporary neuroscience.

The journey of emotional intelligence training is not a linear progression from emotional illiteracy to mastery. Rather, it resembles the spiral staircase in a medieval tower—we encounter similar challenges at different levels, each time with greater sophistication and deeper understanding. Sometimes we ascend rapidly, other times we pause on a landing, catching our breath, consolidating our gains. Occasionally, we may even descend a few steps, only to discover that this apparent regression has prepared us for a more substantial leap forward.

Consider the profound implications of this developmental process. When we train our emotional intelligence, we are not merely acquiring a set of interpersonal skills or stress management techniques. We are engaging in nothing less than the fundamental restructuring of our relationship with reality itself. As neuroscientist Lisa Feldman Barrett demonstrates in her revolutionary work on constructed emotion, our brains are not passive recipients of emotional experiences but active constructors of meaning (Barrett, 2017). This means that the very act of training our emotional intelligence is simultaneously an act of authoring our own emotional reality.

## The Philosophical Foundations of Emotional Development

Before we delve into the practical methodologies of emotional intelligence training, we must first establish the philosophical bedrock upon which these practices rest. The Western tradition, from Aristotle's concept of phronesis (practical wisdom) to William James's radical empiricism, has long grappled with the relationship between emotion and wisdom (Aristotle, 4th century BCE; James, 1904). The Eastern contemplative traditions, with their sophisticated understanding of mindfulness and emotional regulation, offer complementary perspectives that have only recently been integrated into Western psychological science (Wallace & Shapiro, 2006).

The first principle that emerges from this cross-cultural synthesis is what we might call "emotional archaeology"—the systematic excavation of our unconscious emotional patterns. Just as archaeologists carefully brush away layers of sediment to reveal ancient artefacts, we must learn to observe our emotional responses with the same patience and precision. This process reveals not just what we feel, but how we have learned to feel, and most importantly, how we can choose to feel differently.

The second principle concerns the nature of emotional courage. Training emotional intelligence requires us to venture into territories of our psyche that we have long avoided. It demands that we sit with discomfort, that we remain present to pain, that we resist the ancient evolutionary impulse to fight, flee, or freeze in the face of emotional intensity. This is not masochism but wisdom—the recognition that our greatest growth often lies on the other side of our greatest fears.

The third principle involves what the Buddhist tradition calls "beginner's mind" (Suzuki, 1970). No matter how sophisticated our emotional understanding becomes, we must maintain the humility to approach each emotional experience with fresh eyes. Emotional intelligence is not a destination but a way of traveling through life. The moment we believe we have "mastered" our emotions is precisely the moment we become vulnerable to emotional hijacking.

## The Neuroscience of Emotional Transformation

To truly understand the potential for emotional intelligence training, we must venture into the fascinating realm of neuroscience. The human brain, with its hundred billion neurons and quadrillion synaptic connections, represents the most complex structure in the known universe (Kandel, 2006). Within this neural cosmos, emotional intelligence emerges from the intricate interplay between multiple brain regions, each contributing its unique capabilities to our emotional repertoire.

The amygdala, often characterised as the brain's "alarm system," processes emotional stimuli with lightning speed—evaluating potential threats in milliseconds before conscious awareness even emerges (LeDoux, 2015). This rapid-fire assessment system served our ancestors well when faced with sabre-toothed tigers, but in our modern world of subtle social dynamics and complex interpersonal relationships, it can lead to what psychologist Daniel Goleman terms "amygdala hijacking"—emotional reactions that overwhelm our rational faculties (Goleman, 1995).

The prefrontal cortex, by contrast, represents our brain's "executive suite"—the neural real estate responsible for planning, decision-making, and emotional regulation (Miller & Cohen, 2001). When we train our emotional intelligence, we are essentially strengthening the communication pathways between the amygdala and the prefrontal cortex, creating what neuroscientist Matthew Lieberman calls "the neural basis of wisdom" (Lieberman, 2013).

But here's where the story becomes truly remarkable: the brain's capacity for change extends far beyond what we previously imagined. Dr. Richard Davidson's pioneering research on neuroplasticity and meditation reveals that even relatively brief periods of contemplative practice can produce measurable changes in brain structure and function (Davidson & Lutz, 2008). Long-term meditators show increased gray matter density in regions associated with attention, emotional regulation, and self-awareness. They also demonstrate decreased activity in the default mode network—the brain regions associated with mind-wandering and self-referential thinking that often contribute to anxiety and depression.

# Training Self-Awareness: The Foundation of Emotional Wisdom

Self-awareness stands as the cornerstone of emotional intelligence, yet it remains one of the most elusive qualities to develop. Like trying to see your own eyes without a mirror, achieving genuine self-awareness requires sophisticated tools and techniques that allow us to observe our own mental processes from a meta-cognitive distance.

## The Practice of Interoceptive Awareness

Begin each day with what we might call an "embodied check-in"—a systematic survey of your internal landscape. But this is not the casual "How are you feeling?" that we might ask a friend. This is a forensic investigation of your emotional state, conducted with the precision of a scientist and the compassion of a loving parent.

Set three alarms throughout your day—perhaps at 9 AM, 2 PM, and 7 PM. When the alarm sounds, stop whatever you're doing and turn your attention inward. Begin with your breath. Is it shallow or deep? Rapid or slow? Is there tension in your chest, lightness in your head, heaviness in your stomach? The body speaks in a language older than words, and learning to listen to this somatic vocabulary is essential for emotional intelligence (Damasio, 1994).

Next, scan your emotional landscape. But here's the crucial distinction: rather than simply identifying what you feel, explore the texture, intensity, and quality of the emotion. Sadness, for instance, might feel like a gentle melancholy, a sharp grief, or a dull ache of disappointment. Anger might manifest as hot rage, cold fury, or simmering resentment. The more precisely we can map our emotional terrain, the more skilfully we can navigate it.

## The Revolutionary Practice of Emotional Journaling

Journaling for emotional intelligence transcends the typical "Dear Diary" approach that many of us learned in childhood. This is archaeological journaling—a systematic excavation of your emotional patterns, triggers, and transformations. Each evening, dedicate fifteen to twenty minutes to this practice, but approach it with the rigour of a research scientist studying the most fascinating subject on earth: yourself.

Begin with the day's emotional weather report. What was the overall emotional climate of your day? Were there sudden storms of anger or anxiety? Periods of calm contentment? Unexpected downpours of sadness or sunshine bursts of joy? But don't stop at simple meteorological metaphors. Dig deeper. What specific events triggered these emotional shifts? More importantly, what thoughts preceded and followed these emotional experiences?

This is where the practice becomes genuinely transformative. Most people experience emotions as mysterious forces that simply happen to them—like weather systems beyond their control. But emotional intelligence training reveals a startling truth: our emotions are far more malleable than we realise. They arise from the interaction between external events and our internal interpretations of those events. By tracking these patterns in our journal, we begin to see the invisible threads that connect our thoughts, emotions, and behaviours.

Consider maintaining what psychologist Sonja Lyubomirsky calls a "gratitude-complexity journal"—a record that not only acknowledges positive experiences but also explores the nuanced emotions that accompany even difficult situations (Lyubomirsky, 2007). Perhaps a challenging conversation with a colleague triggered frustration, but it also revealed your capacity for patience. Maybe a project failure caused disappointment, but it also sparked innovative thinking. This practice develops what researchers call "emotional granularity"—the ability to distinguish between subtle emotional states and to find meaning in emotional complexity.

## Mindfulness Meditation: The Training Ground of Awareness

Mindfulness meditation represents perhaps the most scientifically validated method for developing self-awareness. But true mindfulness practice extends far beyond the popular conception of "emptying the mind" or achieving a state of blissful tranquillity. Authentic mindfulness is more like becoming a skilled naturalist of your own consciousness—learning to observe the flora and fauna of your mental landscape with patient, non-judgmental attention.

Begin with a simple but profound practice: breath awareness meditation. Sit comfortably, close your eyes, and bring your attention to the sensation of breathing. But here's the crucial instruction that transforms this from relaxation to training: when your mind wanders (and it will, constantly), don't judge this as failure. Instead, celebrate the moment of noticing that your mind has wandered. This moment of recognition is the muscle of mindfulness being strengthened.

As your practice deepens, expand your awareness to include the full spectrum of mental phenomena. Notice thoughts as they arise and dissolve. Observe emotions as they emerge, peak, and fade. Watch physical sensations come and go. But maintain the stance of what Buddhist teacher Joseph Goldstein calls "the loving observer"—present, curious, and compassionate toward whatever arises (Goldstein, 2002).

This practice gradually reveals one of the most liberating insights available to human consciousness: you are not your thoughts, emotions, or sensations. You are the awareness in which they arise. This shift in identity—from being the content of consciousness to being consciousness itself—represents the foundation of true emotional freedom.

## Training Self-Regulation: The Art of Emotional Alchemy

If self-awareness is the foundation of emotional intelligence, then self-regulation is its most practical application. Self-regulation transforms raw emotional energy into skilful action, converting what the ancient alchemists called base metals into gold. But this transformation requires both precision and patience—the delicate touch of a master craftsman working with volatile materials.

### The Neuroscience of Naming: "Name It to Tame It"

Dr. Dan Siegel's research reveals a fascinating quirk of brain function: the simple act of verbally labelling an emotion activates the prefrontal cortex and reduces activity in the amygdala (Siegel, 2012). This process, which Siegel calls "name it to tame it," represents one of the most accessible yet powerful tools for emotional regulation.

But effective emotional labelling requires sophistication beyond simply saying "I'm angry" or "I'm sad." Develop an emotional vocabulary that would make a poet envious. Instead of anger, you might feel irritated, frustrated, incensed, livid, or indignant. Instead of sadness, you might experience melancholy, grief, disappointment, or heartbreak. Each subtle distinction activates different neural networks and suggests different response strategies.

Moreover, practice what we might call "layered emotional labelling." Often, our surface emotions mask deeper, more vulnerable feelings beneath. Anger, for instance, frequently serves as a protective shell around hurt, fear, or disappointment. By learning to identify these emotional layers, we gain access to more sophisticated and effective regulation strategies.

## The 90-Second Rule: Riding the Wave of Neurochemical Reality

Neuroscientist Jill Bolte Taylor's discovery of the "90-second rule" revolutionises our understanding of emotional regulation (Taylor, 2008). When we experience an emotional trigger, our brains release a cascade of neurochemicals—stress hormones, neurotransmitters, and other biochemical messengers. These chemicals flood our system, creating the physical sensations we associate with emotions. But here's the remarkable part: if we don't continue to fuel these chemicals with additional thoughts, they naturally metabolise and leave our bloodstream within ninety seconds.

This means that most of our emotional suffering beyond that initial 90-second window is self-created through the stories we tell ourselves about the triggering event. We replay the situation, imagine worst-case scenarios, rehearse angry responses, or spiral into victim narratives. Each of these mental activities releases fresh waves of stress chemicals, perpetuating and intensifying our emotional reactivity.

The 90-second rule practice is elegantly simple yet profoundly challenging: when you notice a strong emotional reaction arising, set a timer for ninety seconds. During this time, resist the urge to think about the triggering situation. Instead, focus entirely on the physical sensations of the emotion. Where do you feel it in your body? Is it hot or cold, tight or expansive, sharp or dull? Breathe deeply and allow yourself to experience the emotion fully without adding mental commentary.

This practice requires what we might call "emotional bravery"—the courage to feel fully without immediately moving into mental analysis or action. Most of us have spent decades learning to avoid, numb, or distract ourselves from uncomfortable emotions. The 90-second rule asks us to do the opposite: to lean into discomfort with curiosity and compassion.

## Cognitive Reframing: The Art of Perspective Transformation

Cognitive reframing represents one of the most sophisticated tools in the emotional regulation toolkit. Based on the foundational insight of cognitive-behavioural therapy—that our emotions are largely determined by our interpretations of events rather than the events themselves—reframing allows us to consciously shift our perspective to create more empowering emotional responses (Beck, 1976).

But effective reframing extends beyond simple positive thinking or optimistic self-talk. It requires what philosopher Richard Rorty calls "final vocabulary flexibility"—the ability to describe the same situation using radically different conceptual frameworks (Rorty, 1989). When faced with a challenging situation, practice generating at least three different interpretive frameworks:

First, the victim narrative: How is this situation happening to you? What external forces are causing your suffering? This perspective, while potentially disempowering, often contains important information about genuine injustices or systemic problems that need addressing.

Second, the hero narrative: How might this challenge be an opportunity for growth, learning, or service? What strengths might you develop by facing this difficulty? How could this situation contribute to your larger life purpose? This reframe often generates energy and motivation for positive action.

Third, the cosmic perspective: How will this situation matter in ten years? What would this look like from the perspective of someone from a different culture, century, or planet? This ultra-wide-angle lens often reduces the emotional charge of situations by placing them in a larger context.

The goal is not to choose the "correct" interpretation but to recognise that all interpretations are constructions. By consciously choosing interpretations that serve your wellbeing and growth, you reclaim authorship of your emotional experience.

## Advanced Breathing Techniques: Regulating the Autonomic Nervous System

While breath awareness forms the foundation of mindfulness practice, specific breathing techniques can serve as precision tools for emotional regulation. These practices work by directly influencing the autonomic nervous system—the neural networks that control heart rate, blood pressure, stress hormone release, and other unconscious physiological processes.

Box breathing, utilised by Navy SEALs and other elite performers, creates a balanced rhythm that activates the parasympathetic nervous system—our body's "rest and digest" response (Nestor, 2020). Inhale for four counts, hold for four, exhale for four, hold for four. Repeat this pattern for two to five minutes, allowing your nervous system to downregulate from states of hyperactivation.

But consider exploring more sophisticated breathwork practices as your skill develops. The 4-7-8 technique, popularised by Dr. Andrew Weil, involves inhaling for four counts, holding for seven, and exhaling for eight. This extended exhale activates the vagus nerve—the primary pathway of the parasympathetic nervous system—creating deep states of relaxation and emotional regulation (Weil, 2011).

For situations requiring energy and focus rather than relaxation, experiment with energising breath patterns. The Wim Hof breathing method, inspired by ancient yogic practices, involves thirty deep breaths followed by retention on empty lungs. This practice can generate states of calm alertness and emotional resilience that persist for hours (Hof, 2020).

# Training Motivation: Sustaining the Fire of Purpose

Motivation represents the emotional fuel that sustains us through the inevitable challenges of growth and change. But motivation is not simply willpower or determination—it's a complex psychological state that emerges from the alignment of our values, goals, and daily actions. Training motivation requires us to become architects of our own inspiration, consciously designing psychological environments that nurture and sustain our commitment to growth.

## Vision Boarding: Neuroplasticity and Visual Imagination

The practice of vision boarding transcends the realm of wishful thinking when grounded in neuroscientific understanding. Research by Dr. Alvaro Pascual-Leone demonstrates that mental rehearsal activates the same neural pathways as actual experience (Pascual-Leone, 2005). When we repeatedly visualise ourselves achieving our goals, we literally wire our brains for success.

But effective vision boarding requires sophistication beyond simply pasting magazine pictures on poster board. Create what we might call a "multisensory vision ecosystem"—a rich, detailed imaginal environment that engages all your senses and emotions. What does achieving your goals look like, sound like, feel like, even smell and taste like? The more vivid and specific your visualisation, the more powerful its impact on your neural programming.

Moreover, include not just the end results but the process of growth itself. Envision yourself practicing emotional regulation during difficult conversations. Imagine yourself choosing compassion over criticism, patience over reactivity, courage over comfort. These process visualisations prime your brain to recognise and seize opportunities for emotional growth in daily life.

## Emotional Goal Setting: Beyond SMART Objectives

Traditional goal-setting methodologies focus primarily on external, measurable outcomes. But emotional intelligence training requires what we might call "heart-centred goal setting"—objectives that are deeply connected to your core values and emotional wellbeing. For each significant goal, explore these deeper questions:

How will achieving this goal serve not just your personal success but your contribution to others? Research by Adam Grant reveals that prosocial motivation—the desire to benefit others—creates more sustainable drive than purely self-focused ambitions (Grant, 2013).

What emotional states will you need to cultivate to achieve this goal? If your objective is to become a more effective leader, you might need to develop greater emotional resilience, deeper empathy, and more skilful communication abilities. By identifying these emotional prerequisites, you can create targeted training practices.

How will you maintain motivation during the inevitable periods of difficulty and doubt? Design what psychologist Gabriele Oettingen calls "implementation intentions"—specific if-then plans for handling obstacles (Oettingen, 2014). "If I feel overwhelmed by this project, then I will spend ten minutes in mindfulness meditation before taking any action." These pre-planned responses prevent emotional reactivity from derailing your progress.

## The Neuroscience of Celebration: Reinforcing Positive Change

One of the most overlooked aspects of motivation training involves learning to celebrate progress effectively. Dr. Rick Hanson's research on "taking in the good" reveals that positive experiences must be consciously savoured to create lasting neural changes (Hanson, 2013). Our brains are naturally biased toward noticing and remembering negative experiences—an evolutionary adaptation that helped our ancestors survive threats. But this "negativity bias" can undermine motivation by causing us to overlook progress and focus disproportionately on setbacks.

Develop sophisticated celebration rituals that go beyond simple reward systems. When you notice progress in your emotional intelligence—perhaps you remained calm during a stressful meeting or showed compassion to someone who had hurt you—pause and really savour the experience. What does this growth feel like in your body? What does it mean about your capacity for positive change? How might this moment of growth ripple out to benefit others?

Create what we might call a "victory journal"—a record not just of major achievements but of small moments of emotional wisdom. The colleague who thanked you for your patience. The argument you avoided through skilful communication. The moment you chose self-compassion over self-criticism. These seemingly minor victories are actually major rewirings of your neural networks, deserving conscious recognition and celebration.

## Training Empathy: The Bridge to Universal Connection

Empathy represents perhaps the most transformative aspect of emotional intelligence, yet it's often misunderstood as a simple feeling of sympathy or concern for others. True empathy is far more sophisticated—it's the capacity to accurately perceive, understand, and resonate with another person's emotional experience while maintaining clear boundaries between their feelings and your own.

## Perspective-Taking as Spiritual Practice

The practice of perspective-taking transforms empathy from an occasional emotional response into a systematic method for expanding consciousness. Begin with situations from your own life—perhaps a recent conflict or misunderstanding. Instead of remaining locked in your own viewpoint, practice what we might call "consciousness shifting."

Write a detailed account of the situation from the other person's perspective. But go beyond simply imagining their thoughts and feelings. Consider their life history, their current stresses, their fears and hopes, their cultural background and personal values. What might this interaction have meant to them? What needs might they have been trying to meet through their behaviour?

This practice reveals a profound truth: most human behaviour, even behaviour that seems harmful or inexplicable, makes perfect sense when viewed from the actor's internal frame of reference. This doesn't mean excusing harmful actions, but rather developing the emotional sophistication to hold both accountability and compassion simultaneously.

As your perspective-taking abilities strengthen, expand the practice to include people you've never met. Read news stories not just for information but for emotional understanding. When you encounter accounts of human conflict—whether personal, political, or international—practice inhabiting multiple viewpoints. What fears, needs, and values might be driving each party's behaviour?

## Story Listening: Expanding Emotional Bandwidth

In our hyperconnected yet increasingly polarised world, we often encounter only stories that confirm our existing beliefs and perspectives. Training empathy requires us to consciously seek out narratives from people whose experiences differ radically from our own. This practice, which we might call "empathy fieldwork," systematically expands our emotional bandwidth and challenges our assumptions about human nature.

Dedicate time each week to consuming content created by people from different cultural, economic, racial, religious, and ideological backgrounds. But listen not just to the content of their stories but to the emotional subtext. What hopes and fears animate their perspectives? What values guide their choices? What experiences have shaped their worldview?

Pay particular attention to stories that make you uncomfortable or defensive. These reactions often signal encounters with perspectives that challenge our own assumptions—precisely the experiences most likely to expand our empathic capacity. Practice what Buddhist teacher Pema Chödrön calls "staying with the discomfort"—neither pushing away these challenging perspectives nor immediately accepting them, but remaining curious and open to what they might teach us (Chödrön, 1997).

## Compassion Cultivation: From Empathy to Action

While empathy involves understanding others' emotions, compassion adds the element of care and the motivation to help alleviate suffering. Research by Dr. Tania Singer reveals that empathy and compassion activate different neural networks, with compassion associated with more positive emotions and less emotional burnout (Singer & Klimecki, 2014).

Develop a daily compassion practice that begins with self-compassion and gradually expands to include others. Start each morning by offering yourself the same kindness you would show a dear friend facing your current challenges. What words of encouragement, understanding, and support would you offer? How would you hold space for your struggles without judgment or criticism?

Then extend this compassionate awareness to people in your immediate environment. The stressed colleague, the overwhelmed parent, the lonely neighbour. Practice what we might call "stealth compassion"—small acts of kindness that don't call attention to themselves. A genuine compliment, a moment of patient listening, an offer to help with a small task.

As your compassion muscle strengthens, expand your practice to include people you find difficult or challenging. This doesn't mean becoming a doormat or failing to maintain healthy boundaries. Rather, it involves recognising the common humanity that connects you even to people whose behaviour you find problematic. As the saying goes, "Hurt people hurt people." Behind every difficult person is usually someone struggling with their own pain, fear, or confusion.

## Training Social Skills: Emotional Intelligence in Relationship

Social skills represent emotional intelligence in action—the practical application of self-awareness, self-regulation, motivation, and empathy in our interactions with others. But skilful social engagement goes far beyond simple politeness or charm. It requires the ability to read social situations accurately, communicate with precision and warmth, navigate conflict constructively, and inspire positive change in group dynamics.

### The Art of Emotional Validation

One of the most powerful social skills involves learning to validate others' emotional experiences without necessarily agreeing with their perspectives or actions. Validation acknowledges the legitimacy of someone's feelings while maintaining your own autonomy and boundaries. This skill can transform conflicts into opportunities for deeper understanding and connection.

Practice the formula: "It makes sense that you would feel [emotion] about [situation] given [their perspective/values/circumstances]." For example: "It makes sense that you would feel frustrated about the project deadline given how many competing priorities you're managing right now."

Notice that validation doesn't require you to agree that their perspective is objectively correct or that their proposed solutions are wise. You're simply acknowledging that their emotional response is understandable given their internal experience. This acknowledgment often creates enough emotional safety for more productive dialogue to emerge.

## Conflict as Collaborative Problem-Solving

Most people approach conflict as a competitive sport—someone wins, someone loses, and the goal is to emerge victorious. But emotional intelligence reframes conflict as collaborative problem-solving. The real enemy is not the other person but the breakdown in communication, understanding, or cooperation that's preventing both parties from getting their needs met.

Develop a repertoire of de-escalation phrases that redirect conflictual energy toward mutual understanding: "Help me understand what's most important to you in this situation." "What would need to happen for both of us to feel good about this outcome?" "I'm wondering if we might be wanting the same thing but seeing different paths to get there."

These phrases embody what Harvard negotiation expert Roger Fisher calls "principled negotiation"—focusing on interests rather than positions, generating options for mutual gain, and using objective criteria for decision-making (Fisher, Ury, & Patton, 2011).

### Building Rapport: The Neuroscience of Connection

The ability to build rapport quickly and authentically represents one of the most valuable social skills in our interconnected world. But genuine rapport goes beyond surface-level charm or manipulation—it involves creating a genuine sense of mutual understanding and shared experience.

Research by Dr. Mauricio Delgado reveals that feelings of social connection activate the brain's reward centers, releasing dopamine and creating positive associations with the interaction partner (Delgado, 2007). We can consciously facilitate this process by looking for genuine commonalities—shared values, experiences, challenges, or aspirations.

But here's the crucial distinction: authentic rapport-building serves the other person's wellbeing as much as your own. Instead of asking "How can I get this person to like me?" ask "How can I create an interaction that genuinely serves both of us?" This shift in intention often leads to more natural and sustainable connections.

## Creating Your Personal EQ Development Plan: The Architecture of Transformation

Developing emotional intelligence requires more than sporadic efforts or good intentions. It demands what we might call "emotional architecture"—the systematic design of daily practices, weekly reflections, monthly goals, and quarterly assessments that create sustainable growth over time.

### Daily Emotional Fitness Practices

Just as physical fitness requires consistent daily movement, emotional fitness demands regular practices that strengthen your EQ muscles. Design a morning routine that includes:

A five-minute emotional check-in that surveys your internal landscape and sets intentions for the day. What emotions are present? What challenges might trigger reactivity? How do you want to show up in your interactions?

A midday reset practice that interrupts habitual patterns and reconnects you with your deeper values. This might involve three minutes of conscious breathing, a brief mindfulness meditation, or simply asking yourself: "How am I doing with my emotional intentions?"

An evening reflection that reviews the day's emotional experiences, celebrates moments of growth, and identifies opportunities for improvement. What situations triggered strong emotions? How skillfully did you handle them? What would you do differently next time?

## Weekly Integration Practices

Weekly practices should focus on deeper reflection and pattern recognition. Dedicate thirty to sixty minutes each week to reviewing your emotional journal, looking for recurring themes, triggers, and growth opportunities. Consider questions such as:

What emotional patterns am I noticing? Are there specific situations, people, or topics that consistently trigger reactivity? What might these triggers be trying to teach me about my values, fears, or unmet needs?

Where am I seeing growth and progress? Even small improvements deserve recognition and celebration. The moment you chose patience over impatience, compassion over judgment, or courage over comfort represents significant neural rewiring.

What skills need the most attention in the coming week? Perhaps you've noticed a tendency toward emotional reactivity in meetings, or difficulty maintaining boundaries with family members. Choose one specific skill to focus on for the week ahead.

## Monthly Goal Setting and Assessment

Monthly reviews allow for broader perspective and more significant course corrections. Assess your progress across all five dimensions of emotional intelligence:

Self-awareness: Are you becoming more skilled at recognising your emotions as they arise? Can you identify subtle emotional states and their physical sensations? Are you developing greater insight into your emotional patterns and triggers?

Self-regulation: How effectively are you managing strong emotions? Are you able to pause before reacting? Can you use breathing techniques, reframing, or other regulation strategies in real-time situations?

Motivation: How well are you maintaining energy and enthusiasm for your goals? Are you celebrating progress effectively? Do you need to reconnect with your deeper values and purposes?

Empathy: Are you becoming more skilled at understanding others' emotional experiences? Can you perspective-take even in challenging situations? Are you developing greater compassion for both yourself and others?

Social skills: How effectively are you navigating relationships and social situations? Are you able to communicate clearly and kindly? Can you handle conflict constructively and build rapport authentically?

## Quarterly Transformation Reviews

Every three months, conduct a comprehensive assessment of your emotional intelligence development. This involves not just reviewing progress but envisioning the next phase of your growth. Consider working with a coach, therapist, or trusted friend to gain an external perspective on your development.

Review your emotional journal entries from the past quarter. What themes emerge? How have your responses to similar situations changed over time? What growth might be so gradual that you're not noticing it day-to-day?

Gather feedback from people in your life. How have they noticed you changing? What shifts have they observed in your communication style, emotional regulation, or way of handling stress? Sometimes others can see our growth more clearly than we can.

Set intentions for the next quarter that build on your current strengths while addressing areas needing development. But make these intentions specific and behavioural rather than vague aspirations. Instead of "be more patient," commit to "use the 90-second rule three times per week when feeling irritated with family members."

## Conclusion: The Evolutionary Imperative of Emotional Intelligence

As we stand at the threshold of an uncertain future—facing climate change, technological disruption, social polarisation, and other unprecedented challenges—emotional intelligence emerges not as a luxury but as a necessity for human survival and flourishing. The problems we face cannot be solved through technical expertise alone; they require the kind of collaborative wisdom, empathic understanding, and emotional resilience that comes from highly developed emotional intelligence.

Training your emotional intelligence is ultimately an act of service—not just to your own wellbeing but to the larger human community of which you are part. Every moment you choose consciousness over reactivity, compassion over judgment, courage over comfort, you are contributing to the collective emotional intelligence of our species. You are becoming part of the solution to humanity's most pressing challenges.

The journey of emotional intelligence training never truly ends. Like a master craftsperson who continues refining their skills throughout their lifetime, you will discover new depths of emotional wisdom for as long as you remain committed to growth. Each challenge becomes an opportunity for greater mastery. Each relationship becomes a laboratory for practicing love. Each difficult emotion becomes a teacher showing you where your freedom lies.

In the end, training emotional intelligence is nothing less than the training of human consciousness itself—the development of our capacity to respond to life with wisdom, compassion, and skilful action. It is the most important work any of us can undertake, and the most beautiful gift we can offer to a world desperately in need of emotional wisdom.

The future belongs not to those with the highest IQ, but to those with the highest EQ—those who can navigate complexity with grace, connect across differences with compassion, and transform challenges into opportunities for collective growth. This future begins with your next breath, your next choice, your next moment of conscious response to whatever life presents.

The question is not whether you have time for this training. The question is whether you can afford not to begin.

---

## References


Aristotle. (4th century BCE). *Nicomachean Ethics*. Trans. W.D. Ross. Oxford: Oxford University Press.

Barrett, L. F. (2017). *How Emotions Are Made: The Secret Life of the Brain*. Boston: Houghton Mifflin Harcourt.

Beck, A. T. (1976). *Cognitive Therapy and the Emotional Disorders*. New York: International Universities Press.

Chödrön, P. (1997). *When Things Fall Apart: Heart Advice for Difficult Times*. Boston: Shambhala Publications.

Damasio, A. (1994). *Descartes' Error: Emotion, Reason, and the Human Brain.* New York: Putnam Publishing.

Davidson, R. J., & Lutz, A. (2008). Buddha's brain: Neuroplasticity and meditation. *IEEE Signal Processing Magazine,* 25(6), 176-188.

Delgado, M. R. (2007). Reward-related responses in the human striatum. *Annals of the New York Academy of Sciences,* 1104(1), 70-88.

Doidge, N. (2007). *The Brain That Changes Itself: Stories of Personal Triumph from the Frontiers of Brain Science.* New York: Viking.

Epictetus. (circa 100 CE). *Discourses.* Trans. Robin Hard. Oxford: Oxford University Press.

Fisher, R., Ury, W., & Patton, B. (2011). *Getting to Yes: Negotiating Agreement Without Giving In.* 3rd ed. New York: Penguin Books.

Goldstein, J. (2002). *One Dharma: The Emerging Western Buddhism.* San Francisco: HarperSanFrancisco.

Goleman, D. (1995). *Emotional Intelligence: Why It Matters More Than IQ.* New York: Bantam Books.

Grant, A. (2013). *Give and Take: Why Helping Others Drives Our Success.* New York: Viking.

Hanson, R. (2013). *Hardwiring Happiness: The New Brain Science of Contentment, Calm, and Confidence.* New York: Harmony Books.

Hof, W. (2020). *The Wim Hof Method: Activate Your Full Human Potential.* Boulder: Sounds True.

James, W. (1904). *A World of Pure Experience.* Journal of Philosophy, Psychology and Scientific Methods, 1(20), 533-543.

Kandel, E. R. (2006). *In Search of Memory: The Emergence of a New Science of Mind.* New York: W. W. Norton & Company.

LeDoux, J. (2015). *Anxious: Using the Brain to Understand and Treat Fear and Anxiety*. New York: Viking.

Lieberman, M. D. (2013). *Social: Why Our Brains Are Wired to Connect*. New York: Crown Publishers.

Lyubomirsky, S. (2007). *The How of Happiness: A Scientific Approach to Getting the Life You Want*. New York: Penguin Press.

Miller, E. K., & Cohen, J. D. (2001). An integrative theory of prefrontal cortex function. *Annual Review of Neuroscience*, 24(1), 167-202.

Nestor, J. (2020). *Breath: The New Science of a Lost Art*. New York: Riverhead Books.

Oettingen, G. (2014). *Rethinking Positive Thinking: Inside the New Science of Motivation*. New York: Current.

Pascual-Leone, A. (2005). The plastic human brain cortex. *Annual Review of Neuroscience*, 28, 377-401.

Rorty, R. (1989). *Contingency, Irony, and Solidarity*. Cambridge: Cambridge University Press.

Siegel, D. J. (2012). *The Developing Mind: How Relationships and the Brain Interact to Shape Who We Are*. 2nd ed. New York: Guilford Press.

Singer, T., & Klimecki, O. M. (2014). Empathy and compassion. *Current Biology*, 24(18), R875-R878.

Suzuki, S. (1970). *Zen Mind, Beginner's Mind*. New York: Weatherhill.

Taylor, J. B. (2008). *My Stroke of Insight: A Brain Scientist's Personal Journey*. New York: Viking.

Wallace, B. A., & Shapiro, S. L. (2006). Mental balance and well-being: Building bridges between Buddhism and Western psychology. *American Psychologist*, 61(7), 690-701.

Weil, A. (2011). *Spontaneous Happiness: A New Path to Emotional Well-Being*. New York: Little, Brown and Company.

# Chapter 14: The Future of Emotional Intelligence: AI, Education, and Society

## Introduction: The Paradox of Progress

In the labyrinthine corridors of human advancement, where silicon dreams dance with carbon realities, we find ourselves at an extraordinary inflection point. The twenty-first century unfolds before us like a vast, uncharted ocean—its depths concealing both treasures of unprecedented possibility and tempests of existential uncertainty. Technological revolutions cascade through our collective consciousness with the relentless force of avalanches, each innovation reshaping not merely how we work, learn, or communicate, but fundamentally altering our conception of what it means to be human in an increasingly mechanised world (Brynjolfsson & McAfee, 2014).

Artificial intelligence, that most ambitious of human creations, now stands as both mirror and rival—reflecting our cognitive capabilities while simultaneously threatening to eclipse them. Machine learning algorithms weave through vast datasets with supernatural precision, automation systems orchestrate symphonies of efficiency, and neural networks dream electric dreams that sometimes surpass their creators' wildest imaginings (Russell, 2019). Yet in this magnificent cacophony of technological triumph, a profound truth emerges from the shadows—one that speaks not to the supremacy of machines, but to the irreducible essence of human consciousness itself.

Emotional intelligence, that most quintessentially human capacity, will not merely survive the coming transformation; it will become the very foundation upon which our future civilisation stands. Like a lighthouse standing resolute against turbulent seas, emotional intelligence illuminates the path forward through the fog of technological disruption, offering not just survival, but transcendence (Goleman, 2020).

This chapter ventures into the heart of tomorrow's promise and peril, exploring how emotional intelligence positions itself not as antiquated wisdom in a digital age, but as the most sophisticated technology humanity has ever developed—the technology of the heart, the algorithm of empathy, the artificial intelligence that was never artificial at all.

## The Algorithmic Revolution and the Human Response

The rise of artificial intelligence presents us with a paradox worthy of ancient philosophers: as machines become increasingly intelligent, the unique value of human intelligence becomes both more precious and more precarious. Consider the breath-taking capabilities that artificial intelligence has already mastered—data analysis of incomprehensible complexity, pattern recognition that surpasses human perception, calculations performed at speeds that make human cognition appear glacial in comparison (LeCun, Bengio & Hinton, 2015).

These achievements represent more than mere technological progress; they constitute a fundamental reordering of cognitive hierarchy. For centuries, humans prided themselves on their analytical prowess, their mathematical acuity, their capacity for logical reasoning. Now, we witness machines performing these tasks with an efficiency that renders human effort not merely obsolete, but embarrassingly inadequate by comparison.

Yet herein lies the beautiful irony of progress: as machines master the quantifiable aspects of intelligence, they simultaneously illuminate the immeasurable depths of emotional intelligence that remain uniquely, irreducibly human. Artificial intelligence systems, despite their remarkable sophistication, encounter profound limitations when confronted with the subtleties of human emotion (Marcus & Davis, 2019).

Consider the delicate art of genuine empathy—not the algorithmic recognition of emotional patterns, but the profound human capacity to feel another's pain as one's own, to understand suffering not through data points but through the mysterious alchemy of shared consciousness. Or examine the complex terrain of moral judgment, where context, intention, cultural nuance, and ethical intuition converge in ways that resist algorithmic reduction. These capabilities represent not merely skills to be learned, but fundamental aspects of human consciousness that emerge from our embodied, relational, and inherently vulnerable existence (Damasio, 2018).

The most sophisticated AI systems can analyse millions of facial expressions and detect patterns in vocal inflection, yet they cannot comprehend the weight of a mother's worry, the complexity of adolescent identity formation, or the profound healing that occurs when one human truly sees and validates another's emotional experience. They can process vast libraries of human creativity, yet they cannot generate art that springs from authentic personal suffering, love that transcends rational calculation, or leadership that inspires others to transcend their limitations through shared vision and collective purpose.

## The Transformation of Human Value in the Age of Automation

As we stand at the threshold of an age where artificial intelligence assumes dominion over tasks once considered the exclusive province of human cognition, a fundamental recalibration of human value becomes not merely advisable but existentially necessary. The traditional metrics by which we have measured professional worth—technical proficiency, analytical speed, information processing capacity—increasingly pale in comparison to machine capabilities (Frey & Osborne, 2017).

This transformation demands nothing less than a revolution in our understanding of human potential. The future workforce will be characterised not by those who can compute fastest or process information most efficiently, but by those who can navigate the intricate landscape of human emotion with wisdom, grace, and authentic connection. The most valuable professionals will be those who possess what we might call "emotional mastery"—the sophisticated ability to understand, regulate, and channel emotion in service of human flourishing (Bar-On, 2006).

Collaborative intelligence emerges as perhaps the most critical competency of this new era—the capacity to work harmoniously across diverse teams, bridging differences in culture, generation, cognitive style, and worldview. This skill transcends mere tolerance or superficial accommodation; it requires the emotional sophistication to appreciate diversity as a source of collective strength, to navigate conflict as an opportunity for deeper understanding, and to forge unity without sacrificing the richness that emerges from difference (Druskat & Wolff, 2001).

Adaptive resilience represents another cornerstone of future professional competence—the emotional agility to navigate constant change without losing one's centre, to embrace uncertainty as creative opportunity rather than paralysing threat. This capacity requires not merely tolerance for ambiguity, but the emotional intelligence to find stability within instability, to maintain psychological equilibrium while riding the waves of perpetual transformation (Southwick & Charney, 2018).

Perhaps most importantly, the future demands ethical leadership of unprecedented sophistication—decision-making that honours human dignity in all its complexity, that considers not merely immediate outcomes but long-term consequences for human welfare and planetary sustainability. Such leadership requires emotional intelligence of the highest order: the capacity to hold multiple perspectives simultaneously, to feel the weight of responsibility without being paralysed by it, to inspire others toward shared vision while respecting individual autonomy (Gardner, 2011).

## Educational Renaissance: Cultivating Emotional Wisdom

The recognition that emotional intelligence constitutes the core competency of the future necessitates nothing less than a complete reimagining of educational purpose and practice. For too long, our educational systems have operated under the mechanistic assumption that learning consists primarily of information transfer—filling empty vessels with predetermined content, measuring success through standardised assessments that privilege analytical intelligence while ignoring emotional wisdom (Robinson, 2011).

This paradigm, perhaps adequate for an industrial age that valued conformity and predictable skill sets, proves woefully inadequate for a future that demands creativity, emotional agility, and the capacity for lifelong adaptation. The educational institutions of tomorrow must evolve from knowledge factories into environments for cultivating whole human beings—spaces where intellectual development occurs alongside emotional maturation, where academic achievement serves the larger purpose of human flourishing (Seligman et al., 2009).

Social and Emotional Learning (SEL) represents the vanguard of this educational transformation—systematic programmes that explicitly teach the skills most essential for human thriving: self-awareness that enables authentic self-knowledge, emotional regulation that prevents reactive behaviour, empathy that builds bridges across difference, and relationship skills that create communities of mutual support and shared purpose (Durlak et al., 2011).

These programmes recognise that emotional intelligence, like any sophisticated capacity, requires intentional cultivation through practice, reflection, and guided development. Students learn to identify and articulate their emotional experiences, to recognise the emotional states of others, to navigate interpersonal conflicts with grace and wisdom, and to channel their emotional energy in service of meaningful goals.

Mindfulness practices within educational settings offer another crucial dimension of emotional development—training students in the art of present-moment awareness, the capacity to observe their thoughts and emotions without being overwhelmed by them. Such practices cultivate what we might call "emotional presence"—the ability to remain centred and responsive rather than reactive, even in the face of challenging circumstances (Kabat-Zinn, 2003).

Project-based and collaborative learning methodologies create natural laboratories for emotional intelligence development, requiring students to negotiate different perspectives, manage interpersonal tensions, communicate across differences, and work together toward shared objectives. These experiences teach lessons that no textbook could convey—the subtle arts of influence without coercion, leadership without domination, and collaboration that honours both individual contribution and collective achievement (Thomas, 2000).

The integration of conflict resolution education becomes particularly crucial in preparing students for a world characterised by increasing diversity and complexity. Rather than avoiding or suppressing disagreement, emotionally intelligent education teaches students to engage conflict as a creative force—an opportunity for deeper understanding, innovative problem-solving, and strengthened relationships. Students learn that conflict, skilfully navigated, can become a source of growth rather than division (Fisher, Ury & Patton, 2011).

Ethical and moral reasoning courses address perhaps the most sophisticated dimension of emotional intelligence—the capacity to think deeply about values, to consider the broader implications of individual choices, and to develop what we might call "moral imagination"—the ability to envision and work toward futures that honour human dignity and planetary sustainability (Rest et al., 1999).

## Digital Empathy: Emotional Intelligence in Virtual Spaces

The digital revolution has created a paradox of connection—simultaneously bringing humanity closer together while creating new forms of isolation, misunderstanding, and emotional disconnection. Social media platforms promise a global community yet often deliver polarisation and superficial engagement. Virtual workspaces enable international collaboration while sometimes diminishing the subtle emotional cues that build trust and understanding. Online communities can foster profound bonds of mutual support or become breeding grounds for toxicity and dehumanisation (Turkle, 2017).

This digital landscape demands the development of what we might call "digital empathy"—a sophisticated form of emotional intelligence adapted to virtual environments. Digital empathy encompasses the capacity to read emotional subtleties in text-based communication, where tone and intention must be inferred from word choice, punctuation, and context rather than facial expression and vocal inflection. It requires the skill to navigate online conflicts with the same grace and wisdom one would bring to face-to-face disagreements, resisting the temptation toward inflammatory rhetoric that the anonymity of digital spaces sometimes encourages (Konrath, 2013).

Perhaps most importantly, digital empathy involves the cultivation of authentic presence in virtual spaces—the capacity to show up as a whole person rather than a curated persona, to build genuine trust and connection despite physical separation, and to maintain emotional integrity across multiple digital platforms and contexts. This requires tremendous emotional sophistication: the self-awareness to recognise how digital environments affect one's emotional state, the emotional regulation to respond thoughtfully rather than reactively to online provocations, and the empathy to remember that behind every screen lies a human being deserving of dignity and respect (Gardner & Davis, 2013).

The development of digital emotional intelligence also requires awareness of the mental health implications of constant connectivity. The human nervous system, evolved for face-to-face interaction in small communities, often struggles with the overwhelming stimulation of digital environments. Emotionally intelligent digital citizenship involves recognising the signs of digital overwhelm, establishing healthy boundaries with technology, and using digital tools in service of rather than at the expense of human well-being (Twenge, 2017).

## Emotional Intelligence as Social Healing

Beyond individual and professional development, emotional intelligence represents perhaps our greatest hope for addressing the profound social challenges that threaten human civilisation. Economic inequality, climate change, political polarisation, mental health crises, and cultural fragmentation—these existential challenges resist purely technological solutions. They require sophisticated emotional intelligence to build bridges across difference, to hold complex perspectives simultaneously, and to work collaboratively toward solutions that honour both individual needs and collective welfare (Putnam, 2000).

Consider the challenge of political polarisation, which threatens democratic institutions around the world. Technological solutions—better algorithms, improved fact-checking, enhanced security measures—address symptoms rather than root causes. The deeper issue lies in the emotional dynamics of human interaction: the tendency toward tribal identity, the comfort of ideological certainty, the fear of admitting error or changing one's mind. Healing political division requires the emotional intelligence to listen across differences, to hold one's own convictions lightly enough to remain open to new information, and to find common ground without sacrificing important principles (Haidt, 2012).

Climate change presents perhaps the ultimate test of collective emotional intelligence. The scientific evidence for human-caused climate change is overwhelming, yet meaningful action remains elusive—not because of inadequate technology or insufficient resources, but because of emotional and psychological barriers. Addressing climate change requires the emotional intelligence to feel genuine concern for future generations, to tolerate the anxiety of uncertainty without falling into paralysis or denial, and to make personal sacrifices for collective benefit. It demands the capacity for what we might call "intergenerational empathy"—the ability to feel responsibility for people not yet born and consequences not yet visible (Marshall, 2014).

Mental health crises, increasingly prevalent in developed societies, similarly require emotional intelligence at both individual and social levels. While medical interventions and therapeutic techniques play crucial roles, deeper healing occurs through human connection—the capacity to offer presence without judgment, to listen without trying to fix, and to create communities where vulnerability is met with compassion rather than shame. Emotionally intelligent societies create cultures that prioritise mental wellness, reduce stigma around emotional struggle, and provide support systems that honour the full spectrum of human experience (Keyes, 2007).

## Future-Proofing Through Emotional Wisdom

As the future unfolds with increasing unpredictability, individuals who not merely survive but thrive will be those who cultivate emotional intelligence as their most powerful adaptive capacity. This involves continuous growth in self-awareness—the ongoing process of understanding one's emotional patterns, triggers, values, and aspirations with ever-greater clarity and compassion. Self-aware individuals can navigate change more skilfully because they understand their own needs and limitations, allowing them to make choices aligned with their authentic values rather than reactive to external pressures (Craig, 2009).

Emotional agility represents another crucial dimension of future resilience—the capacity to feel emotions fully without being controlled by them, to extract wisdom from emotional experience without being overwhelmed by emotional intensity. Emotionally agile individuals can hold multiple, sometimes contradictory emotions simultaneously, recognising that complexity and ambiguity are inherent features of human experience rather than problems to be solved (David, 2016).

The cultivation of empathy across differences becomes increasingly vital in a world characterised by diversity and rapid change. This empathy extends beyond mere tolerance or intellectual understanding to include genuine curiosity about different perspectives, authentic appreciation for alternative ways of being, and the emotional capacity to find common humanity across apparent differences. Such empathy serves as both personal enrichment and social necessity, enabling collaboration across the boundaries that often divide human communities (Rifkin, 2009).

Communication skills of extraordinary sophistication will distinguish future leaders—not merely the ability to convey information clearly, but the capacity to inspire, heal, challenge, and unite through language. This communication integrates intellectual content with emotional resonance, analytical precision with imaginative vision, individual expression with collective need. It requires the emotional intelligence to read one's audience accurately, to adapt one's message to different contexts and recipients, and to speak truth with both courage and compassion (Brown, 2018).

Perhaps most importantly, future thriving requires the capacity to build and maintain networks of trust and collaboration—relationships characterised by mutual respect, shared purpose, and genuine care for one another's welfare. These networks provide not merely professional advantage but psychological resilience, creative inspiration, and moral support. Building such networks requires tremendous emotional intelligence: the authenticity that invites trust, the reliability that sustains it, and the generosity that deepens it over time (Grant, 2013).

## Innovations and Applications: The Frontier of Emotional Technology

The intersection of emotional intelligence and technological innovation represents one of the most fascinating frontiers of human development. Emotional AI, while unable to replicate the full depth of human emotional experience, shows promise in supporting human emotional intelligence through sophisticated pattern recognition and response systems. These technologies can detect emotional states through facial expression analysis, vocal tone assessment, and physiological monitoring, potentially offering valuable support in healthcare settings where early detection of depression or anxiety could save lives, in educational environments where adapting to students' emotional states could enhance learning, and in customer service contexts where responding appropriately to frustration or confusion could improve human satisfaction (Picard, 2000).

However, the development of emotional AI raises profound ethical questions about privacy, consent, and the commodification of human emotion. The capacity to detect and potentially manipulate emotional states carries enormous potential for both benefit and harm. Ensuring that emotional AI serves human flourishing rather than exploitation requires sophisticated ethical frameworks, robust regulatory oversight, and ongoing dialogue between technologists, ethicists, and society at large (Jobin, Ienca & Vayena, 2019).

Corporate investment in emotional intelligence training represents another significant development, with major organisations recognising that technical skills alone are insufficient for success in complex, collaborative environments. Companies like Google, Salesforce, and Microsoft have implemented comprehensive programmes focusing on mindfulness training, resilience building, feedback skills development, empathy cultivation, and conscious leadership practices. These initiatives represent more than mere employee development; they constitute recognition that organisational success increasingly depends on the emotional intelligence of its members (Cherniss & Goleman, 2001).

Global movements toward emotional literacy in education show promise for creating generations of emotionally intelligent leaders, innovators, and citizens. Programs like the Yale Center for Emotional Intelligence's RULER initiative work systematically to integrate emotional learning into academic curricula, training educators to model and teach emotional intelligence while creating school cultures that prioritise both intellectual and emotional development. These efforts represent investment in humanity's future—recognition that the challenges ahead require not just smarter individuals, but wiser, more emotionally sophisticated communities (Brackett, 2019).

## Conclusion: The Heart of Tomorrow

As we stand at the threshold of a future shaped by artificial intelligence, global challenges, and unprecedented change, we discover that our salvation lies not in the superiority of our machines, but in the depth of our humanity. Emotional intelligence emerges not as an optional enhancement to human capability, but as the essential foundation upon which all meaningful progress depends.

The future belongs not to those who can compute fastest or process information most efficiently—machines will always surpass us in these domains. The future belongs to those who can love most deeply, empathise most authentically, lead most inspiringly, and connect most genuinely across the full spectrum of human difference and complexity.

In a world where information is abundant and automation is ubiquitous, our emotional wisdom becomes our most powerful competitive advantage and our most precious gift to future generations. As we craft the next chapter of human civilisation, let us ensure that it is written not merely with the precision of algorithms, but with the wisdom of hearts that have learned to beat in harmony with the vast, beautiful, fragile symphony of human experience.

The path forward illuminated by emotional intelligence leads not merely to professional success or personal fulfilment, but to the realisation of humanity's highest potential—a civilisation characterised by wisdom, compassion, creativity, and the kind of profound connection that transforms not just individuals, but the entire human family.

---

## References


Bar-On, R. (2006). The Bar-On model of emotional-social intelligence (ESI). *Psicothema*, 18, 13-25.

Brackett, M. (2019). *Permission to feel: Unlocking the power of emotions to help our kids, ourselves, and our society thrive*. Celadon Books.

Brown, B. (2018). *Dare to lead: Brave work, tough conversations, whole hearts*. Random House.

Brynjolfsson, E., & McAfee, A. (2014). *The second machine age: Work, progress, and prosperity in a time of brilliant technologies*. W. W. Norton & Company.

Cherniss, C., & Goleman, D. (Eds.). (2001). *The emotionally intelligent workplace: How to select for, measure, and improve emotional intelligence in individuals, groups, and organizations*. Jossey-Bass.

Craig, C. (2009). *The self-aware universe: How consciousness creates the material world*. Springer.

Damasio, A. (2018). *The strange order of things: Life, feeling, and the making of cultures*. Pantheon Books.

David, S. (2016). *Emotional agility: Get unstuck, embrace change, and thrive in work and life*. Avery.

Druskat, V. U., & Wolff, S. B. (2001). Building the emotional intelligence of groups. *Harvard Business Review*, 79(3), 80-90.

Durlak, J. A., Weissberg, R. P., Dymnicki, A. B., Taylor, R. D., & Schellinger, K. B. (2011). The impact of enhancing students' social and emotional learning: A meta-analysis of school-based universal interventions. *Child Development*, 82(1), 405-432.

Fisher, R., Ury, W. L., & Patton, B. (2011). *Getting to yes: Negotiating agreement without giving in*. Penguin Books.

Frey, C. B., & Osborne, M. A. (2017). The future of employment: How susceptible are jobs to computerisation? *Technological Forecasting and Social Change*, 114, 254-280.

Gardner, H. (2011). *Leading minds: An anatomy of leadership*. Basic Books.

Gardner, H., & Davis, K. (2013). *The app generation: How today's youth navigate identity, intimacy, and imagination in a digital world*. Yale University Press.

Goleman, D. (2020). *Emotional intelligence: Why it matters more than IQ*. Bantam Books.

Grant, A. (2013). *Give and take: Why helping others drives our success*. Penguin Books.

Haidt, J. (2012). *The righteous mind: Why good people are divided by politics and religion*. Vintage Books.

Jobin, A., Ienca, M., & Vayena, E. (2019). The global landscape of AI ethics guidelines. *Nature Machine Intelligence*, 1(9), 389-399.

Kabat-Zinn, J. (2003). *Mindfulness-based interventions in context: Past, present, and future*. Clinical Psychology: Science and Practice*, 10(2), 144-156.

Keyes, C. L. (2007). Promoting and protecting mental health as flourishing: A complementary strategy for improving national mental health. *American Psychologist*, 62(2), 95-108.

Konrath, S. H. (2013). The empathy paradox: Increasing disconnection in the age of increasing connection. In R. Luppicini (Ed.), *Handbook of research on technoself: Identity in a technological society* (pp. 204-228). IGI Global.

LeCun, Y., Bengio, Y., & Hinton, G. (2015). Deep learning. *Nature*, 521(7553), 436-444.

Marcus, G., & Davis, E. (2019). *Rebooting AI: Building artificial intelligence we can trust*. Pantheon Books.

Marshall, G. (2014). *Don't even think about it: Why our brains are wired to ignore climate change*. Bloomsbury Publishing.

Picard, R. W. (2000). *Affective computing*. MIT Press.

Putnam, R. D. (2000). *Bowling alone: The collapse and revival of American community*. Simon & Schuster.

Rest, J., Narvaez, D., Bebeau, M., & Thoma, S. (1999). *A neo-Kohlbergian approach: The DIT and schema theory*. Educational Psychology Review*, 11(4), 291-324.

Rifkin, J. (2009). *The empathic civilization: The race to global consciousness in a world in crisis*. Polity Press.

Robinson, K. (2011). *Out of our minds: Learning to be creative*. Capstone Publishing.

Russell, S. (2019). *Human compatible: Artificial intelligence and the problem of control*. Viking Press.

Seligman, M. E., Ernst, R. M., Gillham, J., Reivich, K., & Linkins, M. (2009). Positive education: Positive psychology and classroom interventions. *Oxford Review of Education*, 35(3), 293-311.

Southwick, S. M., & Charney, D. S. (2018). *Resilience: The science of mastering life's greatest challenges*. Cambridge University Press.

Thomas, J. W. (2000). A review of research on project-based learning. *The Autodesk Foundation*.

Turkle, S. (2017). *Alone together: Why we expect more from technology and less from each other*. Basic Books.

Twenge, J. M. (2017). *iGen: Why today's super-connected kids are growing up less rebellious, more tolerant, less happy—and completely unprepared for adulthood*. Atria Books.

# Chapter 15: Living an Emotionally Intelligent Life: The Path to Fulfilment

## Introduction: The Architecture of Being

In the vast cathedral of human consciousness, where thoughts echo like whispered prayers and emotions surge like ancient hymns, we arrive at the most sacred threshold of our exploration—the moment when understanding transforms into being, when knowledge becomes wisdom incarnate. Emotional intelligence, as we have discovered throughout this journey, transcends the boundaries of mere concept or skill; it emerges as nothing less than a fundamental way of existing in the world, a philosophical framework for navigating the profound complexity of human experience with grace, authenticity, and transcendent purpose (Aristotle, trans. 2009).

To live an emotionally intelligent life is to choose, with each breath and heartbeat, awareness over the comfortable numbness of autopilot existence. It is to embrace compassion as a revolutionary act in a world too often governed by judgment and separation. It demands the cultivation of resilience not as mere endurance, but as the capacity to transform suffering into wisdom, setbacks into stepping stones, and wounds into sources of healing for others. Most profoundly, it requires us to choose connection over the isolation that modernity too frequently offers as an acceptable substitute for authentic human communion (Frankl, 2006).

This penultimate chapter ventures beyond the theoretical framework of emotional intelligence into the lived reality of what it means to embody these principles fully. We explore not merely what emotionally intelligent people do, but who they become—how they move through the world as sources of stability in chaos, beacons of hope in darkness, and architects of transformation in communities starved for authentic leadership and genuine care.

The path we illuminate here is not one of perfection—for perfection is the enemy of growth—but rather one of conscious becoming, of moment-by-moment choices toward our highest potential. It is the path of those who dare to live with their hearts wide open, even in a world that sometimes rewards emotional armor over vulnerable authenticity (Brown, 2010).

## The Sacred Territory of Self-Understanding

The foundation of an emotionally intelligent life rests upon what we might call "radical self-awareness"—not the superficial self-consciousness that plagues many modern individuals, but a profound, compassionate understanding of one's inner landscape that emerges from years of patient, loving observation. This awareness encompasses far more than intellectual knowledge about oneself; it represents an embodied understanding of one's emotional patterns, a visceral recognition of one's triggers and tendencies, and a deep appreciation for the unique combination of gifts, wounds, dreams, and fears that constitute one's authentic self (Siegel, 2012).

Such self-awareness requires what Buddhist psychology terms "mindful witnessing"—the capacity to observe one's thoughts, emotions, and reactions with the same gentle curiosity one might bring to watching clouds drift across an endless sky. This witnessing consciousness neither judges nor attempts to change what it observes; instead, it simply sees with clarity and compassion, recognising that all emotional states are temporary visitors in the vast space of consciousness rather than permanent residents that define one's identity (Kabat-Zinn, 2013).

The cultivation of radical self-awareness demands consistent practices of introspection and reflection. This might manifest as daily journaling that explores not merely external events but internal responses to those events—the subtle shifts in mood that accompany different interactions, the patterns of thought that emerge under stress, the values that guide decisions in moments of uncertainty. It requires the courage to examine one's shadow aspects—those parts of the psyche that Carl Jung identified as containing both rejected positive qualities and suppressed negative impulses (Jung, 1968).

Modern neuroscience confirms what contemplative traditions have long understood: self-awareness is not a fixed trait but a capacity that can be developed through intentional practice. Functional magnetic resonance imaging studies demonstrate that individuals who engage in regular self-reflective practices show increased activity in the prefrontal cortex regions associated with executive function and emotional regulation, while simultaneously showing decreased reactivity in the amygdala regions associated with fear and defensive responses (Davidson & Lutz, 2008).

This neuroplasticity of awareness offers profound hope for human transformation. Regardless of one's starting point—whether one begins the journey of emotional intelligence with high natural capacity or significant challenges—the brain's remarkable adaptability ensures that committed practice yields measurable growth in emotional wisdom and behavioural flexibility.

## The Art of Emotional Mastery

The second pillar of emotionally intelligent living involves what we might term "conscious emotional regulation"—not the suppression or denial of emotional experience, but rather the sophisticated capacity to feel deeply while responding wisely. This mastery represents one of the highest achievements of human psychological development, requiring the integration of emotional sensitivity with behavioural discipline, passionate engagement with thoughtful restraint (Gross, 2014).

True emotional regulation begins with the radical acceptance of emotional experience itself. Our culture often treats emotions as inconvenient interruptions to rational thought, obstacles to productivity, or signs of weakness to be overcome. An emotionally intelligent approach recognises emotions as sophisticated information systems that have evolved over millions of years to guide human behaviour toward survival and thriving. Fear alerts us to potential dangers, anger mobilises energy to address injustice or boundary violations, sadness signals the need for comfort and support, and joy indicates alignment with our deepest values and purposes (Damasio, 2018).

The practice of conscious emotional regulation therefore involves learning to listen to emotional messages without being overwhelmed by emotional intensity. This requires developing what psychologists call "distress tolerance"—the capacity to experience uncomfortable emotions without immediately seeking escape through distraction, numbing, or reactive behaviour. Such tolerance is not passive endurance but active engagement, a willingness to stay present with difficult feelings long enough to understand their wisdom and respond appropriately (Linehan, 2014).

Advanced emotional regulation also involves the cultivation of what we might call "emotional flexibility"—the ability to shift emotional states when circumstances warrant such shifts. This is not emotional suppression or artificial mood manipulation, but rather the natural capacity to move fluidly between different emotional modes as situations require. A parent might move from playful joy with children to serious concern about their safety to tender compassion for their struggles, all within the span of minutes, each emotional state appropriate to its context and fully experienced in its time.

The development of emotional mastery requires understanding the intimate relationship between thoughts, emotions, and behaviours. Cognitive-behavioural research demonstrates that these three domains of human experience continuously influence one another in recursive loops. Changing thoughts can shift emotions, which in turn influences behaviours, which then affects thoughts in an ongoing cycle of mutual influence (Beck, 2011). Emotionally intelligent individuals learn to intervene skilfully at any point in this cycle, using cognitive reframing to shift perspective, emotional regulation techniques to modulate intensity, or behavioural changes to interrupt problematic patterns.

## Purpose as the North Star of Existence

The third dimension of emotionally intelligent living involves the cultivation of what Viktor Frankl termed "logotherapy"—the alignment of daily existence with transcendent meaning and purpose. Without such alignment, even the most sophisticated emotional skills become mere techniques rather than expressions of authentic being. Purpose provides the context within which emotional intelligence finds its deepest expression and greatest power (Frankl, 2006).

Living with purpose requires distinguishing between what psychologists call "hedonic" and "eudaimonic" well-being. Hedonic well-being focuses on pleasure maximisation and pain avoidance—a legitimate but ultimately limited approach to human flourishing. Eudaimonic well-being, by contrast, emphasises meaning, personal growth, and contribution to something greater than oneself. Research consistently demonstrates that while hedonic pleasures provide temporary satisfaction, eudaimonic engagement generates lasting fulfilment and psychological resilience (Ryff & Singer, 2008).

The discovery of authentic purpose often emerges from what we might call "values archaeology"—the patient excavation of one's deepest commitments and most cherished principles. This process requires moving beyond socially conditioned expectations to uncover the unique combination of passions, talents, and concerns that constitute one's authentic calling. It involves asking not merely "What do I want?" but rather "What wants to emerge through me?" and "How can my unique gifts serve the healing and flourishing of the world?" (Palmer, 2000).

Purpose-driven living transforms the experience of challenge and difficulty. When actions are aligned with deeper meaning, obstacles become opportunities for growth rather than reasons for despair. Setbacks become information rather than evidence of failure. Criticism becomes feedback rather than personal attack. This transformation occurs not through denial of difficulty but through the context that purpose provides—the recognition that temporary struggles serve longer-term significance.

The cultivation of purpose also requires what we might call "intention-setting practices"—regular rituals that connect daily activities to larger vision. This might involve morning meditations that dedicate the day's activities to service, evening reflections that evaluate whether actions aligned with values, or weekly planning sessions that ensure time and energy allocation reflects authentic priorities rather than mere urgency or social pressure.

## Empathy as Revolutionary Practice

The fourth pillar of emotionally intelligent living involves the systematic cultivation of empathy—not as occasional kindness but as a fundamental orientation toward all beings encountered in the journey of life. This empathy extends far beyond sympathetic concern to encompass what phenomenologists call "intersubjective understanding"—the capacity to sense and appreciate the subjective experience of others from within their own frame of reference rather than projecting one's own assumptions and expectations (Husserl, trans. 1913).

The development of sophisticated empathy requires overcoming what psychologists term "empathy gaps"—the systematic biases that limit our capacity to understand others. These include the "fundamental attribution error," which leads us to attribute others' behaviours to character flaws while attributing our own behaviours to situational factors; "projection bias," which causes us to assume others share our preferences, values, and reactions; and "affective forecasting errors," which lead us to mispredict how others will feel in various circumstances (Gilbert, 2006).

Advanced empathy involves what we might call "perspective-taking flexibility"—the ability to shift fluidly between different viewpoints, holding multiple perspectives simultaneously without collapsing into relativism or abandoning one's own values. This capacity proves especially crucial in navigating the polarised political and cultural landscape of contemporary society, where the ability to understand opposing viewpoints without necessarily agreeing with them becomes essential for democratic dialogue and social cohesion (Haidt, 2012).

The practice of empathy also requires developing "emotional granularity"—the capacity to distinguish subtle differences in emotional experience, both in oneself and others. Research by Lisa Feldman Barrett demonstrates that individuals with high emotional granularity show greater psychological resilience, more effective emotional regulation, and stronger interpersonal relationships. They can distinguish, for example, between frustration and disappointment, between anxiety and excitement, between love and attachment, and respond appropriately to each distinct emotional reality (Barrett, 2017).

Empathic development involves regular practices that stretch one's capacity for understanding across differences. This might include engaging in "empathy interviews"—structured conversations designed to understand others' experiences without judgment or agenda. It might involve "perspective journaling"—writing about challenging situations from multiple viewpoints, including those of people one disagrees with or dislikes. It might include "compassion meditation"—formal practices that systematically extend goodwill toward oneself, loved ones, neutral persons, difficult people, and all beings (Salzberg, 2011).

## The Architecture of Authentic Relationship

The fifth dimension of emotionally intelligent living involves the conscious creation and maintenance of relationships characterised by what philosopher Martin Buber called "I-Thou" rather than "I-It" connection—relationships that honour the full humanity of all participants rather than treating others as objects to be manipulated or used for personal advantage (Buber, 1970). Such relationships become laboratories for emotional and spiritual growth, spaces where individuals can practice vulnerability, accountability, forgiveness, and unconditional positive regard.

Authentic relationships require what psychologists term "differentiation"—the capacity to maintain one's own identity and values while remaining emotionally connected to others. This involves neither the fusion that characterises co-dependent relationships nor the isolation that marks avoidant attachment patterns, but rather a mature interdependence that honours both individual autonomy and relational connection. Highly differentiated individuals can remain calm and centred even when others around them are anxious or reactive, while simultaneously maintaining empathic connection and appropriate responsiveness (Bowen, 1978).

The cultivation of authentic relationships demands mastery of what John Gottman calls the "Four Horsemen"—criticism, contempt, defensiveness, and stonewalling—patterns of interaction that reliably predict relationship deterioration. Instead of these destructive patterns, emotionally intelligent individuals learn to practice "soft start-ups" when raising concerns, to offer appreciation and admiration regularly, to take responsibility for their own contributions to problems, and to engage in repair attempts when conflicts arise (Gottman & Silver, 1999).

Advanced relational skills also involve the capacity for what we might call "relational mindfulness"—moment-to-moment awareness of the emotional dynamics occurring within interpersonal interaction. This includes noticing when conversations shift from connection to competition, recognising when one's own triggers are activated and might lead to reactive responses, and sensing when others need space, support, challenge, or simple presence. Such awareness allows for real-time course corrections that keep relationships aligned with love and respect rather than unconscious power struggles or emotional manipulation.

The practice of authentic relationship also requires developing comfort with what Brené Brown calls "the vulnerability of being seen"—the willingness to share one's authentic thoughts, feelings, struggles, and dreams even when such sharing involves risk of rejection, misunderstanding, or judgment. This vulnerability is not mere self-disclosure but rather the courage to show up as one's genuine self rather than performing a role designed to please others or avoid conflict (Brown, 2012).

## Leadership as Sacred Service

The sixth pillar of emotionally intelligent living recognises that regardless of formal titles or positions, every individual exercises leadership through the energy, presence, and influence they bring to their interactions and environments. This leadership is not about dominance or control but about what Robert Greenleaf called "servant leadership"—the use of one's gifts, wisdom, and position in service of others' growth and the common good (Greenleaf, 2002).

Emotionally intelligent leadership begins with what we might call "presence-based influence"—the capacity to affect others not primarily through words or actions but through the quality of consciousness one brings to each moment. This presence communicates safety, wisdom, and possibility without requiring explicit verbal communication. Research in social neuroscience demonstrates that emotions are highly contagious, spreading through groups via unconscious mimicry of facial expressions, vocal tones, and body language. Leaders who embody calm confidence, genuine care, and hopeful vision literally transform the emotional climate of their environments (Hatfield, Cacioppo & Rapson, 1994).

Effective emotional leadership also requires mastery of what Daniel Goleman calls "social awareness"—the sophisticated ability to read the emotional currents within groups, to sense when energy is building or declining, to recognise when individuals need support or challenge, and to intervene appropriately to maintain psychological safety while promoting growth and productivity. This awareness extends beyond individual emotions to encompass group dynamics, organisational culture, and systemic patterns that may not be immediately visible but significantly influence collective functioning (Goleman, 2002).

The practice of emotionally intelligent leadership involves regular "systems thinking"—the capacity to perceive how individual actions ripple through larger networks of relationship and influence. This thinking recognises that seemingly isolated problems often reflect deeper systemic issues, that sustainable solutions require addressing root causes rather than merely symptoms, and that effective change often requires patience, persistence, and strategic timing rather than force or urgency (Senge, 2006).

Advanced leadership also demands what we might call "moral courage"—the willingness to act in accordance with ethical principles even when such action involves personal risk or social disapproval. This courage emerges from the integration of clear values, emotional regulation skills, and commitment to purposes larger than self-interest. It enables leaders to speak truth to power, to advocate for marginalised voices, to challenge unjust systems, and to model the change they wish to see in the world (Kidder, 2005).

## Self-Compassion as Sustaining Force

The seventh and perhaps most crucial pillar of emotionally intelligent living involves the cultivation of self-compassion—the capacity to extend to oneself the same kindness, understanding, and support one would offer to a beloved friend facing difficulty. This self-compassion is not self-indulgence or self-pity but rather a form of emotional wisdom that recognises suffering as an inherent part of the human condition and responds to personal struggles with tenderness rather than harsh judgment (Neff, 2011).

Self-compassion consists of three interconnected components: self-kindness rather than self-judgment, common humanity rather than isolation, and mindfulness rather than over-identification with painful experiences. Self-kindness involves treating oneself with gentleness during times of failure, mistake, or suffering rather than engaging in harsh self-criticism that amplifies pain without promoting growth. Common humanity recognises that struggle, imperfection, and loss are universal human experiences rather than personal failures or evidence of individual inadequacy. Mindfulness allows one to observe difficult emotions and thoughts without being overwhelmed by them or pushing them away through denial or distraction.

Research by Kristin Neff demonstrates that individuals with high self-compassion show greater emotional resilience, more stable self-esteem, lower levels of anxiety and depression, and stronger motivation for personal growth and improvement. Paradoxically, self-compassion proves more effective than self-criticism in promoting positive behavioural change, as it creates the psychological safety necessary for honest self-examination and the emotional resources required for sustained effort toward improvement (Neff & Germer, 2018).

The cultivation of self-compassion requires recognising and changing the inner critic—that harsh internal voice that developed during childhood as a misguided attempt to motivate good behaviour or protect against rejection. This voice often reflects internalised messages from critical parents, teachers, or peers rather than actual wisdom about what promotes growth and well-being. Transforming this inner critic into what we might call an "inner mentor"—a supportive voice that offers encouragement, perspective, and gentle guidance—represents one of the most important psychological achievements of mature emotional development.

Self-compassion practices might include "loving-kindness meditation" directed toward oneself, "self-compassion letters" written during times of difficulty, or "self-compassion breaks" that offer oneself comfort during challenging moments. These practices gradually rewire neural pathways associated with self-relation, creating more supportive and nurturing internal environments that sustain rather than deplete emotional resources.

## Daily Rhythms of Emotional Wisdom

The integration of emotional intelligence into daily life requires the establishment of what we might call "contemplative practices"—regular rituals and routines that support ongoing emotional development and sustain the capacity for wise response rather than unconscious reaction. These practices need not be elaborate or time-consuming; their power lies in consistency and intentionality rather than complexity or duration.

Morning practices might include "intention-setting meditation"—brief periods of quiet reflection that connect the day's activities to larger purposes and values. This might involve asking questions such as: "How do I want to show up in my relationships today?" "What energy do I want to bring to challenging situations?" "How can I serve the greater good through my work and interactions?" Such practices orient consciousness toward growth and contribution rather than mere survival or pleasure-seeking.

Midday practices might involve "emotional check-ins"—brief pauses that assess current emotional states and their influence on thoughts, behaviours, and relationships. This might involve asking: "What am I feeling right now?" "How are these emotions affecting my interactions?" "What do these emotions need from me?" Such awareness prevents the accumulation of emotional tension and allows for course corrections before minor issues become major problems.

Evening practices might include "gratitude reflection"—systematic appreciation for positive experiences, personal growth, and contributions received from others throughout the day. Research demonstrates that regular gratitude practice increases life satisfaction, strengthens immune function, improves sleep quality, and enhances social relationships. Gratitude shifts attention from what is lacking or problematic toward what is abundant and meaningful, creating upward spirals of positive emotion and engagement (Emmons, 2007).

Weekly practices might involve "empathy expansion exercises"—deliberate attempts to understand perspectives different from one's own through reading, conversation, or imaginative exercise. This might include engaging with literature, films, or documentaries that explore unfamiliar cultures or experiences, having conversations with people whose backgrounds differ significantly from one's own, or participating in volunteer activities that expose one to different forms of human struggle and resilience.

Monthly practices might include "growth celebration rituals"—formal acknowledgment of progress made in emotional development, relationships improved, challenges navigated skilfully, or contributions made to others' well-being. Such celebrations reinforce positive change and maintain motivation for continued growth even when progress feels slow or invisible.

## The Ripple Effects of Emotional Awakening

The commitment to living an emotionally intelligent life creates what systems theorists call "positive feedback loops"—patterns of influence that amplify beneficial outcomes across widening circles of relationship and community. The individual who embodies emotional wisdom becomes a source of stability and inspiration for family members, colleagues, friends, and even strangers encountered in daily life. This influence operates not through preaching or teaching but through modelling—demonstrating what becomes possible when human beings live from their highest emotional capacities rather than their most primitive reactive patterns.

Within families, emotionally intelligent individuals create what psychologists call "secure attachment" environments—relational contexts characterised by safety, attunement, and unconditional positive regard. Children raised in such environments develop stronger emotional regulation skills, greater empathy, more resilient self-esteem, and better capacity for forming healthy relationships throughout their lives. Partners of emotionally intelligent individuals report higher relationship satisfaction, greater emotional intimacy, and more effective conflict resolution. The emotional wisdom of one family member literally raises the emotional intelligence of the entire family system (Siegel & Hartzell, 2003).

Within organisations, emotionally intelligent individuals contribute to what researchers call "psychological safety"—collective environments where individuals feel free to express ideas, admit mistakes, ask questions, and take creative risks without fear of punishment or humiliation. Such environments show significantly higher levels of innovation, productivity, learning, and employee satisfaction. Teams with emotionally intelligent members demonstrate better communication, more effective problem-solving, and greater resilience during periods of change or stress (Edmondson, 2019).

Within communities, emotionally intelligent individuals often become what sociologists call "social entrepreneurs"—individuals who identify unmet needs and create innovative solutions that benefit the common good. They serve as bridges across cultural divides, mediators in conflicts, advocates for marginalised voices, and creators of inclusive spaces where diverse groups can come together around shared purposes. Their emotional wisdom enables them to navigate complex social dynamics while maintaining focus on collaborative solutions rather than competitive advantage.

The global impact of individuals committed to emotional intelligence cannot be overstated in an era characterised by unprecedented challenges requiring collaborative responses. Climate change, economic inequality, technological disruption, political polarisation, and mental health crises all demand sophisticated emotional capacities that enable cooperation across difference, sustained commitment to long-term solutions, and resilience in the face of complexity and uncertainty.

## Conclusion: The Invitation to Wholeness

As we reach the conclusion of this exploration into the depths and heights of emotional intelligence, we find ourselves not at an ending but at a threshold—the threshold between understanding and embodiment, between knowing and being, between aspiration and actualisation. The journey we have travelled together through these pages represents more than an intellectual exercise; it constitutes an invitation to a way of life that honours both the magnificent complexity and the profound simplicity of human existence.

Living an emotionally intelligent life is not about achieving perfection—indeed, the pursuit of perfection often becomes the enemy of authentic growth. Rather, it is about embracing what we might call "conscious imperfection"—the willingness to remain eternally curious about oneself and others, eternally committed to growth, eternally open to the lessons that emerge from both success and failure. It is about becoming a student of the human condition in all its beauty and brokenness, finding wisdom in wounds and strength in vulnerability.

The world we inhabit today desperately needs individuals who dare to live from their emotional wisdom rather than their reactive patterns, who choose connection over separation, who respond to fear with love and to hatred with compassion. In an age of artificial intelligence and technological marvels, our most advanced technology remains the human heart—when it is open, aware, and aligned with purposes greater than self-interest.

Your commitment to emotional intelligence represents more than personal development; it constitutes a form of social activism, a contribution to the healing and evolution of human consciousness itself. Every moment of emotional awareness, every choice to respond rather than react, every act of empathy that bridges difference, every expression of authentic vulnerability that invites others into deeper truth—these become threads in the larger tapestry of human transformation.

The invitation before you is not to become someone other than who you are, but to become who you have always been beneath the conditioning, fear, and unconscious patterns that may have obscured your essential nature. It is an invitation to live as the full human being you were born to be—awake, compassionate, resilient, connected, and contributing to the magnificent project of creating a more loving world.

This journey of emotional intelligence begins anew each morning when you open your eyes and choose awareness over automaticity, each moment when you pause between stimulus and response, each interaction when you see the person before you as a fellow traveller deserving of dignity and understanding. It continues through every challenge that invites you to grow, every relationship that calls forth your capacity for love, every opportunity to serve something greater than yourself.

The world needs your heart—not the defended heart that has learned to protect itself through armor and distance, but the open heart that has learned to transform pain into wisdom, fear into compassion, and separation into connection. This heart is your gift to the world and the world's gift to you.

Go forward with courage, knowing that your commitment to emotional intelligence joins you with countless others who have chosen the path of conscious living. Together, you are writing the next chapter of human evolution—not through technological advancement alone, but through the much more profound advancement of human consciousness itself.

The future depends not on artificial intelligence, but on authentic intelligence—the intelligence of the heart, the wisdom of emotional maturity, the courage to live fully human in a world that often settles for less. This is your invitation. This is your opportunity. This is your time.

Live it fully. Live it wisely. Live it with your whole heart.

---

# References

Aristotle. (2009). *The Nicomachean ethics* (D. Ross, Trans.). Oxford University Press. (Original work published 4th century BCE)

Barrett, L. F. (2017). *How emotions are made: The secret life of the brain*. Houghton Mifflin Harcourt.

Beck, J. S. (2011). *Cognitive behaviour therapy: Basics and beyond* (2nd ed.). Guilford Press.

Bowen, M. (1978). *Family therapy in clinical practice*. Jason Aronson.

Brown, B. (2010). *The gifts of imperfection: Let go of who you think you're supposed to be and embrace who you are*. Hazelden Publishing.

Brown, B. (2012). *Daring greatly: How the courage to be vulnerable transforms the way we live, love, parent, and lead*. Gotham Books.

Buber, M. (1970). *I and thou* (W. Kaufmann, Trans.). T&T Clark. (Original work published 1923)

Damasio, A. (2018). *The strange order of things: Life, feeling, and the making of cultures*. Pantheon Books.

Davidson, R. J., & Lutz, A. (2008). Buddha's brain: Neuroplasticity and meditation. *IEEE Signal Processing Magazine*, 25(6), 176-188.

Edmondson, A. (2019). *The fearless organization: Creating psychological safety for learning, innovation, and growth*. Wiley.

Emmons, R. A. (2007). *Thanks! How the new science of gratitude can make you happier*. Houghton Mifflin Harcourt.

Frankl, V. E. (2006). *Man's search for meaning*. Beacon Press. (Original work published 1946)

Gilbert, D. (2006). *Stumbling on happiness*. Knopf.

Goleman, D. (2002). *Primal leadership: Realizing the power of emotional intelligence*. Harvard Business Review Press.

Gottman, J., & Silver, N. (1999). *The seven principles for making marriage work*. Crown Publishers.

Greenleaf, R. K. (2002). *Servant leadership: A journey into the nature of legitimate power and greatness* (25th anniversary ed.). Paulist Press.

Gross, J. J. (2014). *Handbook of emotion regulation* (2nd ed.). Guilford Press.

Haidt, J. (2012). *The righteous mind: Why good people are divided by politics and religion*. Vintage Books.

Hatfield, E., Cacioppo, J. T., & Rapson, R. L. (1994). *Emotional contagion*. Cambridge University Press.

Husserl, E. (1913). *Ideas: General introduction to pure phenomenology* (W. R. Boyce Gibson, Trans.). Macmillan.

Jung, C. G. (1968). *The archetypes and the collective unconscious* (2nd ed.). Princeton University Press.

Kabat-Zinn, J. (2013). *Full catastrophe living: Using the wisdom of your body and mind to face stress, pain, and illness* (Revised ed.). Bantam Books.

Kidder, R. M. (2005). *Moral courage*. William Morrow.

Linehan, M. M. (2014). *DBT Skills training manual* (2nd ed.). Guilford Press.

Neff, K. (2011). *Self-compassion: The proven power of being kind to yourself*. William Morrow.

Neff, K. D., & Germer, C. K. (2018). *The mindful self-compassion workbook: A proven way to accept yourself, build inner strength, and thrive*. Guilford Press.

Palmer, P. J. (2000). *Let your life speak: Listening for the voice of vocation*. Jossey-Bass.

Ryff, C. D., & Singer, B. H. (2008). Know thyself and become what you are: A eudaimonic approach to psychological well-being. *Journal of Happiness Studies*, 9(1), 13-39.

Salzberg, S. (2011). *Real happiness: The power of meditation*. Workman Publishing.

Senge, P. M. (2006). *The fifth discipline: The art and practice of the learning organization* (Revised ed.). Doubleday.

Siegel, D. J. (2012). *The developing mind: How relationships and the brain interact to shape who we are* (2nd ed.). Guilford Press.

Siegel, D. J., & Hartzell, M. (2003). *Parenting from the inside out: How a deeper self-understanding can help you raise children who thrive.* Jeremy P. Tarcher.

# Chapter 16: Fifty Daily Practices to Strengthen Your Emotional Intelligence: The Alchemy of Transformation

## Introduction: The Sacred Art of Daily Becoming

In the grand theatre of human consciousness, where each dawn presents a new stage upon which the drama of existence unfolds, we discover that emotional intelligence is not forged in the crucible of momentous events alone, but rather in the quiet sanctity of daily practice—in those seemingly insignificant moments when we choose awareness over automaticity, compassion over judgment, wisdom over reaction. Like the ancient alchemists who sought to transform base metals into gold through patient, methodical processes, the cultivation of emotional intelligence requires the sacred art of daily transmutation—the gradual refinement of our most primitive impulses into our most noble capacities (Jung, 1968).

The practices offered in this chapter represent more than mere exercises; they constitute what we might call "spiritual technologies"—systematic approaches to rewiring the neural pathways that govern our emotional responses, restructuring the cognitive frameworks that shape our perceptions, and realigning the behavioural patterns that determine our impact upon the world. Each practice, however simple it may appear on the surface, contains within it the potential for profound transformation when approached with intentionality, consistency, and the kind of reverent attention that recognises the extraordinary hiding within the ordinary (Kabat-Zinn, 2013).

The ancient Greeks understood this principle through their concept of "askesis"—not asceticism in the sense of deprivation, but rather the disciplined practice of exercises designed to cultivate virtue and wisdom. Modern neuroscience has vindicated this ancient wisdom, demonstrating that the brain's remarkable neuroplasticity ensures that repeated experiences literally reshape neural architecture, creating new pathways while weakening old ones, until what once required conscious effort becomes effortless second nature (Doidge, 2007).

These fifty practices emerge from decades of research in psychology, neuroscience, contemplative traditions, and clinical experience. They have been tested not only in laboratory settings but in the far more demanding laboratory of daily life—by individuals seeking to become more emotionally intelligent parents, partners, leaders, and citizens. Some may seem deceptively simple; others may challenge you to venture beyond your comfort zone. All have been carefully selected for their capacity to create measurable changes in emotional awareness, regulation, motivation, empathy, and social skill when practiced with dedication and patience.

## The Architecture of Self-Awareness: Awakening to Inner Truth

Self-awareness, the cornerstone of emotional intelligence, requires what we might call "inner archaeology"—the patient excavation of the layers of conditioning, reactivity, and unconscious patterns that obscure our authentic emotional experience. The practices in this domain serve as both excavation tools and illumination devices, revealing the hidden topography of our inner landscape with increasing clarity and compassion.

**Morning Emotional Naming Ritual** Begin each day by sitting quietly for three minutes and asking yourself: "What am I feeling as I enter this new day?" This practice of emotional naming serves multiple neurological functions. Research by UCLA neuroscientist Matthew Lieberman demonstrates that the simple act of labelling emotions activates the prefrontal cortex while diminishing activity in the amygdala, literally reducing the intensity of difficult emotions while increasing cognitive control (Lieberman et al., 2007). The morning ritual establishes what psychologists call "affective awareness"—consciousness of one's emotional starting point that serves as a baseline for the day's experiences.

**Embodied Emotions Journal** Rather than merely recording events, maintain a journal that explores the felt sense of emotions in your body. Notice: Where does anxiety manifest as sensation? How does joy express itself somatically? What does anger feel like before it becomes thought? This practice draws upon the ground-breaking research of Antonio Damasio, who demonstrated that emotions are fundamentally embodied experiences—somatic markers that guide decision-making often before conscious thought occurs (Damasio, 2018). By developing body-based emotional awareness, you cultivate what might be called "somatic intelligence"—the capacity to read your own internal guidance system with precision and trust.

**The Three-Point Body Scan** Three times daily—morning, midday, and evening—pause for sixty seconds to scan your body systematically from head to toe, noticing areas of tension, relaxation, comfort, or discomfort. This practice, derived from mindfulness-based stress reduction protocols, serves as an early warning system for emotional states that have not yet reached conscious awareness. Research by Jon Kabat-Zinn demonstrates that regular body scanning increases interoceptive awareness—sensitivity to internal bodily signals—which correlates strongly with emotional regulation and decision-making capacity (Kabat-Zinn, 2003).

**The Sacred Pause** Before responding to any emotionally charged situation, institute a "sacred pause"—a brief moment of conscious breathing that creates space between stimulus and response. This practice embodies Viktor Frankl's profound insight that "between stimulus and response there is a space. In that space is our power to choose our response. In our response lies our growth and our freedom" (Frankl, 2006). Neuroscientically, this pause allows the prefrontal cortex to come online, enabling what Daniel Siegel calls "response flexibility"—the capacity to choose among multiple possible responses rather than defaulting to automatic reactivity (Siegel, 2012).

**Emotional Vocabulary Expansion** Use an emotion wheel or feelings chart to identify and name the subtle gradations of your emotional experience. Rather than settling for broad categories like "good" or "bad," distinguish between frustration and disappointment, between excitement and anxiety, between contentment and joy. Research by Lisa Feldman Barrett demonstrates that individuals with high "emotional granularity"—the ability to distinguish between similar emotions—show greater psychological resilience, more effective emotion regulation, and better social relationships (Barrett, 2017).

## The Discipline of Self-Regulation: Mastering Inner Weather

Self-regulation represents perhaps the most sophisticated achievement of emotional intelligence—the capacity to feel deeply while acting wisely, to honour the information emotions provide while choosing responses aligned with values rather than impulses. These practices cultivate what we might call "emotional aikido"—the ability to work with emotional energy rather than against it, redirecting rather than suppressing, transforming rather than denying.

**The Ninety-Second Neurological Reality** Neuroanatomist Jill Bolte Taylor's research reveals that the physiological lifespan of an emotion is approximately ninety seconds—the time required for the chemical cascade triggered by emotional stimuli to be completely flushed from the bloodstream. Emotions that persist beyond this window are sustained by continued thinking about the triggering event. Practice allowing emotions to complete their natural cycle by neither suppressing them nor amplifying them through rumination, but simply witnessing their arising and passing with curious, compassionate attention (Taylor, 2008).

**Cognitive Reframing as Creative Alchemy** When faced with frustrating circumstances, consciously practice what psychologists call "cognitive reframing"—shifting perspective to reveal growth opportunities hidden within challenges. This is not positive thinking or denial, but rather what we might call "transformational perception"—the sophisticated ability to hold multiple perspectives simultaneously and choose those that promote learning and resilience. Research by cognitive behavioural therapy pioneers like Aaron Beck demonstrates that systematic cognitive reframing literally rewires neural pathways, creating more adaptive thinking patterns over time (Beck, 2011).

**Physiological Coherence Through Box Breathing** Practice box breathing—inhaling for four counts, holding for four, exhaling for four, holding empty for four—whenever experiencing emotional overwhelm. This technique, drawn from yogic pranayama practices and validated by HeartMath Institute research, creates physiological coherence—a state in which heart rhythm, breathing, and blood pressure patterns synchronise, promoting emotional balance and cognitive clarity (Childre & Martin, 1999). The practice serves as a bridge between mind and body, using breath as a tool for conscious regulation of both physiological and psychological states.

**Language as Emotional Architecture** Consciously replace reactive language patterns with responsive ones. Instead of "You make me angry," practice "I notice feeling angry when..." This linguistic shift, rooted in nonviolent communication principles developed by Marshall Rosenberg, transforms the experience of emotional responsibility from external blame to internal empowerment, creating space for dialogue rather than defensiveness (Rosenberg, 2003).

**Evening Integration Ritual** Each evening, spend five minutes reviewing moments when you successfully chose response over reaction, celebrating these victories regardless of their magnitude. This practice leverages what positive psychology research calls the "broaden-and-build" effect—positive emotions expand awareness and build psychological resources over time, creating upward spirals of growth and resilience (Fredrickson, 2001).

## The Cultivation of Motivation: Aligning Action with Authentic Purpose

Motivation in the context of emotional intelligence transcends mere goal achievement; it encompasses what Abraham Maslow called "self-actualisation"—the ongoing process of becoming who one is capable of becoming, aligned with values deeper than external rewards or social expectations. These practices cultivate intrinsic motivation—the joy that emerges from engaging in activities that express authentic values and contribute to meaningful purposes.

**Values Archaeology Through Daily Reflection** Each morning, write three sentences connecting your planned activities to your deepest values and purposes. This practice draws upon Self-Determination Theory research demonstrating that individuals whose daily actions align with intrinsic values show higher levels of well-being, persistence, and performance than those motivated primarily by external rewards (Deci & Ryan, 2000). The practice serves as a daily reminder that even mundane tasks can become meaningful when connected to larger purposes.

**Future Self visualisation** Spend five minutes each morning visualising your ideal future self—not in terms of external achievements, but in terms of character qualities, relationships, and contributions. Research by psychologist Hal Hershfield demonstrates that individuals who can vividly imagine their future selves make better long-term decisions and show greater perseverance in pursuing meaningful goals (Hershfield, 2011). The practice creates what might be called "temporal coherence"—alignment between present actions and future aspirations.

**Micro-Victory Celebration** Identify and celebrate small progress markers daily, recognising that transformation occurs through accumulation of seemingly insignificant advances rather than dramatic breakthroughs. This practice leverages the neuroscience of positive reinforcement—the brain's tendency to repeat behaviours associated with positive emotions. Teresa Amabile's research on "the progress principle" demonstrates that recognising small wins is more motivating than large, infrequent rewards (Amabile & Kramer, 2011).

**Gratitude as Motivational Fuel** Begin and end each day by identifying three specific elements of your life experience for which you feel genuine appreciation. Robert Emmons' extensive research on gratitude demonstrates that regular gratitude practice increases life satisfaction, optimism, and resilience while decreasing depression and anxiety. Gratitude shifts attention from scarcity to abundance, creating the emotional foundation for generous, creative action (Emmons, 2007).

**Storytelling Your Journey** Weekly, share your dreams, challenges, and progress with someone who supports your growth.

This practice leverages what narrative psychology research reveals about the power of story in creating meaning and sustaining motivation. When we can articulate our experiences as coherent narratives with ourselves as protagonists rather than victims, we develop what psychologists call "narrative identity"—a sense of continuity and purpose that sustains motivation through difficulty (McAdams, 2011).

## The Practice of Empathy: Expanding the Circle of Care

Empathy represents the bridge between self-understanding and social connection, the capacity that enables us to transcend the limitations of our own perspective and experience the world through other consciousnesses. These practices systematically expand what we might call "empathic range"—the breadth and depth of our capacity to understand and care for others across differences in culture, experience, and worldview.

**Reflective Listening as Sacred Practice** In every significant conversation, practice reflecting back not only the content but the emotional undertone of what others share. This technique, central to humanistic psychology approaches developed by Carl Rogers, serves multiple functions: it ensures accurate understanding, communicates caring attention, and creates space for deeper sharing. Research demonstrates that feeling truly heard and understood is one of the most powerful predictors of relationship satisfaction and personal healing (Rogers, 1961).

**Perspective-Taking Meditation** Daily, spend five minutes imagining a challenging situation from another person's viewpoint—particularly someone with whom you disagree or feel conflict. This practice, validated by social psychology research, literally expands neural networks associated with theory of mind—the capacity to understand that others have thoughts, feelings, and experiences different from our own. Regular perspective-taking increases prosocial behaviour and reduces prejudice across group boundaries (Galinsky & Moskowitz, 2000).

**Loving-Kindness as Social Technology** Practice traditional loving-kindness meditation, systematically extending goodwill toward yourself, loved ones, neutral persons, difficult people, and all beings. Neuroscientist Richard Davidson's research demonstrates that loving-kindness practice increases activity in brain regions associated with empathy and compassion while decreasing activity in areas linked to anxiety and negative emotion. The practice literally rewires the brain for greater compassion (Lutz et al., 2004).

**Curiosity Over Judgment** When encountering behaviour that triggers judgment or criticism, consciously shift from "What's wrong with this person?" to "What might this person be experiencing that leads to this behaviour?" This reframe, central to nonviolent communication approaches, creates space for understanding rather than condemnation, opening possibilities for connection rather than separation.

**Diverse Story Engagement** Regularly consume narratives—books, films, podcasts—that offer windows into experiences vastly different from your own. Research by psychologist Keith Oatley demonstrates that fiction reading specifically increases empathy and social understanding by allowing us to practice "theory of mind" in low-stakes environments where we can explore other perspectives without real-world consequences (Oatley, 2016).

## The Art of Social Skill: Weaving Webs of Connection

Social skills in emotional intelligence extend far beyond mere politeness or charm; they encompass the sophisticated capacities required to create authentic connections, navigate complex interpersonal dynamics, and influence others in ways that serve mutual flourishing rather than manipulation or domination. These practices cultivate what we might call "relational artistry"—the ability to co-create interactions that leave all participants feeling seen, valued, and inspired.

**Conscious Relationship Initiation** Begin every interaction—whether with family members, colleagues, or strangers—with genuine presence and warmth. Research by John Gottman demonstrates that the first few moments of any interaction set the emotional tone for everything that follows. What he calls "soft start-ups" in relationships create positive emotional atmospheres that facilitate connection and cooperation (Gottman & Silver, 1999).

**Nonverbal Awareness and Attunement** Consciously observe and mirror positive body language, facial expressions, and vocal tones in conversations. This practice leverages mirror neuron research demonstrating that human beings unconsciously synchronise nonverbal behaviour with others, creating feelings of rapport and connection. However, authentic mirroring differs from manipulation—it emerges from genuine attunement rather than strategic imitation (Iacoboni, 2008).

**Conflict as Creative Opportunity** When disagreements arise, practice what Harvard Negotiation Project researchers call "getting to yes"—focusing first on understanding underlying interests and needs rather than defending positions. This approach, validated by decades of conflict resolution research, transforms adversarial dynamics into collaborative problem-solving opportunities (Fisher, Ury & Patton, 2011).

**Appreciation as Social Investment** Offer at least one specific, sincere appreciation daily to someone in your life. Research by positive psychology pioneers demonstrates that expressing gratitude and appreciation strengthens relationships, increases positive emotions in both giver and receiver, and creates upward spirals of mutual goodwill. The key is specificity—rather than general praise, identify particular behaviours or qualities you genuinely value (Seligman et al., 2005).

**Bridge-Building Across Difference** Actively seek opportunities to connect with individuals whose backgrounds, beliefs, or experiences differ significantly from your own. Social psychology research consistently demonstrates that positive contact across group boundaries reduces prejudice, increases empathy, and expands social networks. The practice requires moving beyond tolerance toward genuine curiosity and appreciation for diversity as a source of collective wisdom (Allport, 1954).

## Integration and Transformation: The Daily Revolution

The true power of these practices emerges not from their individual application but from their synergistic integration into a coherent way of life. Like instruments in a symphony orchestra, each practice contributes its unique voice to a larger harmony that transforms not only the practitioner but all those within their sphere of influence.

**The Compound Effect of Micro-Practices** Research in behavioural psychology demonstrates what Darren Hardy calls "the compound effect"—small, consistent actions accumulate over time into dramatic transformations. A daily practice maintained for merely one percent of your day (approximately fifteen minutes) creates 91 hours of focused development annually—equivalent to more than two full work weeks dedicated to emotional intelligence cultivation (Hardy, 2010).

**Neuroplasticity and the Creation of New Neural Highways** Modern neuroscience reveals that the adult brain remains remarkably plastic throughout life, continuously forming new neural connections based on repeated experiences. Rick Hanson's research on "experience-dependent neuroplasticity" demonstrates that conscious practices literally rewire brain structure, strengthening neural pathways associated with emotional regulation, empathy, and social skill while weakening pathways linked to reactivity and defensiveness (Hanson, 2013).

**From Practice to Identity: The Alchemy of Character** Aristotle understood that virtue emerges not from occasional noble acts but from the habituation of excellent choices until excellence becomes second nature. Modern psychology validates this ancient wisdom through research on identity formation and behavioural change. When practices become consistent enough to shift self-concept—when we begin to see ourselves as emotionally intelligent people rather than people trying to become emotionally intelligent—transformation accelerates exponentially (Aristotle, trans. 2009).

## The Ripple Effects: Personal Transformation as Social Revolution

The commitment to daily emotional intelligence practices creates what systems theorists call "positive contagion"—beneficial changes that spread through networks of relationship and influence. Your personal development becomes a gift to everyone whose life intersects with yours, creating widening circles of transformation that extend far beyond what you might imagine possible.

**Family Systems Transformation** When one family member commits to emotional intelligence practices, research demonstrates measurable improvements in family communication, conflict resolution, and overall relationship satisfaction. Children of emotionally intelligent parents show better academic performance, stronger peer relationships, and greater psychological resilience. Partners report increased intimacy, trust, and collaborative problem-solving capacity (Gottman, 2001).

**Organisational Culture Evolution** Emotionally intelligent individuals within organisations create what researchers call "psychological safety"—collective environments where people feel safe to express ideas, admit mistakes, ask questions, and take creative risks. Teams with emotionally intelligent members demonstrate higher performance, greater innovation, and better adaptation to change. The practices of individual members literally transform organisational culture from the inside out (Edmondson, 2019).

**Community Healing and Social Change** Communities benefit immeasurably from the presence of emotionally intelligent individuals who serve as bridges across differences, mediators in conflict, advocates for justice, and creators of inclusive spaces. Research on social capital demonstrates that communities with higher levels of emotional intelligence show greater civic engagement, reduced crime rates, better public health outcomes, and more effective responses to collective challenges (Putnam, 2000).

## Practical Guidelines for Implementation

**Start Small, Think Big** Begin with two or three practices that resonate most strongly with your current needs and interests. Consistency matters more than quantity. A single practice maintained daily for a month creates more transformation than ten practices attempted sporadically.

**Create Environmental Supports** Design your physical and social environment to support practice. Place reminders in visible locations. Share your commitment with supportive friends or family members. Create accountability systems that encourage rather than judge.

**Embrace Imperfection as Part of Perfection** Expect setbacks, forgotten practices, and periods of resistance. These are not failures but natural parts of the growth process. Self-compassion during difficult periods proves more motivating than self-criticism.

**Track Progress Through Multiple Metrics** Monitor development through various indicators: emotional awareness, relationship quality, stress levels, conflict resolution effectiveness, and contribution to others' well-being. Transformation often occurs gradually and becomes visible only through sustained observation.

**Celebrate Evolution, Not Just Achievement** Acknowledge growth in emotional intelligence as an ongoing journey rather than a destination to reach. Each day of practice contributes to a lifetime of expanding wisdom, compassion, and effectiveness.

## Conclusion: The Daily Revolution of the Heart

In a world increasingly dominated by artificial intelligence and technological solutions, these fifty practices represent a profound return to the most sophisticated technology humanity has ever developed—the human heart operating at its full capacity. They offer a path toward what we might call "authentic intelligence"—wisdom that emerges not from processing information but from processing experience with consciousness, compassion, and courage.

Your commitment to these practices joins you with countless others throughout history who have understood that personal transformation and social evolution are inextricably linked. Every moment of increased self-awareness, every choice of response over reaction, every act of empathy that bridges differences, every expression of authentic care—these become threads in the larger tapestry of human awakening.

The revolution our world desperately needs will not emerge from political movements or technological breakthroughs alone, but from the quiet, persistent work of individuals who choose daily to become more conscious, more compassionate, more fully human. Your practices matter not only for your personal fulfilment but for the healing and evolution of human consciousness itself.

Begin today. Begin small. Begin with love.

The world is waiting for your heart—not the defended heart that has learned to protect itself through armor and distance, but the open heart that has learned to transform reactivity into responsiveness, judgment into curiosity, separation into connection.

This is your invitation to daily revolution—the gentle, persistent transformation of yourself in service of a more emotionally intelligent world.

---

## References

Allport, G. W. (1954). *The nature of prejudice*. Addison-Wesley.

Amabile, T., & Kramer, S. (2011). *The progress principle: Using small wins to ignite joy, engagement, and creativity at work*. Harvard Business Review Press.

Aristotle. (2009). *The Nicomachean ethics* (D. Ross, Trans.). Oxford University Press. (Original work published 4th century BCE)

Barrett, L. F. (2017). *How emotions are made: The secret life of the brain*. Houghton Mifflin Harcourt.

Beck, J. S. (2011). *Cognitive behaviour therapy: Basics and beyond* (2nd ed.). Guilford Press.

Childre, D., & Martin, H. (1999). *The HeartMath solution*. HarperSanFrancisco.

Damasio, A. (2018). *The strange order of things: Life, feeling, and the making of cultures*. Pantheon Books.

Deci, E. L., & Ryan, R. M. (2000). The "what" and "why" of goal pursuits: Human needs and the self-determination of behaviour. *Psychological Inquiry*, 11(4), 227-268.

Doidge, N. (2007). *The brain that changes itself: Stories of personal triumph from the frontiers of brain science*. Viking.

Edmondson, A. (2019). *The fearless organization: Creating psychological safety for learning, innovation, and growth*. Wiley.

Emmons, R. A. (2007). *Thanks! How the new science of gratitude can make you happier*. Houghton Mifflin Harcourt.

Fisher, R., Ury, W. L., & Patton, B. (2011). *Getting to yes: Negotiating agreement without giving in*. Penguin Books.

Frankl, V. E. (2006). *Man's search for meaning*. Beacon Press. (Original work published 1946)

Fredrickson, B. L. (2001). The role of positive emotions in positive psychology: The broaden-and-build theory of positive emotions. *American Psychologist*, 56(3), 218-226.

Galinsky, A. D., & Moskowitz, G. B. (2000). Perspective-taking: Decreasing stereotype expression, stereotype accessibility, and in-group favoritism. *Journal of Personality and Social Psychology*, 78(4), 708-724.

Gottman, J. M. (2001). *The relationship cure: A 5 step guide to strengthening your marriage, family, and friendships*. Three Rivers Press.

Gottman, J., & Silver, N. (1999). *The seven principles for making marriage work*. Crown Publishers.

Hanson, R. (2013). *Hardwiring happiness: The new brain science of contentment, calm, and confidence*. Harmony Books.

Hardy, D. (2010). *The compound effect*. Vanguard Press.

Hershfield, H. E. (2011). Future self-continuity: How conceptions of future selves transform intertemporal choice. *Annals of the New York Academy of Sciences*, 1235, 30-43.

Iacoboni, M. (2008). *Mirroring people: The new science of how we connect with others*. Farrar, Straus and Giroux.

Jung, C. G. (1968). *The archetypes and the collective unconscious* (2nd ed.). Princeton University Press.

Kabat-Zinn, J. (2003). *Mindfulness-based interventions in context: Past, present, and future. Clinical Psychology: Science and Practice*, 10(2), 144-156.

Kabat-Zinn, J. (2013). *Full catastrophe living: Using the wisdom of your body and mind to face stress, pain, and illness* (Revised ed.). Bantam Books.

Lieberman, M. D., Eisenberger, N. I., Crockett, M. J., Tom, S. M., Pfeifer, J. H., & Way, B. M. (2007). Putting feelings into words: Affect labeling disrupts amygdala activity in response to affective stimuli. *Psychological Science*, 18(5), 421-428.

Lutz, A., Slagter, H. A., Dunne, J. D., & Davidson, R. J. (2004). Attention regulation and monitoring in meditation. *Trends in Cognitive Sciences*, 12(4), 163-169.

McAdams, D. P. (2011). *The stories we live by: Personal myths and the making of the self* (Revised ed.). Guilford Press.

Oatley, K. (2016). Fiction: Simulation of social worlds. *Trends in Cognitive Sciences*, 20(8), 618-628.

Putnam, R. D. (2000). *Bowling alone: The collapse and revival of American community*. Simon & Schuster.

Rogers, C. R. (1961). *On becoming a person: A therapist's view of psychotherapy*. Houghton Mifflin.

Rosenberg, M. B. (2003). *Nonviolent communication: A language of life* (2nd ed.). PuddleDancer Press.

Seligman, M. E. P., Steen, T. A., Park, N., & Peterson, C. (2005). Positive psychology progress: Empirical validation of interventions. *American Psychologist*, 60(5), 410-421.

Siegel, D. J. (2012). *The developing mind: How relationships and the brain interact to shape who we are* (2nd ed.). Guilford Press.

Taylor, J. B. (2008). *My stroke of insight: A brain scientist's personal journey*. Viking.

## Epilogue: The Journey Continues

As you turn the final pages of this book, know this: You are not at an ending. You are standing at **a beginning**—a threshold into a deeper, more vibrant way of living, leading, loving, and growing. The very act of reaching this culmination represents what Csikszentmihalyi (1990) would recognise as a moment of profound potential energy, where consciousness stands ready to expand into new territories of human experience.

Emotional intelligence is not a destination you arrive at—it is **a path you walk**, one step at a time, one choice at a time, across the landscapes of your inner and outer worlds. This journey echoes the ancient Greek concept of *eudaimonia*, not as fleeting happiness but as Aristotle (2009) envisioned it: a flourishing life lived in accordance with virtue and wisdom. Yet unlike the philosophical abstractions of antiquity, emotional intelligence offers us concrete, measurable pathways toward this flourishing existence.

Consider for a moment the profound transformation that occurs when we shift from emotional reactivity to emotional responsiveness. Goleman (2005) demonstrated through extensive neurological research that this shift literally rewires our brains, strengthening the prefrontal cortex while diminishing the amygdala's hijacking of our rational faculties. Every conversation you engage in with more presence becomes an act of neuroplasticity—literally sculpting your brain toward greater wisdom. Every emotion you meet with more compassion creates new neural pathways that Siegel (2012) calls "integration," where disparate parts of the mind work in harmonious coordination.

The ripple effects of these individual transformations extend far beyond personal benefit. Bar-On (2006) documented how emotionally intelligent individuals create what he termed "contagious emotional climates"—environments where positive emotional states spread exponentially through families, organisations, and communities. Every challenge you navigate with more resilience doesn't merely strengthen your own capacity; it models possibility for others who witness your journey. Every person you encounter with more empathy contributes to what Fredrickson (2013) identified as "positivity resonance"—moments of genuine connection that literally synchronise heart rates and brainwaves between individuals.

Every dream you pursue with more authentic passion becomes what Palmer (2000) calls "living divided no more"—a state where our deepest values align with our outward actions, creating integrity in its truest sense. **These are victories. These are transformations. These are ripples you send into the world.**

## The Architecture of Emotional Mastery

The journey you are embarking upon rests upon what we might call the architecture of emotional mastery—a structure built not of stone and steel, but of awareness, intention, and practice. This architecture, as described by Mayer and Salovey (1997) in their foundational four-branch model, encompasses the ability to perceive emotions accurately, use emotions to facilitate thinking, understand emotional language and signals, and manage emotions in oneself and others.

Yet this clinical description, while accurate, fails to capture the lived experience of emotional intelligence development. It is akin to describing a symphony by listing its notes—technically correct but missing the music itself. The true architecture of emotional mastery reveals itself in the quiet moments when you pause before reacting in anger, recognising what Thich Nhat Hanh (2001) calls "the space between stimulus and response"—that sacred pause where choice lives.

This architecture manifests in your increasing capacity to hold paradox: to be simultaneously strong and vulnerable, confident and humble, passionate and peaceful. As Brené Brown (2012) eloquently demonstrates in her research on vulnerability, the courage to be emotionally authentic paradoxically becomes our greatest source of strength. The architecture supports your growing ability to navigate what Keats (1817) termed "negative capability"—the capacity to remain present with uncertainty and doubt without irritably reaching after fact and reason.

## You Are a Lighthouse

In a world often clouded by fear, anger, division, and numbness, emotionally intelligent individuals are like **lighthouses**—and this metaphor deserves deeper exploration, for it reveals profound truths about the nature of human influence and leadership.

Lighthouses do not chase ships. They do not shout instructions across the waves or attempt to forcibly guide vessels to safety. Instead, they embody what Lao Tzu (2006) understood when he wrote that the highest form of leadership is that which is barely felt by those being led. A lighthouse's power lies in its constancy, its reliability, its unwavering commitment to its purpose regardless of external conditions.

**Anchored in self-awareness**, you shine steadily no matter the storm. This anchoring, as Kabat-Zinn (2003) discovered through decades of mindfulness research, creates what neuroscientists call "equanimity"—a balanced state of mind that remains calm in the face of both pleasure and pain, success and failure. When you are anchored in self-awareness, you become what Rogers (1961) described as "fully functioning"—responsive rather than reactive, authentic rather than defensive, growth-oriented rather than fear-based.

**Beaming compassion** across turbulent emotional seas, you embody what the Dalai Lama (2001) calls "universal compassion"—not mere sympathy or pity, but the active wish for all beings to be free from suffering. This compassion, research by Davidson and Lutz (2008) reveals, literally changes brain structure, increasing gray matter in regions associated with emotional regulation and empathy while reducing activity in areas linked to stress and anxiety.

**Guiding others** safely toward trust, hope, and possibility, you practice what Kouzes and Posner (2017) identified as authentic leadership—influence that emerges not from position or power, but from the magnetic pull of genuine integrity and care. You become what Gandhi (2008) meant when he urged us to "be the change you wish to see in the world"—not through preaching or teaching, but through the quiet power of embodied wisdom.

**Illuminating paths** of connection, dignity, and love, you contribute to what King Jr. (1963) envisioned as the "beloved community"—a society based on justice, equal opportunity, and love of one's fellow human beings. Your very presence becomes what Nouwen (1998) called "a healing presence"—one that creates space for others to discover their own capacity for wholeness.

You do not need to be perfect to be a lighthouse. This truth bears repeating, for it strikes at the heart of one of emotional intelligence's most liberating insights. Perfectionism, as research by Brené Brown (2010) demonstrates, is not the path to worthiness—it is a shield we use to protect ourselves from vulnerability, but which ultimately prevents the very connection and growth we seek. You only need to be willing to keep the light on—especially when the night is dark.

## The Neuroscience of Transformation

The journey of emotional intelligence development is fundamentally a story of neuroplasticity—the brain's remarkable ability to reorganise and adapt throughout life. When Kandel (2006) won the Nobel Prize for his work on memory and learning, he proved that our brains are not fixed entities but dynamic, ever-changing systems that respond to experience and intention.

Every moment of mindful awareness literally reshapes your neural landscape. When you choose to pause and breathe before responding to a triggering situation, you strengthen what Siegel (2010) calls the "mindful brain"—neural pathways that connect the thinking prefrontal cortex with the emotional limbic system. This connection, what researchers term "top-down regulation," allows wisdom to inform emotion rather than being overwhelmed by it.

The practice of self-compassion, as researched extensively by Neff (2011), creates measurable changes in brain regions associated with emotional regulation and stress response. When you treat yourself with the same kindness you would offer a dear friend, you activate the parasympathetic nervous system—what Porges (2011) calls the "social engagement system"—creating a state of calm alertness optimal for both learning and connection.

Perhaps most remarkably, the development of empathy and compassion toward others creates what Rizzolatti and Craighero (2004) identified as "mirror neuron" activation—brain cells that fire both when we perform an action and when we observe others performing the same action. This neurological mirroring is the biological foundation of empathy, suggesting that our capacity for connection is literally wired into our nervous systems.

## Keep Practicing, Keep Rising

There will be days when you stumble, react impulsively, or forget your highest intentions. This is not failure—it is the very essence of what it means to be human. The Japanese concept of *wabi-sabi*, as explored by Koren (2008), celebrates the beauty found in imperfection and impermanence. Your emotional journey is not a linear progression toward some imagined state of perpetual calm, but rather what Pema Chödrön (2000) describes as "making friends with yourself"—accepting the full spectrum of your humanity while gently guiding yourself toward greater wisdom.

This is an invitation: **to return to yourself, to recommit, to rise stronger.** Each return to awareness after a period of unconsciousness strengthens what Siegel (2012) calls "resilience"—not the brittle strength that refuses to bend, but the flexible strength that bends without breaking and returns to centre stronger than before.

Consider the profound wisdom embedded in the practice of what Buddhists call "beginning again." Each moment offers a fresh start, a new opportunity to choose consciousness over reactivity. This principle, validated by decades of research on habit formation by Duhigg (2012), suggests that sustainable change occurs not through massive efforts but through countless small choices compounded over time.

Emotional intelligence is a lifelong dance—a dynamic, living relationship with yourself, with others, and with the unfolding mysteries of life. This dance requires what Rumi (1995) called "the intimate act of surrender"—not passive resignation, but active participation in the larger intelligence that moves through all life. It demands what Rilke (2005) meant when he urged us to "live the questions"—embracing uncertainty as a gateway to growth rather than a problem to be solved.

Each step you take with greater awareness, compassion, and resilience **writes a new story**—for you, for those you love, and for a world in need of healing. This story becomes part of what Campbell (2008) identified as the "hero's journey"—not a tale of conquest over external foes, but of integration of the shadow aspects of ourselves, resulting in the capacity to return to the world as healers and wisdom-bearers.

## The Ripple Effect of Individual Transformation

The transformation of individual consciousness creates what chaos theorists call the "butterfly effect"—small changes in initial conditions that cascade into large-scale transformations across entire systems. When you choose emotional intelligence, you become what Gladwell (2000) would recognise as a "connector"—someone whose influence extends far beyond their immediate circle through the power of authentic relationship.

Research by Fowler and Christakis (2009) on social networks reveals that happiness and other positive emotional states spread through up to three degrees of separation—meaning your emotional intelligence doesn't just affect your immediate family and friends, but their friends and their friends' friends. This creates what they term "emotional contagion on a network scale," suggesting that your individual practice contributes to collective transformation in ways you may never fully realise.

The implications extend beyond personal relationships into organisational and societal transformation. Companies with emotionally intelligent leaders, according to research by George (2000), demonstrate higher levels of employee engagement, customer satisfaction, and financial performance. Communities with higher levels of social-emotional intelligence, as documented by Putnam (2000) in his research on social capital, show greater resilience in the face of challenges and higher levels of civic participation and trust.

Your emotional intelligence journey thus becomes what Teilhard de Chardin (1975) envisioned as participation in the evolution of consciousness itself—contributing to what he called the "noosphere," the collective mental and spiritual layer of human awareness that encompasses and transcends the biosphere.

## A Final Invitation

As you move forward from this book, I invite you to remember that you stand at the confluence of ancient wisdom and cutting-edge science, of timeless spiritual insights and revolutionary psychological discoveries. The path of emotional intelligence you are embarking upon has been walked by contemplatives and mystics throughout history, yet it has never been more accessible or more urgently needed than it is today.

You have **the power to choose consciousness over reaction**. This choice, moment by moment, becomes what Frankl (2006) called "the last of human freedoms"—the ability to choose one's attitude in any given set of circumstances. This power transforms you from victim of circumstance to author of experience, from passive recipient of life to active creator of meaning.

You have **the strength to meet pain with wisdom**. This strength emerges not from denying or avoiding pain, but from what Levine (1997) calls "turning toward the difficult"—facing our suffering with the same compassionate attention we would bring to a crying child. In this turning toward, pain transforms from enemy to teacher, from obstacle to gateway.

You have **the courage to open your heart in a world that sometimes feels closed**. This courage, as explored by Hooks (2000) in her work on love as resistance, becomes a radical act of transformation—choosing connection over separation, love over fear, hope over despair, even when the world around us seems to reward the opposite choices.

You have **the vision to lead not by force, but by inspiration and empathy**. This vision creates what Senge (2006) calls "presence"—the capacity to sense the emerging future and help bring it into being. It transforms leadership from manipulation to invitation, from coercion to inspiration, from power over others to power with others.

You are capable of living an emotionally intelligent life—not just for your own fulfilment, but as a gift to the world. This gift, like all true gifts, becomes more valuable the more freely it is given. Your emotional intelligence becomes what Lewis Hyde (2007) calls "a gift economy"—a system of circulation where value increases through sharing rather than hoarding.

## The Extraordinary Hidden Power

**The extraordinary hidden power of emotional intelligence is not just within you. It is you.** This recognition represents what the mystics have always known but science is only now proving: consciousness is not something we have, but something we are. Your awareness, your capacity for love, your ability to choose wisdom over reactivity—these are not merely psychological skills but expressions of the fundamental nature of reality itself.

When quantum physicist Max Planck (1944) declared that "consciousness is fundamental, and matter is derived from consciousness," he anticipated what emotional intelligence practitioners discover through lived experience: we are not separate beings trying to connect, but expressions of an underlying unity learning to recognise itself through relationship.

This understanding transforms the entire project of emotional intelligence from self-improvement to self-recognition, from becoming someone different to remembering who you have always been. It shifts the focus from acquiring new capabilities to uncovering the wisdom that has always resided within you, waiting for the right conditions to emerge.

Live boldly. This boldness is not reckless bravery but what Thoreau (2004) called "quiet desperation" transformed into quiet confidence—the willingness to be authentically yourself in a world that, as E.E. Cummings (1958) observed, "is doing its best, night and day, to make you everybody else."

Love deeply. This depth of love extends beyond romantic or familial affection to what Fromm (1956) identified as "the art of loving"—an active commitment to the growth and happiness of another, ultimately extending to all beings everywhere.

Lead wisely. This wisdom-based leadership embodies what Greenleaf (2002) called "servant leadership"—influence exercised not for personal gain but for the flourishing of those being led and the larger community they serve.

**And never forget: you are the light.** Not merely a bearer of light, not simply someone who has found the light, but light itself—consciousness recognising its own luminous nature through the vehicle of your unique humanity.

The journey continues, dear reader, not because it must, but because you choose it to. In that choice lies your power, your gift, and your profound contribution to the healing of our world.

**With deep gratitude and hope for your journey,**

**Marien**

---

## References


Aristotle. (2009). *The Nicomachean Ethics*. Oxford University Press.

Bar-On, R. (2006). The Bar-On model of emotional-social intelligence (ESI). *Psicothema*, 18(1), 13-25.

Brown, B. (2010). *The Gifts of Imperfection*. Hazelden Publishing.

Brown, B. (2012). *Daring Greatly*. Gotham Books.

Campbell, J. (2008). *The Hero with a Thousand Faces*. New World Library.

Chödrön, P. (2000). *When Things Fall Apart*. Shambhala Publications.

Christakis, N. A., & Fowler, J. H. (2009). *Connected: The Surprising Power of Our Social Networks*. Little, Brown and Company.

Csikszentmihalyi, M. (1990). *Flow: The Psychology of Optimal Experience.* Harper & Row.

Cummings, E. E. (1958). *95 Poems.* Harcourt, Brace & World.

Dalai Lama. (2001). *An Open Heart: Practicing Compassion in Everyday Life.* Little, Brown and Company.

Davidson, R. J., & Lutz, A. (2008). Buddha's brain: Neuroplasticity and meditation. *IEEE Signal Processing Magazine,* 25(6), 176-188.

Duhigg, C. (2012). *The Power of Habit.* Random House.

Frankl, V. E. (2006). *Man's Search for Meaning.* Beacon Press.

Fredrickson, B. L. (2013). *Love 2.0: How Our Supreme Emotion Affects Everything We Feel, Think, Do, and Become.* Hudson Street Press.

Fromm, E. (1956). *The Art of Loving.* Harper & Row.

Gandhi, M. K. (2008). *The Essential Gandhi: An Anthology of His Writings on His Life, Work, and Ideas.* Vintage Books.

George, J. M. (2000). Emotions and leadership: The role of emotional intelligence. *Human Relations,* 53(8), 1027-1055.

Gladwell, M. (2000). *The Tipping Point.* Little, Brown and Company.

Goleman, D. (2005). *Emotional Intelligence.* Bantam Books.

Greenleaf, R. K. (2002). *Servant Leadership: A Journey into the Nature of Legitimate Power and Greatness.* Paulist Press.

hooks, b. (2000). *All About Love: New Visions.* William Morrow.

Hyde, L. (2007). *The Gift: Creativity and the Artist in the Modern World.* Vintage Books.

Kabat-Zinn, J. (2003). *Mindfulness-Based Interventions in Context: Past, Present, and Future.* Clinical Psychology: Science and Practice, 10(2), 144-156.

Kandel, E. R. (2006). *In Search of Memory: The Emergence of a New Science of Mind.* W. W. Norton & Company.

Keats, J. (1817). *Letter to George and Tom Keats*. December 21, 1817.

King Jr., M. L. (1963). *Strength to Love*. Fortress Press.

Koren, L. (2008). *Wabi-Sabi: For Artists, Designers, Poets & Philosophers*. Imperfect Publishing.

Kouzes, J. M., & Posner, B. Z. (2017). *The Leadership Challenge*. Jossey-Bass.

Lao Tzu. (2006). *Tao Te Ching*. Vintage Books.

Levine, P. A. (1997). *Waking the Tiger: Healing Trauma*. North Atlantic Books.

Mayer, J. D., & Salovey, P. (1997). What is emotional intelligence? In P. Salovey & D. Sluyter (Eds.), *Emotional Development and Emotional Intelligence* (pp. 3-31). Basic Books.

Neff, K. (2011). *Self-Compassion*. William Morrow.

Nhat Hanh, T. (2001). *Anger: Wisdom for Cooling the Flames*. Riverhead Books.

Nouwen, H. J. M. (1998). *The Return of the Prodigal Son*. Doubleday.

Palmer, P. J. (2000). *A Hidden Wholeness*. Jossey-Bass.

Planck, M. (1944). *Das Wesen der Materie*. Lecture in Florence, Italy.

Porges, S. W. (2011). *The Polyvagal Theory*. W. W. Norton & Company.

Putnam, R. D. (2000). *Bowling Alone: The Collapse and Revival of American Community*. Simon & Schuster.

Rilke, R. M. (2005). *Letters to a Young Poet*. Dover Publications.

Rizzolatti, G., & Craighero, L. (2004). The mirror-neuron system. *Annual Review of Neuroscience*, 27, 169-192.

Rogers, C. R. (1961). *On Becoming a Person*. Houghton Mifflin.

Rumi, J. (1995). *The Essential Rumi*. HarperOne.

Senge, P. M. (2006). *The Fifth Discipline*. Doubleday.

Siegel, D. J. (2010). *Mindsight*. Bantam Books.

Siegel, D. J. (2012). *The Developing Mind*. Guilford Press.

Teilhard de Chardin, P. (1975). *The Phenomenon of Man*. Harper Perennial Modern Classics.

Thoreau, H. D. (2004). *Walden*. Princeton University Press.

# Recommended Reading and Resources: A Comprehensive Guide for the Lifelong Journey of Emotional Intelligence

## Introduction: The Infinite Library of Human Wisdom

The journey of emotional intelligence is not merely lifelong—it is infinite, spiralling ever deeper into the mysteries of consciousness, connection, and human potential. Like the mythical Library of Alexandria, the repository of knowledge available to the modern seeker of emotional wisdom spans millennia of human insight, from ancient philosophical treatises to cutting-edge neuroscientific research, from contemplative practices refined over thousands of years to revolutionary psychological methodologies emerging from contemporary laboratories.

Consider this curated collection not as a mere bibliography, but as what Borges (1962) envisioned in his "The Library of Babel"—an infinite repository where every possible insight into the human condition exists, waiting to be discovered by the dedicated explorer. The more perspectives, tools, and insights you explore, the deeper and richer your growth will become, creating what complexity theorists call "emergent properties"—new capacities that arise from the intersection and integration of multiple knowledge systems (Holland, 1998).

These works have empowered countless individuals around the world—from corporate executives discovering the transformative power of vulnerability to educators revolutionising classroom dynamics through emotional literacy, from therapists healing generational trauma through compassionate presence to parents raising emotionally intelligent children who will shape our collective future. They can enrich your path too, serving as what Campbell (2008) called "the thousand faces of the hero's journey"—multiple expressions of the same fundamental quest for wholeness and wisdom.

The resources that follow represent what we might call "the great conversation" of human emotional development—a dialogue that spans cultures, disciplines, and centuries, united by the recognition that our capacity to understand and skilfully navigate the landscape of human emotion is perhaps our species' greatest evolutionary achievement and our most profound hope for collective flourishing.

# Essential Foundational Texts: The Pillars of Emotional Intelligence

## The Scientific Revolution in Emotional Understanding

**Goleman, D. (1995). *Emotional Intelligence: Why It Can Matter More Than IQ*. Bantam Books.**

This foundational classic represents what Kuhn (1962) would recognise as a paradigm shift—a fundamental reframing of how we understand human intelligence and potential. Goleman's synthesis of decades of psychological research challenged the prevailing orthodoxy that privileged analytical intelligence above all other forms of cognitive capacity. The book's enduring power lies not merely in its comprehensive review of research, but in its radical proposition that emotional competencies—self-awareness, empathy, emotional regulation, social skills—often prove more predictive of life success than traditional measures of intellectual ability.

What makes this work particularly significant is its integration of what Gardner (1983) termed "multiple intelligences" with emerging neuroscientific research on the emotional brain. By demonstrating that emotional intelligence could be measured, taught, and developed, Goleman transformed abstract psychological concepts into practical tools for human development, creating what Gladwell (2000) would call a "tipping point" in popular understanding of human potential.

**Goleman, D. (2006).** ***Social Intelligence: The New Science of Human Relationships.*** **Bantam Books.**

Building upon his foundational work, Goleman's exploration of social intelligence delves into what Porges (2011) calls the "social engagement system"—the neurobiological mechanisms that enable us to connect, communicate, and collaborate with remarkable sophistication. This work bridges individual emotional intelligence with collective emotional wisdom, exploring how emotional contagion, empathic accuracy, and social awareness create the fabric of human civilisation itself.

The book's examination of mirror neurons and social brain networks provides scientific validation for what contemplatives have long understood: we are fundamentally interconnected beings whose individual emotional states profoundly influence collective well-being. This understanding transforms emotional intelligence from personal development tool to social responsibility, from individual skill to collective necessity.

**Goleman, D., Boyatzis, R., & McKee, A. (2013).** ***Primal Leadership: Realizing the Power of Emotional Intelligence.*** **Harvard Business Review Press.**

This seminal work addresses what Warren Bennis (2009) identified as the central challenge of contemporary leadership: how to inspire and influence others in an age where traditional authority structures are increasingly obsolete. The authors' concept of "resonant leadership"—leadership that creates positive emotional climates through emotional intelligence—offers a compelling alternative to command-and-control models that dominated organisational thinking for centuries.

The book's exploration of leadership styles and their emotional impacts provides what Senge (2006) calls "practical wisdom"—insights that bridge theoretical understanding with real-world application. By demonstrating how emotional intelligence translates into organisational performance, innovation, and sustainability, the authors make the business case for what is ultimately a deeply human approach to influence and change.

## The Courage to Be Vulnerable: Revolutionary Insights on Authentic Leadership

**Brown, B. (2018). *Dare to Lead: Brave Work, Tough Conversations, Whole Hearts*. Random House.**

Brown's work represents what Rogers (1961) called "a revolutionary way of being"—an approach to leadership that requires the courage to be vulnerable, the wisdom to embrace uncertainty, and the strength to lead with love rather than fear. Her research on shame, vulnerability, and courage provides scientific validation for what poets and mystics have long understood: our greatest strength often emerges from our willingness to acknowledge our limitations and imperfections.

The book's practical framework for "daring leadership" offers concrete tools for what Kegan and Lahey (2009) call "developmental leadership"—influence that not only achieves results but transforms both leaders and followers in the process. Brown's integration of rigorous research with deeply personal storytelling creates what narrative therapists call "re-authoring"—the opportunity to rewrite our understanding of what it means to lead and be led.

**Brown, B. (2010). *The Gifts of Imperfection: Let Go of Who You Think You're Supposed to Be and Embrace Who You Are*. Hazelden Publishing.**

This profound exploration of authenticity and wholehearted living challenges what Winnicott (1965) called the "false self"—the adaptive persona we develop to meet external expectations at the cost of our true nature. Brown's research on vulnerability, shame resilience, and authentic living provides a roadmap for what Maslow (1968) termed "self-actualisation"—the full realisation of human potential through authentic self-expression.

The book's emphasis on "imperfection as a pathway to courage, compassion, and connection" offers a radical alternative to perfectionist cultures that, as research demonstrates, actually inhibit performance, creativity, and well-being (Curran & Hill, 2019). Brown's work provides both theoretical framework and practical strategies for cultivating what she calls "wholehearted living"—a way of being that integrates vulnerability with strength, authenticity with effectiveness.

## The Art of Transformative Communication

**Rosenberg, M. B. (2015).** ***Nonviolent Communication: A Language of Life*****. Puddle Dancer Press.**

Rosenberg's revolutionary approach to communication represents what Gandhi (2008) envisioned as "satyagraha"—the force of truth expressed through compassionate action. Nonviolent Communication (NVC) offers a systematic methodology for transforming conflict into connection, judgment into understanding, and reactive patterns into conscious choice.

The four-step NVC process—observation without evaluation, expression of feelings, identification of needs, and clear requests—provides what Bateson (1972) called "a difference that makes a difference"—a fundamental shift in how we conceptualise and practice human communication. By focusing on universal human needs rather than strategies for meeting those needs, NVC transcends cultural, ideological, and personal differences to create what Buber (1970) termed "I-Thou" relationships characterised by mutual respect and authentic connection.

Research by Wacker and Dziobek (2018) demonstrates that NVC training significantly improves emotional intelligence, empathy, and conflict resolution skills while reducing interpersonal stress and aggression. The approach's emphasis on self-empathy and emotional regulation aligns with contemporary neuroscience research on emotional processing and social cognition.

**Stone, D., Patton, B., & Heen, S. (2010). *Difficult Conversations: How to Discuss What Matters Most*. Penguin Books.**

This practical masterpiece, emerging from the Harvard Negotiation Project, addresses what most people consider their greatest interpersonal challenge: how to navigate conversations that matter when emotions run high and stakes are significant. The authors' framework for transforming difficult conversations into learning conversations provides what Argyris (1990) calls "double-loop learning"—the capacity to examine and modify the underlying assumptions that create recurring interpersonal difficulties.

The book's exploration of the "three conversations" happening in every difficult interaction—the "what happened" conversation, the feelings conversation, and the identity conversation—offers a sophisticated understanding of conversational dynamics that integrates cognitive, emotional, and existential dimensions of human communication.

## Emotional Flexibility and Resilience

**David, S. (2016). *Emotional Agility: Get Unstuck, Embrace Change, and Thrive in Work and Life*. Avery.**

David's concept of emotional agility represents a significant evolution in our understanding of emotional intelligence, moving beyond basic emotional awareness and regulation to what she calls "emotional flexibility"—the capacity to navigate emotions with curiosity, courage, and intentionality rather than being controlled by them. Her research at Harvard Medical School demonstrates that emotional agility is more predictive of success and well-being than traditional measures of emotional intelligence.

The book's four-step process—showing up, stepping out, walking your why, and moving on—provides a practical framework for what Hayes (2019) calls "psychological flexibility"—the ability to stay present with difficult emotions while taking values-based action. This approach integrates insights from Acceptance and Commitment Therapy with contemporary research on emotion regulation and goal pursuit.

**Brach, T. (2003). *Radical Acceptance: Embracing Your Life with the Heart of a Buddha*. Bantam.**

Brach's integration of Western psychology with Buddhist contemplative wisdom offers what Epstein (2013) calls "therapy without a therapist"—a profound approach to emotional healing that recognises our inherent capacity for wisdom and compassion. The concept of "radical acceptance" challenges Western psychology's focus on changing or fixing problematic emotions, instead offering a path of unconditional presence that paradoxically creates the conditions for natural transformation.

The book's exploration of the "trance of unworthiness" that afflicts so many people in contemporary culture provides both diagnostic insight and therapeutic intervention, offering what Kristin Neff (2011) calls "self-compassion" as an alternative to self-criticism and self-improvement. Research demonstrates that radical acceptance practices significantly reduce anxiety, depression, and stress while increasing resilience, life satisfaction, and emotional well-being (Baer, 2003).

# Contemporary Advances: The Cutting Edge of Emotional Intelligence Research

## Neuroscientific Foundations

**Siegel, D. J. (2012). *The Developing Mind: How Relationships and the Brain Interact to Shape Who We Are*. Guilford Press.**

Siegel's ground-breaking integration of neuroscience, attachment theory, and contemplative practice provides what he calls "interpersonal neurobiology"—a comprehensive understanding of how relationships literally shape the structure and function of the brain throughout life. His concept of "integration"—the linkage of differentiated elements of mental functioning—offers a neurobiological foundation for emotional intelligence that bridges individual psychology with relational dynamics.

The book's exploration of "mindsight"—the ability to see the internal world of self and others—provides both theoretical framework and practical exercises for developing what contemplatives call "metacognitive awareness" and psychologists term "theory of mind." Research demonstrates that mindsight practices create measurable changes in brain structure and function, particularly in regions associated with emotional regulation, empathy, and self-awareness (Siegel, 2010).

**Davidson, R. J., & Lutz, A. (2008). Buddha's brain: Neuroplasticity and meditation. *Signal Processing Magazine*, 25(6), 176-188.**

This seminal research paper demonstrates that contemplative practices literally rewire the brain, creating structural and functional changes that enhance emotional regulation, attention, and compassion. Davidson and Lutz's work provides scientific validation for what contemplatives have claimed for millennia: that systematic mental training can fundamentally transform human consciousness and capacity.

Their research on "neuroplasticity"—the brain's capacity to reorganise throughout life—challenges longstanding assumptions about fixed personality traits and cognitive limitations, suggesting that emotional intelligence can be significantly enhanced through appropriate training and practice.

**Porges, S. W. (2011).** ***The Polyvagal Theory: Neurophysiological Foundations of Emotions, Attachment, Communication, and Self-regulation*****. W. W. Norton.**

Porges's revolutionary polyvagal theory provides a neurobiological explanation for emotional regulation, social connection, and trauma response that has transformed our understanding of human emotional functioning. His identification of the "social engagement system"—a neural pathway that enables calm, connected states of being—offers both theoretical framework and practical interventions for enhancing emotional intelligence and interpersonal effectiveness.

The theory's emphasis on the autonomic nervous system's role in emotional experience provides a bridge between mind and body that informs trauma therapy, leadership development, and relationship enhancement. Research demonstrates that polyvagal-informed interventions significantly improve emotional regulation, stress resilience, and social connection (Dana, 2018).

## Positive Psychology and Human Flourishing

**Seligman, M. E. P. (2011).** ***Flourish: A Visionary New Understanding of Happiness and Well-being*****. Free Press.**

Seligman's evolution from studying depression and learned helplessness to investigating human flourishing represents what he calls "psychology's second revolution"—a shift from merely treating mental illness to actively building human strengths and virtues. His PERMA model (Positive emotions, Engagement, Relationships, Meaning, Achievement) provides a comprehensive framework for well-being that integrates emotional intelligence with broader life satisfaction and effectiveness.

The book's emphasis on character strengths and virtues offers what Peterson and Seligman (2004) call "a manual of the sanities"—a systematic exploration of human psychological assets that contribute to flourishing. Research demonstrates that strengths-based interventions significantly enhance life satisfaction, work performance, and relationship quality while reducing depression and anxiety.

**Fredrickson, B. L. (2013).** ***Love 2.0: How Our Supreme Emotion Affects Everything We Feel, Think, Do, and Become.*** **Hudson Street Press.**

Fredrickson's research on positive emotions and their role in human flourishing provides scientific support for what poets and mystics have long proclaimed: love is not merely an emotion but a fundamental force that shapes human experience, relationships, and development. Her concept of "positivity resonance"—moments of shared positive emotion that literally synchronise nervous systems—offers a neurobiological explanation for empathy, connection, and collective well-being.

The book's exploration of how brief moments of positive connection accumulate to create lasting changes in personality, resilience, and life satisfaction provides practical strategies for cultivating what she calls "micro-moments of love" in daily life. Research demonstrates that loving-kindness meditation and other heart-centred practices create measurable improvements in emotional intelligence, social connection, and physical health.

## Leadership and Organisational Development

**Kegan, R., & Lahey, L. L. (2009).** ***Immunity to Change: How to Overcome It and Unlock the Potential in Yourself and Your Organization.*** **Harvard Business Review Press.**

This revolutionary approach to personal and organisational change addresses what most development efforts fail to consider: the hidden psychological mechanisms that maintain status quo behaviour despite conscious intentions to change. Kegan and Lahey's concept of "competing commitments" and "big assumptions" provides a diagnostic framework for understanding resistance to change that integrates cognitive, emotional, and behavioural dimensions.

Their methodology for overcoming "immunity to change" offers what they call "developmental coaching"—an approach that addresses not just what people do, but how they think and feel about what they do. Research demonstrates that immunity-to-change interventions create lasting behavioural change in contexts where traditional approaches fail.

**Kouzes, J. M., & Posner, B. Z. (2017). *The Leadership Challenge: How to Make Extraordinary Things Happen in Organizations*. Jossey-Bass.**

Based on more than thirty years of research involving millions of leaders worldwide, this comprehensive study identifies the practices that enable ordinary people to accomplish extraordinary things. The authors' Five Practices of Exemplary Leadership—Model the Way, Inspire a Shared Vision, Challenge the Process, Enable Others to Act, and Encourage the Heart—provide a research-based framework for leadership development that emphasises emotional intelligence, authentic communication, and collaborative empowerment.

The book's emphasis on "encouraging the heart" recognises what Daniel Pink (2009) calls "the surprising truth about what motivates us"—that emotional recognition, meaningful connection, and purpose-driven engagement often matter more than traditional incentives and rewards. Research demonstrates that leaders who practice these behaviours create higher levels of employee engagement, innovation, and organisational performance.

# Specialised Applications: Emotional Intelligence in Specific Contexts

## Education and Child Development

**Cohen, J. (Ed.). (2001).** ***Caring Classrooms/Intelligent Schools: The Social Emotional Education of Young People.*** **Teachers College Press.**

This comprehensive exploration of social-emotional learning (SEL) in educational contexts demonstrates how emotional intelligence can be systematically developed in children and adolescents through curriculum, pedagogy, and school culture. Cohen's work bridges individual emotional development with collective learning environments, showing how emotionally intelligent schools create conditions for both academic achievement and character development.

Research by Durlak et al. (2011) demonstrates that SEL programmes improve students' social-emotional skills, attitudes about self and others, connection to school, positive social behaviour, and academic performance while reducing conduct problems and emotional distress.

**Siegel, D. J., & Hartzell, M. (2003).** ***Parenting from the Inside Out: How a Deeper Self-Understanding Can Help You Raise Children Who Thrive.*** **Tarcher/Perigee.**

This ground-breaking integration of attachment research, neuroscience, and contemplative practice offers parents a framework for raising emotionally intelligent children through their own emotional development. The authors' emphasis on "making sense" of one's own childhood experiences as a foundation for effective parenting provides what they call "earned security"—the capacity to provide responsive, attuned caregiving regardless of one's own early experiences.

Research demonstrates that parents who develop emotional intelligence and mindful awareness raise children with greater emotional regulation, empathy, resilience, and social competence (Siegel & Hartzell, 2003).

## Healthcare and Therapeutic Applications

**Van der Kolk, B. A. (2014). *The Body Keeps the Score: Brain, Mind, and Body in the Healing of Trauma*. Viking.**

This masterpiece of trauma research and treatment demonstrates how emotional intelligence must include what Van der Kolk calls "body awareness"—the capacity to sense, understand, and regulate the somatic dimensions of emotional experience. His integration of neuroscience, attachment theory, and body-based therapies provides a comprehensive approach to healing that recognises trauma's impact on the entire person.

The book's exploration of how traumatic experiences "live" in the body offers practical strategies for developing what Levine (1997) calls "somatic intelligence"—the capacity to use bodily sensations as information for emotional regulation and healing. Research demonstrates that body-based interventions significantly improve trauma recovery, emotional regulation, and overall well-being.

**Germer, C. K. (2009). *The Mindful Path to Self-Compassion: Freeing Yourself from Destructive Thoughts and Emotions*. Guilford Press.**

Germer's integration of mindfulness meditation with self-compassion training provides what Neff (2011) calls "an emotionally positive and less contingent way of relating to oneself." His practical approach to developing self-compassion offers both theoretical understanding and experiential exercises for transforming self-criticism into self-kindness, isolation into common humanity, and over-identification into mindful awareness.

Research demonstrates that self-compassion training significantly improves emotional regulation, resilience, life satisfaction, and interpersonal relationships while reducing anxiety, depression, and stress-related symptoms (Neff & Germer, 2013).

## Ancient Wisdom for Modern Times: Cross-Cultural Perspectives on Emotional Intelligence

### Eastern Contemplative Traditions

**Chödrön, P. (2000). *When Things Fall Apart: Heart Advice for Difficult Times*. Shambhala Publications.**

Chödrön's accessible presentation of Buddhist psychology offers what she calls "practical teachings for difficult times"—wisdom practices that cultivate emotional resilience, compassion, and what Buddhists call "equanimity" in the face of life's inevitable challenges. Her concept of "staying with the experience" provides an alternative to Western psychology's emphasis on changing or fixing difficult emotions.

The book's exploration of "groundlessness" as a fundamental aspect of human experience offers what existential psychologists call "anxiety tolerance"—the capacity to remain present with uncertainty without premature closure or defensive reactivity. Research demonstrates that Buddhist-inspired practices significantly improve emotional regulation, stress resilience, and psychological well-being (Goyal et al., 2014).

**Kornfield, J. (2008). *The Wise Heart: A Guide to the Universal Teachings of Buddhist Psychology*. Bantam.**

Kornfield's integration of Buddhist contemplative psychology with Western psychotherapy provides what he calls "a psychology of liberation"—an approach to emotional and spiritual development that recognises both the importance of healing personal wounds and transcending the ego-based consciousness that creates those wounds. His synthesis of ancient wisdom with contemporary psychological insights offers a comprehensive framework for human development.

The book's exploration of what Buddhists call "the noble qualities of the heart"—compassion, loving-kindness, sympathetic joy, and equanimity—provides both theoretical understanding and practical cultivation methods for developing emotional intelligence that serves not only personal well-being but collective liberation.

## Indigenous and Traditional Wisdom

**Some, S. (1998).** ***The Healing Wisdom of Africa: Finding Life Purpose Through Nature, Ritual, and Community*****. Tarcher/Putnam.**

Some's presentation of West African Dagara wisdom offers what he calls "technologies of the sacred"—ritual and community practices that maintain emotional, spiritual, and social balance within traditional cultures. His exploration of how emotional difficulties are understood and addressed within indigenous contexts provides alternative perspectives on mental health and emotional well-being that emphasise collective healing over individual therapy.

The book's emphasis on the role of grief, ritual, and community connection in emotional healing offers what contemporary trauma therapists are rediscovering: that emotional intelligence includes not just individual skills but collective practices that support individual and community well-being.

**Menakem, R. (2017).** ***My Grandmother's Hands: Racialised Trauma and the Pathway to Mending Our Hearts and Bodies*****. Central Recovery Press.**

Menakem's ground-breaking exploration of racialised trauma demonstrates how emotional intelligence must include what he calls "cultural competency"—the capacity to understand how historical and systemic trauma affects individuals, families, and communities across generations. His integration of somatic therapy with cultural analysis provides a framework for healing that addresses both individual and collective dimensions of emotional experience.

The book's emphasis on "body-based practices" for healing racialised trauma offers practical strategies for developing what might be called "cultural emotional intelligence"—the capacity to navigate the emotional complexities of multicultural, multi-racial relationships and communities.

# Essential Research Articles and Academic Papers

## Foundational Research

**Mayer, J. D., & Salovey, P. (1997). What is emotional intelligence? In P. Salovey & D. Sluyter (Eds.), *Emotional development and emotional intelligence: Educational implications* (pp. 3-34). Basic Books.**

This seminal paper establishes the theoretical foundation for emotional intelligence as a distinct form of intelligence involving the ability to perceive, understand, and manage emotions in oneself and others. The authors' four-branch model provides the scientific framework that distinguishes emotional intelligence from personality traits, social skills, or general intelligence.

**Bar-On, R. (2006). The Bar-On model of emotional-social intelligence (ESI). *Psicothema*, 18, 13-25.**

Bar-On's comprehensive model of emotional-social intelligence integrates emotional competencies with social skills and personality factors, providing what he calls "a cross-section of interrelated emotional and social competencies, skills and facilitators that determine how effectively we understand and express ourselves."

## Neuroscience and Emotional Intelligence

**Boyatzis, R. E., & McKee, A. (2005).** ***Resonant Leadership: Renewing Yourself and Connecting with Others Through Mindfulness, Hope, and Compassion.*** **Harvard Business Review Press.**

This research-based exploration of leadership effectiveness demonstrates how emotionally intelligent leaders create what the authors call "resonance"—positive emotional climates that enhance creativity, collaboration, and performance while reducing stress and burnout.

**Goleman, D. (1998). What makes a leader?** ***Harvard Business Review*****, 76(6), 93-102.**

This influential article synthesises research demonstrating that emotional intelligence competencies are more predictive of leadership effectiveness than technical skills or cognitive intelligence, fundamentally challenging traditional assumptions about leadership development and selection.

## Applications and Interventions

**Durlak, J. A., Weissberg, R. P., Dymnicki, A. B., Taylor, R. D., & Schellinger, K. B. (2011). The impact of enhancing students' social and emotional learning: A meta-analysis of school-based universal interventions.** ***Child Development*****, 82(1), 405-432.**

This comprehensive meta-analysis of 213 school-based social-emotional learning programmes demonstrates significant improvements in students' social-emotional skills, attitudes, behaviour, and academic performance, providing strong evidence for the effectiveness of emotional intelligence education.

**Brackett, M. A., Rivers, S. E., & Salovey, P. (2011). Emotional intelligence: Implications for personal, social, academic, and workplace success.** ***Social and Personality Psychology Compass*****, 5(1), 88-103.**

This comprehensive review examines the empirical evidence for emotional intelligence's impact across multiple life domains, providing strong support for its role in personal well-being, relationship quality, academic achievement, and workplace effectiveness.

## Digital Resources and Online Learning Platforms

### Massive Open Online Courses (MOOCs)

**Yale University's "The Science of Well-Being" (Coursera)** Instructor: Dr. Laurie Santos. This ground-breaking course, one of the most popular in Coursera's history, integrates positive psychology research with practical interventions for enhancing well-being. Santos's presentation of research on happiness, resilience, and life satisfaction provides both theoretical understanding and evidence-based practices for emotional flourishing.

**University of California, Berkeley's "The Science of Happiness" (edX)** Instructors: Dr. Dacher Keltner and Dr. Emiliana Simon-Thomas. This comprehensive exploration of positive psychology research offers practical strategies for cultivating emotional well-being, social connection, and life satisfaction based on cutting-edge scientific research.

**Google's "Search Inside Yourself" Program** Originally developed by engineer Chade-Meng Tan, this programme teaches mindfulness-based emotional intelligence specifically designed for workplace application. The curriculum integrates contemplative practices with neuroscience research and practical business applications.

### Specialised Online Programs

**The Center for Mindful Self-Compassion's Online Courses:** Founded by Christopher Germer and Kristin Neff, these programmes provide systematic training in self-compassion practices that significantly enhance emotional regulation, resilience, and well-being.

**The Greater Good Science Center's Online Courses:** Based at UC Berkeley, these courses translate cutting-edge research on compassion, gratitude, mindfulness, and forgiveness into practical interventions for personal and professional development.

## Podcasts: The Contemporary Oral Tradition

### Leadership and organisational Development

**"The Dare to Lead Podcast" with Brené Brown:** This influential podcast features conversations with global leaders, researchers, and creatives on vulnerability, courage, empathy, and authentic leadership. Brown's interviews provide both inspiration and practical strategies for leading with emotional intelligence in complex, challenging environments.

**"The Learning Leader Show" with Ryan Hawk:** Featuring interviews with world-class leaders, this podcast explores the practices, mindsets, and emotional competencies that enable extraordinary leadership and organisational performance.

### Psychology and Personal Development

**"The Science of Happiness" by the Greater Good Science Center:** This evidence-based podcast explores research on emotional well-being, compassion, resilience, and mindfulness, offering practical applications of scientific findings for daily life.

**"Unlocking Us" with Brené Brown:** Brown's deep dives into emotional experiences, relationships, and personal growth provide both research-based insights and practical wisdom for living with greater authenticity, courage, and connection.

**"On Being" with Krista Tippett:** This contemplative podcast explores the intersection of spirituality, psychology, and social justice through conversations with leading thinkers, offering profound insights into the nature of human experience and flourishing.

### Business and Innovation

**"The EQ Applied Podcast" by Justin Bariso:** Focusing specifically on practical applications of emotional intelligence in business contexts, this podcast provides real-world examples and strategies for enhancing professional effectiveness through emotional competency.

**"Masters in Business" with Barry Ritholtz (Bloomberg):** While primarily focused on finance and economics, this podcast frequently explores the role of emotional intelligence in business leadership, decision-making, and organisational culture.

## Assessment Tools and Diagnostic Instruments

### Scientifically Validated Assessments

**The Mayer-Salovey-Caruso Emotional Intelligence Test (MSCEIT):** This ability-based assessment measures the four branches of emotional intelligence: perceiving emotions, using emotions to facilitate thinking, understanding emotions, and managing emotions. Unlike self-report measures, the MSCEIT evaluates actual emotional intelligence abilities through performance-based tasks.

**The Emotional Quotient Inventory 2.0 (EQ-i 2.0):** Based on Bar-On's model of emotional-social intelligence, this comprehensive assessment measures fifteen competencies across five key areas: self-perception, self-expression, interpersonal skills, decision-making, and stress management.

**The Emotional Intelligence Appraisal (EIA):** Developed by Bradberry and Greaves, this assessment measures four core emotional intelligence skills: self-awareness, self-management, social awareness, and relationship management, providing both individual scores and developmental recommendations.

### 360-Degree Feedback Tools

**The Emotional and Social Competency Inventory (ESCI):** Based on Goleman's emotional intelligence competency model, this 360-degree assessment gathers feedback from supervisors, peers, and direct reports to provide comprehensive insights into emotional and social competencies in workplace contexts.

**The Leadership Circle Profile:** This comprehensive leadership assessment integrates emotional intelligence competencies with leadership effectiveness measures, providing insights into both conscious competencies and unconscious limiting patterns that affect leadership impact.

## Practical Tools and Applications

### Mobile Applications for Emotional Intelligence Development

**Mood Meter (Yale Center for Emotional Intelligence):** This research-based app helps users recognise, understand, label, express, and regulate their emotions using the RULER approach developed at Yale. The app provides real-time emotional tracking and evidence-based strategies for emotional regulation.

**Ten Percent Happier:** Founded by Dan Harris, this meditation app focuses specifically on practical mindfulness training for sceptics and busy professionals, offering guided meditations that enhance emotional regulation, stress resilience, and interpersonal effectiveness.

**Insight Timer:** This comprehensive meditation platform offers thousands of guided meditations, talks, and courses from leading emotional intelligence teachers and researchers, creating a global community of practitioners committed to emotional and spiritual development.

## Journaling and Reflection Tools

**The Five-Minute Journal:** This structured journaling approach enhances emotional intelligence through daily gratitude practice, intention setting, and reflection, creating positive emotional habits that compound over time.

**The Emotion Regulation Workbook (online resources):** Companion resources to Julie Smith's research-based workbook, providing practical exercises for developing emotional awareness, regulation strategies, and interpersonal effectiveness.

## Communication and Relationship Tools

**The Gottman Card Decks:** Based on decades of relationship research by John and Julie Gottman, these card decks provide structured exercises for enhancing emotional intimacy, communication skills, and conflict resolution in personal and professional relationships.

**Nonviolent Communication Practice Sheets:** Practical worksheets and exercises for developing Marshall Rosenberg's four-step communication process, available through the Center for Nonviolent Communication's online resources.

# Cutting-Edge Research Centres and Academic Programs

## Leading Research Institutions

**Yale Center for Emotional Intelligence:** Founded by Peter Salovey and directed by Marc Brackett, this centre conducts ground-breaking research on emotional intelligence and develops evidence-based interventions for schools, families, and organisations. Their RULER programme has been implemented in thousands of schools worldwide.

**Greater Good Science Center (UC Berkeley):** Led by Dacher Keltner, this centre studies the psychology, sociology, and neuroscience of well-being, translating scientific research into practical applications for individuals and communities.

**Center for Healthy Minds (University of Wisconsin-Madison):** Founded by Richard Davidson, this centre investigates the neural mechanisms of emotion, attention, and compassion, demonstrating how contemplative practices create measurable changes in brain structure and function.

**Stanford Center for Compassion and Altruism Research and Education:** This interdisciplinary centre studies the neural, physiological, and psychological bases of compassion and altruism, developing interventions that enhance empathic concern and prosocial behaviour.

## Graduate Programs in Emotional Intelligence and Related Fields

**Naropa University - Contemplative Psychology Programs:** These innovative graduate programmes integrate traditional psychology with contemplative practices, preparing therapists and counsellors who understand both Western psychological methods and Eastern wisdom traditions.

**California Institute of Integral Studies - Integral Counselling Psychology:** This programme integrates multiple therapeutic modalities with spiritual and somatic approaches, preparing clinicians who can work with the full spectrum of human experience.

**Lesley University - Expressive Arts Therapy:** These programmes recognise the role of creative expression in emotional processing and healing, training therapists who can facilitate emotional intelligence development through artistic modalities.

# International Perspectives and Cross-Cultural Applications

## Global Initiatives

**UNESCO's Social and Emotional Learning Program:** This international initiative promotes emotional intelligence education as a component of quality education for all, providing frameworks and resources for implementing SEL programmes across diverse cultural contexts.

**The Dalai Lama Center for Peace and Education:** This organisation promotes what the Dalai Lama calls "educating the heart" through programmes that integrate emotional intelligence with contemplative wisdom and social justice education.

## Cultural Adaptation Research

**Emotional Intelligence in Collectivist Cultures:** Research by Bar-On, Maree, and Elias (2007) explores how emotional intelligence manifests differently in collectivist versus individualist cultures, providing frameworks for culturally responsive emotional intelligence development.

**Indigenous Approaches to Emotional Wisdom:** Scholarly work by Native American, African, and other indigenous researchers demonstrates how traditional cultures have long cultivated emotional intelligence through ceremony, storytelling, and community practices that Western psychology is only beginning to understand and integrate (Gone, 2013; Koenig & Spano, 2007).

## Emerging Frontiers: The Future of Emotional Intelligence

### Artificial Intelligence and Emotional Intelligence

**Russell, S. (2019). *Human Compatible: Artificial Intelligence and the Problem of Control.* Viking.**

As artificial intelligence becomes increasingly sophisticated, Russell's exploration of AI alignment raises profound questions about the role of emotional intelligence in human-AI interaction. His work suggests that teaching machines to recognise, understand, and respond appropriately to human emotions may be crucial for developing AI systems that enhance rather than replace human flourishing.

The emergence of emotionally responsive AI systems creates new imperatives for human emotional intelligence development—if machines can simulate empathy and emotional understanding, what uniquely human emotional capacities must we cultivate to maintain our relevance and dignity in an AI-augmented world?

**Picard, R. W. (2000). *Affective Computing.* MIT Press.**

Picard's pioneering work on affective computing explores how machines can be designed to recognise, interpret, and respond to human emotions. Her research suggests that the future of human-computer interaction will require sophisticated understanding of emotional communication, creating new applications for emotional intelligence in technological design and implementation.

## Virtual Reality and Empathy Training

**Bailenson, J. (2018). *Experience on Demand: What Virtual Reality Is, How It Works, and What It Can Do*. W. W. Norton.**

Bailenson's research on virtual reality's potential for empathy development demonstrates how immersive technologies can create "perspective-taking experiences" that enhance emotional intelligence more effectively than traditional training methods. His studies show that VR experiences of being elderly, disabled, or of different races create lasting increases in empathic concern and prosocial behaviour.

This technology offers unprecedented opportunities for what he calls "empathy at scale"—the possibility of giving millions of people direct, embodied experiences of perspectives radically different from their own.

## Neurofeedback and Emotional Regulation

**Demos, J. N. (2005). *Getting Started with Neurofeedback*. W. W. Norton.**

Advances in neurofeedback technology now allow real-time monitoring and training of brain states associated with emotional regulation, attention, and empathy. Demos's work demonstrates how individuals can learn to consciously influence their own neural activity, potentially accelerating emotional intelligence development through direct brain training.

Research by Gruzelier (2014) shows that neurofeedback training can significantly improve emotional regulation, stress resilience, and cognitive performance, suggesting that technological enhancement of emotional intelligence may become increasingly available and effective.

# Specialised Professional Applications

## Healthcare and Medical Training

**Levinson, W., Roter, D., Mullooly, J. P., Dull, V. T., & Frankel, R. M. (1997). Physician-patient communication: The relationship with malpractice claims among primary care physicians and surgeons.** ***JAMA*****, 277(7), 553-559.**

This landmark study demonstrates that physicians with better communication skills—particularly empathy and emotional responsiveness—are significantly less likely to be sued for malpractice, regardless of their technical competence. The research catalysed widespread integration of emotional intelligence training into medical education.

**Shapiro, J. (2002). How do physicians teach empathy in the primary care setting?** ***Academic Medicine*****, 77(4), 323-328.**

Shapiro's research on empathy training in medical education explores how healthcare providers can maintain a compassionate connection with patients while protecting themselves from emotional overwhelm and burnout. Her work demonstrates that emotional intelligence training improves both patient satisfaction and physician well-being.

## Legal Profession and Conflict Resolution

**Goleman, D. (1995). Emotional intelligence in the legal profession.** ***Law Practice Management*****, 21(6), 54-57.**

This application of emotional intelligence principles to legal practice demonstrates how attorneys can enhance their effectiveness through improved emotional regulation, empathy, and communication skills. Research shows that emotionally intelligent lawyers achieve better outcomes for clients while experiencing less stress and burnout.

**Bush, R. A. B., & Folger, J. P. (2004).** ***The Promise of Mediation: The Transformative Approach to Conflict.*** **Jossey-Bass.**

This ground-breaking approach to conflict resolution emphasises what the authors call "empowerment and recognition"—helping conflicting parties develop greater self-awareness and empathy for each other's perspectives. Their transformative mediation model demonstrates how emotional intelligence can turn adversarial legal processes into opportunities for growth and understanding.

## Military and Law Enforcement Applications

**Grossman, D. (2009).** ***On Combat: The Psychology and Physiology of Deadly Conflict in War and in Peace.*** **Warrior Science Publications.**

Grossman's research on combat psychology demonstrates the crucial role of emotional regulation, stress management, and ethical decision-making in high-stakes situations. His work has influenced military and law enforcement training programmes worldwide, emphasising emotional intelligence as essential for both effectiveness and moral conduct under extreme pressure.

**Goleman, D. (2013).** ***Focus: The Hidden Driver of Excellence.*** **HarperCollins.**

Goleman's exploration of attention and focus includes significant discussion of emotional intelligence applications in military and law enforcement contexts, where the ability to maintain calm awareness while managing intense emotions can be literally life-or-death.

# Creative and Artistic Applications

## Arts-Based Emotional Intelligence Development

**McNiff, S. (2004).** ***Art as Medicine: Creating a Therapy of the Imagination*****. Shambhala.**

McNiff's exploration of expressive arts therapy demonstrates how creative expression can serve as both diagnostic tool and therapeutic intervention for emotional intelligence development. His work shows how painting, music, movement, and other art forms can access and process emotions that resist verbal expression.

Research by Stuckey and Nobel (2010) demonstrates that arts engagement significantly improves emotional regulation, stress resilience, and overall well-being, suggesting that creative practices may be essential components of comprehensive emotional intelligence development.

**Cameron, J. (2016).** ***The Artist's Way: A Spiritual Path to Higher Creativity*****. Tarcher/Perigee.**

Cameron's influential programme for creative recovery integrates emotional intelligence principles with artistic development, demonstrating how creative expression and emotional awareness mutually enhance each other. Her practices of "morning pages" and "artist dates" have helped millions of people develop both creative capacity and emotional intelligence.

## Music and Emotional Intelligence

**Levitin, D. J. (2006).** ***This Is Your Brain on Music: The Science of a Human Obsession*****. Dutton.**

Levitin's neuroscientific exploration of music demonstrates how musical engagement enhances emotional intelligence through improved emotional recognition, regulation, and expression. His research shows that musical training creates structural brain changes that improve empathy, emotional processing, and social cognition.

**Sacks, O. (2007).** ***Musicophilia: Tales of Music and the Brain.*** **Knopf.**

Sacks's clinical observations of music's therapeutic effects provide compelling evidence for music's role in emotional healing and development. His case studies demonstrate how musical engagement can restore emotional connection and expression even after severe brain injury or neurological disease.

## Environmental and Ecological Perspectives

### Nature-Based Emotional Intelligence

**Louv, R. (2008).** ***Last Child in the Woods: Saving Our Children from Nature-Deficit Disorder.*** **Algonquin Books.**

Louv's research on the relationship between nature exposure and child development demonstrates that connection with natural environments is essential for healthy emotional development. His concept of "nature-deficit disorder" highlights how urbanisation and technology use may be compromising children's emotional intelligence development.

Studies by Berman, Jonides, and Kaplan (2008) show that nature exposure significantly improves attention, reduces stress, and enhances emotional regulation, suggesting that environmental connection may be a crucial but overlooked component of emotional intelligence development.

**Williams, T. T. (1991).** ***Refuge: An Unnatural History of Family and Place.*** **Pantheon.**

Williams's integration of personal grief narrative with environmental observation demonstrates how ecological awareness and emotional intelligence are intimately connected. Her work suggests that developing empathy for the natural world enhances our capacity for human empathy and emotional wisdom.

### Sustainable Leadership and Emotional Intelligence

**Scharmer, O. (2016). *Theory U: Leading from the Future as It Emerges*. Berrett-Koehler.**

Scharmer's framework for transformational leadership integrates emotional intelligence with systems thinking and ecological awareness, demonstrating how leaders can develop what he calls "presencing"—the capacity to sense and actualise emerging possibilities for positive change.

His work suggests that addressing complex global challenges like climate change, inequality, and conflict requires leaders who can integrate rational analysis with emotional wisdom and ecological sensitivity.

## Somatic and Body-Based Approaches

### Embodied Emotional Intelligence

**Levine, P. A. (1997). *Waking the Tiger: Healing Trauma*. North Atlantic Books.**

Levine's development of Somatic Experiencing demonstrates how emotional intelligence must include what he calls "felt sense"—the body's capacity to provide information about emotional states and needs. His work shows how trauma disrupts the natural flow between emotion and embodied response, and how healing requires restoring this connection.

Research by Van der Kolk (2014) confirms that emotional intelligence development requires integration of cognitive, emotional, and somatic awareness—thinking, feeling, and sensing must work together for optimal emotional functioning.

**Caldwell, C. (2018). *Bodyfulness: Somatic Practices for Presence, Empathy, and Waking Up in This World*. Shambhala.**

Caldwell's integration of somatic psychology with contemplative practice provides what she calls "bodyfulness"—an embodied approach to emotional intelligence that includes the wisdom of physical sensation and movement. Her work demonstrates how practices like yoga, dance, and martial arts can enhance emotional awareness and regulation.

### Movement and Emotional Expression

**Chace, M. (1993).** ***Marian Chace: Her Papers*****. American Dance Therapy Association.**

Chace's pioneering work in dance/movement therapy demonstrates how physical expression can both reveal and transform emotional patterns. Her observation that "the body doesn't lie" highlights how movement can access authentic emotional expression that bypasses psychological defences.

Contemporary research by Koch et al. (2019) shows that embodied movement practices significantly improve emotional regulation, self-awareness, and interpersonal connection, supporting the integration of somatic approaches with traditional emotional intelligence training.

## Measurement and Assessment Innovation

### Advanced Assessment Technologies

**Emotional AI and Facial Recognition:** Companies like Affectiva and Emotient have developed artificial intelligence systems that can recognise emotional expressions with remarkable accuracy, creating new possibilities for real-time emotional intelligence assessment and training. These technologies raise important questions about privacy, consent, and the commercialisation of emotional data.

**Voice Analysis and Emotional Detection:** Research by Scherer (2003) demonstrates that vocal patterns can reveal emotional states with high accuracy, leading to development of voice-based emotional intelligence assessment tools that could provide continuous, unobtrusive monitoring of emotional patterns.

**Physiological Monitoring:** Advances in wearable technology now allow continuous monitoring of heart rate variability, skin conductance, and other physiological markers of emotional state, potentially enabling real-time feedback for emotional regulation training.

## Final Integration: A Living Library of Transformation

### The Ecology of Learning

This comprehensive collection represents what systems theorists call an "ecology of learning"—an interconnected web of resources that support development from multiple perspectives and through multiple modalities. Like a natural ecosystem where diversity creates resilience and adaptability, this library of emotional intelligence resources gains its power through the dynamic interaction between different approaches, methodologies, and wisdom traditions.

The beauty of this collection lies not in any single resource, but in what emerges from their interaction—the spaces between books where insights cross-pollinate, where ancient wisdom meets cutting-edge science, where individual development connects with collective transformation. As you explore these resources, pay attention not only to their individual contributions but to the patterns and connections that emerge across different domains and approaches.

## Creating Your Personal Learning Architecture

Consider this library not as a curriculum to be completed but as a living ecosystem to be explored according to your own interests, needs, and developmental edge. Some recommendations for navigating this abundance:

**Start with Your Current Edge**: Begin with resources that address your most pressing emotional intelligence challenges or interests, whether that's leadership development, relationship enhancement, stress management, or creative expression.

**Balance Ancient and Modern**: Integrate time-tested wisdom traditions with contemporary scientific insights, allowing each to inform and enrich the other.

**Include Multiple Modalities**: Combine reading with experiential learning through podcasts, online courses, apps, and embodied practices like meditation, movement, or creative expression.

**Find Your Learning Community**: Join online groups, attend workshops, or create local study groups around these resources to support your learning through relationship and accountability.

**Practice Integration**: After engaging with any resource, take time to reflect on how its insights apply to your daily life and relationships. The goal is not information accumulation but transformation through embodied practice.

**Maintain Beginner's Mind**: Approach each resource with what Zen Buddhism calls "shoshin"—beginner's mind—remaining open to insights that might challenge your existing assumptions or expand your understanding.

## The Continuing Conversation

Remember that emotional intelligence is not a problem to be solved but a conversation to be continued—a lifelong dialogue between your evolving self and the ever-changing world around you. These resources represent voices in that conversation, each offering their unique perspective on the fundamental questions of human development: How do we understand ourselves and others? How do we navigate the complexities of emotion and relationship? How do we live with wisdom, compassion, and authentic power?

As you engage with these resources, you become part of this great conversation, adding your own voice, insights, and experiences to the collective understanding of human emotional potential. Your learning becomes a gift not only to yourself but to all those whose lives you touch through your increasing emotional intelligence and wisdom.

Let learning be your constant companion—not as a burden or obligation, but as joy and adventure. Let curiosity guide your exploration—remaining open to unexpected insights and surprising connections. Let compassion lead your actions—using your growing emotional intelligence not for personal gain alone but in service of collective healing and flourishing.

The extraordinary hidden power within you will only continue to grow as you walk forward—heart open, mind awake, spirit strong—contributing your unique gifts to the ancient and ever-new project of human emotional evolution.

# References

Argyris, C. (1990). *Overcoming organisational Defenses.* Allyn & Bacon.

Baer, R. A. (2003). Mindfulness training as a clinical intervention: A conceptual and empirical review. *Clinical Psychology: Science and Practice*, 10(2), 125-143.

Bailenson, J. (2018). *Experience on Demand: What Virtual Reality Is, How It Works, and What It Can Do.* W. W. Norton.

Bar-On, R., Maree, J. G., & Elias, M. J. (Eds.). (2007). *Educating People to Be Emotionally Intelligent*. Praeger.

Bateson, G. (1972). *Steps to an Ecology of Mind*. University of Chicago Press.

Bennis, W. (2009). *On Becoming a Leader*. Basic Books.

Berman, M. G., Jonides, J., & Kaplan, S. (2008). The cognitive benefits of interacting with nature. *Psychological Science*, 19(12), 1207-1212.

Borges, J. L. (1962). *Labyrinths: Selected Stories and Other Writings*. New Directions Publishing.

Boyatzis, R. E., & McKee, A. (2005). *Resonant Leadership*. Harvard Business Review Press.

Brackett, M. A., Rivers, S. E., & Salovey, P. (2011). Emotional intelligence: Implications for personal, social, academic, and workplace success. *Social and Personality Psychology Compass*, 5(1), 88-103.

Buber, M. (1970). *I and Thou*. T&T Clark.

Bush, R. A. B., & Folger, J. P. (2004). *The Promise of Mediation*. Jossey-Bass.

Caldwell, C. (2018). *Bodyfulness*. Shambhala.

Cameron, J. (2016). *The Artist's Way*. Tarcher/Perigee.

Campbell, J. (2008). *The Hero with a Thousand Faces*. New World Library.

Chace, M. (1993). *Marian Chace: Her Papers*. American Dance Therapy Association.

Cohen, J. (Ed.). (2001). *Caring Classrooms/Intelligent Schools*. Teachers College Press.

Curran, T., & Hill, A. P. (2019). Perfectionism is increasing over time: A meta-analysis of birth cohort differences from 1989 to 2016. *Psychological Bulletin*, 145(4), 410-429.

Dana, D. (2018). *The Polyvagal Theory in Therapy*. W. W. Norton.

Demos, J. N. (2005). *Getting Started with Neurofeedback*. W. W. Norton.

Durlak, J. A., Weissberg, R. P., Dymnicki, A. B., Taylor, R. D., & Schellinger, K. B. (2011). The impact of enhancing students' social and emotional learning: A meta-analysis of school-based universal interventions. *Child Development*, 82(1), 405-432.

Epstein, M. (2013). *The Trauma of Everyday Life*. Penguin Press.

Gandhi, M. K. (2008). *The Essential Gandhi*. Vintage Books.

Gardner, H. (1983). *Frames of Mind: The Theory of Multiple Intelligences*. Basic Books.

Germer, C. K. (2009). *The Mindful Path to Self-Compassion*. Guilford Press.

Gladwell, M. (2000). *The Tipping Point*. Little, Brown and Company.

Goleman, D. (1995). Emotional intelligence in the legal profession. *Law Practice Management*, 21(6), 54-57.

Goleman, D. (1998). What makes a leader? *Harvard Business Review*, 76(6), 93-102.

Gone, J. P. (2013). Redressing First Nations historical trauma: Theorizing mechanisms for indigenous culture as mental health treatment. *Transcultural Psychiatry*, 50(5), 683-706.

Goyal, M., Singh, S., Sibinga, E. M., Gould, N. F., Rowland-Seymour, A., Sharma, R., ... & Haythornthwaite, J. A. (2014). Meditation programs for psychological stress and well-being: A systematic review and meta-analysis. *JAMA Internal Medicine*, 174(3), 357-368.

Grossman, D. (2009). *On Combat*. Warrior Science Publications.

Gruzelier, J. H. (2014). EEG-neurofeedback for optimising performance. *Neuroscience & Biobehavioural Reviews*, 44, 124-141.

Hayes, S. C. (2019). *A Liberated Mind*. Avery.

Holland, J. H. (1998). *Emergence: From Chaos to Order*. Perseus Publishing.

Kegan, R., & Lahey, L. L. (2009). *Immunity to Change*. Harvard Business Review Press.

Koch, S., Riege, R. F., Tisborn, K., Biondo, J., Martin, L., & Beelmann, A. (2019). Effects of dance movement therapy and dance on health-related psychological outcomes. *The Arts in Psychotherapy*, 64, 52-59.

Koenig, B., & Spano, R. (2007). *Native American Perspectives on Health and Traditional Ecological Knowledge*. Center for Humans and Nature.

Kornfield, J. (2008). *The Wise Heart*. Bantam.

Kuhn, T. S. (1962). *The Structure of Scientific Revolutions*. University of Chicago Press.

Levine, P. A. (1997). *Waking the Tiger*. North Atlantic Books.

Levinson, W., Roter, D., Mullooly, J. P., Dull, V. T., & Frankel, R. M. (1997). Physician-patient communication: The relationship with malpractice claims among primary care physicians and surgeons. *JAMA*, 277(7), 553-559.

Levitin, D. J. (2006). *This Is Your Brain on Music*. Dutton.

Louv, R. (2008). *Last Child in the Woods*. Algonquin Books.

Maslow, A. H. (1968). *Toward a Psychology of Being*. Van Nostrand Reinhold.

McNiff, S. (2004). *Art as Medicine*. Shambhala.

Menakem, R. (2017). *My Grandmother's Hands*. Central Recovery Press.

Neff, K. D. (2011). *Self-Compassion*. William Morrow.

Neff, K. D., & Germer, C. K. (2013). A pilot study and randomized controlled trial of the mindful self-compassion program. *Journal of Clinical Psychology*, 69(1), 28-44.

Peterson, C., & Seligman, M. E. P. (2004). *Character Strengths and Virtues*. Oxford University Press.

Picard, R. W. (2000). *Affective Computing*. MIT Press.

Pink, D. H. (2009). *Drive: The Surprising Truth About What Motivates Us*. Riverhead Books.

Rogers, C. R. (1961). *On Becoming a Person*. Houghton Mifflin.

Russell, S. (2019). *Human Compatible*. Viking.

Sacks, O. (2007). *Musicophilia*. Knopf.

Scharmer, O. (2016). *Theory U*. Berrett-Koehler.

Scherer, K. R. (2003). Vocal communication of emotion: A review of research paradigms. *Speech Communication*, 40(1-2), 227-256.

Seligman, M. E. P. (2011). *Flourish*. Free Press.

Senge, P. M. (2006). *The Fifth Discipline*. Doubleday.

Shapiro, J. (2002). How do physicians teach empathy in the primary care setting? *Academic Medicine*, 77(4), 323-328.

Siegel, D. J. (2010). *Mindsight*. Bantam Books.

Siegel, D. J., & Hartzell, M. (2003). *Parenting from the Inside Out*. Tarcher/Perigee.

Some, S. (1998). *The Healing Wisdom of Africa*. Tarcher/Putnam.

Stone, D., Patton, B., & Heen, S. (2010). *Difficult Conversations*. Penguin Books.

Stuckey, H. L., & Nobel, J. (2010). The connection between art, healing, and public health: A review of current literature. *American Journal of Public Health*, 100(2), 254-263.

van der Kolk, B. A. (2014). *The Body Keeps the Score*. Viking.

Wacker, R., & Dziobek, I. (2018). Preventing empathic distress and social stressors at work through nonviolent communication training: A field study with health professionals. *Journal of Occupational Health Psychology*, 23(1), 141-150.

Williams, T. T. (1991). *Refuge*. Pantheon.

Winnicott, D. W. (1965). *The Maturational Processes and the Facilitating Environment*. International Universities Press.

## Don't miss out!

Visit the website below and you can sign up to receive emails whenever Marien-Edgard Ngbali BEMI publishes a new book. There's no charge and no obligation.

https://books2read.com/r/B-A-AYAEB-GMZSG

BOOKS 2 READ

Connecting independent readers to independent writers.

Did you love *The Extraordinary Hidden Power of Emotional Intelligence*? Then you should read *The Extraordinary Hidden Power of Indifference: Harnessing Detachment to Find Calm and Clarity.*[1] by Marien-Edgard Ngbali BEMI!

[2]

**What if the key to inner peace wasn't passion—but indifference?**

In a world that demands our attention, triggers our emotions, and bombards us with endless expectations, *indifference* is often misunderstood—seen as cold, uncaring, or apathetic. But what if indifference, when practised with wisdom and intention, is not weakness but power?

***The Extraordinary Hidden Power of Indifference*** reveals a radical yet refreshing path to emotional sovereignty, mental clarity, and true personal freedom. With rich insight and philosophical

---

1. https://books2read.com/u/4NJ7Pz

2. https://books2read.com/u/4NJ7Pz

depth, Marien-Edgard Ngbali Bemi takes you on a journey through the transformative force of **constructive detachment**—a conscious refusal to be consumed by chaos, people's opinions, or the need for external validation.

From ancient Stoicism and Eastern philosophy to modern leadership, mental health, and spiritual growth, this book explores: The difference between apathy and enlightened indifferenceHow to master non-reaction in a world addicted to outrageThe psychological and spiritual power of detaching from outcomesHow to thrive emotionally without absorbing other people's energyThe art of digital indifference in a hyper-connected ageTools to cultivate calm, resilience, and emotional disciplineWhy peace is not found in more caring—but in *caring selectively*

**This is not about feeling less. It's about choosing what deserves your feelings.**

Whether you're exhausted by drama, overwhelmed by noise, or seeking a deeper connection to your purpose, this book offers a quiet revolution: a new way to live with strength, serenity, and focus. *The Extraordinary Hidden Power of Indifference* is a must-read for those who wish to live more deliberately—and unshakably—in today's turbulent world.

**Let go. Stay grounded. Reclaim your peace.**

# Also by Marien-Edgard Ngbali BEMI

Échos de l'Est de la République Démocratique du Congo : Poèmes d'une Terre en Guerre Perpétuelle.
Ecos do Leste da República Democrática do Congo: Poemas de uma Terra de Guerra Perpétua.
Echi dall'est della Repubblica Democratica del Congo: poesie da una terra di guerra perpetua.
Demokratik Kongo Cumhuriyeti'nin Doğusundan Yankılar: Sürekli Savaş Ülkesinden Şiirler.
Jesus-Christ, the Refugee!
Jésus-Christ, le réfugié!
Gesù-Cristo, il rifugiato!
¡Jesucristo, el Refugiado!
Jesus Cristo, o Refugiado!
İsa-Mesih, Mülteci!
Jesus-Christus, der Flüchtling!
The Genocide in the Democratic Republic of the Congo: Unveiling the Forgotten Tragedy.
Le génocide en République démocratique du Congo : Révéler la tragédie oubliée.
Il genocidio nella Repubblica Democratica del Congo: Svelare la tragedia dimenticata.
El genocidio en la República Democrática del Congo: Desvelando la tragedia olvidada.
O Genocídio na República Democrática do Congo: Desvendar a tragédia esquecida.

Der Völkermord in der Demokratischen Republik Kongo: Die vergessene Tragödie ans Licht bringen.

The Palestinian genocide: a scandal and a disgrace for our civilised world!

Le génocide palestinien : un scandale et une honte pour notre monde civilisé !

Echoes from the East of the Democratic Republic of Congo: Poems from a Land of Perpetual War.

Ecos del Este de la República Democrática del Congo: Poemas de una tierra en guerra perpetua.

El genocidio palestino: ¡Un escándalo y una vergüenza para nuestro mundo civilizado!

The Extraordinary Hidden Power of Indifference: Harnessing Detachment to Find Calm and Clarity.

Gaza, le nouvel Auschwitz : Comment l'histoire se répète dans l'indifférence internationale !

The Extraordinary Hidden Power of Emotional Intelligence

## About the Author

Marien-Edgard Ngbali BEMI est professeur de Français et coordinateur de la théorie de connaissance à « British International School Istanbul » en Turquie. Il a enseigné diverses matières scolaires dans différents pays : R.D. Congo, Royaume Uni et Turquie. Il a fait ses études en R.D. Congo, en Italie et au Royaume Uni. Polyglotte parlant plusieurs langues, il est détenteur de nombreux diplômes universitaires dont une licence en théologie, une double maîtrise en philosophie et en éducation. Il est en outre auteur de quelques articles et de plusieurs livres.

www.ingramcontent.com/pod-product-compliance
Lightning Source LLC
LaVergne TN
LVHW101612210926
848480LV00008B/48